Aristocracy and the
Middle-Classes in
Germany

Aristocracy and the
Middle-Classes in
Germany

SOCIAL TYPES IN GERMAN LITERATURE

1830–1900

REVISED EDITION

ERNEST K. BRAMSTED

WITH A FOREWORD BY G. P. GOOCH

THE UNIVERSITY OF CHICAGO PRESS: CHICAGO & LONDON

This book was originally published in 1937 under the author's former name, Ernst Kohn-Bramstedt, by P. S. King & Son, Ltd., 14 Great Smith Street, London, S.W. 1., England.

Library of Congress Catalog Card Number: 64-15031

THE UNIVERSITY OF CHICAGO PRESS, CHICAGO & LONDON
The University of Toronto Press, Toronto 5, Canada

KARL MANNHEIM

In Memoriam

PREFACE

M O R E than twenty-five years have passed since this book was first published. It then met with a very friendly reception in England and the United States whilst in Germany's Third Reich it was conveniently ignored. The attempt to provide a specific contribution to the sociological study of literature and to correlate social history and literary history has been generally acknowledged by the critics as being feasible and fruitful. It is particularly gratifying to the author that in the important *Theory of Literature* by René Wellek and Austin Warren the present book has been described as "an admirably clearheaded study," furnishing evidence that "students of social attitudes and aspirations can use literary material, if they know how to interpret it properly."[1] Professors Wellek and Warren have also expressed their agreement with the caution expressed in the Introduction to this book that "only a person who has a knowledge of the structure of a society from other sources than purely literary ones, is able to find out if, and how far, certain social types and their behaviour are reproduced in a novel in an adequate or inadequate manner."[2]

In this preface to the present edition I intend to comment briefly on some relevant publications that have appeared since the first edition. The sociological study of literature has been handicapped frequently by the fact that too often literary historians have insufficient knowledge of the specialized work of social historians and vice versa.[3] However, today a number of social historians

---

[1] René Wellek and Austin Warren, *Theory of Literature*, London, 1949, p. 100.

[2] See below p. 4.

[3] A lack of knowledge of the social history of the period is a major handicap in the study by Werner Oberle, *Der Adelige Mensch in der Dichtung: Eichendorff, Gotthelf, Stifter, Fontane*, Basel, 1950.

do take note of the illustrating significance of literary material, while at least some students of literature direct their attention to the sociological implications as distinct from the merely aesthetic aspects of the novel and the play.

Perhaps one of the most interesting of recent attempts to assess the meaning of social attitudes as portrayed in fiction has been made by Raymond Williams in his perceptive book *Culture and Society, 1780–1950*.[1]

Carefully tracing the various meanings of the idea of culture in England since the period of the Industrial Revolution, Mr. Williams offers us, to quote his own words, "an account and an interpretation of our responses in thought and feeling to the changes in English society since the late eighteenth century."[2]   In this context he is not only concerned with contrasting the attitudes of men like Edmund Burke and William Cobbett, Robert Southey and Robert Owen, and with discussing the different interpretations of the grim realities of the Industrial Age by J. S. Mill and Carlyle; he also considers what he calls "The Industrial Novel," that is, half a dozen representative novels written in the middle of the nineteenth century.   These books by Mrs. Gaskell, Dickens, Disraeli, Charles Kingsley, and George Eliot are relevant to the theme since they "not only provide some of the most vivid descriptions of life in an unsettled industrial society, but also illustrate certain common assumptions within which the direct response was undertaken."[3] Mr. Williams succeeds because he is familiar with responses to the situation from sources other than fiction. He finds that while Cobbett's "criticism of the System is in many ways very similar to that of Dickens [in *Hard Times*] and rests on so many similar valuations," yet the politician Cobbett had a much better grasp of the significance of the trade union movement.[4]   Again, for an assessment of George Eliot's attitude in *Felix Holt*, an

[1] London, 1958.
[2] *Culture and Society, 1780–1950*, Penguin Books Edition, p. 11.
[3] *Op. cit.*, p. 99.
[4] *Op. cit.*, p. 107.

attitude which recognizes the existing social evil but is afraid of becoming involved in social issues, Cobbett serves as "a touchstone." His "conduct at his own trial after the labourers' revolt of 1830," we are told "is a finer demonstration of real maturity than the fictional compromises here examined."[1]

When we turn from England to Germany and to the relations between the two classes discussed in the present book, it seems that in recent years only one major contribution has been made by a social historian to the study of the German aristocracy. We refer to the analysis, undertaken by Heinz Gollwitzer for the period 1815– 1918, of the political and social position of the so-called mediatized nobles or *Standesherrn* who lost their sovereignty and territories during the Napoleonic reforms.[2] He sheds a new light on the outlook of the "German Whigs," the type of "liberal aristocrat," which I discuss in this book.

Important questions of rank and caste, of "proper" marriages and misalliances, the chances of the mediatized nobles to rise, their position in the eyes of their kings and of other sovereigns are examined with expertise. We learn much about the patriarchial authority of the head of such families and the relative dependence of the younger brothers, and of the women, widows, and children. Some of these highly placed members of a group of the nobility which had lost its political function though not its social prestige preferred to lead a patriarchal life on their estates while others turned courtiers, often filling major positions at the many German courts. Probably a novelist could have provided a livelier picture of this group. Professor Gollwitzer himself points to the advantages, in this respect, of the writer of fiction who is free of the restraint set by verifiable facts which determine the approach of the historian. He also rightly

---

[1] *Op. cit.*, p. 115.

[2] Heinz Gollwitzer, *Die Standesherren: Die politische und gesellschaftliche Stellung der Mediatisierten; Ein Beitrag zur deutschen Sozialgeschichte*, Stuttgart, 1957.

points out that the upper strata of the German aristocracy have rarely been depicted in German literature. Indeed there never has been produced in German literature a social picture of the brilliance and subtlety of Marcel Proust's *À la recherche du temps perdu*. A convincing analysis of Proust's masterpiece set against the findings of French social historians is a task still to be undertaken. Proust has well illustrated how "the sense of caste that separates the aristocrat from the bourgeoise is operative also within the nobility." There was a clearly defined aristocratic hierarchy. "A member of one circle scorns the one below and will stop at nothing to be admitted into the one above."[1]

The study of nineteenth century realism in European literature, and particularly that of German writers, has been stimulated by George Lukacs, the Hungarian literary critic. Although the present writer finds his Marxist concepts of history and literature and his often one-sided polemics in favour of the Russian masters unacceptable, it would be churlish not to acknowledge the wealth of his shrewd remarks on individual writers and their social attitude, his wide knowledge and his often felicitous formulations. Mr. Lukacs judges literature and society from a progressive point of view. He and his friends see in history "a purposeful development where formerly only a blind, senseless confusion surrounded them." Having been severely criticized by some less knowledgeable and more narrow-minded comrades as a "deviationist," Lukacs seems till to maintain that "Marxists watch the birth pangs of a new world and assist in mitigating the pains of labour."[2]

It has been rightly said of Lukacs, who regards both naturalism and aesthetic formalism as undesirable extremes, that he has developed among Marxists "the most coherent theory of realism,"[3] a theory which in fact owes

---

[1] Harold March, *The Two Worlds of Marcel Proust*, London, 1948, pp. 186–187.

[2] George Lukacs, *Studies in European Realism*, London, 1950, p. 2.

[3] R. Wellek, *The Concept of Realism in Literary Scholarship*, Groningen, 1961, p. 11.

as much to the aesthetics of classical German idealism as to Marxism. To Lukacs naturalism is indefensible as it shows only the surface of life, whereas realism points to essentials and creates types "which are both representative and prophetic." This literary type has a number of criteria, such as individual characteristics, representativeness, anticipatory power foreshadowing future trends and, last but not least, articulate expression or self-consciousness.[1] Altogether realism, as Lukacs understands it, means that a work of literary art has the function not only of a mirror but also operates as "a X-ray screen and even as a divining rod."[2]

All this leads to very marked value-judgments. Lukacs asks point blank: "Which of the two, Balzac or Flaubert, was the greatest novelist, the typical classic of the nineteenth century?" The question is, do you prefer a work of art which proclaims the unity of the external with the internal world or their separation? Did the modern novel reach its climax in Gide, Proust, or Joyce, or earlier in the works of Balzac and Tolstoy? Lukacs has no doubt that the answer must be in favour of the latter.[3]

It is this valuation which one has to keep in mind when perusing Lukacs' spirited, though by no means always convincing, work on German realists in the nineteenth century.[4] Admittedly during that period the German novel did not produce a figure of the world rank of a Balzac or Tolstoy, but is this really sufficient justification for measuring Fontane solely by the yardstick of Tolstoy, as Lukacs prefers to do? To him the difference in the literary calibre of the two novelists is not only one of talent but is also the outcome of the different social developments in Russia and in Prussian Germany which are said to have proved helpful in the case of Tolstoy and restrictive in that of Fontane.[5] Lukacs does not deny

[1] See Peter Demetz, *Marx, Engels und die Dichter*, Stuttgart, 1959, pp. 271–74.
[2] P. Demetz, *op. cit.*, p. 276.
[3] G. Lukacs, *Studies in European Realism*, p. 2.
[4] G. Lukacs, *Deutsche Realisten des 19. Jahrhunderts*, Berlin, 1951.
[5] G. Lukacs, *Deutsche Realisten*, p. 306.

that "Fontane belongs to the most important realists of
the second half of the nineteenth century," but rather
diminishes his significance by the remark that *Anna
Karenina* compares with *Effi Briest* as "the Great October
Revolution of 1917" in Russia does with the Revolution
of November, 1918 in Germany.[1]   As a result Lukacs
has little appreciation of the highly individualistic and
rather independent attitude of the old Fontane, which I
have emphasized in my Conclusion.

One is more prepared to agree with some of the
general observations on the German novel after 1848
made by Lukacs.   Although he is inclined to put too
much blame on the quick capitalist development in
Germany for the lack of literary significance and for the
philistine features in the novels of Gutzkow, Freytag,
and Spielhagen, Lukacs is right in his remark that in
German literature "everything truly valuable and antici-
pating the trend to the future has been pushed to the
periphery."   This, he says, is true even in a geographic
sense.   "One has only to think of the Swiss Gottfried
Keller and C. F. Meyer, of Theodor Storm in Holstein.
By the way, the only productive and original playwright
is the Austrian Anzengruber."[2]   The movement to the
periphery has also a psychological relevance.   "Anything else of lasting literary value has been pushed back
to the periphery of literature as can be seen in the case
of Raabe and, in spite of his success with the public, in
that of Fritz Reuter."[3]

Perhaps the best part of Lukacs' analysis of the German
realists is his study of Gottfried Keller, whose mature,
earthy and often attractive stories and novels reveal 'what
could have become of German literature, if the democratic revolution of 1848 had succeeded.   This would
have meant the victory over the ideological diseases of
the German mind and with it of German literature."[4]

[1] *Ibid.*
[2] *Op. cit.*, p. 12.
[3] *Ibid.*
[4] *Op. cit.*, p. 13.

Indeed the literature produced after 1848 in the territory which was later to become Bismarck's Second Empire has markedly philistine and uninspiring characteristics. There no longer existed strong literary movements and schools such as Classicism, Romanticism, or the group of the Young Germans (which I discuss in chap. ix). There was, in Lukacs' words, "a growing inability of highly talented writers to regard the local events of provincial life in an overall national and social perspective."[1]   But to blame a Raabe or Fontane because they were inclined to come to terms with the existing order or disorder is too limited a criterion by which to assess their work.

In my Conclusion I state that "in the frenzy of the boom period, in the exultation of the era of successful bourgeois finance, his pietistic mixture of *Innerlichkeit*, individualism and diffident pessimism found no demand amongst the bourgeoisie."[2]   It is this flight inward, into *Innerlichkeit* which is so significant of not a few of the heroes in German literature.   It is true, the German novel in the nineteenth century shares with the French novel of the time, with Stendhal and Balzac, the theme of disillusionment.   In the end its heroes, too, have few illusions left, if any.   But as Hans Mayer has observed in a penetrating essay,[3] only with German writers does disillusionment result in this typical introvert reaction of an "escape into *Innerlichkeit*."   It has had its forerunners in some of Jean Paul's heroes, it excels—as we can see in the following pages—in Hans Unwirrsch of Raabe's *Hungerpastor*, it has continued in the twentieth century with Hermann Hesse's Peter Camenzind and with some figures in the work of Hans Carossa and of Ernst Wiechert.   The demand from a considerable German public for this type seems to have receded only since 1945.   Professor Mayer has shown that to some extent

[1] *Op. cit.*, p. 151.
[2] See below, p. 338.
[3] Hans Mayer, "Der Deutsche Roman des 19. Jahrhunderts," in *Deutsche Literatur und Weltliteratur: Aufsätze*, Berlin, 1955, pp. 268–84.

the heroes of Fontane, of Th. Vischer's *Auch Einer* and of Keller's *Martin Salander* belong to this category.[1]   Disapproving of the roughshod methods of an industrialized and property-proud society, they all flee from the overcrowded cities to the country, into their study, to the fringe of society.   There is certainly a good deal of resignation in Fontane's, Storm's, and Vischer's heroes. However it is simplifying the categories too much to see in this escape into a private inner life nothing but "an expression of a deeply artistic, that means a deeply grievous, clash with the world of the bourgeoisie now also advancing everywhere in Germany, a clash with the economy and society of a fully developed capitalism."[2] Rooted in seventeenth century pietism, the tradition of German *Innerlichkeit* found a new expression in the German Youth Movement of the twentieth century which is without parallel in other European countries and cannot therefore be simply explained as a by-product of modern imperialism or capitalism.

Since the present work first appeared, a good deal of attention has been paid by literary historians and lovers of literature—two categories, incidentally, which are by no means identical—to such lonely "outside" figures as Raabe and Fontane.[3]   We discuss below the cleavage between the "ideal public" and the "actual public" which is so indicative of Fontane.[4]   It has been shown

[1] *Op. cit.*, p. 276.

[2] *Op. cit.*, p. 279.

[3] See the relevant chapters in Lukacs' *Deutsche Realisten* and, in Roy Pascal, *The German Novel*, Manchester, 1953; also Fritz Martini, *Die Deutsche Literatur des Bürgerlichen Realismus 1848–1898*, Stuttgart, 1962; and the survey of recent publications in this field by the same author "Deutsche Literatur in der Zeit des Bürgerlichen Realismus: Ein Literaturbericht," in *Deutsche Vierteljahrschrift für Literaturwissenschaft und Geistesgeschichte*, XXIV, 1960, pp. 581–666.   For further material on Fontane see the essays by D. Barlow, "Fontane and the Aristocracy," *German Life and Letters*, New Series, VIII, 1955, pp. 182–91, and E. K. Bramsted, "Marriage and Misalliance in Thackeray and Fontane," *German Life and Letters*, III, 1939, pp. 285–97.

[4] See below, chap. vi.   See also the article by P. Magill, "The German Author and His Public in the Mid-Nineteenth Century," *Modern Language Review*, CXLIII, 1948, pp. 492–99.

that in the end, in resignation, this sage found himself with a public very different from the aristocracy he had hoped earlier would provide his keenest readers. Reflecting on his public a few years before his death, old Raabe displayed a similar realism. As he remarked in a handwritten *curriculum vitae* in 1906, "Only for the writings of my first work period which extends to the book last mentioned [his *Hungerpastor*] have I found readers, for the rest only lovers of books, but these are, I think, the truly finest public which exists among the German people to-day."[1]

Writers, consciously or unconsciously, reflect and illustrate trends and attitudes of the society in which they live. But however wide the appeal of their work, most of them are little inclined to identify themselves altogether and always with the taste and the outlook of one social unit (class, stratum, group) or another. In short, they cannot, and probably in most cases would not aspire to the shortlived glory of becoming the literary "Beatles" of their time.

London   E. K. BRAMSTED
Sydney

[1] Quoted in H. Mayer, *op. cit.*, p. 284.

FOREWORD

THIS learned and original book deserves a warm welcome from students of modern German history and literature. While Bismarck was founding and ruling the Hohenzollern Empire, far-reaching social transformations were in progress of which neither the political nor the literary historians tell us as much as we need to know. Where shall we look for the most authentic information as to the decline of the feudal aristocracy, the transition from a mainly agricultural to a mainly industrial state, the rise of the bourgeoisie, the emergence of the Jew, with all the shifting of political influence and social values which such changes inevitably bring in their train? In the German novel above all, answers Dr. Bramsted, who approaches his subject as a trained sociologist, working along the lines of such eminent pioneers as Max Weber, Sombart and Mannheim.

Though the German novel can hardly be said to rank with the English, the French and the Russian, and though Goethe is the only German novelist of the first rank, the nineteenth century produced a long series of works of the highest significance for the study of national life. Since the mutual illustration of the history of literature by social history and of social history by the history of literature is the purpose of our author, he is concerned, not with the intrinsic merits of the works under discussion, but with their illustrative function. Thus many old favourites which have been resting on the top shelves of the libraries are taken down again and studied from a new angle. For however literary reputations may wax and wane, our interest in the past, above all in the recent past, remains. Some Russians maintain that the gloomy picture of the national character which emerges from their wonderful novels and dramas is unfair and incomplete, and we are often warned not to form our impressions of French character and morality from a century of novelists from Stendhal to Proust. Be that as it may, no one is likely to argue that the fiction of England and Germany in the nineteenth century bears false witness. That the picture should be complete in every detail is too much to expect, and we have plenty of other evidence to fill up the gaps. Yet no reader will close this volume, filled as it is with skilful analyses of many books, good, bad and indifferent, without finding his vision of modern Germany enlarged, coloured and vivified.

It is a story of unceasing change, and Dr. Bramsted is careful not to confuse one generation with another nor to claim evidential value for works beyond the limits of their authors' experience. The study both of German society and German literature must be pursued not merely chronologically but regionally. For the differences in temperament and tradition between North and South, between East Prussia and the Rhineland, were and are too deep to be removed by the political unifications of Bismarck and his successors. One of the merits of this work is to remind us of the numerous elements which have gone to the making of a great nation, and of the need of bearing in mind not only the date but the birthplace, the residence, the social and professional status, the political and religious colour of the writer.

Dr. Bramsted's picture gallery contains portraits of men whose work is little known outside the circle of specialists as well as of those whose names are still household words. Yet for the scientific purposes of the sociological inquirer the one category may be as valuable as the other. The author of *Soll und Haben*, the most popular German novel of the century, receives the attention he deserves as the spokesman of the optimism of the comfortable and cultivated bourgeoisie as it began advancing towards the centre of the stage after 1830.

But Immermann and Gutzkow, Spielhagen and Fontane hold the mirror up to the life they knew no less faithfully than Gustav Freytag himself.

The volume ends with a penetrating study of the place of the writer in society, carrying on the story recently begun in Professor Bruford's *Germany in the Eighteenth Century*. The making of an Intelligentsia is due as much to authors as to schools and universities, and in describing a state of society they are often, consciously or unconsciously, transforming it before our eyes. For novelists, like other men, have their ideologies, and they preach through types and situations as effectively as the journalist, the parson and the professor. Writers make readers, and with a wide diffusion of culture what Dr. Bramsted calls society based on status comes to an end. Such changes occur so gradually that we do not always realize their vast importance till the process is almost complete. And even when our eyes are opened it is a privilege to be shown how it came about.

G. P. GOOCH.

ACKNOWLEDGMENT

THIS book is the result of research work undertaken from 1934 to 1936 at the London School of Economics and Political Science. Its bulk formed a Ph.D. thesis approved by the University of London.

The publication has been made possible with the generous help of grants from the Publication Fund of the University of London, the Professional Committee and the Zangwill Memorial Fund, to all of which I tender my respectful thanks.

I am greatly indebted to Professor M. Ginsberg, who suggested the subject to me and who has shown keen interest in its development. My sincere thanks are due to Professor Karl Mannheim, whose friendly advice and stimulating criticism I have enjoyed both in Frankfort-on-Main and London since 1931. Frequent discussions with him as well as his books have influenced my attitude in regard to certain problems of the sociology of culture touched upon in the present work. My debt to him will be obvious from the references.

These studies would never have been completed without the generous encouragement and the valuable suggestions of Dr. G. P. Gooch, to whom my special thanks are due. Further, I have to thank Dr. W. Rose, Head of the Modern Language Department, London School of Economics, for the very kind interest he has shown in my work.

Mr. H. Instein has taken considerable pains in revising the English of my book. He, as well as Dr. R. Wellek, have read the proofs and have, together with Mr. A. F. Wells, greatly assisted in finding adequate English expressions for difficult German concepts and idioms.

London   E. K. B.

CONTENTS

PART II

THE PLACE OF THE WRITER IN GERMAN SOCIETY
1830–1900

INTRODUCTION

THE SOCIOLOGICAL APPROACH TO LITERATURE

THE aim of this book is twofold. First, it endeavours to analyse and describe relations between the aristocracy and the middle-classes of Northern Germany during the period from 1830 to 1900, using as one of its main sources the nineteenth-century novel. Such a method of investigation immediately raises a number of questions: What rôle did the writers, *quâ* special group, play in the struggle between the two classes? Were the men of letters spectators or actors in this struggle? Were they riveted to the class front or could they disentangle themselves from the immediate class issues and so obtain a relatively independent survey of the society in which they lived?

The second aim is to make some contribution to the sociology of German writers in the nineteenth century by analyses of the careers of individual authors, and of whole groups of writers, who were engaged in the clash between the aristocracy and the bourgeoisie.

Since this study uses literature as a source for the examination of class-distinctions, it is perhaps necessary to make a few introductory observations on the relation between literature and society, as well as on the analysis of class-relations.

I

To what extent can one rely on literature in depicting society? What likelihood is there that the social novel

will help to a better understanding of society? By
means of particular instances and sequences of events
it can portray the specific character of social situations
or of social types and illustrate even the smallest features
of everyday life.   To-day a serious social novel implies
just as exact an empirical knowledge of its subject as
does a scientific sociological analysis.   Although, in contrast with science, the novel does not verify its results
with the help of a statistical method, it works with a
combination of observation and intuition, involving the
risk of inaccuracy, but conferring the advantage of a
greater approximation to life.

Notwithstanding the different means of expression
used in art and science, the characterization in the
modern social novel (as, for instance, in the novels of
Balzac, Zola, Fontane, Galsworthy, V. Sackville-West,
Sinclair Lewis) bears some similarity to the "ideal type"
in modern sociology.   According to Max Weber,[1]
sociology elaborates "types of the course of social behaviour"; on the other hand literature, in so far as it
is concerned with social relations, describes typical ways
in which people of different classes or groups behave,
think and feel.   When, in *The Man of Property*, Galsworthy draws the character of Soames Forsyte, this
leading figure is intended not only to be illustrative of
an individual fictitious case but also to characterize the
behaviour of a certain historical type—the "economic
man" of the Victorian age.[2]

Just as the sociologist should be able to analyse the
deviations of an individual case by referring it to the
construction of an ideal type, so also in an important
novel does the individual character display his distinc-
tive traits only against the background of the general
type.   When a writer describes the Prussian Junker's
persistence, courage, egoism, lust for power and love of

[1] Max Weber, *Wirtschaft und Gesellschaft, Grundriss der Sozialökonomik*,
Tübingen, 1922, iii. I, 14.
[2] Cf. H. V. Routh, *Money, Morals and Manners as Revealed in Modern
Literature*, London, 1935, p. 214.

carousing, we can, from our historical knowledge, accept this picture as typical of a distinct species of man. But as soon as a mad Junker or an unsociable Junker is represented, an individual case only is dealt with which diverges, more or less, from the historical type and is understood precisely by this deviation from the "normal type."

In political life a deputy represents a party, a speaker a social group, a king a state; similarly in literature an individual's behaviour, his way of thinking and feeling, can be regarded as representative of that of groups or classes. The thoughts and feelings of social types, as for example of the unemployed, of the millionaire, of the supporter of the Salvation Army or of Fascism, can be portrayed in examples of individual persons, and their typical motives and effects can be interpreted psychologically.

For the sociological aspect of the novel we mention here only one example: in Meredith's novel *The Egoist* the principal character, a young aristocrat, definitely refuses to receive into the circle of his friends and admirers a poor relative, till then unknown to him, because the latter does not bear the stamp of the gentleman, "on his hat, his coat, his feet or anything that was his." [1] Here is sketched the manner of thought and action of a certain type of individual in society: a manner which can be understood only by reference to the then prevailing ideal of the English gentleman with its typical disdain of class-fellows who diverge from this ideal.

The limitations and shortcomings of fiction, in the study of society, are due in the main to two factors: the structure of the novel as a work of art, and the characterological and sociological conceptions of the writer, i.e. his "personal equation." A novel is never simply a catalogue of facts. It has its own laws of composition, no matter whether it lays more stress on, and is more concerned with, actions than characters, or vice

[1] G. Meredith, *The Egoist*, chap. i.

versa.[1] It unites the elements of imagination with observation, fiction with social truth. The social content of a work of art is therefore wrapped in a texture of æsthetic elements, which are subject, amongst others, to the laws of contrast or of continuity.

It would be one-sided and narrow to argue that the sociological approach is the only one possible towards literature; a philological and æsthetic interpretation will by no means be rendered superfluous by it.[2] But it is the important and indispensable task of the sociological approach to trace carefully the social elements and distinguish strictly between arbitrariness and freedom of fancy and the picture of social reality with its many characteristic phenomena. This can be done only if, in the course of analysis, one treats the literary document not in isolation, but in connection with the social world which it reflects. Only a person who has a knowledge of the structure of a society from other sources than purely literary ones, is able to find out if, and how far, certain social types and their behaviour are reproduced in a novel in an adequate or inadequate manner. What is pure fancy, what realistic observation and what only an expression of the desires of the author must be separated in each case in a subtle manner.

One has to distinguish between *the attitude of the ethical writer and that of the æsthetic writer towards society.* The ethical man of letters is impressed by the tension between society as it is and society as, according to his view, it ought to be. He is a social critic; he reveals,

---

[1] For the novel of action and the novel of character see the valuable book by Edwin Muir, *The Structure of the Novel*, Hogarth Lectures, No. vi, London, 1928, and for the general problems of an analysis of a work of art, see R. Wellek and A. Warren, *Theory of Literature*, London, 1949, chap. xii.

[2] The differences between the immanent and the sociological interpretation of literature are analysed by K. Mannheim, *Ideologische und soziologische Interpretation geistiger Gebilde*, *Jahrbuch für Soziologie*, Karlsruhe, 1926, ii. 424 ff., and by E. K. Bramsted, *Probleme der Lietratursoziologie*, *Neue Jahrbücher für Wissenschaft und Jugendbildung*, Leipzig, 1931, vii. 719 ff.; an interesting survey of the whole field of sociology of literature has recently been given by A. Guérard, *Literature and Society*, Boston, 1935; see also Wellek and Warren, *op. cit.*, chap. ix.

preaches, accuses, and is dominated by a tendency to cutting satire. On the other hand, the social æsthete is given more to portraying society as it is, with its strong and weak points, its beauty and its ugliness. The one is more concerned with morality and immorality, the other with harmony and disharmony in a social order. The one frees himself from the pressure of social reality by biting satire, the other by soothing humour. The ethical writer wants to alter the world, the æsthetic author only to contemplate it, the realism of the one is critical, that of the other poetical.

For sociological and historical purposes, the works of the ethical writer are often very important as sources for awakening recognition of existing social defects and the resentment which has accumulated in a given social stratum. But the works of the social æsthete reflect more everyday life, the conditions and opinions of certain groups. They demonstrate to some degree what really happened, how the mechanism of co-operation and competition operated in a stated society.[1]

Only by skilful and careful handling can a study of literature become a vital supplement to research into social history, and, in its turn, the history of literature can obtain necessary correction by an analysis of its sociological determinants. The mutual illustration of the history of literature by social history and of social history by the history of literature is the method employed in this book. On the one hand, the structure of society in a certain period is illustrated and illumined by reference to the social contents of literature; on the other hand, the single, apparently accidental, works of literature acquire a symbolic function in connection with the society

---

[1] The contrast between these two types of writers can be seen particularly well in the brothers Heinrich and Thomas Mann. Swift, Thackeray, H. von Kleist, Wedekind, are other cases of a tendency towards the ethical, whilst Goethe, Balzac, Fontane, incline towards the æsthetic pole. Many writers, of course, represent a mixed type or incline in different periods of their development more to one or to the other type. Galsworthy, for example, shows undoubtedly in his early writings an ethical attitude (see *The Island Pharisees*), but in his later work an æsthetic one (e.g. *Swan Song*).

of their age when studied in relation to social history, as well as by occasional analysis with a cautious application of general sociological and psychological categories.

But it is by no means sufficient merely to find out what social types are illustrated in literature (inquiry into the facts); beyond that it has to be clearly shown how far the literary types are reflections of social reality, how far they cartoon or idealize it, if and why certain types of society are preferred and others neglected in literature and why some real types are not represented in it at all (explanation of the causes).

If we discover that the renegade type—the aristocratic leader of the liberal opposition—is almost completely glossed over in the German novel after 1840, although in reality he played a vital rôle, or that the figure of the ugly, morally inferior Jew has been portrayed in representative German novels with one-sided predilection, a sociological explanation of this fact has at least to be attempted.   The analysis of the causes and motives could scarcely indeed provide mathematical evidence; the social determinants of the individual writers are easier to disentangle than is the general influence of social and political factors on the formation of the whole literature of an age, but the difficulty of the inquiry into the causes cannot belittle the importance of this method; for the latter—as Professor W. H. Bruford recently has aptly said—is "in inverse proportion to the degree of accuracy that can be attained in the result. Social influences are no more intangible than the personality of an author or the literary value of a work, and perhaps no less worthy of study." [1]

II

The term "class" has often been used in the sense of a terminological realism, as an independent "entity." To-day a certain reaction to this approach has taken place in sociological research, and the latent difficulties

---

[1] W. H. Bruford, *Germany in the Eighteenth Century.*   Cambridge, 1935, p. 291.

and differences are stressed more than before.[1]   One no longer starts directly from the concept of class, but distinguishes between "class-situation" and "class in the making."[2]   "Class-situation" means simply the determination of the place of individuals or groups in the whole of society.   An individual is in a given social position, no matter if this is formed by a group, a generation or a class.   Situation is the determining factor.   It forces the individual to orientate himself about this situation, to adapt himself to it and to discuss it.   In this sense class-situation operates as a means to "keep people in their places."[3]   But class-consciousness is only developed if people in the same social situation react similarly to it and join in common action.   In such case the people who are in the same social position become conscious of their situation in the whole of society and strive for that attitude which corresponds most to their interests.

The question of the origin of class-distinctions is less important for our purpose than the question of their character and effect.   The main cause of class-distinctions is the different participation of sections of the population in the ownership of the means of production and in political power, respectively.   The phenomenon of class-distinctions is manifested in the differences of standard of life, cultural level and education.   If the cause of class-distinctions is to be sought in the different participation in economic or political power, their most significant effect consists in the different prestige, which the different classes in society obtain.[4]   This

[1] See especially the chapter "Social Classes" in Prof. Ginsberg's *Sociology*, London, 1934, pp. 159–81; and R. H. Tawney, *Equality*, London, 1931, p. 65.

[2] These terms are used by Prof. K. Mannheim in an as yet unpublished book on the sociology of the intelligentsia.   I am greatly indebted to Prof. Mannheim for letting me read his work in manuscript form.

[3] M. Ginsberg, *op. cit.*, p. 160.

[4] Within a class, differing degrees of prestige exist owing to the function, activity, political significance and age of the members of subgroups.   Prestige is not only determined by class-distinctions, but by many other factors as, for example, the whole structure of a political system.   The prestige of a union of former war-soldiers is higher in a fascist dictatorship than in a democracy.

prestige causes different modes of reaction in the members of a class towards class-equals and class-strangers. That of the socially inferior class towards a superior class often results in an inferiority complex, in resentment, envy and imitation; conversely, the superiority-feeling of a higher class towards people who are socially inferior is often expressed by disdain, contempt or pity. The feelings between equals are characterized by solidarity and acknowledgment on the one hand, by rivalry and jealousy on the other.

Social phenomena, such as class-hatred, the behaviour of the parvenu, snobbery, which result from the consciousness of class-distinctions, being not so much objective facts and part of overt behaviour but very complex attitudes, have so far been much better illustrated in fiction (e.g. by Balzac, Thackeray, Dostoievsky) than in the usual sources afforded by the social sciences.

Complex attitudes involve a fusion of emotions and thoughts. Although sometimes the economic as well as the political aspect of class-distinctions is dealt with in literature, the importance of the literary exposition is, in the main, still to be found in the psychology of the behaviour of people of different social groups and classes. For with regard to psychological attitudes, the often unconscious intuitive penetration of the poet and writer yields not seldom much shrewder information than the documents and deeds upon which the scientific historian's expositions are based.

III

The relation between the aristocracy and the middle-class in the nineteenth century is characterized by the fact that the aristocracy was a survival from the age of *status*, whilst the bourgeoisie, apart from the patricians, formed a *class*. In the proper sense of the term the main difference between the old society and the new class-society is twofold.[1]

[1] Cf. Max Weber, *Wirtschaft und Gesellschaft, Grundriss der Sozialökonomik,* iii. I, 631–40.

(1) In the society based on status,[1] social prestige depends on the defined legal privileges which are attributed to the different Estates; but in a class-society it depends primarily on the possession of the means of production and of the market opportunity of different classes.

(2) The former society has a relative rigidity and exclusiveness, while the latter is relatively open and mobile.

In a society based on status, ascent from lower strata was largely subject to the approval of the leading Estates, whilst in the early period of this society it often took place independently and spontaneously. Modern class-society, in which the different classes are often antagonistically organized, is characterized by a greater professional and social mobility as well as by the distribution of political power over several centres. In the Estates-system the traditional privilege of power begot wealth in the class-system wealth often became the source of political power. In the first case the aristocracy controlled the means of production because it was the chief repository of political power: in the second case the capitalist-class has power because it controls the means of production.[2] Property has a more central function in capitalistic class-society than in society based on status; it forms not only the basis of the way of life considered normative for those strata, but it also gives opportunity for new acquisition of wealth, for an endless accumulation of capital. In the ruling stratum of the older society, acquisition *quâ* acquisition was taboo, or at least subordinate; in class-society it became indispensable and central.

So far the problem of the relationship of aristocracy and bourgeoisie has always been regarded as solved from the moment that the professional limits between the Estates were dropped—when the commoners were

---

[1] It is very difficult to express the German term "*ständische Gesellschaft*" in English. We shall use "society based on status" and "Estates-system."

[2] Cf. W. Sombart, *Der moderne Kapitalismus*, i, p. 586 f., 2nd Ed., München, 1916.

allowed to acquire landed-property, and the aristocrats to trade.[1]

But an important problem arises from the fact that the aristocracy, even in the capitalistic society of the nineteenth century and despite the loss of its former juridical, military and administrative functions,[2] still played a significant social and political rôle, and that this rôle caused certain reactions on the part of the middle-class.   The prestige of the European aristocracy undoubtedly decreased in the nineteenth century, but did not disappear.   Aristocracy was on the defence, but it nearly always held its ground.

In the nineteenth century tension and rapprochement between the tradition of the aristocracy and the economic power of the plutocracy are very noticeable.   Not indeed in France, where the political power of the feudal stratum was radically eliminated by the revolution of 1789 despite subsequent reactions.   But in England and Germany the political power of the aristocracy was still important.   Each of these two countries solved the problem of the survival of aristocratic power in a different manner, but both did it by compromise.   In England a comparatively harmonious solution of the relation between the two forces was found by a mutual acknowledgment of the rights of each.   England became therefore "at once as businesslike as Manchester and as gentlemanly as Eton, and, if its hands can be as rough as those of Esau, its voice is as mellifluous as that of Jacob." [3]   For the English aristocracy cleverly pursued a double tactic.   It opened the doors for the reception of fresh blood from the middle-class, and it remained also in contact with capitalistic development by sending its younger sons into industry and commerce.

In Germany the amalgamation was far less harmonious

[1] From the point of view of the social sciences so far only Carl Brinkmann has dealt with the rôle of aristocracy in capitalist society (*Grundriss der Sozialökonomik*, Tübingen, 1926, ix. 1).

[2] For the function of the aristocracy in the society based on status see the remark of H. Heller, *Allgemeine Staatslehre*, Leiden, 1934, p. 114.

[3] R. H. Tawney, *Equality*, p. 75.

and double-sided. The aristocracy mostly kept aloof from the new capitalistic development. It was only due to the superior tactics of Bismarck (of whom the aristocracy itself was for many years distrustful), that the Junkers could maintain their political and social hegemony in alliance with the army and the bureaucracy. After this decisive re-establishment of the threatened conservative feudal stratum in Prussia (which was a result of the victories in 1866 and 1870–1), a division (more or less) of functions took place between political power (aristocracy and ennobled bureaucracy) and economic power (bourgeoisie).[1] In England the aristocracy maintained its political prestige almost undisputed because the middle-class was, in principle, allowed to participate in it. In Germany, aristocratic prestige at first was threatened by the economic and political rise of the middle-class, but was later made secure by the political impotence and failure of the bourgeoisie. The aristocracy to some extent envied, yet felt itself superior to, the middle-class. The bourgeoisie, in turn, partly hated the aristocracy for its hegemony but sometimes imitated its behaviour. A peculiar psychological situation arose. It is important to analyse this situation in order to understand German development in the nineteenth and twentieth centuries, and as it has been reflected distinctly in literature, it will form an essential subject of this study.

Relations between two classes are characterized by the fact that they can be examined from economic, political and psychological points of view. Therefore the first part of this book attempts to elaborate different aspects of the distinctions between the nobility and middle-class in North Germany during the nineteenth century. The starting-point is the beginning of the age of Liberalism after the French Revolution of July 1830. Though the economic and juridical limits between the aristocracy and middle-class were already dropped by the reforms of Stein and Hardenberg in

---

[1] See A. Rosenberg, *Die Entstehung der deutschen Republik, 1871–1918,* Berlin, 1928, and P. Kosok, *Modern Germany,* New York, 1933.

1808, the real advance of the middle-class and of its writers began intensively only after 1830. The following fifty years of German intellectual history have been rightly called: "a fight for tradition."[1] But it was in part also a fight for or against the remnants of feudalism, for or against the political and social hegemony of the aristocracy, for or against the political influence of a prospering bourgeoisie.

A few words should be said about the materials used in this research. As many German novels of the nineteenth century as possible which deal with or touch upon the main problems have been examined. Not their literary value, but only their illustrative function was essential to this purpose. As this book is not a study in the history of literature as such, but in the sociology of literature, I have not aimed at giving a detailed description of all the novels concerned, but selected from them according to the different aspects of the sociological problem. Moreover, it was intended to employ mainly such literary material as a documentation for which a counter-proof was available in sources of non-fiction, such as autobiographies, memoirs, political leaflets, sociological treatises, expositions of historians, etc.

In Part I the life and works of the authors are analysed with reference to the relations between the two classes in question; in Part II, however, the writers are regarded as a social group of its own and some sociological aspects of their situation are more closely examined.

[1] Cf. H. Bieber, *Der Kampf um die Tradition*, Stuttgart, 1931.

PART I

ARISTOCRACY AND THE
MIDDLE-CLASSES
1830–1900

CHAPTER I

THE SITUATION TOWARDS THE END OF THE ESTATES-SYSTEM

I

GERMAN society, up to the end of the eighteenth century, was based upon the principle of status. It was characterized by a precise demarcation of the different Estates and by the absolute power of the princes who, with the aid of a professional bureaucracy and a standing army, were able ruthlessly to enforce their will on these Estates. The prince in the territorial-state determined in their details the privileges and boundaries of the different classes. The absolute police and mercantilist state had destroyed the last remnants of middle-class self-sufficiency just as it had broken the independence of the Junkers. Its principle was "divide et impera"—carefully divide the Estates which history had brought into being, and rule over them. The two chief Estates, aristocracy and middle-class, had at one and the same time both negative and positive privileges; the positive privilege of one Estate meant the negative privilege of the other. The aristocracy had the sole right of owning landed property and the patriarchal authority that was bound up with it; it had also an unwritten right to the higher ranks of the army and to the chief administrative and diplomatic posts. The Commons, on the other hand, owned the sole right of trade and manufacture as an advantage against the aristocracy, and freedom from military service as an advantage over the peasantry.

The three Estates—aristocracy, commons and peasantry—not only were socially separated from each other, but showed far-reaching internal divisions within themselves. The aristocracy was divided according to the status of the nobles, the Commons according to the nature of their occupation, and the peasantry according to the type of their holdings.[1]

The Nobility.—The hereditary nobility had for centuries been sharply divided into a higher and lower nobility.[2] Members of the higher nobility were those possessing a seat and vote in the Reichstag, beginning with the electoral princes and ending with imperial counts. They traced their descent from the free knights of the Middle Ages who were granted fiefs by the King in return for military and administrative services. The lower nobility derived its descent from the *ministeriales*, who had originally been unfree household officials of the King or greater magnates and who had, as a reward for their services, received land and aristocratic privileges, both of which became hereditary. After this stratum had risen from serfdom to freedom and ennoblement, it very soon closed its ranks, and later recognized only noble offspring as candidates for the nobility.

The lower nobility was further divided into two groups: into knights immediately subject to the Empire, and territorial nobility. The imperial knights, who were to be found chiefly in Swabia and South-Western Germany, were, until the disappearance of the Holy Roman Empire in 1806, immediately subject to the

---

[1] The hierarchy of grades between the Estates and within each Estate gave rise to group prejudices no less strong than they are to-day: the higher aristocracy very often despised the lower, the plutocrats disdained the landed-classes, the councillors of the middle-class felt superior to the clerks, the banker looked down on the shopkeeper, the Professor on the elementary school-teacher. Cf. Johanna Schultze, *Die Auseinandersetzung zwischen Adel und Bürgertum in deutschen Zeitschriften der letzten drei Jahrzehnte des 18. Jahrh.* (*1773–1806*), Berlin, 1925, p. 3 f.

[2] Johann Michael v. Loen, *Der Adel*, Ulm, 1752, on which our exposition is chiefly based, differentiates between an upper, middle and lower aristocracy, whereby the upper aristocracy includes the princes, the middle aristocracy the Counts, "Freiherrn," and the so-called "ever-free" nobles immediately subject to the Empire, and the lower aristocracy the country nobility and city nobility subject to the princes of a territorial state. The upper and middle nobility cannot be subject to a prince.

Emperor and the Imperial Court of Chancery (*Reichs-kammergericht*), whilst the territorial knights were subject to the prince of the territory, within which their estates lay.

According to centuries-old tradition, intermarriage between upper and lower nobility was interdicted; it was regarded as a misalliance, concerning whose validity or invalidity legal subtlety exercised itself in long-winded arguments. The strict segregation of the German nobility into two closed camps resulted in a deeply-rooted caste spirit (in contrast with the English nobility), and the inbreeding occasioned thereby meant that any vital contact with the people was wellnigh impossible. There was, then, besides this acknowledged upper and lower nobility, the so-called "semi-nobility," to use an expression of Loen; that is, an intermediate class which consisted partly of déclassé hereditary nobles and partly of a socially-rising, but not yet fully-recognized, letters-patent nobility. In this sense we can distinguish a negative semi-nobility and a positive semi-nobility. The negative déclassé semi-nobility exhibited a discrepancy between appearance and reality, between what it pretended to be and what it really was, between ancestry and possessions. The déclassé noble, according to Loen, was "sometimes as noble as the Emperor, but often as needy as a wage-earner, sometimes a good French marquis but at the same time a wretched teacher of languages." [1] To the semi-nobility, also, belonged the French ladies of noble birth who, after the emigration, taught as demoiselles in middle-class families, thus living and serving beneath their own class. Conversely, we find that the ennobled commons, the "honourable families," are the positive semi-nobility. They were not of noble birth, but descendants of chancellors, councillors, doctors, officials, magistrates, and rich merchants.[2] They sought to compensate for their lack of noble blood by living the life of a noble. "They lead a *vitam nobilitatis decentem*, bearing arms and avoiding

[1] v. Loen, *op. cit.*, pp. 61 ff.   [2] v. Loen, *op. cit.*, p. 64.

all degrading occupations."[1] We possess no precise
information as to the number of conferments of nobility
in the eighteenth century.   Yet there were, at that time,
as later, three types of ennoblement: nobilitation by
purchase (plutocracy), ennoblement of deserving officials,
statesmen and officers, and ennoblement of eminent
scholars and writers.[2]

At the end of the eighteenth century, an enlightened
monarch like Joseph II ennobled large numbers of
bankers and merchants.   It cost at that time round about
twenty thousand gulden to become a count, six thousand
gulden to be a baron, and three hundred and eighty-six
gulden for a plain ennoblement.[3]   The exaltation of a
merchant to the aristocracy could only be achieved,
asserts Loen, if the noble:

(1) Has sufficient means at his disposal "to uphold
this dignity with honour and vigour."
(2) If he justified his claim by obtaining free-noble
estates and bequeathing them to his descendants.
(3) If he restricted his sons to careers befitting their
class, that is, if they married ladies of noble
birth and occupied themselves with service in
the army or at court, or cultivated the sciences:
they must, in any case, give up all degrading
occupations.[4]

The ennoblement of scholars arose first at the end of
the seventeenth and beginning of the eighteenth century
in Germany, and it was an indirect indication of loss of
prestige of scholarship, for in the seventeenth century a

[1] v. Loen, *op. cit.*, p. 65.
[2] e.g. Leibniz, Wolff, Haller and later Schiller and Goethe. The ennoblement of writers and painters was also no rare occurrence in sixteenth- and
seventeenth-century Western Europe, e.g. Molière, Rubens, Cranach, Merian,
van Dyck, etc.
[3] W. H. Bruford, *Germany in the Eighteenth Century*, p. 61.
[4] Ennoblement is not advisable, says Loen (*op. cit.*, p. 158 f.), if the noble
has not sufficient resources or if his business includes keeping an open shop.
This condemnation of shop-owners is still important at the end of the nineteenth century in affecting the composition of the Prussian corps of reserve
officers. The son of a shopkeeper could not become a lieutenant in the Reserve.

doctorate in Jurisprudence or theology was still considered to be equivalent to noble rank. The value of
the doctorate was already declining in the eighteenth
century on account of its frequent bestowal, and even the
pettiest nobles now refused to be called "Doctor."
Moreover, the title of Professor was no qualification for
the court, since the prestige of a court-councillor far outweighed any academic rank.

If we examine the structure of the nobility of old
lineage in the eighteenth century, we shall notice four
main groups: country-nobility (estate-owners), court-
nobility, military-nobility in the cities and administrative
nobility.

Whilst the first group of relatively independent,
widely-privileged country-nobles represented a relic of
feudal times, the position of the three other groups was
determined by the decisive change of function which
they suffered in the period of absolutism and the standing
army.[1]   Until then, the nobility had been a military and
political factor of far-reaching independence and importance, but the absolute ruler of Prussia bent it to his
service—of course, not without rewarding it with an
exceptionally privileged position—and the independent
feudal-nobility became a courtly subject-nobility, the
independent knights a modern corps of State officers.

Whereas the territorial noble exercised a patrimonial
jurisdiction, and, like the English country squire,
administered the law on his estate and in the surrounding
district, there were reserved for him at the same time,
by a kind of indigenous right, the chief military and

---

[1] A reactionary aristocratic writer like Marwitz characteristically acknowledges only the country nobility as the true aristocracy, whilst he describes
the immense crowd of landless nobles of the eighteenth century as "pretended
nobles"; his descending scale of values is as follows: landed nobility—military
nobility—town nobility—court nobility. "A great deal of mischief and cor-
ruption came by degrees from this pretended nobility. The better part of it
served in the army (and in this activity approximated somewhat to its original
purpose), the worse part, however, idled in the cities or at court: but both
dissipated their paternal inheritance which had been turned into liquid capital
on the security of estates of brothers or cousins" (F. A. L. v. d. Marwitz, *Preussischer Adel*, ed. Fr. Schinkel, Breslau, 1932, p. 264).

administrative posts.[1]   With the latter was bound up admission to court, and it was this life at court that furnished so strong an attraction when compared with the monotonous existence in the country.   For there, if possessed of the requisite versatility, the noble could reckon on some political power, social recognition, refined luxury and intercourse with his equals.[2]

Even the last defender of the hierarchy of Estates confessed in his retrospect "that the officer-ranks as a whole (apart from artillery and hussars), and the higher civil posts, were filled with nobles."[3]   But this preference was not so absolute in the civil service.   It was precisely in Prussia that there were several high officials (military-councillors, court-councillors, Presidents, and Privy councillors) of middle-class origin, since they recommended themselves to the absolute rulers by their legal training and practical knowledge.[4]   It is significant that Frederick the Great gave wide preference to nobles in government, but filled the important post of Secretary to the Cabinet almost exclusively from the ranks of loyal commoners, and not from those of nobles covetous of power.[5]   The higher middle-class officials, however, had always to yield precedence to nobles of the same official standing, and they were reminded of the fact so often that their professional training furnished only a moderate compensation for shortcomings in blood and tradition.[6]

The social gradation of the nobility, which we have examined, corresponds only in part with the different attitudes which the nobles assumed towards culture.

[1] The aristocracy was still, according to the Prussian Land Law of 1794, "assigned the place of honour in the state for which it had fitted itself" (Johanna Schultze, *op. cit.*, p. 114).

[2] W. H. Bruford, *op. cit.*, p. 63.

[3] L. v. d. Marwitz, *op. cit.*, p. 61.

[4] Johanna Schultze, *op. cit.*, p. 115.

[5] Cf. R. Koser, *Geschichte Friedrichs d. Gr.*, 4th Ed., Stuttgart, 1913, ii. 28 ff.

[6] For the relationship between middle-class and aristocratic officials in Prussia see A. Lotz, *Geschichte des deutschen Beamtentums*, Berlin, 1909, pp. 207–8.

Here there existed many regional and sociological
variants. Joseph von Eichendorff has classified the
aristocracy very neatly in this respect[1] : he differentiates—

(*a*) The patriarchal country-nobility, such as was to
be met with in Silesia, "the most numerous,
healthiest, and by far the most entertaining
group." It was composed of small estate-
owners who sought to brighten a life of almost
insular seclusion with annual events such as
harvests, hunts, and journeys to annual fairs or
the nearest town. To be good gentlemen-
farmers was the ideal of the men, the reputation
for good domestic management was the pride
of the women. They made no pretence to
æsthetic claims, their education differed little
from that of their subjects, and this, says
Eichendorff, explains the intimate understanding between the two groups. "They understood the people because of this, and were still
understood by the people."

(*b*) The exclusive, ornamental nobility who copied
French pretentiousness. These were anxious
to keep abreast of the modish culture, copied
the style of Versailles and engrossed themselves
in a traditional æsthetic life.[2] They showed in
their manner contempt for the first group,
whom they regarded as plebeian country bump-

[1] Jos. Freiherr v. Eichendorff, *Der Adel und die Revolution, Sämtliche Werke,
Historisch-kritische Ausgabe von Becker-Kosel-Sauer*, Regensburg, 1911, x.
383–406.

[2] The stereotype of this pretentious "leisure-class" is well described by
Eichendorff: "Like their gardens, each possessed no clear and definite individuality, nor did they have national features, but only a completely general
class-appearance; there was everywhere, to the extent of deadliest boredom,
the same 'Courtoisie,' the same banal catchwords, likes and dislikes. . . .
Their stables were turned into magnificent temples, where an almost ghostly
cult held sway, with beautiful horses and handsome Swiss cows. In the
interior of castles there was a kaleidoscope of dazzling dilettantism in all its
artifices and colours: the young ladies indulged in music, painted, or played
battledore and shuttlecock with theatrical grace, the mistress of the house fed
occasional chickens and doves, or pulled gold lace—and everyone really did
nothing" (Eichendorff, *op. cit.*, x. 393).

kins, and were in turn despised by the latter
for their seemingly affected fine airs.

(c) The pleasure-seekers and spendthrifts, the mobile
element in the nobility, "cavaliers floundering
in the mire of love." The majority had been
spoilt by long years of travel abroad and sought
to make themselves conspicuous by crazy eccen-
tricities. They were exceedingly dangerous
for the nobility as a whole; they were destructive elements that undermined its prestige, for
this group spread the contagion of an inordinate
desire for pleasure amongst the lower layers of
society which at that time still looked up
credulously and admiringly to the nobility.[1]

The different reactions of these three aristocratic
groups to the repercussions of the French Revolution
are very interesting. The Junkers were pure reactionaries and hated the foreign revolution, the pretentious
smiled elegantly and ignored the "impertinent attempt
of the rabble to make world history," "indeed, it was
considered by them for a long time degrading merely to
speak of it"; the eccentrics, on the other hand, seized
upon the revolution as a highly piquant amusement and
"often tumbled head over heels into the flaming crater." [2]

This short review of the different groups of nobles
shows that it would be quite wrong to disregard the
far-reaching social and cultural differences between the
court-nobility, the officer-nobility quartered in the city,
the administrative nobility which periodically consumed
in the towns the revenues from its estates, and the completely secluded country-nobility in the provinces. It
was inevitably the middle-class critics of the nobility,

---

[1] Eichendorff, *op. cit.*, p. 395.

[2] Apart from this, there existed the small cultural élite of a progressive
aristocracy which, as in the case of Baron Grimm and Count Schlabrendorf,
turned to the French Revolution from serious conviction. "The new matter
had by no means penetrated to the people, it was purely a secret knowledge of
the so-called cultured classes, and therefore represented to a large extent by
aristocrats" (Eichendorff, *op. cit.*, p. 397. Cf. also W. Wenck, *Deutschland
vor 100 Jahren*, Leipzig, 1890, ii. 60 ff.).

who recognized, with the shrewd perception of an enemy, the manifold tension and snobbishness within the nobility.[1]

The French aristocracy before the revolution of 1789 had formed itself into seven grades, each of which transferred to its inferior the contempt that it had to suffer from its superior stratum: in the same way there existed also in the North German nobility, in addition to its common class-consciousness, a scale of internal snobbery. The poor and uninfluential noble was despised by the rich landowner, the rich landowner, in turn, belittled by the fashionable courtier, the mere courtier was pitied by the real courtly families, those who had a blot on their escutcheon were looked at askance "by the full-blooded noble," and finally the noble who bore a name that was blameless but little known was looked down on by the illustrious families.[2]   But the widest gap existed between the noble who could live on his "income from landed property" and the noble who was obliged to live on a "professional income."

The Middle-Class.—The absolute territorial state had succeeded in overcoming and subjecting both the feudal-nobility and the urban bourgeoisie, but the damage suffered by the cities that were formerly economically and politically independent was far more severe and enduring than the loss of function suffered by the nobility.[3]   All the old democratic tendencies towards a self-governing commonalty were suppressed and had disappeared.   The German cities, in so far as they were not independent imperial cities, were subject to the autocratic will of the territorial prince.   Common assemblies of the citizens were forbidden in the eighteenth century

---

[1] e.g. the moderate conservative *Geheime Kabinettsrat* A. Wilhelm Rehberg, who knew the aristocracy intimately, in his *Über deutschen Adel*, Göttingen, 1803.

[2] Rehberg, *op. cit.*, p. 178.

[3] For the legal and political situation at the end of the eighteenth century see the illuminating exposition of H. Preuss, *Die Entwicklung des deutschen Städtewesens*, vol. i, Leipzig, 1906.   Cf. also Bruford, *Germany in the Eighteenth Century*, part iii.

as highly dangerous organizations. The city council degenerated into the spineless servant of the rulers and the cities themselves became a kind of domain and garrison belonging to the State. The autocratic pressure from above was passed down to the citizens by the council which ruled its subjects with unlimited powers. But this brings us now to the social organization within the Commons. The Commons, as an Estate, was at that time a very comprehensive and negative conception. It consisted, mainly, of all inhabitants who belonged by birth neither to the nobility nor to the peasantry.[1] It embraced, therefore, with very few exceptions, the Christian population of the cities. But we must differentiate between the dissimilar situations of the cities immediately subject to the Empire and those subject to the territorial prince.

In the imperial cities the most important gradation was that between the patriciate, potential councillors, and the rest of the citizens. In many imperial cities an oligarchy had made the government hereditary: in Nürnberg, for example, only twenty families, mostly noble, were qualified to rule: in eighteenth-century Frankfort the régime alternated between two families, between whom the council positions were apportioned. Membership of the council in many cities was for life, and since the council could supplement itself by co-option, there was created of necessity an exclusiveness which soon led to hereditary transmission in conciliar offices.

Much more characteristic of the decay in power and lack of independence of the commons was the social and legal organization of the bourgeoisie in the provincial cities of the eighteenth century. For here the upper stratum was constantly striving to surrender its civic rights and place itself directly under the protection of the absolutist institutions of the court and garrison. At that time there arose, therefore, in several German provincial cities, especially in residential and garrison-towns,

[1] H. Preuss, *op. cit.*, p. 189.

three groups: freed citizens, citizens proper and protected citizens. (*Gefreite Bürger, Bürger, Schutzbürger.*)

The *Gefreite Bürger* were those members of the upper
grade who had had themselves freed by the court from
their civic qualifications, rights and duties.

To the normal category, the *Bürger*, belonged the
middle-grade of the cities: artisans, agricultural-workers,
shop-owners, and innkeepers, a group which was at the
time spoken of somewhat contemptuously in literature
as "a set of small shopkeepers."

The *Schutzbürger*, the protected citizens, included men
whose livelihood was uncertain and dependent, such as
labourers, married journeymen and pedlars.

In the year 1783, Berlin had, for example, a population of 141,000 inhabitants, of whom no less than
57,000 were freed (exempted) from civic obligations:
their composition was:

    33,000—garrison (including dependents).
    14,000—officials (including dependents).
    10,000—lackeys and serving men.

Besides these the whole court-nobility, all civil servants,
even the court-purveyors and court-artisans, together
with all foreign colonists, were also exempted.[1]

A strong light is thrown on the political weakness of
this class by the fact that the upper stratum of the residential cities preferred to be considered as privileged
subjects of the Prince rather than as privileged citizens.
And even if the pressure of the State on the cities in the
feudal east was stronger than in the west, there prevailed
practically everywhere (with the exception of a few
economically successful imperial towns like Frankfort-
on-Main) a timidly passive philistinism which disappeared only very slowly through the reforms of the
nineteenth century.

II

The Prestige of the Nobility.—The priority of the
nobility in the eighteenth century was undisputed and

[1] H. Preuss, *op. cit.*, pp. 171 ff.

indisputable. It did, however, suffer criticism and opposition from numerous bourgeois writers; aristocratic privileges were questioned very often in books and periodicals. In the last thirty years of the century special objections were raised against the several groups of the nobility. Again and again the country nobility was described as coarse and uncultured, the court nobility as conceited, foppish and useless.[1] We shall discuss later this ethical criticism of the eighteenth century which helped prepare the ground for the social reforms of 1808. It could by no means shake the prestige enjoyed by the nobility in society, for the social postulates for such a revolution as in France were lacking in the politically disunited Germany. Only if we keep in mind the significance and power of the nobility, can the vigour, as well as the limits, of the hostile attacks of the middle-class writers in the nineteenth century be understood.

We must here once again turn to our distinction between the attitude of the ethical writer and that of the æsthetic writer towards society. The first type combated the prestige of the nobility at that time as spokesman of the Commons; the second described it and acknowledged it as an existing power. The first type belonged to the defiant, suppressed intelligentsia of opposition, the other to the loyal intelligentsia which had either already gained a footing in the upper grade, or hoped to gain such a footing. For a critical evaluation, the second type is more important than the first in throwing light on the social distribution of power and the actual strength of nobility and Commons. Two authors of this type will be especially significant for our purpose: Goethe, the ennobled son of a patrician, and Christian Garve, the conservative social philosopher and admirer of Frederick the Great.[2]

---

[1] Johanna Schultze, *op. cit.*, p. 12.

[2] Goethe depicts the precedence of the aristocracy in *Wilhelm Meisters Lehrjahre*, whilst Christian Garve describes the relationship of aristocratic and middle-class prestige in his essay *Über die Maxime Rochefoucaulds: das bürgerliche Air verliert sich zuweilen bei der Armee, niemals am Hofe* in *Versuche über verschiedene Gegenstände aus der Moral, der Literatur und dem gesellschaftlichen Leben*, Breslau, 1802, i. 295–452. See also the studies of W.

The dualism of noble and non-noble—as we see from these sources—still possessed an extraordinary social importance at the end of the society based on status. The social gap between a noble and a commoner was, according to Garve, far more significant at that time than the gap between a poor landed noble and a powerful court-noble on the one hand, or between a petty bourgeois employee and a banker on the other.[1]   For amongst bourgeois officials "the youngest candidate is of the very stuff from which the foremost member of a council is formed"; but "the man of common ancestry can never, in actual fact, become a man of good birth."[2] The noble has a whole string of privileges which make him feel at his ease in society. He possesses, for example, the privilege of wearing a specially elegant costume and the *ius præcedentiæ*—the right of precedence in a society consisting of nobles and commoners. Above all, however, his word of honour has an extremely high value: for the word of a "cavalier" is worth as much as a statutory declaration.[3]

The prestige of the nobility is largely an æsthetic one: it expresses itself in the inclination of the court- and

Wittich, *Der soziale Gehalt von Goethe's Roman Wilhelm Meisters Lehrjahre*, in Max Weber, *Erinnerungsgabe*, Munich, 1923, ii. 278–306, and of W. H. Bruford, *Goethe's Wilhelm Meister as a picture and a criticism of society*, in *Publications of the English Goethe Society*, London, 1933. The interpretation of Goethe's attitude towards eighteenth-century society by L. Balet, *Die Verbürgerlichung der deutchen Kunst, Literatur und Musik im 18. Jahrhundert*, Strassburg, 1936, pp. 210 ff., is biased and insufficient.

[1] This conservative view of the middle-class social philosophers is naturally still more stressed by the extreme aristocratic opposition which later turns against the removal of this framework of classes. Their most determined advocate, L. v. d. Marwitz, says: "It is not possible to seek the origin of the aristocracy anywhere else than in military service. Favour and money have indeed nothing noble in themselves, and therefore no ground for nobility. Kings can distribute titles as a mark of favour or for the sake of money, and also give away the name of noble—by this means they can create elegant men, but not nobles. In ninety-nine cases out of a hundred the speculator or boorish shopkeeper will be visible in the children of bankers and merchants, of ideologists and citizens of the world; the trade instincts hide in them, ideas of profit are always before their eyes, i.e. *they are and remain common*. The son of a noble (who may be foolish for all I care) will always shun a mean action" (F. A. L. v. d. Marwitz, *Preussischer Adel*, p. 204).

[2] Garve, *op. cit.*, p. 347.   [3] v. Loen, *op. cit.*, p. 232.

state-aristocracy towards a refined sociability. This
sociability has its economic foundations in the wealth
which still stands at the disposal of part of the nobility;
but it has, moreover, its psychological root in the special
capability of the noble classes for employing this wealth
in an untroubled leisure.[1] The rich men of other classes
are either busier, for they pursue the trade to which they
owe their wealth, or else they have been imbued with
the idea of working and cannot rid themselves of the old
habits. But the nobility has this leisure, for its varied
functions do not overburden it. The aristocrat who lives
in the country is concerned at the most with the supervision of his estates, and at least six months a year remain
to him for social diversions; the administrative and political nobility leaves the greater part of the routine-work
to bourgeois subordinates; and the nobles who are officers
are in the same way nearly always free from serving.[2]

It is because of this traditional leisure that the nobility
develops its characteristic air, the free courtly "tone"
which appears to the educated commoner so desirable
to imitate, yet so impossible of imitation.

It is a fact [affirms Garve, with a heart by no means light] that
the greatest refinement of manners, the highest refinement of
social intercourse, the truly good "tone" is not to be found in the
merchant cities, nor in the universities and houses of the Muses,
but in the capitals and court cities.[3]

Here the noble air of refinement and elegance crystal-
lizes—and the bourgeois air appears, in comparison with
it, merely as an accumulation of uncertain and unhappy
attempts at imitation. "It is indeed definitely decorous,
but it is not quite the right article; it is a species of
courtesy, but one which betrays the school of the small
circle in which it has been learnt."[4] The negative
criteria of the bourgeois airs are fourfold:

  (1) Exaggerated and sweeping politeness. (Ten-
      dency towards affectation and false ceremonial.)

---

[1] Cf. Garve, *op. cit.*, p. 337.   [2] Garve, *op. cit.*, p. 338.
[3] Garve, *op. cit.*, p. 308.   [4] Garve, *op. cit.*, p. 402.

(2) Uneasy shifting between false modesty and pride
     which gives the commoner an ambiguous and
     embarrassed attitude. From this arises

(3) the frequent inferiority complex of the unprivi-
     leged, an uncomfortable uncertainty in regard
     to "the degree of frankness and constraint" to
     be assumed towards other persons, especially
     those of a superior class.

(4) Physical and spiritual limitations due to their
     professions. The body and mind of the noble
     reveal the man of the world: the body and mind
     of the commoner show, in contrast, the pro-
     fession which he pursues daily. The noble is
     always to be recognized by his easy superiority
     and gracious manner; the commoner, on the
     other hand, by the peculiarities of his profession,
     e.g. as artisan, book-keeper, or scholar.[1]

In these characteristics we can find the essential sociological distinction between noble and commoner. The
noble, as is to be seen both at court and in the state, is represented by his very being, the commoner purely by his
achievement. The noble can strive for the harmonious
cultivation of all his powers, whilst the commoner must
concentrate on a one-sided cultivation of individual functions: the one creates by what he represents, the other
represents what he creates. The fundamental thesis of
the declining society of Estates is: *Harmony and personality
belong only to the uppermost social stratum, that is to say,
are accessible and peculiar only to the upper and lower nobility.*
   "A commoner may acquire merit, by excessive efforts,
he may even educate his mind; but his personal qualities
are lost, let him struggle as he will."[2] The ideal of
an æsthetic way of life always emphasizes the idea
of an organic correlation and harmony between the
whole and its parts.[3] In the society of Estates, how-

---

[1] Garve, *ibid.*   [2] Goethe, *Wilhelm Meisters Lehrjahre*, book v, ch. iii.
[3] We might notice here *en passant* that the Estates-system stresses, similarly
to the modern totalitarian state, the political ideology of the harmony of the
whole and its parts (see v. d. Marwitz, *Preussischer Adel*, pp. 266 ff.).

ever, such an ideal of harmony can only be realized by
the noble type.

Whereas the nobleman, who mixes with the most elegant, is
obliged to acquire an elegant behaviour himself and whereas, since
neither door nor gate is closed to him, this behaviour becomes an
unconstrained one; since he has to pay with his figure, his person,
be it at court or in the army, he has taken care to attach value to
it and to show that he attaches value to it. A certain festive
graciousness in ordinary things, a kind of thoughtless elegance in
serious and important ones, becomes him well, because he lets it
be seen that he is well-balanced in everything he does.[1]

Self-control and inner equilibrium are therefore the
essential demands of society from the noble in his
capacity as a "public person."[2] He acts always as a
representative, as one who will be seen in public:

He is a public person, and the more cultivated his movements,
the more sonorous his voice, the more restrained and moderate his
whole manner is, the more he is complete, and if he remains ever
the same towards high and low, towards friend and relative, then
no exception can be taken to him: one cannot wish him otherwise.
If he can outwardly control himself at any moment of his life,
then nothing more can be demanded of him; and everything else
that he possesses within and around himself, ability, talent, wealth
—all these seem to be only adjuncts.[3]

For Goethe, as for Garve, it constitutes an essential
characteristic of the Estates-system that the nobility
lives without any handicap of social limitations, whilst
the commoner has to live with a strong consciousness
of them: "Inasmuch as the noble knows absolutely no
boundaries in his ordinary life, inasmuch as one can
create out of him kings or king-like figures, he may,
therefore, appear everywhere before his peers with a quiet
self-confidence; he may press forward everywhere, whilst

---

[1] Goethe, *Wilhelm Meisters Lehrjahre*, v. 3.

[2] With this conception of an easy bearing and inner balance, the attitude
of the court-nobility approaches the English gentleman-ideal, which for a
long time was characterized by fine manners and good breeding. See A.
Hoyler, *Gentleman-Ideal und Gentleman-Erziehund, Munich*, 1933, pp. 8–33.

[3] Goethe, *Wilhelm Meisters Lehrjahre*, v. 3.

for the commoner there is no better thing than the pure, silent feeling of the boundary-line which is drawn for him. He may not ask: "What are you?" but only: "What have you? What judgment, what knowledge, what ability, how much wealth?" If the noble gives everything by exhibiting his person, the commoner gives nothing, and can give nothing through his personality . . . This one shall work and produce, that one shall achieve and create: he shall cultivate single abilities in order to be useful, and it is already postulated that there shall be no harmony in his being, nor may there be, because he, in order to make it useful in some way, must neglect everything else." [1]

From the different conceptions of representation in the nobility and achievement in the middle-classes there follow quite contrasted paths of social rise for both classes. Even the start is different. For, with the nobles, glory is always the glory of a family, with the commons it is the glory of an individual; therefore the noble will always distinguish himself as a member of his Estate and his family. The commoner, however, as an individual can only rise and justify himself by his own achievement. The specific quality required by a noble to rise higher resides in the alertness of a man of the world, that of a commoner in his ability in useful matters. The former advances through his versatility on the world-stage, the latter through his knowledge of practical affairs. The career of a courtier fulfils itself mostly outside the stifling air of the office, in a dexterous participation in balls, parties, festivities at court, in which one strives to

[1] Goethe, *ibid.* It is worth noticing that Goethe thinks here in a sociological manner when he sees the cause of class-differences not so much in the vices of aristocracy and bourgeoisie, but rather in the social structure of the society of Estates itself. He makes Wilhelm Meister say: "It is not the arrogance of the nobles and the obsequiousness of burghers that is responsible for these differences, but the organization of society itself." The next sentence is just as characteristic of the passivity of Goethe's æsthetic attitude as contrasted with the spirit of opposition of the more ethical writers, such as Lessing: "It matters little to me, whether anything will change in this, and what will change; it is sufficient for me, as things now stand, to think of myself, and of how I am to save myself and attain what is for me an indispensable necessity."

obtain the favour of the mighty and the illustrious, of the prince or of an influential minister.

The organization of a society based on status and the inferiority complex which it induced in the commoner give rise in Garve, as in other bourgeois writers, to a characteristic resignation, a surrender of the unattainable objectives of social ambition, a compromise with the reality of an unrevolutionary society. The elegant life, the existence of a "public person," is by its nature barred to the commoner. The oppressive feeling of the impossibility of entering the leading upper-class at a time when the privileged nobility in France was being swept away by the revolution, was then widespread amongst the middle-class and indeed allowed the very cultural revolutionary movement of the "Storm and Stress" to run away helplessly in the sand. The rising generation of the middle-class had at that time, in its narrow German conditions, only a limited perspective. It lived—as Goethe expressed it later—"outwardly inspired in no way to significant action with only the prospect of having to hang on to a dragging, spiritless, bourgeois life." [1]

The social barriers formed by an exclusive society produced in the finer minds a melancholy and a weariness of life—the classical expression of this mood was Goethe's *Werther*—and in the coarser ones stupidity and indifference.

> Everything that is called noble [said Risbeck, comparing German conditions with those of France], even if the nobility should only be founded on the name, and everything that appertains to the court, is closed to the German commoner. His knowledge, his experience of social situations are therefore more confined than those of our own citizens. He has no feeling for the innumerable relationships of ordinary life which the inhabitants of an average French town can experience and appreciate fittingly. [2]

Goethe's *Wilhelm Meister* believes that he can find,

---

[1] Goethe, *Dichtung und Wahrheit*, part ii, book xiii.

[2] K. Risbeck, *Briefe eines reisenden Franzosen über Deutschland*, 1783, vol. i; quoted in H. Weil, *Die Entstehung des deutschen Bildungsprinzips*, Bonn, 1930, p. 250.

as a commoner, a way of attaining to that harmony which is otherwise reserved for the nobility only. The actor's profession, so he thinks, will make it possible for him to act as a "public person." So he chooses a profession which at that time, from the social point of view, was no less foreign to the bourgeois than the existence of a noble. "On the stage," he reflects, "the cultured man appears as much a personality in his glamour as in the upper classes; mind and body must correspond in every effort, and I will be able to be and appear here to as good an advantage as anywhere else." [1]

Wilhelm Meister's development shows, and is intended to show, that the ideal of harmony is incompatible with the actor's status which is socially inferior and is at bottom somewhat despised by the nobility. In the end, Goethe's hero becomes a surgeon, realizing that a commoner, in order to attain to something in the modern world, must specialize.

The deep resignation which sometimes may have overcome the talented commoner in viewing the opportunities for entering the nobility, was significantly expressed in Garve's work: "There remains here nothing else for the noble spirited man to do but courageously to surrender that which he finds valuable but cannot attain." Self-sufficiency and confinement to his own social sphere comprise the true virtues of the good commoner. "If we realize our own awkward existence or our bourgeois air, then this realization is already an advantage which can console us to a certain extent." [2]

If Garve acquiesces in resignation, Goethe seeks for a non-political synthesis of blood and intellect, of tradition and achievement. Goethe's hopes correspond in this only to the actual fact of a formation of small cultural élites recruited from the court as well as from the bourgeoisie, from nobility as well as from Jews. These early cultural amalgamations of noble and bourgeois elements came into being round about 1800 in one or

---

[1] Goethe, *Wilhelm Meisters Lehrjahre*, book v, chap. iii.
[2] Garve, *op. cit.*, p. 439.

two small courts, like Weimar and Darmstadt, but more particularly were they to be found in the salons of the Berlin Jewesses. It was precisely the contact of members of extreme classes or professions (noble, Jew, actor) that made this new form of social intercourse especially attractive and interesting.[1]

Goethe formulated the ideology of this actual "rapprochement" and of the fusion of the criteria of ancestry and achievement, of birth and genius. "Birth, class and wealth," such was the doctrine of the patrician statesman, "are by no means incompatible with genius and taste. This has been taught us by foreign nations which counted a great number of noblemen amongst their best minds." [2]

III

The criticism of society by middle-class writers differentiates itself in the eighteenth century from the æsthetic attitude, such as we have found it in Garve and Goethe, by its dissatisfaction with prevailing society and by its protest against the arbitrary superiority of the nobility. In comparison with later middle-class criticism of the nobility, it is characterized both by its intensity and its growing conviction of the impossibility of a radical alteration by political means, which was the ever-present possibility for the following generations. Criticism of the nobility in the eighteenth century is a moral criticism of politically powerless citizens, that of the nineteenth century is a moral criticism of a middle-class which is slowly becoming class-conscious and political.

The extreme judgments in a critical review of aristo-

---

[1] In aristocratic circles it was, above all, the aristocrats in official positions (diplomatists) who, stirred by ideas of enlightenment, dropped the strict exclusion of the cultured burgher. For the composition and function of the Berlin Salons see H. Weil, *Die Entstehung des deutschen Bildungsprinzips*, chap. iii, pp. 199–236.

[2] Goethe, *Wilhelm Meisters Lehrjahre*, book iii, chap. v. That Goethe's public was not identical with one special class or group, but formed itself beyond the existing social barriers, has been recently pointed out by M. Sommerfeld, in his valuable essay, *Goethe und sein Publikum*, in *Goethe in Umwelt und Folgezeit*, Leiden, 1935, pp. 36–59.

cracy and middle-class are based chiefly on the dualism of might and right. The aristocracy and the despotic rulers of the petty states possessed might, but the middle-class had right. The one commanded prestige and glamour, the other virtue and morality. As long as it was impossible to rob the aristocracy of political power, at least morality was denied to it—that middle-class morality of orderliness and honest work, of marital fidelity and the acceptance of its place in existing society, which was to be raised as a battle-cry against the aristo-cracy in the nineteenth century. The catalogue of aristocratic vices which we find in the dramatists of the eighteenth century, both great and small,[1] as well as in writers of didactic works and light novels, changes colour more and more towards the end of the eighteenth century until it acquires in the nineteenth century, as we shall see later, its characteristic form and summation. The middle-class boasted of its modesty, honesty and diligence as virtues in contrast with the aristocratic vices of frivolity, arrogance and lack of principle.

How did the aristocracy react to this bourgeois resentment and denunciation as expressed in the dramas of Lessing and the young Schiller, in the poems of Bürger and Pfeffel, in children's periodicals such as Weisse's *Kinderfreund?* As long as it was in power (before the great Prussian reforms of 1808), it could afford to ignore the attacks with aloofness. But when the bourgeoisie grew more active and the higher en-lightened bureaucracy pushed through fundamental reforms, the aristocracy sought either to nullify these hostile arguments or to make them ridiculous by exaggera-tion. The former was attempted by the ponderously honest Freiherr von der Marwitz, the latter by the adroit Freiherr von Eichendorff.

While Marwitz simply disputed the justification of the moral reproaches of middle-class writers and declared

---

[1] Cf. Clara Stockmeyer, *Soziale Probleme im Drama des Sturm und Drang*, Frankfort-on-Main, 1922.

that he had never met, in actual life, the aristocratic caricatures described by them,[1] Eichendorff displayed the moral figures of the bourgeois writers and their attribution of all vices to the Jesuits and aristocrats and all virtues to the lower classes as pure abortions begotten of over-heated imagination.[2] He parries the middle-class attacks by admitting indeed the reproach of the growing meaninglessness of the aristocracy, but claims at the same time that the middle-class is losing its own meaning and is depriving the world of its divine attributes. Since this Catholic romanticist interprets society from the point of view of a glorified picture of the Middle Ages, he reflects how much the aristocracy has declined since that time, and records the curse of the middle-class to be its surrender to capital.[3]

The decisive event in the position in society of aristocracy and middle-class was, in Prussia, the Stein-Hardenberg legislation of 1808. It signified in practice the end of the society based on status since it removed two essential characteristics: the restriction of the *Stände* to fixed professions, and the intervention of the state in municipal administration. The division of the people into three hereditary Estates of aristocracy, middle-class and peasantry, was destroyed: citizens and peasants were free to pursue middle-class professions, and the cities now received the right to administer themselves through

---

[1] "In all these poems and writings the aristocrats were represented as rough, ignorant, haughty and proud of their rank; they torment their peasants with arbitrary tallages, drive them out of house and home, are perverted lovers of hunting, who ruin the cornfields of their peasants with their huge hunting expeditions." "In all children's books, the Junker is always a fool and a coarse fellow, the son of the citizen the embodiment of virtue." (v. d. Marwitz, *Preussischer Adel*, p. 58.)

[2] Eichendorff, *Sämtliche Werke*, x. 402–6.

[3] Eichendorff, *op. cit.*, p. 403 f.: "The burghers once built churches for the glory of God; now they are building factories and workers-tenements." "The cities were changed from a world-power to a money-power." Similarly, v. d. Marwitz in the end charges both classes with causing the decline of the State of Estates: "Neither was better or worse than the other, but both classes tore themselves loose from the state and indulged in vile self-seeking. Their whole thought was concentrated on the gratification of the moment: they were completely ignorant of the fact that there was a spiritual whole of which they were parts" (*Preussischer Adel*, p. 266 f.).

bodies elected by themselves. The principles of ownership and individual ability respectively were to replace
heredity and tradition in political and economic life.
This innovation, introduced by a rationalist bureaucracy,
naturally encountered the strongest opposition from the
nobility. Therefore one need not wonder that in the
aristocratic casino in Berlin people said: better to lose
three battles of Auerstaedt than tolerate such a law.[1]

The middle-class, hitherto repressed and politically
powerless, had proved its fitness in the national armies
of the Wars of Liberation, where it had shown that
courage and presence of mind were not the monopoly
of the aristocracy. Through the institution of the
territorial army (*Landwehr*) which was led by middle-
class reserve-officers, the bourgeoisie had played a great
part in the victories of 1813–15 and therefore it became
more strongly conscious of its claim to a constitution
and a share in the administration of the State. But the
hopes of the middle-class were bitterly shattered after
their return from the field. The aristocracy rapidly
regained its political influence, sabotaged a great deal
of the work of reform, and continued in its intransigent
attitude. In this way the conflict between aristocracy
and middle-class became more sharply defined.[2]

The aristocracy sought to regain its lost ground at any
price; it planned a "Union of the German Aristocracy
for the protection of common interests" and adroitly
organized its opposition everywhere. Its literary defence was undertaken by two different groups of writers.
The first was a sprinkling of literary aristocrats who
were driven by their resentment to take up the pen in
their unpractised hands. The second consisted of
romantic intellectuals who glorified the aristocracy in a
fantastic way and who diverted the reader from social
reality by their clever propaganda. The aristocratic

[1] H. Preuss, *op. cit.*, p. 218. Cf. F. Schnabel, *Deutsche Geschichte im 19.
Jahrhundert*, Freiburg i. Br., 1933, i. 356–8; see also R. Aris, *History of
Political Thought in Germany from 1789 to 1815*, London, 1936, pp. 391–406.
[2] Cf. M. von Boehn, *Biedermeier. Deutschland von 1815–1847*, Berlin,
n.d., 2nd Ed., pp. 277 ff.

writers, together with their more skilled bourgeois helpers, developed a common ideology for the justification of the old Estates, and of aristocratic dominion:[1] but with this difference, that a hard-boiled Junker like Marwitz worked on the basis of a realistic consciousness of power, whilst the political romanticists decked out their ideas with all the ornamentations of philosophical dialectic and intellectual architecture in order to arouse attention and to rise to success. The argumentation of an Adam Müller or Friedrich Schlegel on behalf of the aristocracy was the cunning play of a versatile intellect which could change its allegiance without any actual class-ties and which, led on by its pleasure in words, was very little concerned as to how far it believed in the truth of its own phrases.

The later romanticists, as a whole, and especially Adam Müller, Görres, Fouqué, Baader, Eichendorff, and Steffens hold firmly to the idea of the state of Estates and romanticize the Estates as "living, organic, collectivities, to which the individual is joined, thereby binding himself inwardly and vitally to the state as a whole."[2] These romanticists embark upon polemics no less fiercely than do their nationalist successors of to-day; they combat the disintegrating spirit of freedom from the west by the preservation of the aristocracy and even by the re-erection of the bygone guild-organization.

If we find amongst the romanticists writers of both aristocratic and middle-class origin, it is significant that generally it is the middle-class elements who, obeying the law of renegades, are the most vituperative. The aristocratic romantics, like Eichendorff or Fouqué, have not broken with their caste through their literary activity,

---

[1] For the fusion of the old principle of Estates with romantic thought and its importance for the German historical and philosophical trend of ideas in the nineteenth century as contrasted with the sociological ideas of the Western nations, see Karl Mannheim, "Conservative Thought," in his *Essays on Sociology and Social Psychology*, ed. Paul Kecskemeti, London, 1953, pp. 74–164.

[2] P. Kluckhohn, *Persönlichkeit und Gemeinschaft, Studien zur Staatsauffassung der deutschen Romantik*, Halle, 1925, p. 91 f.

but it has caused a certain gap between them and the aristocracy: they are able to appreciate personal intercourse with class-conscious burghers, and are not seldom to be found discussing with them the rights and conception of aristocracy.

Fouqué, for example, in his correspondence with a burgher, with whom he was on terms of familiarity, discusses the problem of aristocracy openly, in a reasonable and naïve way.[1]   Even if he does argue against a reform of the aristocracy on the English model, this correspondence shows that he is just as far from an unyielding aristocratic dogmatism as is the conciliatory catholic Eichendorff.

Quite different are the professional litterati of middle-class origin like Adam Müller, the wit and rhetorician who became in succession an Anglomaniac in Göttingen, defender of the Estates-system against centralism in Berlin, and a functionary of the absolutist central state in Austria.   With the extraordinary versatility of a badly paid intellectual, this type was at one and the same time a philosopher of history and propagandist, a "typical concocter of justifications,"[2] who quickly found an ideological superstructure for any political cause that employed him.   How far Müller's eloquence went in glorifying and romanticizing the aristocracy, is shown by one single passage from his book *Die Elemente der Staatskunst*:[3]

The nobility is the first and only necessary legal institution in the state: in contrast to individuals and their momentary power, it represents the power of freedom of the invisible and absent members of society: and so it lays the foundation, through its exalted and exclusive struggle with the bourgeoisie, of the possibility of

---

[1] Cf. *Etwas über deutschen Adel, über Ritter-Sinn und Militär-Ehre*, in *Briefen von Friedr. Baron de la Motte Fouqué und Friedrich Perthes*, Hamburg, 1819.

[2] K. Mannheim, *op. cit.*, pp. 116, 124.

[3] *Die Elemente der Staatskunst*, Berlin, 1809, i. 264.   This book resulted from public lectures before "His Excellency the Prince of Saxony-Weimar and a gathering of statesmen and diplomats," in the winter of 1808–9 in Dresden.

representation, of the *liberté générale* as well as of the *intérêt générale* and *volonté générale* in the person of a single, ruling, sovereign being.

Besides the actual political romanticism which consciously glorified and defended the aristocracy, there is also the positive picture of aristocracy in romantic poetry which was very much read by the youth of the middle-class. In contrast to the sober consideration of social reality, as it is to be found in Goethe's mature novels, romantic poetry, so to speak, soars over social reality. Precisely for this reason it contains a hidden idealization of the landed aristocracy and a belittlement of certain bourgeois types. It praises the independent "good-for-nothing" (*Taugenichts*), who frees himself from the bonds of middle-class everyday life, from parental home and town, preferring the adventurousness of a free existence. This hero nearly always enjoys fabulous experiences with charming ladies of noble birth in old castles, and nearly always suffers opposition from petty-bourgeois philistines, who think merely of material ends and have no understanding for higher truths. So long as romanticism did not (as for example in E. T. A. Hoffmann's *Meister Martin* or in Novalis' *Heinrich von Ofterdingen*) praise the bygone guild-life of the worthy artisans, it usually saw in the burgher merely an empty-headed philistine. This is clearly shown—to take a characteristic example—by Clemens Brentano's malicious essay, *The Philistine before, in and after History* (1811), which betrays its sociological function through its place of origin—the "Christian-German Table-Society" in Berlin. The Table-Society was a conservative round-table composed of hereditary nobles, officers, higher bureaucrats and a few middle-class scholars and artists. It was directed against the Hardenberg reforms that favoured the middle-class, and characteristically excluded "philistines" as a third category, in addition to Jews and women. The philistine was for this *Fronde*, however, the presumptuous burgher who did not bow down to the order of society as handed down by history, but who exhibited "a self-satisfied, arrogant self-confidence." [1]

Immediately after the Wars of Liberation the aristocracy and middle-class faced each other like two hostile powers who mistrustfully observe their opponent's movements. The aristocracy followed the economic progress of the middle-class with increasing suspicion: the middle-class, led partly by renegades like Varnhagen von Ense (who acted somewhat like spies in aristocratic society), saw with uneasiness the aristocracy's recovery of political strength and social position.

Aristocratic hatred of middle-class reforms and reformers sought to strike at the latter through their low birth, hoping thereby to weaken their influence. The aristocrat, as we saw, could be proud of his family, the bourgeois only of his personal achievements: but alas, for him! if the son of a middle-class reformer should dare to flatter himself with his father's achievements, by which to raise a claim to a middle-class family tradition! The man, who is otherwise quite reasonable, would then be sharply rebuked by the aristocracy for his arrogant pride and reproached for the arrogance with which he maintained that "there has never been a more famous family pride and that the merits of such a father would never be sufficiently honoured in the son." [2] The animosity against middle-class reformers like Scharnhorst and against their intellectualism was so strong that an attempt was made to belittle at least their outward appearance, even their physical stature. They were said to lack military bearing and proper physical development. Scharnhorst, for example, the great middle-class military reformer of the Wars of Liberation, is spoken

---

[1] Clemens Brentano, *Ges. Schriften*, Frankfort-on-Main, 1852, v. 379 ff.   In accordance with the fashion of that time, Brentano here developed a kind of philosophy of oscillation between the two negative poles, Jew and Philistine.   He saw into both extremes and spoke of "the genius in the Jew turned sour and become a crafty fear" and of "the genius in the philistine turned sweet and become an arrogant self-confidence."

[2] L. v. d. Marwitz, *Preussischer Adel*, p. 198.

of as follows: "Scharnhorst had nothing at all military in his appearance or manner: he looked much more like an old, pensive writer, he had by no means such magnificent normal loins as Rauch permits him to stretch out in his statue, but thighs of a common type." [1]

In the period of early liberalism the aristocracy was able to hold in check the still politically unorganized middle-class and to assert itself socially everywhere. Varnhagen, the aristocratic wit and enemy of aristocracy, the liberal interpreter of the Wars of Liberation, described the situation in Prussia in 1825 in the following words:

> The aristocracy gains in strength daily: first at court, then in the army and administration. It is true, of course, that the individual aristocrat is not looked up to so much as he used to be, but the aristocracy as a whole has perhaps gained in this respect. Our noble, landed, families are establishing an aristocratic power by which the royal power is guided. Every native who is not descended from the aristocracy is only a semi-Prussian. [2]

Especially in East-Elbia, even in the following decades, did the dependence of the lower classes on the nobility, on the military and civil administration, on the court-purveyor attitude continue. [3]

But in the larger cities the aristocracy could no longer seriously endanger the continually growing strong self-confidence of the middle-class. There thus remained for it only the "pinprick" policy by which it managed to irritate the burgher in his sensitive spot—his desire for social acceptance. [4] Professors enjoyed a high prestige in middle-class circles, and the middle-class was not a little hurt when their idol, the professor, was not acceptable at court. Similarly, the aristocratic husbands of mixed marriages were subjected to an inner conflict,

[1] L. v. d. Marwitz, *Preussischer Adel*, p. 198.

[2] M. v. Boehn, *Biedermeier. Deutschland von 1815–1845*, p. 276.

[3] See H. Preuss, *Die Entwicklung des deutschen Städtewesens*, i. 348 f.

[4] This held good not only for Prussia, but also for Austria, where especially in Vienna as the meeting-place of Hungarian, Bohemian, Polish, Italian and German nobles in the Metternich period, the permanent humiliation and repression of the burghers was displayed. Cf. the *Wiener Eindrücke* by Karl Gutzkow, *Ges. Werke*, Frankfort-on-Main, 1845, iii. 329 f.

for entry at court was forbidden to their bourgeois wives. Bismarck's mother, for example, a middle-class professor's daughter, could not appear at court. In the court theatre at Weimar, the first row of seats was still, after 1815, divided up for nobles and for burghers, and at the same time the title of "Fräulein" was still reserved for aristocrats.[1]

It was the July Revolution of 1830 in France which first aroused the German middle-class and served as a flaming torch to give the young cause of liberalism new aggressiveness. Less in Prussia than in a few North-German middle-states, political differences arose and the *Hambacher Fest* (1832) showed for the first time the integrating effect of the liberal and democratic movement. At the same time there began after 1830 a slow advance of middle-class industrialization, and with the disposition to form political parties the tension between aristocracy and middle-class now took on a practical shape. This tension lies behind the political struggle of the revolution of 1848–49. We shall endeavour, then, in the following chapters, to illustrate and analyse the different economic and political aspects of the struggle between the two classes.

---

[1] See M. v. Boehn, *op. cit.*, p. 280. According to Bruford (*loc. cit.*, p. 54), even as late as 1816 the post-offices were notified that they were not to forward letters to middle-class girls if they were addressed as "Fräulein."

The sociological change in meaning of the term "Fräulein" is worth noticing: in 1930 "Fräulein" as a mode of address had completely depreciated amongst the lower middle-class. A clerk would think it now insulting and socially degrading if she were addressed in the office as "Fräulein" (without the addition of her name).

CHAPTER II

THE CHANGE IN ECONOMIC EQUILIBRIUM
1830–1848

In any comparative study of the economic and social systems of Germany, France and England one is struck by the late and slow development of Germany in the first half of the nineteenth century from agrarianism to industrialism, and from feudalism to democracy.[1] Karl Marx has rightly compared the economic situation of Germany in 1843 with that of France in 1789. The causes are manifold, political as well as economic. Germany's division into a number of small states for a long time hindered the growth of a national economic unity, and the agrarian crises of 1820–31 had a depressing effect upon economic enterprise. The lack of a political centralization crippled the process of democratization and weakened the impetus of the liberal movement. The apportionment of Germany into small states meant the absence of a unified *tiers état* which could, as in England and France, have acted with decision and taken over, in part at least, state-control. Not until after 1830 did the German middle-class, profoundly influenced by the success of the French July Revolution, slowly start its political organization. Yet on the other hand, the economic ascent of German industry and capitalist banking in every sphere did not begin until after 1848.

If, so far as the middle-class was concerned, the

---

[1] Cf. C. Brinkmann, *Wirtschafts- und Sozialgeschichte*, Munich, 1927, and A. Sartorius v. Waltershausen, *Deutsche Wirtschaftsgeschichte, 1815–1914*, 2nd Ed., Jena, 1923.

political and social situation advanced but little after 1815, the aristocracy was still faced with significant changes. For them the Freiherr von Stein reforms of 1808 were of far-reaching importance. However much the aristocracy might seek to sabotage their execution, this franchise made a decisive breach in an ancient tradition. For centuries the Prussian nobility had been subjected to the principle that money-making by trade or industry was not consonant with social standing and therefore taboo. Even landed-property had always been for purposes of consumption and not a means of profit. In classical times and in the Middle Ages it had been considered both by the landed aristocracy and the urban politicians as a serious offence against normal class standards if an estate were regarded as a basis for economic gain instead of the basis for a way of life befitting one's estate. "Whoever crossed the line between the two forms of economic behaviour—wealth and profit-bearing capital—in too perceptible a manner, and became an *entrepreneur*, was regarded in Antiquity as a person of base mind, in the Middle Ages as a man lacking knightly qualities."[1]

The edict of 1808 signifies the recognition of middle-class acquisitive labour by the Prussian state, or rather by the bureaucracy that directed it. The absolute monopoly of the aristocracy in regard to estate-ownership was broken, the ownership of land made accessible to the middle-classes, and trade and industry spread to the aristocracy. Now, for the first time the two classes stood on the same footing as owners of estates.

The aristocracy developed different attitudes in face of the gradual advance of middle-class enterprise with its rationalized capitalist methods.[2] A significant number of nobles adapted themselves to the new movement

---

[1] Max Weber, *Wirtschaft und Gesellschaft, Grundriss der Sozialökonomik*, iii. I, 560.

[2] For the reaction of the aristocracy and the early capitalist economy see the exposition of C. Brinkmann, *Die Aristokratie im kapitalistischen Zeitalter, Grundriss der Sozialökonomik*, 1926, ix. i. Further, the illuminating article of T. Hobhouse, *Aristocracy, Encyclopedia of the Social Sciences*, ii. 183–90.

towards a rational agrarian economy, and engaged in the exploitation of their agricultural products in great distilleries and sugar refineries.[1] Further, one or two regional groups of nobles, especially in Silesia, engaged in the new, industrial exploitation of their estates (mining); aristocrats like the Princes Pless and Henkel von Donnersmark, the Counts Schaffgotsch and Ballestrem, and others, realized that much bigger business could be done in the nineteenth century with ore and coal than with corn and potatoes.[2]

Yet prior to 1870 the German nobility lacked, in general, that spirit of enterprise which takes the risk of losing its money in strange and hitherto untried ventures. Thus, the landed nobility, who, apart from a few big bankers, furnished at that time the capital-owning stratum, stood aside during the building-up of West German heavy industries in the middle of the nineteenth century and left the financing almost entirely in the hands of foreign capitalists.

Besides this indifference, there is to be found amongst other nobles an avowed disinclination to or incapacity for accommodating themselves to technical and industrial development. Either the aristocrat would not adapt himself because he considered the middle-class profit-making economy unrefined and not becoming to his class, or else he could not adapt himself because he was degenerate and lacking in the mental energy that the new struggle for existence demanded. This type of noble rejected the "middle-class" principle of labour for the sake of profit, thereby condemning the so-called "revenue-economy" in which expenditure has to be strictly regulated according to income; he clung much more to the seigneurial idea of "expenditure economy" in which income is determined for the moment by the necessary expenditure,[3] and it is therefore very char-

---

[1] F. Tönnies, *Deutscher Adel im 19. Jahrhundert* (*Neue Rundschau*, 1912, ii. 1050).

[2] R. Lewinsohn, *Das Geld in der Politik*, Berlin, 1930, pp. 32 ff.

[3] W. Sombart, *Der Bourgeois*, Munich, 1913, pp. 10 and 138 f.

acteristic that even at the beginning of the twentieth century a large minority of junker-estates were still being worked without sharing in capitalist tendencies.[1]

Of the different aristocratic types, the one that failed to adapt itself enjoys a surprisingly one-sided preference in literature between 1830 and 1870. Nowhere, so far as we have been able to discover, has the aristocrat who has succeeded in adapting himself to the market-economy and in becoming a business-magnate, been depicted in literature. If, therefore, we present only the fate of the aristocratic failure, as it is revealed in literature in accordance with our approach to the problem, the fact must by no means be overlooked that in reality there existed the type of an aristocratic entrepreneur and industrialist.[2]

We must first ask ourselves: how is this one-sided portrayal of the aristocrat by middle-class writers to be explained? To some extent it was due to the literary technique of Realism, that is, to the striving to depict, above everything, the characteristic types of contemporary society. (The type of the aristocratic failure was new and therefore more interesting than that of the successful one which had always existed.) To a greater extent, however, the preference of literature is founded on the *anti-aristocratic tendency*, which, open or concealed, finds some expression in almost all the middle-class writers.[3] It is with great pleasure, even if at times not without sympathy, that Gutzkow, Spielhagen, Fanny Lewald, Freytag and others describe the economic decline of the aristocracy. The inefficiency and thoughtlessness of the aristocratic landowners, as contrasted with the capability and intelligence of the middle-class entre-

[1] W. Sombart, *Die Deutsche Volkswirtschaft im 19. Jahrhundert*, 7th Ed., Berlin, 1927, p. 330.

[2] The economically powerful position of the large agrarian estates in 1860 is overstressed in the controversy with Brinkmann by G. Hermes, *Statistische Studien zur wirtschaftlichen und gesellschaftlichen Struktur des zollvereinten Deutschland, Archiv f. Sozialwissenschaft und Sozialpolitik*, 1929, vol. 63, pp. 121 ff.

[3] Fontane is indeed the only middle-class writer without any anti-aristocratic resentment.

preneurs and merchants, furnishes them with a never-
ending theme.   Apart from this, the loss of meaning of
the aristocracy as an Estate is illustrated and discussed:
and the incongruity that has grown up between the
claims to prestige and the economic condition of the
debt-ridden agrarian aristocracy is debated with avidity.
In the view of writers the aristocracy appears on the
defensive: it is increasingly threatened by the capacity
for achievement possessed by its middle-class rivals.

The declining position of the aristocracy can be seen
most strongly in the condition of the landed nobility
of the provinces.   The officer and court-nobility were
doubtless able to conceal the difficult economic situation
in which they sometimes found themselves or to compensate for it by the glamour and the prestige of the
institutions to which they belonged.   As a town-aristo-
cracy, they were far more sympathetic to the political
and cultural innovations, than the more backward rural
nobility which resided in castles and estates that were
often remote and difficult of access.   In any case, the
struggle between the advancing spirit of middle-class
enterprise and the old feudal class was most visible in the
provinces.

It is therefore no accident that the first novel that
gives us a culturally significant picture of the altered
condition of the aristocracy has chosen the provinces as
the background for its plot.   *Die Epigonen*, by Karl
Immermann (1836), clearly illustrates the contrast between the decline of the aristocracy and the rise of
middle-class industrialism in the Rhineland, whilst the
humorous story *Münchhausen* (1838), by the same
author, forms an acid satire on the loss of power and
the backwardness of the Westphalian aristocracy.

Immermann could never eliminate from his writings
the atmosphere of the higher Prussian bureaucracy with
which he was connected through origin and profession.
It is of some sociological significance that he had thus a
certain detachment from, as well as survey over, the
different strata of society.   When he wrote these two

novels he was serving as Judge of the Provincial Court in Düsseldorf. Neither as student, nor later as writer, was Immermann eager to make social contacts; he remained a conservative individualist.

It is significant that as a student he opposed the new and characteristic social organization of academic youth, the *Burschenschaft*. Immediately after the Wars of Liberation the *Burschenschaft* was a youth-movement of a political character. Its function was to unite and integrate the youth of different social origin and different German states.[1] Whilst as students the leading writers of the Young German movement belonged to the *Burschenschaft* (e.g. Laube, Heine, Gutzkow), Immermann as the loyal son of an official openly opposed it in Halle and was rewarded by the commendation of the Prussian King.

Later, too, Immermann's contacts with the Young German writers remained loose. It is true that the Young Germans for the most part appreciated his achievement,[2] and Heine even collaborated with him in a struggle against the aristocratic author Platen. But the political standpoints of the group and those of Immermann were too divergent for a closer bond.[3] In contrast with the Young Germans who remained mobile and open-minded, enlarging their outlook through voluntary and involuntary travel, Immermann belonged

[1] Cf. Fr. Schnabel, *Deutsche Geschichte im Neunzehnten Jahrhundert*, ii. 241 ff. See also the treatise of E. Brinkmann, *Der Nationalismus und die deutschen Universitäten im Zeitalter der deutschen Erhebung*, Heidelberg, 1932, which is rich in material, but is unsatisfactory owing to its lack of form and to its prejudices.

[2] Immermann became acquainted with Gutzkow and Laube only very shortly before his early death ; the posthumous notice of him by Laube is indicative of his positive appreciation by the "Young Germans" (*Gans und Immermann, Deutsche Pandora*, Berlin, 1841, iv. 3 ff.).

[3] The ambiguity in Immermann is well expressed by Gutzkow: "If Immermann spoke of intellectual interests he was revolutionary; but whenever it was a matter of Germany's political condition, he was the Prussian official and one-time volunteer" (*Werke*, ed. W. Deetjen, i. p. lxxiv). For the difference between Heine's and Immermann's attitude towards culture see G. M. Bacon, *The Personal and Literary Relations of H. Heine to Karl Immermann* (Ph.D. Thesis, University of Michigan, 1910), pp. 73 ff.

to an intellectual type deeply rooted in regional culture. His position as an official restricted him locally and mentally. He was, indeed, transferred from one province to another by the decree of his employer, the State, but he had no opportunity for foreign travel. He is characterized not by mobility but by a permanent connection with the centre of provincial court-culture. At the end of the eighteenth and for the first three decades of the nineteenth century there was a tendency for petty courts like Weimar, Dresden, Darmstadt and Munich to be the centre-points of cultural impulses and innovations, due to contacts between a permanent court and a fluctuating cultural élite. Düsseldorf experienced a cultural Renaissance in the period of 1822–30 through co-operation between a petty-court and the newly-founded Academy of Art directed by W. Schadow.[1] The constant factor here was the court-circle, and the variable element the young Academy students of fine art.[2]   The artist-colony embraced people from every part of Germany; the Court of Prince Frederick consisted of nobles who were connected with the city.

The painters, with whom Immermann connected himself, found patrons and protectors in the courtiers, whilst the Court experienced an artistic revival through its theatrical performances and gay plays.[3]   At the same time the Düsseldorf Theatre which Immermann directed with powerful energy in his leisure hours was distinguished by the high cultural level it attained.

If Immermann associated at Court with artists in the years 1827–30, his long-standing friendship with Else von Lützow (the later divorced wife of General von

[1] See the impressive description by Immermann, *Düsseldorfer Anfänge*, *Werke*, v. 189–278.

[2] *Ibid.*, p. 189: "The Düsseldorf artists are intellectual nomads. To-day they tie their steed to this stake, to-morrow to that bush."

[3] *Ibid.*, p. 223: "The frame gave the picture a still higher relief. This golden frame was namely the interest of the court and society in our efforts. The muses had then become completely the fashion in the highest circles and were considered as belonging to society; lectures, living tableaux, and talks on this and that followed each other in quick succession on the smooth parquet."

Lützow), also brought him into close contact with aristocratic circles.[1] Whilst this author became more and more settled in Düsseldorf, he was yet not averse to the stimulation and news of the wide world given him by mobile writers and artists like Heine, M. Beer, Laube, Felix Mendelssohn and others, who stayed with him when passing through.[2] The provincial official type who made contributions to culture was embodied also in two of Immermann's most intimate friends and colleagues: the important historian of art Karl Schnaase [3] and the poet Friedrich von Uechtritz [4] who acted simultaneously with him as jurists in the Düsseldorf Court of Justice.

These Düsseldorf painters, scholars and poets maintained a common attitude to art and history. Romantic tendencies with their preference for historical themes found a strong echo amongst them. The Düsseldorf school of painting specialized in historical pictures, whilst Immermann portrayed historical myths in his works "Alexis" and "Merlin." Similarly, Schnaase, the art historian, regarded "history the most important and the surest representation of the being of beauty": [5] his central idea was the conservative ideology of a national mind (*Volksgeist*), and involved a peculiar pantheism which sees in history the development of the living. This circle thought "dynamically." Immermann also paid homage to it when he showed in his great novels that behind the destructive tendencies of the age there lived the "organic" *Volkstum*, rooted in the peasantry. His predilection for conservative, provincial culture

---

[1] H. Mayne, *loc. cit.*, p. 84.

[2] This applied especially to the Jewish dramatist M. Beer, of whom Immermann says: "He had seen and heard an infinite number of things, for he had been in almost all the capitals of Europe, his wealth and social talent opened an entry for him everywhere. He was therefore able to bring life in my quiet hermitage with an abundance of information" (*Düsseldorfer Anfänge*, p. 229).

[3] See W. Waetzoldt, *Deutsche Kunsthistoriker*, Leipzig, 1924, ii. 71–3, for Schnaase's connection with the Düsseldorf circle of painters.

[4] For Uechtritz, see H. Mayne, *loc. cit.*, pp. 233 ff.

[5] W. Waetzoldt, *loc. cit.*, pp. 80–3.

brought him into contrast with radical Liberalism and
Rationalism in Berlin. He found no response amongst
the literary cliques of the Prussian capital, and it is
significant that in Laube's obituary he was regarded
precisely as the counterpole to E. Gans, the important
advocate of a progressive policy in Berlin.[1]

Immermann's novels are especially valuable as a
sociological source because he does not take a one-sided
attitude of middle-class bias. The *Epigonen* is not ten-
dentious, but seeks rather to delineate the aristocratic
decline and the middle-class rise to power as a historical
phenomenon. Its melancholy author sees the darker
aspects rather than the merits of the historical development. He senses with discomfort the many breaks in
development, and the dangers that are bound up with
the gradual transition from feudal-agrarian to middle-
class industrial society.

The aristocracy was absolutely on the defensive.
Since the middle-class felt an impulse to press forward
with the help of its intellect and efficiency, the aristocracy
found itself, according to Immermann, in a dangerous
situation. Whilst it is precisely the obstacles facing
him that called forth energy in the man of the middle-
class, the aristocrat was in danger of perishing because
of his easy life.[2] Therefore in those of its members
who were incapable of making up for the fateful burden
of a privileged birth with talent and pre-eminent gifts,
there sprang up an attempt to save the endangered
existence for themselves and their descendants by the
employment of every kind of palliative.

Various methods of propping up their threatened
prestige were feasible and attempted: one of these

---

[1] H. Laube, *Gans und Immermann, Deutsche Pandora*, iv. 92 ff.

[2] *Die Epigonen*, iii, 8th Bk., chap. xi, p. 127. This defensive situation is
also clearly indicated in the later novel of Levin Schücking, *Die Ritterbürtigen*
(1846), which is written from an intimate knowledge of the Westphalian
aristocracy. Here the wiser aristocracy is dominated by the fear of soon
losing all their public functions. "We shall be poor," so runs the dialogue
between two aristocrats, "in comparison with any ordinary industrialist, lacking in influence beside any ordinary official, and the man with the loudest voice
will then have the chief say in public life" (2nd Ed., I, p. 88).

attempts was the institution of the *Fideikommiss* to preserve estates as inalienable property.[1] This was the path taken by the conservative type which was filled with an unshakable desire for security. On the other hand, the lighter and livelier natures preferred the display of a worldly life of luxury on a big scale, which they thought to be an aristocratic monopoly.

They knew or felt that a member of the middle-class would for a long time be unable to follow them to the gaming-tables of princes, into the boudoirs of high-born beauties, and in all the amenities of a life devoted to enjoyment and personal pleasure; further, that such glittering and shimmering ingredients were able to create for them a way of life that was characteristic of themselves and, as they thought, unattainable by the plebeians. They passed therefore from their estates to the courts, watering-places, meeting-places of the world of fashion, swept like winged divinities or semi-divinities through the ranks of inferior men, even treading on their heads.[2]

Every section of the aristocracy, however, wanted to repress the consciousness of its actual weakness by playing with the former symbols of its power. In the *Epigonen*, the Duchess wishes to organize a mediæval tourney. For long weeks before, the liveliest activity reigns over all the estates and knightly castles. Only nobles of unblemished birth and all ladies of the neighbourhood whose rank would qualify them to become canonesses are invited, whilst the newly-ennobled and middle-class landowners are excluded. Since the results of the rehearsals for the knightly tournament are deplorable, it is decided to change the character of the celebration, and they organize only a "Caroussel," an entertainment of the time of Louis XIV.[3] All these attempts at a revival of the dignity of the aristocratic class come to nought: many a noble estate falls into

---

[1] For the institution of the *Fideikommiss* as a protection against the competition of urban capital, see the article *Adel* by G. v. Below, *Handwörterbuch der Staatswissenschaften*, 3rd Ed., i. 41–8.

[2] Immermann, *loc. cit.*, pp. 127 ff.

[3] *Die Epigonen*, ii, 4th Bk, chap. i, ii, vi.

middle-class hands;[1] the worldly luxury of the debt-ridden aristocracy makes no impression on the self-reliant middle-class; the flight into the past appears degenerate and ridiculous.

The loss in meaning and in power suffered by the aristocracy seems to Immermann to be unpreventable. They are both subjected in his satire *Münchhausen* to a grotesque exaggeration which, however, does sharply reveal the precise failings and backwardness of this class, from a middle-class point of view. The Freiherr Schnick-Puckelig-Erbsenscheucher and his daughter Emerenzia live in a completely decayed castle in the provinces and are absolutely penurious. They have, in Hegel's words, "a false consciousness"—their consciousness of belonging to a ruling caste stands in ridiculous contrast to their economic and social position. Their forbears had been successful with the Prince of the country; by means of an ideology invented for the occasion, they had claimed irrevocable privileges.

Their caste-ideology declared "that all ecclesiastical benefices and all military posts belonged to the von Schnucks, who were scattered as usual throughout the whole country; and they claimed to form the iron wall round the throne."[2] When the von Schnucks had consumed the revenues of their lands, they began to run through more money as generals at the expense of regiments: and then almost all their sons became prelates or councillors in the service of the Prince. This satirical picture tears the mask off the pretentions of the nobility to monopolize the best positions in the state purely on the ground of noble birth, or to be more accurate, because of its power as a courtly clique.[3]   Its

---

[1] This happened very often between 1820 and 1830 in the stress of the agricultural crisis which was a result of the limited possibilities of German agriculture for export. At that time 80 per cent of the aristocrat landlords lost their estates. Cf. Sartorius v. Waltershausen, *Deutsche Wirtschaftsgeschichte*, p. 39.

[2] *Münchhausen, Werke*, ed. Deetjen, i, 1st Bk., p. 55 f.

[3] Heine argues similarly in 1831 when he speaks of the "invisible alliance" of the aristocrats who through a silent agreement, having got hold of all the ruling positions in the state and having kept out the middle-class *roturiers*,

caste-ideology is shrewdly denounced as something long
outmoded, in the name of an overwhelming "majority
of right-thinking people who have had a hard life of
struggle." [1] The last scion of the formerly privileged
von Schnuck family is in a deplorable situation, for
one day he will discover that the council in which
he wants to take his privileged seat as a councillor
is just as fictitious as the whole princely house of
Hechelkram.

Participation in the new industrial prosperity offers
itself to him as a last resort for improving his economic
position. Baron Münchhausen, the master of lies, suggests to him a partnership in an utopian scheme for the
condensation of air which will yield him a dividend
of 136 per cent. This subjects the last Freiherr von
Schnuck to a typical conflict between class-ideology and
financial necessity. [2] The dignity of the aristocracy is
an exclusive one and differentiates between permissible
and unpermissible transactions, between transactions
compatible with class-honour and those that are not.
"Can I, as a nobleman of old family, justify myself in
the eyes of my ancestors for participating in an enterprise which, when viewed clearly, has no other object
but trade and commerce and profit, and which will be
shared by all sorts of people of low origin?" [3]—such is
the question the Baron asks himself. The malicious

dispose of practically all the higher posts in the army and in the diplomatic
service. See H. Heine, Introduction to *Kahldorf über den Adel. In Briefen
an den Grafen M. von Moltke,* Nürnberg, 1831, p. 21.

[1] The writer complains ironically to an anonymous lady reader that in the
account of the ideology of the aristocracy he has, to his regret, to repeat old
stories which the novelist of fifty years ago must have written already. But
then he permits the lady reader to remind him that it is indeed speaking of
the past and that it is only by dint of imagination that he makes the invention
of the von Schnucks apply to the present or to the near future. The tremendous
majority of all right-thinking people will therefore see to it that this
ideology based on lies will belong for ever to the "prehistoric sagas" (*ibid.,*
p. 156).

[2] The same conflict is still reflected in literature decades later, e.g. for
the period of bubble-companies after 1870 in Spielhagen's novel *Sturmflut*
(1875).

[3] *Münchhausen, Werke,* i, 3rd Bk., chap. viii, p. 253.

answer of Münchhausen forms a sophistical argument which many an aristocrat may have employed, in this time of progressive capitalism, in order to pacify his class-conscience.

Münchhausen replied that in certain respects the aristocracy had marched with the times, that everyone engaged in business nowadays, Count, Freiherr and Prince like the smallest shop-keeper, without harming their prestige.[1] For the aristocratic Estate, like the consecrated character of the priesthood, was immortal: a count could practise usury on the exchange and take the bread out of the mouths of the Jews and remain none the less an unsullied Christian count as before, and even if another crusade to Jerusalem should take place, none of his people would forbid him to join the enterprise.[2]

Whilst a positive solution is found in the satire for the relation of the aristocrat to capitalism, the solution is a tragically negative one in the serious novel, *Die Epigonen*. According to the latter, the aristocratic attitude and the middle-class capitalist attitude are irreconcilable contradictions. Three generations of a ducal family are portrayed as three different types, and their economic behaviour corresponds to the three methods employed by the aristocracy in their attempt to bolster up their threatened prestige.

The Duke's grandfather was a simple "Country-Junker" who, economical and even niggardly, generally preferred to discuss with his stewards and peasants the management of the estate, "and the aims dearest to his heart were to improve his holdings, round them off with new acquisitions, and leave behind, in addition to his real property, a considerable capital in cash. In order

---

[1] In the first decades of the nineteenth century the aristocrats in fact seldom made financial transactions directly, but carried them out in indirect ways, very often through the medium of a Jewish dealer (see S. Neumann, *Die Stufen des preussischen Konservatismus*, Berlin, 1930, p. 38; also G. Freytag's novel, *Soll und Haben*, and Fontane's *Stechlin*). In 1848 a deputy in the St. Paul's Parliament said in the debate on the aristocracy: "The present aristocracy uses its estates as an object of bargaining and haggling like any speculator" (F. Tönnies, *loc. cit.*, p. 1056).

[2] *Münchhausen, Werke*, i, 3rd Bk., chap. viii, p. 253.

to attain them, he ate from pewter-plates and denied himself every pleasure." [1]

His son is, in contrast, the luxurious type: ostentatious, sentimental, imaginative, his whole frivolous being centred on pleasure.   Foreign travel, enthusiastic friendships, extensive love affairs, make up the content of his life.   The third generation is distinguished neither by its acquisitive instinct, nor by extravagance, but by its endeavour to keep up a dignified appearance.   The last Duke is traditional in the extreme, and completely filled with the idea of aristocratic dignity.   Legitimacy of blood and ancestors is for him the meaning of life.   To it he clings all the more closely as the economic situation of his family deteriorates.

The family of the Duke shows the *typical economic decline of the aristocracy*.   The economic indifference of the last representative of the junior line, the decadent pleasure-loving Count Julius, supplies the small middle-class entrepreneurs with opportunities for advancement. He quickly squanders a considerable inheritance in a multitude of adventures and in dazzling sumptuousness at court.   Then a middle-class capitalist, whose ambition it is to utilize the Count's estate as a factory-site, sets to work with his shrewd methods.   He repeatedly lends the Count considerable sums until he has him completely in his hand.   In the end the estates of the Count pass into his possession, the Count being accorded only free quarters in the castle of his fathers with a reasonable annual income.

The new middle-class owner pursues the industrialization of the former princely estate with vigour.   He buys up in addition some monastic land, and a giant industry arises with the co-operation of different industrial branches.   Mines, a brewery and a distillery, a

---

[1] *Die Epigonen*, iii, 8th Bk., pp. 128 ff.—The two types of the country Junker and the luxurious aristocrat are to be found at the same period (end of the eighteenth century) also in Silesia.   See the essay mentioned above of Eichendorff, *Der Adel und die Revolution*; also the observations on the country Junker in G. Steinhausen, *Geschichte der deutschen Kultur*, 3rd Ed., 1929, p. 499.

weaving-factory, and a porcelain factory all accumulate. The whole region changes its aspect, metamorphosed by the energy of the middle-class entrepreneur.

Immermann based his description on actual experience, having before his eyes the factories of Nathusius in Althaldensleben near Magdeburg[1] as an excellent example of the destruction of agriculture by incipient industrial capitalism and as an example of the synthesis of rationalized agriculture and industry. Gottlieb Nathusius[2] had achieved great success in the tobacco-business by a shrewd exploitation of the tobacco-monopoly, and when the price of land fell to unprecedented levels in the Kingdom of Hanover because of the agrarian crisis, he sank his capital in landed property. He bought up the monastic lands of Althaldensleben, whose area he gradually increased to almost a square-mile by the purchase of aristocratic ancestral estates.[3]

In the year 1824 the poet had paid a visit to the rich landowner Nathusius in Althaldensleben and had written about it in a letter to Frau von Lützow:

> You will perhaps have heard of the extensive possessions and all-embracing activities of this man who from a beggar has become a millionaire, manufacturing his own paper-money that is acknowledged by all money-changers. . . . Carts heavily laden with tobacco-leaves now rumble through the proud avenues

---

[1] Cf. F. Schulthess in the *Karl Immermann Gedächtnisschrift zum 100. Geburtstage*, Hamburg, 1896, p. 98.

[2] For the life of Nathusius see the biography by E. v. Nathusius, unfortunately lacking in scientific presentation (*J. G. Nathusius, Ein Pionier deutscher Industrie*, Stuttgart, 1915).

[3] *Hannoversches Magazin*, 1830, pp. 698 ff.: "The Nathusius works, with the exception of a large tobacco factory and a counting-house in Magdeburg, are situated on two fine, big, immediately contiguous estates, Althaldensleben and Hundisberg, 3 miles from Magdeburg. Recently, an addition to these has been made by the purchase of two huge, somewhat distant, estates (Meiendorf and Gehrendorf), for 200,000 Taler. Althaldensleben is a secularized monastery with spacious, and generally massive buildings, which for the most part have been utilized as workshops, with some additions. In place of monastic indolence there is now an enormous bustle of manifold economic and other industries which have re-vivified, populated, and made prosperous a once insignificant spot." A similar change had taken place in the former aristocratic estate of Hundisburg and is similarly described.

leading up to the castles, where once dazzling equipages were wont to drive; the former banqueting halls are used as granaries, and a few humble small rooms suffice for the owner's own requirements. . . . He, personally, is the simplest of men: it is the success, his activity has achieved, not the pleasure that acquisition could have brought him, that attracts and delights him.[1]

In his novel Immermann has only transferred the theatre of capitalist expansion from the province of Magdeburg in the West-German district to one where, in fact, the old aristocratic lordships (e.g. the Lords of Salm, Sayn and Croy) lay right next to industrial areas. *The contrast between the aristocratic and capitalistic modes of life* is visibly embodied in the figures of the Duke and the middle-class industrialist. The Duke is of stately and distinguished appearance, the capitalist a small wretched figure with square knee-buckles, faded stockings and heavy shoes. In contradistinction to the Duke, he places no importance on his appearance, but a great deal on the rationalist maxims by which he guides his life. His economic mind, which always thinks mathematically, is characterized by a dislike of any kind of sentimentality and tenderness. Life, so he thinks, cannot be erected on a foundation of sentiment, emotion and courtesy.

One must know how to calculate intelligently, one must expect from oneself and from others no other principle, except that that which is not forbidden is permissible; this will furnish an efficient foundation-stone for one's destiny, and in it the Good and the Beautiful will find their proper place.[2]

With his contempt for all adventurers and idlers, and with his appreciation of order, homeliness and middle-class virtue,[3] this entrepreneur is the exact embodiment of the calculating and feelingless "bourgeois" whose nature and historical development have been described

---

[1] Schulthess, *loc. cit.*, p. 99.
[2] *Die Epigonen*, ii, 4th Bk., chap. ix, p. 243.
[3] *Ibid.:* "Everything exists in the world only through orderliness, homeliness, citizen-ship. Whoever disputes this, be he who he may, is hateful to me."

by Sombart.[1] His passion for order makes his objection to the uneconomic expenditure-economy of the aristocrat comprehensible.   Land, for the Duke, is something to be preserved out of reverence for tradition and for æsthetic pleasure; for the entrepreneur it is, on the contrary, an object of trade, a source of economic profit. The latter therefore despises the aristocrats' lack of economic instinct which prevents them from opening a limestone-quarry, although it would supply them annually with a secure income; "because they never had to make exertions for anything, they never dream of increasing their wealth, hardly even of saving it." [2]   *Side by side with this contempt for the economic impotence of the aristocracy appears a hatred of its political pretentiousness.*   The gloomy memories of the former repression which was inflicted on the middle-class "canaille" by the aristocracy have produced in the capitalist a militant class-consciousness. "We people of the middle-class have an indescribably short remembrance of our suffering. . . .   For my part, at least, I will always strain every effort to destroy the old feudal towers and castle-dungeons." [3]   The antithesis between the seigneurial and middle-class capitalist modes of life and thought is especially apparent in the relation of the two types to love and death.

The entrepreneur, cool and calculating, is of a non-erotic and unsentimental nature: his relation to his counter-type, Count Julius, is like that of sober reason to excited imagination.   Whilst the burgher has not the faintest idea of the *ars amandi*, the Count, whom he has expropriated, is a Don Juan whom no feminine heart can resist.   His grand seigneurial air and his generous ways captivate women and he even seduces the wife of his exploiter, who is bored by her empty existence in the cold world of ledgers and accounts.   In this situation she is easily susceptible to the charm of the aristocrat's superior way of life.   We are not inter-

---

[1] W. Sombart, *Der Bourgeois*, Munich, 1913. Sombart does not, however, mention the classical description of this type by Immermann.

[2] *Die Epigonen*, ii, 4th Bk., chap. ix, p. 245.   [3] *Ibid.*

ested here in the consequences of this clandestine mis-alliance—the birth of a son who, to the sorrow of his legal father, has inherited all the feudal instincts and desires of his high-born begetter—but in the visible contrast between the erotic and the calculating type, between the man with his one-sided industrial ambition and the other with his all-round enjoyment of life. To quote Sombart:

> A good householder . . . that is a good burgher and a lover, of whatever rank, are irreconcilable antitheses.	Either economic interests, in the broadest sense, or love-interests form the central point of all life's importance.	One lives either to work or else to love.	Work implies saving, love implies spending.[1]

Immermann himself has noticed, as we saw, that the success of his activities meant everything for his historical model, and the enjoyment of his acquired wealth nothing.

In contrast also are the middle-class and aristocratic attitudes to death.	Both the Duke and the entrepreneur expect an imminent death, the Duke braced for suicide, his middle-class opposite prepared for a natural end.

The Duke hides his suicidal intentions right to the end, and, indeed, he deliberately maintains on occasions the "disgrace" of such an end, since the subsequent inquest is degrading.	Although his constitution in no way tends in that direction, he insists that he will one day die of a stroke.	He succeeds by this means in deceiving the world, and after he has put all his affairs in order, he manages to die in a manner that opportunely presents itself for an aristocrat who does not want to offend outward custom.[2]

The aristocrat is guided up to the last moment by the idea of keeping up appearances; the burgher is inspired by the principle of rationalism.	The satisfaction of the noble lies in preserving an outward glamour that hides the bitter reality, that of the capitalist in the cal-

---

[1] W. Sombart, *op. cit.*, p. 263.
[2] *Die Epigonen*, iii, 8th Bk., chap. xi, p. 134, and 9th Bk., chap. iv, p. 162.

culating conscientiousness with which he regulates the
affairs of his world in anticipation of death.   In both
cases the irrational is included in the habits of life, but
to the end the one thinks of appearances and the other
of calculation.   The one is dominated to the end by the
idea of dignity, the other by the idea of order.   To a
priest who wants to talk the ailing entrepreneur out of
thoughts of death, the latter answers: "Leave me please
to my calculations, I find them pleasant.   When I die,
it will be like the closing of a commercial year, like an
ordinary business account.   Everything will go on in
the old way, no chair need be moved because of it." [1]
But unexpected events spoil the scheme of the over-
certain rationalist.

If, after this analysis of Immerman's comprehensive
presentation of the antithesis between the two powers,
we ask for his solution of the problem, we shall find
a kind of negative neutrality in his novel.   He realizes
the anachronism of aristocratic pretensions as well as
the æsthetic insufficiencies of the capitalist middle-class.
The aristocracy's loss of influence is as little liked by
him as the one-sided vulgarity of the capitalist.[2]

Besides the hostility and hatred for the aristocracy
harboured by the middle-class, the *Epigonen* also notes
its secret admiration and attempts to imitate it.   The
materialistic merchants and capitalists see their greatest
enemy in the aristocracy, but to the æsthetes and intellectuals it represents their secret ideal.   The entrepreneur's middle-class attorney who negotiates with the
Duke the handing-over of the castle is conscience-
stricken at his mission when he glimpses the culture of
the aristocracy.   He realizes the superiority of the
courtly aristocratic attitude of life to the unformed middle-
class one, and contrasts the tasteful and elegant splendour
in the castle with the vulgarity of the industrial quarter.

---

[1] *Die Epigonen*, iii, 9th Bk., chap. iv, p. 161.
[2] The same applies also to another rural and intellectually related writer,
Levin Schücking (cf. K. Pinthus, *Die Romane Levin Schückings*, Leipzig, 1911,
p. 71).

Similar to that of the lawyer is the reaction of a doctor who, otherwise described as the most thorough-going type of modern sceptic, compares the æsthetic charm of this aristocratic style, if one wants to put it that way, with the beauty of the dying swan.

The same twofold attitude towards the aristocracy is also to be found in Immermann himself. It can be stated that *Immermann desired the aristocracy as his public and protector, but opposed it as a source of competition.* Although, as a Prussian official, he took no side in the latent struggle between aristocracy and middle-class, his middle-class consciousness was yet sharply awakened when confronted with the aristocratic writers as rivals. In 1831, for instance, the *Briefe eines Verstorbenen* by Prince Pückler-Muskau enjoyed a wide popularity, due to no small extent to the social qualifications of the author. Immermann, embittered by the unfavourable reception of one of his own works, turned against the zealous friends of the prince who prophesied that a new, an elegant, literature would begin with that book.

I think [said he, with cutting emphasis] that our good old literature will remain what it has always been, *an honest middle-class one.* At least, it would be a sign of complete decrepitude if, after all the stupidities it has already committed, it should also permit itself to be aristocraticized.[1]

In contradistinction, Immermann wished for the aristocracy as a reading-public,[2] and desired it indeed as a protector. Perhaps in this he had before him as a model the English aristocracy, which for centuries had acted as the patron of writers.[3] The aristocracy, in the

---

[1] *Werke,* ed. Deetjen, vi. 296.

[2] The desire of Immermann to find a reading public in the aristocracy is also indirectly expressed in a letter to Varnhagen: "And ought not our aristocrats, who are unfortunately only too unliterary, to make a more profound acquaintance with literature, if they would compel themselves to think a little—which is what our former literature demands—instead of lounging on the comfortable Pückler Bridge?" (*ibid.,* vi. 297).

[3] Cf. L. L. Schücking, *The Sociology of Literary Taste,* London, 1944, pp. 9–14.

opinion of Immermann, could only find again a *raison-d'être*, which it had lost as an Estate, by undertaking a new function as protector and patron of intellectual things.[1]

Whilst the "Young Germans" wanted to sweep away the aristocracy as completely anachronistic, Immermann only wished to reform it and bring it into closer relationship with the world of literature. In the long run he dreamed of an aristocracy of intellect and beauty, and stood in sharp contrast to the didactic tendencies of early liberalism, which regarded the expansion of knowledge and culture in widening circles as a positive advantage.[2]

Thus the solution in Immermann's novels is not a realistic, but a romantic, one. He takes flight from the disquietening state of class-struggle in a characteristic agrarian romanticism. He anticipates the criticism that the destruction of the soul of the world is caused by the "dry mechanization" of industry. This argument has been voiced again and again in German literature, and furnished the theme of Rathenau's book *Zur Mechanik des Geistes* in the twentieth century.[3] The utopia of his agrarian romanticism is in contrast both to feudalism as well as to capitalism. The conclusion of the *Epigonen* is symbolical of this:

The aristocracy had strained terribly at its own roots, its vices had brought irremediable confusion into the houses of the middle-

---

[1] *Werke*, i, 2nd Bk., chap. x, pp. 184 ff.: "The Estate as such," he makes the Deacon say in the dialogue in *Münchhausen*, "did not plunge into the waves of the movement which began with Lessing and brought about an unlimited expansion of the entire field of German thought, science and poetry. Instead of refined persons being born to act as the patrons of all distinguished talent, many of the great ones among us still regard talent as a natural enemy, or as burdensome and uncomfortable and certainly as something we can quite well do without. There are whole districts in our German fatherland where it is still considered degrading for a noble to read a book; instead he blusteringly bustles through his useless days as in the time of the hunting ballad of Bürger."

[2] See *Die Epigonen*, i, 2nd Bk., chap. x for the liberal attitude towards culture. G. G. Gervinus' writings are especially characteristic. Cf. his *Einleitung in die Geschichte des 19. Jahrhunderts*, Leipzig, 1853, p. 166.

[3] Cf. H. Freyer, *Die Bewertung der Wirtschaft im philosophischen Denken des 19. Jahrhunderts*, Leipzig, 1921, p. 145.

class. The Third Estate, armed with its weapon, money, avenged itself in a remorseless war of extermination. It too, however, failed to achieve its object; out of all the struggles, out of the explosion of the underground mines which had driven aristocratic desires and plebeian greed into hostility, out of the conflict of the known and the unknown, out of the confusion of laws and rights, spring new strange combinations which none of those concerned dreamed of. The heritage of feudalism and industry falls in the end to one who belongs to both classes, and yet to neither.[1]

The impact of industrialization gave rise to various reactions. It filled the middle-class capitalist with an optimism and sensation of power. In the desperate workers, however, who began to sense their exploitation by capital in the transition from hand to machine industry,[2] it produced a hatred against the machines as the cause of their misfortunes. In 1844 Upper-Silesian weavers were inspired by this idea to destroy textile machines.[3] Eleven years previously the provincial intellectual and Prussian civil servant, Immermann, had suggested the destruction of the factories at the end of his novel.

Above all else, the factories should perish and the land be given over again to cultivation. Those institutions for the artificial satisfaction of artificial needs, appear to me as nothing but pernicious and evil. The earth belongs to the plough, to the sunshine and the rain which fertilize the seed, to the diligent, unassisted hand of the worker. The present speeds towards an avid mechanization with lightning swiftness: its passage we cannot hinder, yet we are not to be blamed if we fence-off a little green

[1] *Die Epigonen*, iii, 9th Bk., p. 213.
[2] See Immermann's description of the industrial changes amongst the workers, and note his belief in the degrading and unhealthy effects of factories: "Whilst behind the ploughs he saw faces glowing with health, he found at the machines others with sunken cheeks and hollow eyes, whose likeness pronounced them to be the brothers or cousins of those healthy ones" (*Die Epigonen*, iii, 7th Bk., p. 19).
[3] For the Upper-Silesian Weavers' Riots of 1844 see the essay of G. Freytag, *Soziale Trauerspiele in der preussischen Provinz Schlesien* in *Vermischte Aufsätze aus den Jahren 1848–1894*, ed. E. Elster, Leipzig, 1903, ii. 319–33. Also the famous presentation of this critical situation in G. Hauptmann's drama, *Die Weber*, and the chapter "Die Unterirdischen" in Ricarda Huch's *Alte und neue Götter*, Berlin, 1930, pp. 233–8.

tract for us and ours and fortify this island as long as possible against
the surge of the industrial waves that rush by.[1]

The agrarian romanticism of Immermann is based on
a conservative idea of *Volk*. By *Volk* he means "the
best of the free burghers and the worthy, active, educated, diligent middle-class." It is a stratum which
includes neither aristocrat nor industrialist, but the provincial petty-bourgeoisie and the prosperous peasantry.
The *Volk* in this sense is the contrary of the Society in
capital cities; it is organic and the latter mechanic.
Whereas many perversions arise out of the mingling
of tedium and excitement in the "sublime circles of
Society," the *Volk* embodies proper and normal conditions.
It is identical with genuine humanity,

for in the *Volk* the fundamental relationships of mankind are *still*
awake, the right attitude of the sexes is *still* clearly defined, big
talk *still* means nothing and only the trade or profession that one
has counts, leisure follows work with regular orderliness, that joy
is *not yet* banished from pleasure,[2] which finds its natural expression in Sunday-dances, weddings and target-shooting. This sober
mean lies outside the aristocratic mode of life that the nobility
and even the literary cliques of the capital, with its mannerisms,
prefer.[3]

The common sense of the people, its physical and
psychological healthiness as contrasted with the deca-
dence of the upper stratum, is described in "Der Ober-
hof," a serious section in the satire *Münchhausen*. In it
the mayor of a Westphalian village represents the
aristocracy of the prosperous and powerful peasantry.
Old uses and customs like the popular secret tribunals

---

[1] *Die Epigonen*, iii, 9th Bk., last chap., pp. 213 ff.

[2] *Münchhausen*, 2nd Bk., chap. x, p. 183. It is significant that the agrarian
romanticism is represented in this work by a priest who had in his youth
moved in Society as the tutor of a young aristocrat and who now discovers,
as a deacon in a provincial city, the degeneracy of the higher Estates and the
true nature of the "immortal *Volk*."

[3] Immermann's conservative ideas possess some similarity to the old
Estate-conservatism of *Justus Möser* who, sixty years earlier in Westphalia,
interested himself deeply in the old, original peasant stratum. For Möser,
see K. Mannheim, *Conservative Thought*.

(*Fehmegerichte*) play a significant part. The marriage of a Swabian imperial count with a healthy and attractive girl of the people instead of with his cousin, a spoilt Society woman, is supposed to point out symbolically the power that lies in the "immortal *Volk*." It alone can rejuvenate the degenerate upper stratum, the aristocracy in particular.

The fact of the gradual removal of class-barriers is to lead not to the victory of the industrial middle-class, but to a conservative return to the true powers of popular strength and tradition as embodied in the simple people, especially the prosperous peasantry of the western province of Prussia.[1] The way out of the confusion of the feudal-agrarian decline and middle-class industrial rise is thereby seen not in the *fata morgana* of a classless society, but in a new co-operation of the former Estates which are to receive their best impulses from the upholders and protectors of the national spirit, i.e. from the rural population.[2]

[1] This agrarian romanticism, as a middle-class shade of conservative thought, propagates in contrast to the "decayed" upper-strata, only a peasantry and a rural bourgeoisie, and therein differentiates itself essentially from the conservative defensive position of Adam Müller who, as the paid spokesman of the Prussian aristocracy, twenty years previously placed noble and peasant on one front. "Noble and peasant Estates," so he feared, "are perishing; there will be in the end only merchants, artisans and Jews." Ad. Müller, *Theorie der Staatshaushaltung* (1818) quoted in Fr. Schnabel, *Deutsche Geschichte im 19. Jahrhundert*, i. 471.

[2] The congenial attitude of Immermann induces present-day National-Socialism to see now in him one of its spiritual forerunners. Cf., for example, the essay by W. H. Keim, *Immermanns Deutschheit, in Zeitschrift für Deutschkunde*, 1935, pp. 228–41.

CHAPTER III

THE POLITICAL ASPECT—THE CONFLICT IN PRUSSIA, 1848

I

THE writers hitherto dealt with have partly described the difference in the economic and social positions of the aristocracy and middle-class, and partly waged a literary battle for or against the privileges of the aristocracy. It is true, indeed, that they occasionally express individual political opinions, but they do not discuss the situation of aristocracy and middle-class in connection with the growing political consciousness of society. Public interest in politics had been latent for a long time, but it now became manifest in the revolution of 1848 which was inspired by its French prototype. The privileges of the aristocracy were the subject of numerous discussions and pamphlets in 1848 and were debated in detail in the St. Paul's Parliament at Frankfort.[1] They formed a fundamental item in the struggle between liberal and legitimist forces, between the conservative order of the State and the liberal democratic mass movement.

In the revolution of 1848–9 there stood on the one side the majority of the middle-class, which embraced both the rich bourgeoisie, the petty-bourgeoisie and peasants.[2] These, led mainly by professional men, demanded a share in political power and expressed a desire for a government based on a free parliamentary

[1] F. Tönnies, *Deutscher Adel im 19. Jahrhundert*, *Neue Rundschau*, Berlin, 1912, ii. 1053.
[2] Cf. H. v. Srbik, *Deutsche Einheit*, Munich, 1935, i. 318 ff.

68

constitution, in place of the arbitrary government of the King and his aristocratic grandees.   On the other side was the conservative feudal stratum which possessed, in the army and administration, the machinery of the state and which also formed an intermediate link between the bureaucracy and the church.

Both the liberal middle-class and the feudal stratum had to raise forces for the struggle and organize their supporters.   As always in history, this organizing was carried out on both sides by political élites.   If we wish to understand the action and reaction of 1848–9 and comprehend fully the attitude of the aristocracy and middle-class in this struggle, then we must examine the structure and rôle of the leading political élites on both sides.   This we shall do by analysing character-istic works of two writers of different social origin and divergent political views, each of whom aims at bringing out clearly the existence of the enemy front, and unmask-ing its leaders and adherents.   We believe by that we shall gain a deeper insight into the manifold tensions and links, and into the antitheses and syntheses between the aristocracy and the middle-class of that period.   Before, however, analysing the political élites and their followers as presented to us by Gutzkow and Ungern-Sternberg, we must first briefly examine the character of élites in general and the structure of the élites in Ger-many during the first half of the century in particular.

The structure of élites and their function in the framework of society has recently been made the sub-ject of sociological analysis by thinkers like Pareto and K. Mannheim.[1]

There is in every society, according to Pareto, an élite, a *"classe supérieure"* which is distinguished by its superiority from the broader *"classe inférieure."*   To this élite belong all those who have been successful in public

---

[1] See V. Pareto, *Traité de Sociologie Générale*, Paris, 1919, vol. ii, especially §§ 2026–46.   Also *Les Systèmes Socialistes*, Paris, 1902, Introduction to vol. i, pp. 6–35.   K. Mannheim, *The Crisis of Culture*, in *The Sociological Review*, London, 1934, xxvi. 105–29.

life and have achieved power (such as officers, politicians, business-men, financiers, scientists, etc.). This upper stratum consists of numerically small groups which play a leading part in the direction and formation of political, economic and cultural life. Whereas Pareto distinguishes only between governing élites ("*élite gouvernementale*" [1]), Mannheim speaks of four main types of élite: the political, the organizing, the intellectual and contemplative, the artistic and religious élites.[2]

The function of the political and organizing élites consists in integrating numerous individual wills into a collective will, whilst the function of the intellectual-contemplative and æsthetic-religious élites lies in developing the organs of scientific knowledge and in educating tastes in the direction of introversion, of artistic and religious contemplation beyond the immediate struggle for existence.

But the élites are by no means stable powers. The constitution of the governing (or political and organizing) élites, at any rate, is subject to continual change. History, according to Pareto, is characterized by an unceasing "circulation of élites." [3]   If we have a governing élite A, there arises out of the masses C (the "*classe inférieure*") a group B possessed of claims to being an élite.   With the assistance of the "*classe inférieure*" from which it originated and to which it usually promises power and wealth, it suppresses and overthrows élite A, and then itself proceeds to govern the "*classe inférieure.*" Later on the process is repeated and a new élite D emerges to overthrow the ruling élite B.   History is thus continually determined by the struggle of minorities which, without always being conscious of doing so, use the masses as tools for the aquisition of positions of power.

It is hardly our task here to discuss the validity of Pareto's theory of the circulation of élites.   Yet it seems necessary to emphasize, as against Pareto's view, that the

---

[1] Pareto, *Traité*, ii, § 2032.   [2] K. Mannheim, *loc. cit.*, p. 108.

[3] Pareto speaks of "le Mouvement de Circulation qui porte les élites, nées des couches supérieures et qui fait descendre et disparaître les élites au pouvoir" (*Les Systèmes Socialistes*, i. 34).

composition of the political and organizing élites (*"élite gouvernementale"*) is by no means always identical with that of the simultaneously existing non-political élite. It is possible that whilst the old élite A still holds political power, the rival élite B, arising from the politically subject stratum, is already fulfilling the functions of an élite in non-political spheres (e.g. economics and culture). Such was the state of affairs in Germany in the second half of the eighteenth and in the first decades of the nineteenth century in regard to the composition of the political and non-political élites. The political and military power in Prussia from the time of Frederick the Great until 1847 (if we omit the brief Stein-Hardenberg episode) lay in the hands of the old feudal élite; whilst at the same period the industrialist and cultural élites consisted mainly of the bourgeoisie, of the middle-class, which was almost completely excluded from political power. Politics, at the end of the eighteenth and in the first decades of the nineteenth century, remained almost exclusively a matter for princes and aristocrats (high officials of middle-class origin who had made themselves indispensable in the service of the State were usually ennobled and rapidly absorbed into the nobility of birth); such leading rôle as was played by the middle-class was in the industrial, commercial and cultural spheres.

What is important for our purpose, now, is the fact that in the nineteenth century, round about 1830, there can be traced within the middle-class a definite move away from the cultural non-political élite towards the formation of a political and economic élite.[1] At the beginning of the nineteenth century a relatively numerous middle-class cultural élite still devoted itself with extraordinary intensity to philosophical and artistic interests. With increasing industrialization and the growth of

---

[1] The causes of this shifting of emphasis from activities and interests in a cultural sphere to those of a political and economic nature, doubtless bound up with the increasing economic prosperity of the middle-class, cannot be discussed here.

capitalism, the middle-class began to turn its attention away from purely cultural pursuits and concentrate on building up a political opposition. It was no longer satisfied with its former non-political rôle. It desired to suppress the political power of the feudal aristocracy and to usurp its place. A new middle-class, liberal opposition, consisting partly of professional men and officials and partly of capitalist entrepreneurs, emerged to face the old ruling élite of the aristocracy and force it into party-government and parliamentarianism. Under pressure from its opponents, the aristocracy changed its basis and modernized itself by confronting the liberals with a conservative party and a conservative ideology—this not without considerable assistance from middle-class literati.

Whilst the composition of the middle-class cultural élite and the aristocratic ruling élite differed essentially round about 1800, there existed in 1848 a marked correlation, and even a partial coincidence between the political opposition and the cultural élite, as is shown by the composition of the Paul's Parliament in Frankfort-on-Main and of other parliaments. This alliance was dominated by the type of the political professor as embodied, for instance, by Gervinus and particularly by political historians such as Dahlmann and Droysen.[1] Art and science were now consciously placed at the service of the political, national and liberal aims of the middle-class, their autonomy being *ipso facto* disavowed.[2] The culture that had hitherto been a monopoly of educated middle-class minorities was now propagated amongst the middle-classes by these minorities themselves.

[1] For Gervinus, see M. M. Rychner, *G. G. Gervinus*, Bern, 1922. For the political historians, cf. G. P. Gooch, *History and Historians in the Nineteenth Century*, Rev. Ed., London, 1952, chap. viii, pp. 122–50.

[2] Characteristic of this, for instance, is the following extract from Gervinus: "Our poetry has had its time; and if German life is not to stand still, then we must entice the talents, that now have no object, into the world of reality and the state where a new spirit can be poured into new matter" (*Geschichte der deutschen Dichtung*, 4th Ed., Leipzig, 1853, vol. iv, p. vii.) "I should only like to see now all art and all science placed at the service of politics at this great turning point of national life" (*Gervinus Leben. Von ihm selbst*, Leipzig, 1893, p. 265).

Liberalism after 1815 was represented by a small but very active group: but the masses remained indifferent to it.[1]   Nevertheless, the leaders felt themselves in every way to be the representatives and attorneys of the middle-class movement.   They were almost entirely men of academic education, with a legal or historical training.[2] Mostly professors, lawyers, or journalists, they believed in the power of principles, in the eternal validity of justice and freedom.   They wished to decide political issues by the democratic means of discussion and public voting; therefore conferences and congresses became the typical organizations of political liberalism, and these were considerably facilitated after 1850 by the improvement in means of communication.   Here again it is symbolical that this opposition used scientific and art congresses for the dissemination of political ideas (e.g. the congresses of the Germanists and historians, and the Schiller Festival of 1959).

Whereas the middle-class liberals claimed the right to govern the state by reason of its wealth and culture, the conservative feudal stratum took its stand on the principles of blood and tradition.   The political opposition prevailed in South Germany, but very soon came up against the organized resistance of the aristocratic court stratum in Prussia.   The liberal élite was scattered throughout the country, especially amongst the towns, and its activities were carried on in the light of publicity, but the conservative champions by no means concentrated primarily on the organization of party, press and parliamentary discussion, which means now lay also at its disposal.[3]   The liberal élite appealed to the middle-class in order to achieve power through it, and for it;

---

[1] F. Schnabel, *Deutsche Geschichte im Neunzehnten Jahrhundert*, ii. 94.

[2] In the Prussian Second Chamber the percentages of professional men amongst the deputies was as follows: 1849, 68 per cent; 1855, 63 per cent; 1862, 65·5 per cent; 1866, 58·8 per cent; see H. Schroth, *Welt-und Staatsideen des deutschen Liberalismus in der Zeit der Einheits- und Freiheitskämpfe 1859–66*, Berlin, 1931, p. 107.

[3] See E. Jordan, *Die Entstehung der konservativen Partei und die preussischen Agrarverhältnisse von 1848*, München, 1914.

the conservative aristocratic élite appealed in Prussia,
above all, to the King as the foremost possessor of
power, in order to preserve its own power with his
help, for it surrounded the crown as being the apex
of the State, and since 1848 it had its place at court
in the form of a clique whose aims were not easy of
detection.

II

The clear description of the feudal reactionary élite
at court and its organization for the political struggle
that is given in Gutzkow's novel *Die Ritter vom Geiste,*
is by no means the least thing that makes it an
important source of sociological knowledge, for the
novel does not merely describe this camarilla and its
auxiliaries, but puts it in its proper place in a vast
comprehensive picture of contemporary society.   In this
novel court and aristocracy, middle-class intelligentsia
and artisan class, workers and criminals, are all inter-
woven in a treatment that is rambling and by no means
uniform.

The work represents in Germany a new type of
novel so to speak; one which, to a certain extent, may
be described as a sociological novel.   The sociological
novel made its appearance in England, France and Germany approximately at the same time, and in this phenomenon there can be noted a *marked correlation between
changed conditions in society and the new type of novel,*
between the development of the industrial middle-class
and the tendency towards artistic realism.   With increasing industrialization and consequent participation of the
middle-class as a whole in political struggles, there begins
to appear simultaneously in Western Europe and in
Germany, side by side with the sentimental and educational novel in which an individual, a "hero," occupies
the foreground, a novel dealing with the conditions and
character of different classes, groups and circles.   In the
period that saw the beginning of the mass-movement, the
discovery was made that environment, class-distinctions,

the interaction of political forces, are deciding factors in human existence.[1]

In Germany Karl Gutzkow thought with his nine-volume work *Die Ritter vom Geiste* to replace the old novel of the *Nacheinander* with the new novel of the *Nebeneinander*, to substitute the novel in which events follow one another by the novel in which events happen concurrently. Following the example of the French writers Balzac and Eugène Sue, he desired to draw, instead of the usual longitudinal section of the life of a few, a latitudinal section of the whole of contemporary society, in the same way, so he puts it, "as one would sketch a cross-section of a warship or a mine."[2] The more the events of 1848 diminished the distance between the different classes of society, the more must this progressive writer have been inspired to describe the relationships and connections of the various classes —how they were composed, and how they worked with or against each other. Two things are characteristic of this type of novel: its desire for totality and its polemical attitude.

The desire for totality consists in the conscious purpose of investigating all classes in society, and of bringing them closer together—at least in the novel, in the course of such investigation. Gutzkow in the preface to his work says significantly: "There lies the whole world, with the present like a spread-out sheet! There we see

---

[1] The new realism in literary description is closely connected with the growing influence of a "public opinion." For the rules of living and playing peculiar to the aristocratic superstratum remained no longer, in the light of increased publicity, a kind of secret knowledge possessed by this stratum itself, but were now exposed to the critical searchlight of public discussion. In the European novel of political and social realism between (roughly) 1830 and 1870, this "revelation" of the ways of life of the ruling upper-classes (aristocracy, high finance), of both its political intrigues and its recreations, played an important part. The milieu-novel could only appear and find a response at a time when the difference of milieu and social existence seem to the majority of readers to be important and worthy of attention; the struggle of political forces, however, became a theme of a novel at the moment that politics ceased to be a matter purely for the cabinet and the diplomatic circle, and was rather the concern of a large public through the increasing power of the middle-class.

[2] Preface to 3rd Edition of the *Ritter vom Geiste*.

kings and beggars meeting! . . . Throne and cottage, market-place and forest are placed in close proximity." [1] In this meeting and gathering of the different groups and classes into close proximity, a democratic tendency finds clear expression.[2]

The purpose of the novel is not only to describe, but also to present a point of view and win support for it. "There an immense carpet is spread out, a philosophy of life, new and original, alas polemic, in one word: *Weltanschauung.*" [3] The polemical writer does not address himself to a vague public, but feels himself to be the apostle of a community. He appeals therefore to a definite conviction, to a definite kind of taste.[4] In this work there is expressed an anti-aristocratic, liberal and humanitarian sentiment which stresses the obligations of a progressive intelligentsia. Before we examine the social content of this representative novel in relation to our problem, we must turn briefly to the sociological determinants in Gutzkow's development previous to the writing of *Die Ritter vom Geiste.*[5]

Karl Gutzkow is the only one of the writers of the "Young Germany" circle whose origin may be called practically proletarian.[6] He was born in Berlin on 17 March, 1811, the son of a groom in the prince's stable, his father's position being an official one. His father later obtained a subordinate position in the war-ministry. The parents of the precocious child lived in one room and shared with their neighbours a communal kitchen

---

[1] Preface to 1st Edition of the *Ritter vom Geiste*, 1850, p. 7.

[2] This was also felt by contemporaries; cf. A. Jung, *Briefe über Gutzkows Ritter vom Geiste*, Berlin, 1856, pp. 20 ff.

[3] See the introduction to the 1st Edition of the *Ritter vom Geiste*, p. 8.

[4] *Op. cit.*, p. 9: "The missionaries of freedom and of faith in the times owe it to their communities to show them how the whole fullness of life can be illuminated by a new light."

[5] For further details of Gutzkow's life see the article *Gutzkow* in *Allgemeine Deutsche Biographie*, x. 227–36. Also L. Männer, *Gutzkow und der demokratische Gedanke*, Munich, 1921, pp. 4–28; cautious use should be made of Gutzkow's autobiography, *Rückblicke auf mein Leben*, Berlin, 1875.

[6] It is wrong to speak of Gutzkow's origin as being a middle-class one, as does M. Schönfeld in *Gutzkow's Frauengestalten*, Berlin, 1933, p. 60.

where his mother was continually quarrelling with the neighbour's wife. The boy realized at an early age the difference in the style of life led by poor and rich and became acquainted with the social dualism of the upper- and lower-classes. Through one of his playmates he was able to gain an early glimpse into the home of gentle and cultured people, and afterwards, as a scholar at the "Gymnasium," he obtained an entry, through a school-fellow, into the house of the Prussian Minister von Kamptz.

From 1821 to 1829 Gutzkow attended the Friedrich Werdersche Gymnasium in Berlin. Like Laube, he also had to earn part of his school fees by giving private lessons. The ambitious youngster soon became estranged from his narrow-minded parents and began to make his own way with the obstinacy of a proletarian; he early was aware of his intellectual superiority over his socially-superior school-fellows and he replaced the servility to princes and aristocrats, as taught him by his father, with a sharp-eyed criticism of the ruling class. Gutzkow's career followed the usual course of a gifted but poor youth between 1780 and 1840. He strove at first to become a parson, because the study of theology was the cheapest and was the one that led most quickly to an adequately paid post. After a few terms of study he gave up this idea owing to his growing estrangement from theology, and under the influence of his fiancée's petty-bourgeois mother he began to study to be a secondary-school teacher. But very soon he chose to follow the career of a journalist and writer, an extremely hazardous proceeding at that time. From 1830 to 1834 Gutzkow studied theology and philosophy in Berlin, Munich and Heidelberg, but at the same time began to busy himself more and more with journalism. At the age of twenty he had already published the *Forum der Journalliteratur*

On account of his difficult disposition, Gutzkow made far fewer social than professional contacts. As a student he became, like all the other adherents of the "Young

German Movement," a member of a secret society called
the "Societas Bibatoria," and as a writer he soon showed
the typical mobility of the "Young Germans." Under
the influence of the writings of Börne he developed an
enthusiasm for the doctrines of St. Simon and began to
criticize sharply such middle-class institutions as marriage
and the Church. The writer sought first of all the
patronage of the powerful dictator of criticism, Wolfgang
Menzel, whom he assisted in the publication of his influential *Cottasches Literaturblatt*. Later, however, when
Menzel became more and more reactionary, Gutzkow
broke away from him and attached himself to writers of
his own way of thinking, such as Laube, Th. Mundt and
Wienbarg. In 1835 appeared Gutzkow's revolutionary
novel *Wally oder die Zweiflerin*, which was of considerable political significance. His former patron, Menzel,
denounced the book in the German *Bundestag* as an attack
on the Christian religion, and with such success that it
was not only confiscated and its author imprisoned for
three months in Mannheim, but several writers with
similar tendencies were branded as the subversive "Young
Germany" clique and their writings prohibited.

After 1835 Gutzkow avoided a clash with the reactionary system, busied himself with editing various
periodicals, including the much-read *Telegraf für Deutschland* (1837–42), and wrote a number of character-
studies and novels. He lived in Frankfort, Hamburg,
and in 1840–2 in Paris; then again in Frankfort. He
was continually spied upon by Metternich's secret
police, without knowing it, and travelled a great deal.
This constant change of residence, which was both
voluntary and involuntary, was significant of the "Young
German" writer of this period.[1] After 1834 Gutzkow
made successful attempts at play-writing, and eleven
years after his condemnation by the *Bundestag*, he became,
like Laube, stage-manager at the Court Theatre in
Dresden.

Partly an official, partly a libertarian publicist, the

[1] See analysis of this type in chap. ix, below.

ambitious man also took part in the March revolution in Berlin. At the instance of conservative politicians (Prince Lichnowsky and Count Arnim-Boytzenburg) he undertook a mission of conciliation; he delivered a pacifying speech to the masses in front of the royal castle and, at the same time, inspired them with the idea of arming the people and forming a citizen-army (*Bürgerwehr*).[1] In two pamphlets Gutzkow discussed the ideas of freedom and unity, sketched out a programme for the future, and offered to the present only Utopias.[2] In 1849 at the dissolution of the theatre he lost his post in Dresden, and he took up once again the life of a free-lance writer. In 1850–2 he made a strong impression on the literary world with his *Ritter vom Geiste*.[3]

On account of his manifold activities, Gutzkow came into contact with ministers and court-circles as well as with the middle-class. He combined a decidedly democratic attitude with a keen observation of all classes of people, and although he was lacking in economic perception, he yet possessed, through his origin, a well-developed sense of the different mentality of rulers and ruled. As a boy he had already lived in two social worlds; as a student he was brought into contact, through the girl to whom he was first betrothed, with the "bigoted, self-complacent, gossiping petty-bourgeoisie," whilst his second betrothed (whom he eventually married) was the stepdaughter of a Swedish consul-general and belonged to the upper middle-class. After he was married, he entered into friendly relations with Therese von Bacharacht, the intelligent wife of a diplomat, and through her influence he gained an entry into the highest circles

[1] See *Rückblick auf mein Leben*, pp. 340 ff. Gutzkow's subsequent insinuation (1875) that the speech was made against his will is problematical. In 1848 he was also member of the committee of conciliation.

[2] See L. Männer, *op. cit.*, p. 24.

[3] For the lively response evoked by this work see A. Jung, *op. cit.*, and J. L. Hoffmann, *Über Gutzkow's Ritter vom Geiste, Almanach des literarischen Vereins in Nürnberg*, 1854; "A book that has had *such an unprecedented success in all circles of society*" (Hoffmann, p. 206).

of society, into the homes of ministers and leading writers.

However, although possessed of all the elasticity of the intellectual, he always retained deep down in himself a certain plebeian pride, a kind of primitive prejudice against the aristocracy. "Since I was once brought up to servility," he writes in his diary, shortly after his condemnation by the *Bundestag*, "I will forever hate that which is aristocratic," and again . . . "for what I hate most is the aristocracy." [1]   Although this prejudice is still very noticeable in the *Ritter vom Geiste*, his work does picture the reactionary aristocracy and court circles much more vividly and truthfully than does Freytag's somewhat colourless representation or Spielhagen's distortion.   Gutzkow's description of society has indeed in many parts only the "partial truth" that can be obtained by any man viewing it from a certain social position, yet he does endeavour throughout to obtain an objective synthesis of all elements in society, such as is characteristic of the comparatively mobile intelligentsia.[2]   Let us now turn to the novel itself.

It does not specifically name the locality that forms its background, but its wide-sweeping content refers constantly to the state of Prussia and particularly to the metropolis of Berlin and surrounding district.[3]   In the forefront of the novel stands the conflict of two political élites, namely the realistic, reactionary élite at court, gathered around the King, and a secret society of idealistic youths trying to achieve a transformation of public life through an Utopia.   We shall first describe the reactionary élite at court, with its subsidiary groups and auxiliary organizations, and then proceed to a descrip-

---

[1] L. Männer, *op. cit.*, p. 42.

[2] Mielke-Homann, *Der Deutsche Roman des 19. und 20. Jahrhunderts*, 7th Ed., Dresden, 1920, p. 176: Gutzkow's view of life in this work "in comparison with that of his earlier youth, had developed a striking objectivity."

[3] In comparison with the English and French type of society novel of the same period, it is marked by a certain narrowness and provincialism, a lack of contact with the greater world around, which is characteristic of the Prussians at that time.

tion of the progressive secret society of the *Ritter vom Geiste*.

In 1848 there was formed at the court in Berlin the so-called Camarilla, which we have already mentioned. It began to take shape from the moment that the King of Prussia was compelled by the pressure of the liberal and democratic movement to make far-reaching concessions to the bourgeoisie and to accept middle-class liberal ministers. The aristocracy sought, by means of a secret governmental clique of its own, to counteract the activities of the liberal government and to influence the King in favour of conservative aims. The glimpse of the building-up and of the activities of this court élite that we get in Gutzkow's novel [1] coincides to a great extent with the description of the Camarilla as given by historians. In Gutzkow a primary court élite is to be found gathered around the King and Queen, that gives the lead in tone and is separated from a secondary, broader, organizing élite that has its meeting-place in the salons of aristocratic ladies. The "little circles" in Gutzkow largely correspond in composition to the Camarilla, the "*ministère occulte*" which had established itself under the patronage of the Queen in order "to prevent the King from again falling into so helpless a position as in the March days." [2]

This clique formed itself from aristocrats and high middle-class officials. Amongst its members were to be found several generals, a Court Marshal, a Cabinet Minister, a judge, a lord-lieutenant, an ecclesiastical councillor, and a few university professors (including the historian Leo and perhaps also the leading conservative political theorist, F. J. Stahl).[3] The group comprised, therefore, not only personal friends of the King, strong monarchists aiming at the restoration of the royal prerogative, but also representatives of the feudal classes

---

[1] Especially in the chapter "Die Gesellschaft und die 'Kleinen Cirkel'" (Society and the "little circles"), ii. 387–409.

[2] H. v. Petersdorff, *König Friedrich Wilhelm IV*, Stuttgart, 1900, p. 17.

[3] Petersdorff, *op. cit.*, p. 22.

whose domination was being threatened. "In supporting the independent right of royal decisions as against
Parliament and the responsible ministers, the Camarilla
supported at the same time the interests of the feudal
circles." [1]

The existence of such a secondary government in the
dim background was as much in keeping with the
romantic mind of the King as with the well-calculated
designs of the aristocracy. In every rigidly exclusive
circle of loyal, like-minded friends, who feel themselves
bound together by common views and a common way of
life, there exists a leaning towards unreality and romanticism. Frederick-William IV was just the sort of man
to act as the centre of an esoteric circle. For the practical, everyday things of life bored him; he was an intro-
verted type that hated "utilitarian" and "administrative
people." [2] Gutzkow has the Camarilla in mind when
he says: [3]

The heart of events was never to be found in the ministries,
but beat only in the evening between the hours of eight and
twelve, within the so-called "little circles" which gathered around
the reigning couple. . . . Membership of the "little circles" was
not only the greatest distinction that the Court could bestow, but
also a proof of its most intimate trust. Only those could enter
it who pledged to the royal family a "real" understanding of the
times. The little circles ruled the country and controlled the
direction of foreign policy. There ambassadors revealed their
missions, there were read the despatches that had just arrived by
courier or by telegraph. Famous scholars, who enjoyed a special
confidence, would there give their views of the times over a
simple cup of tea, or they would relate what they had recently
observed in the course of their travels. [4]

According to Gutzkow's account, the circle consisted
of a few deposed statesmen of the old régime, some

[1] F. Hartung: *Verantwortliche Regierung, Kabinette und Nebenregierungen
im konstitutionellen Preussen 1848–1918, Forschungen zur Brandenburg. und
Preuss. Geschichte,* Munich, 1931–2, xliv. 1–45, 302–73.

[2] V. Valentin, *Geschichte der deutschen Revolution 1848–1849,* Berlin, 1931,
i. 30.

[3] *Die Ritter vom Geiste,* 1st Ed., ii. 399.   [4] *Op. cit.,* ii. 399–400.

widely-read but uncritical scholars, a sprinkling of foreign ambassadors' wives, and some ladies of the court, including particularly the shrewd and severe leading court governess (*Oberhofmeisterin*), who had superintended the Queen's education. The guiding spirit of the circle, however, was the King's favourite, General Voland von der Hahnenfeder, in reality Josef Maria von Radowitz whom Bismarck once called "valet to the King's imagination." [1]

Here was the seat of the indirect, shadowy counter-government, "the source of events." "The 'little circles' were the ministries' nightmare.[2] Only very seldom could one of the men whom the wave of the moment lifted up into Court gain an entry to them. For that, one needed qualities apart from mere knowledge of state-craft and government. One had, so to speak, to be in harmony with the young royal couple, especially with the young Queen. How few of the dry bureaucrats, blunt warriors, cunning lawyers were thus attuned! *And yet they all realized that it was in the little circles that the password of the System was issued.* Some of the plans formulated there might be frustrated once by the resistance of a minister, perhaps a second time, but then they succeeded. Thousands of secret threads coming from the little circles would suddenly weave themselves around apparently the most secure position, and bring it crashing down."[3] Gutzkow describes these circles—so we could say to-day—as a typical *devotion-group*, i.e. an association of persons who place themselves voluntarily at the service of a superior. The superior determines its selection not according to the possession of expert knowledge and qualifications, but rather according to

[1] For Radowitz, see F. Meinecke : *Radowitz und die deutsche Revolution*, Berlin, 1913.

[2] Cf. Hartung, *op. cit.*, p. 7: "The existence of the Camarilla was naturally a tremendous burden for the ministers who had to determine the King's policy and be responsible for it to Parliament. For they had not only to deal with the King, but with the influence of a secret secondary government that was difficult to trace."

[3] *Die Ritter vom Geiste*, ii. 400–1.

capacity to identify themselves with his feelings and aims. The author overlooks the fact that the members of this political court circle use the King as a tool and means to an end, in just the same way that they allow him to use them as such; the process is an alternating one.[1]

Next to the little circles, the counter-revolutionary primary élite, there comes the *conservative salon* as the meeting-place of a broader *secondary aristocratic élite*. Between the little circles and the conservative salon there is a difference in the social level; the secondary élite takes up eagerly, copied and displayed to wider circles the impulses, ideas, and models that were originated and developed by the primary élite. It is not so much a leader in tone, as a mediator thereof; it does not create a political and social style of life, but propagates and classifies it; it is, in the real sense of the word, an organizing élite.[2] The cultural and political example set at court by Frederick-William IV after his accession to the throne achieved, strangely enough, only a gradual success within the circle of the secondary élite.

At the beginning, nothing was so out of fashion as the young royal couple. Hardly any one took any notice of them, their tastes were ridiculed and they were both declared to be of limited intelligence. But shortly afterwards there came a change. The royal couple became the fashion. Their ideas began to set the tone. Everybody stepped into line with the new sun which, although it now stood so high, had required two years of uphill struggle to penetrate the clouds of "Society." [3]

[1] The following sentence characterizes Gutzkow's point of view: "What is so all-powerful in a monarchy is that which has been faithfully interpreted as the idea of the prince and of his most intimate circle by a dozen clever and devoted slaves, who proceed to propagate it with holy zeal" (*ibid.*, ii. 401).

[2] A counter-example for the same period in England is given by Disraeli's novel, *Endymion*. Here a secondary government is not developed at court, but precisely in the political salons of the Whigs and Tories, and a number of ladies of high standing in society play here the part of secret political wire-pullers which the ladies in the conservative salons in Prussia strove to play at that time, but in vain.

[3] *Die Ritter vom Geiste*, ii. 392.

Like every politically-dominating group, the court-monarchy also selected certain æsthetic qualities as a norm. Although the possessor of power is only one factor in the formation of cultural fashions, he does play in the history of western culture an important selective rôle. The absolutist court of the seventeenth century had acted as arbiter of fashion, and it pleased Frederick-William IV also, as a "romantic on the royal throne," to perform the same function.

Suddenly [says Gutzkow of the style at court] simplicity, soulfulness, modesty, narrowness and domesticity came into fashion. The "ingenious" was abandoned.   One did not exactly read pious or bigoted literature, but one read books that were innocent, pure, uplifting and naïve.   The frivolous accounts of the ways of the big world were ignored.   One took the side of the simple, the naïve, the countrified.[1]

The ambitious ladies of the conservative salons in Gutzkow's novel adapted themselves accordingly.   Frau Geheimrat Pauline von Harder, for instance, the clever wife of an intellectually narrow Court Intendant, had formerly engaged in literary activity, and she used to gather in her salon the cultural élite of Berlin.   But now she began to notice the precedence possessed by politics and organizing activities over art and science in the revolutionary period of 1848.   With the growing interest in politics, the extraordinary prestige that was enjoyed by intellectual celebrities in Berlin, especially by the great representatives of scholarship between 1800 and 1848, was indeed declining.   Whilst, hitherto, the broad stratum of "the cultured" had interested themselves, in a non-political period, in all the facts and personal details of the life of a Hegel or an Alexander von Humboldt,[2] there followed now a marked shifting of interest in the direction of politics, accompanied by a decline in reputations of purely scientific or artistic distinction.   Only celebrities

---

[1] *Die Ritter vom Geiste*, ii. 392.
[2] Cf., for instance, the characteristic chapter in Laube's *Neue Reisenovellen*, Mannheim, 1837, i, 275-324, entitled "Berliner Berühmtheiten."

who had opportunely adjusted themselves to politics in 1848 and following years had any chance of retaining their esteem in public life.

The old intellectual names [says Gutzkow] such as she [i.e. Frau von Harder] had used to gather at her house almost every evening, were faded stars. Painters, sculptors, poets, scholars— who cared about them at a time when votes, and votes only, were the watchword? She, also, had refrained from inviting the great men of former times. Who spoke of them? Who admired a poem, a picture, an astronomical discovery? Poor buried ones! You could only arise from the dead if you were prepared to join in the crazy political outbursts and celebrate your rebirth in the demonstrations of the patriotic club.[1]

The salon of Frau von Harder forms the centre for the organization of counter-revolutionary propaganda. Here is organized the boycott of all merchants and artisans who do not vote in favour of the government.[2] In this drawing-room we see exposed the technique of the political struggle by means of which the hard-pressed feudal stratum tries to regain its lost ascendancy. To the standing-army of Frau von Harder, who pursues this struggle both openly and in secret, there belong aristocrats, officers, officials, all united through their hostility to revolutionary chaos. Above all, however, it is the country-nobility who give free play here to their feelings of hatred and scorn for the revolution. Completely carried away by the idea of "lords' right" (*Herrenrecht*), and by an autocratic view of life, they are enraged at the recurrent threat of loss of privileges, and at the proposed taxation of their property.[3]

[1] *Die Ritter vom Geiste,* ii. 398 ff. This passage is a significant testimony of the amorphous character of the public and of the uncertainty of fame that was dependent on it in the beginnings of mass-democracy.

[2] *Ibid.,* ii. 394: "She was one of the chief inspirers of the counter-revolutionary attacks, she helped to found the 'Reubund,' she canvassed at elections with unprecedented intrigue, she organized on a large scale the prevention of a livelihood to all the merchants and artisans who would not vote unconditionally in the way that the aristocrats and officials demanded."

[3] Gutzkow says of the excited country-nobility: "When the gentlemen von Zeisel, von Sänger, Count Benzheim, von Saengebusch met together, they gave vent to a fanaticism that Siegbert did not dare to contradict, since all

The circles represented in Frau von Harder's salon were by no means guided by principles of humanity in the choice of their fighting methods. The counter-revolution of 1848–9 displayed, in comparison with the relatively more moderate revolution, greater brute force. "Patriotism, morality and loyalty to the ruling house," says a modern historian, "advanced to the attack. The revolution had seen the criminal only in a Metternich; but the counter-revolution branded a whole social stratum as rogues." [1]   In Gutzkow's account, the leaders of the counter-revolutionary storm-troops who meet at Frau von Harder's are an aristocratic land-owner and a high official of the administrative military staff.

Kammerherr von Ried organized peasants' clubs that attacked democratic societies whenever occasion was opportune, beating almost to death such as did not profess themselves ready to sing straightway a certain patriotic hymn. These patriotic bands were organized practically throughout the monarchy and were led by gendarmes or by ex-soldiers who had put on again their civilian working-clothes, but who had not overmuch inclination for civilian labour.[2]

As there was not then in existence a class-conscious proletariat, these organizations were successful—as we can also see from other contemporary sources—in creating a secret fighting troop from men of the lowest strata, such as porters, barrow-pushers, sewer-men and dockers. "The war-councillor Wisperling," we are told, "was one of those creeping natures who knew how to employ a full purse in the enlistment of sewer-men and

discussion was impossible. They condemned the times and the men, called the newly-appointed statesmen robbers, demanded that the despoilers of the land, the democrats, be declared outlaws, and often Count Benzheim would say: 'They ought to be shot like mad dogs.' " (*Die Ritter vom Geiste*, vii. 382.) For the counter-revolutionary agitation of the nobility in the provinces, see E. Jordan, *op. cit.*, and also R. Springer, *Berlin's Strassen, Kneipen und Clubs im Jahre 1848*, Berlin, 1850, p. 192.

[1] V. Valentin, *op. cit.*, ii. 585 ff.

[2] *Die Ritter vom Geiste*, iv. 48. On the organization of the peasantry by aristocratic propagandists for counter-revolutionary purposes, see R. Springer, *op. cit.*, p. 192.

stevedores for such loyal demonstrations of cudgel-
ling." [1]

We see therefore how from this salon—which contains, besides representatives of the landed-aristocracy
and military bureaucracy, also representatives of ecclesiastical institutions like the "Home Mission" (*Innere
Mission*)—the threads go out to organized fighting troops.
In addition, the salon is instrumental in organizing clubs
for the more numerous of its adherents. The desire to
form clubs and associations of like-minded people was
of significance for the liberal movement, which demanded
freedom of assembly.[2] For the liberal-democratic
bourgeoisie in Berlin in 1848 the political club was a
typical social form. In accordance with the law of
mutual adjustment of political fronts, the reactionaries
copied this club-formation and organized their adherents
into clubs such as the *Preussen Verein für konstitutionelles
Königtum* in Berlin, and the *Verein für König und Vaterland* in the province of Brandenburg.[3]

[1] These references to the excesses of the counter-revolutionary bands are
confirmed, also as regards Berlin, by other contemporary documents. R.
Springer, for instance, says of the "Political Club": "This club, which had
exhibited from the beginning the most determined efforts for democracy, was,
in the eyes of the conservatives, the most abominable smithy where the strokes
of agitation were forged. . . . The fanatics of peace did not disdain to distribute money amongst the dregs of the population so as to incite them to mis-
handle bodily the peaceably assembled democrats." "The club, like a hunted
beast, had to change its places of refuge, but despite that could not escape ill-
treatment at the hands of knackers and wood-cutters." (*Op. cit.*, pp. 64–5.)
A. Wolff, *Berliner Revolutions-Chronik*, Berlin, 1852, iii. 311 f. and 321 f.,
mentions sewer-men as well as knackers.

[2] Cf. F. Schnabel, *op. cit.*, ii. 210.

[3] The composition of these two organizations is interesting; they are completely different although they both serve the same ends of fighting the revolution and strengthening the monarchy. The Berlin society is a combination
of aristocrats, officials, titular intelligentsia and, significantly, members of the
middle-class loyal to the system. The invitation to the inaugural meeting
was signed chiefly by elevated artisans (including the court-upholsterer,
slaughterer and shoemaker), followed by aristocrats and officials (including
several counts and other aristocrats, a barrister [*Justizrat*], a major-general,
a general-staff-accountant, and a few members of the ministries of commerce
and health and of the Chancellery).

The "Society for King and Fatherland," on the other hand, which pursued
the same aims in the provinces where the population participated much less
in the democratic movement than in Berlin on account of the pressure of the

Under pressure of the revolution, there took place a rapprochement between aristocrats and middle-class circles loyal to the old régime, and it was in these clubs that they met on a social footing. This amalgamation of the various reactionary elements obtained perhaps its most significant organization in 1849 in the so-called *Treubund für König und Vaterland* (Association of the Faithful for King and Country), which opposed to the idea of a national and liberal unity that of a Prussian, patriotic particularism.[1] Our author offers us interesting sidelights on the social structure of these monarchist associations. The historical *Treubund* appears in his book, but bearing the slightly disguised and easily recognized appellation of *Reubund* (Society of Repentance),

for its founders [he says] intended to prove to the ruling house, by influencing public opinion in every possible way, that the people, whose real representatives they claim to be, now repented the manner in which they extorted certain concessions in the last upheavals.[2]

In Gutzkow's *Reubund* are to be found squires (*Landräte*), aristocratic government officials (*Regierungsräte*) without money, aristocratic guards' officers and middle-class court purveyors, professors and clerics.[3]   No lady who was married to an officer or an official omitted to join this club.   The actual *Treubund* had a special female section for Prussian women who desired to educate the rising generation to a veneration for the Hohenzollerns. "A model house was planned whose aim was to achieve a cheaper and more moral life," and to educate the

aristocratic landowners, had the typical character of a men's club (*Herrenklub*). Its 90 members included almost all the aristocratic landowners, and also one non-noble lieutenant-colonel, one non-noble manufacturer, and one country-preacher.

See A. Wolff: *Berliner Revolutions-Chronik. Darstellung der Berliner Bewegungen im Jahre 1848 nach politischen, sozialen und literarischen Beziehungen*, ii. 575, and iii. 212 ff.

[1] For the *Treubund*, cf. V. Valentin, *op. cit.*, ii. 473 ff.
[2] *Die Ritter vom Geiste*, i. 47.
[3] Valentin gives no figures as to the composition of the *Treubund*.

children of the poorer classes. This organization had
four different grades : The Henrietta (green), Sophie
(white), Louise (pink) and Elisabeth (pale-blue) grades.
Its organ was called *Gott mit uns* (God with us), in which
the editor, Count Otto Schlippenbach, presented typical
reactionary views on the structure of society "which, like
nature around us, has to consist of an upper and a lower
part." [1]

This association was, then, a systematically organized
machine for conservative political propaganda. In
Gutzkow's novel, the propaganda is carried out by a
young aristocratic lady, Fräulein von Flottwitz, the
daughter of a retired officer and sister of numerous
officers and cadets. In her work for the (*T*)*reubund*, she
represents thinly disguised class-interests.

She is grateful [the author says, not without sarcasm] for the
benefits that her poor family has received, and is still receiving,
from the state. Without the former conservative government,
whose restoration she and the whole Reubund likewise desired,
they might perhaps have had to starve. Her old father might
perhaps be deprived of part of his means of subsistence, which
he believed he was justified in counting on after the frightful
difficulties of the peace treaty of 1815.[2]

This (*T*)*reubund* was, if we are to believe Gutzkow,
organized on the model of the Freemasonic lodges,
except that, on account of the propagandist motives,
the exclusiveness of the latter was omitted. "One had
one's lodges, one's first and second degrees, there were
brothers, sisters, signs of recognition, hidden handshakes
and secret initiations," [3] according to Probst Gelbsattel,
the leader of protestant orthodoxy. The (*T*)*reubund*,
whose chief aim was to influence the masses and achieve
publicity, and in which the aristocracy and higher officials
had to set a good example, created for the ambitious and
patriotic burgher a *specific opportunity of a rapprochement*
with the ruling upper strata. The burgher saw in it

---

[1] V. Valentin, *op. cit.*, ii. 473 f.   [2] *Die Ritter vom Geiste*, i. 52 f.
[3] *Ibid.*, i. 190.

definite prospects of arranging an advantageous marriage for his daughters.[1]

"Thus on the pretext of principle," states, with a sigh, a conservative cleric in the novel, "every pater familias who has a daughter to dispose of and who has no hopes of being accepted in a finer club or in the big Casino, comes flocking to join us." [2]

It seems a remarkable thing that we find also in Frau von Harder's conservative salon, just as in the *Reubund*, a certain type of intelligentsia.

If we view the situation of society in 1848, we can divide the intelligentsia, broadly, into two types, the *intelligentsia loyal to the old régime* and the *opposition intelligentsia*. It would be natural to expect that the intellectuals amongst the bureaucrats should belong to the first type, for their inclinations were determined by their official position, and that the members of the free professions should support the second. In point of fact, however, we do find members of the free professions amongst the loyalist intelligentsia, for some of them, such as doctors and lawyers, drew their clientele from the aristocratic, conservative stratum of society, and their political views were therefore influenced by immediate economic interests.

Gutzkow draws a clear and detailed picture of the middle-class loyalist intellectuals, but depicts the opposition intellectuals rather vaguely. We are presented with characteristic representatives of that socially superior, usually unofficial intelligentsia, which is bound up with the traditional ruling strata through its professional duties, social intercourse and political work and which, therefore, forms one of the pillars of the system. We

---

[1] It is to be regretted that representatives of middle-class landed-proprietors, of the spheres of industrial, commercial and financial capitalism, are almost wholly lacking in the novel. Only the owner of a machine-factory appears, and then once, as a minor character. Gutzkow prefers too much (in contrast to Balzac) the definitely intellectual, the game of political intrigue, to be able to describe the life of the upper bourgeoisie with the soberness of its endeavours and conflicts.

[2] *Die Ritter vom Geiste*, iii. 256. The "Casino" was a very exclusive aristocratic society.

can designate this group, which to a very large extent
has been turned by honours and titles into the satellites
of the ruling stratum of junkerdom and bureaucracy,
as an *escorting or titular intelligentsia*.[1] The representatives of it in the novel are a barrister (*Justizrat*), a
physician (*Sanitätsrat*), and a highly-placed protestant
clergyman (*Probst*), three figures who together play an
important part within the conservative circle; as advisers
and confidants of the aristocratic upper stratum, they
exercise a powerful influence. The functions of the
legal, medical and spiritual adviser have this in common,
that they give to their executors a far-reaching and
freely conceded influence over the people to whom
they minister. In the novel the representatives of the
titular intelligentsia are, moreover, linked together by
membership of a freemasonic lodge; further, the lawyer
and the physician are friends, whilst the *Probst* is the
father-confessor of the physician's family. These types
know the life of the great world, are worldly-like courtiers
and skilful in guarding their interests. They combine
the manners of the man of the world with the knowledge
of the specialist.

They are opportunists and shelter behind the dominant
system, not because it is their system but just because
it is dominant. They follow a certain line only because
it pays them best, but they do not adhere to it too completely; they have secret reservations and keep themselves
elastic. The lawyer Schlurk, for example, has the typically calculating mentality of the experienced jurist. He
is described as an absolutely negative character who does
everything out of self-interest and he says with placid
cynicism, "if nonsense succeeds, well let us join in with
nonsense." [2]

Such a continual relative adjustment appears in times
when the political structure is unstable and a continual

---

[1] V. Valentin probably has this titular intelligentsia before his eye when
he mentions the self-confidence of the professional men "which clung,
lacking and desirous of honour, to the socially superior classes" (*op. cit.*, ii. 558).

[2] *Die Ritter vom Geiste*, i. 183 ff.

change of system occurs. From the knowledge the skilled lawyer gathers by contact with all strata and classes of society in the course of his practice, he is inclined to trace the cause of all events to money and indulgence. His opportunist manœuvring shows itself in his being sobered by revolutionary experiences, and his beginning to see in all political activities only a means for furthering his career:

I was a member of every Bible Society, of every mission and Gustavus-Adolphus society; I belonged first to the constitutional *"Angstklub"*; I am now . . . officially a member of the *Reubund*; why should I stop to explain to people why I am not a genuine supporter of it? [1]

This opportunist must vote for the right just now, but gains his living from many people who support the left, perhaps secretly holds left opinions himself. He is a type, however, that is very different from the politically-minded lawyer, who attained to great influence in Western Europe.[2]

This lawyer is far too much of a hedonist not to realize that only through an enforced stabilization of the reactionary régime will safety and prosperity be again guaranteed for the property-owning classes. As a man of property he appreciates the value of a régime of order. Schlurk remarks on one occasion: "It is of some value if reaction succeeds in enabling us once more to visit watering-places in comfort." [3] Although he has very few illusions about the ruling class, he is yet continually filled with the ambition to belong to it, to be its legal adviser, administrator, a favourite in society who himself keeps a fine establishment, to be indispensable to it.

The doctor is also characterized by changeability,

---

[1] *Die Ritter vom Geiste*, i. 183 ff.

[2] Lawyer Schlurk appears only once, as a moderate liberal candidate. As F. Schnabel has aptly remarked, the independence, which explains the high respect enjoyed by the lawyer-politicians in western Europe, was lacking in Germany at that time owing to her still relatively undeveloped economic conditions. (*Deutsche Geschichte im 19. Jahrhundert*, ii. 203.)

[3] *Die Ritter vom Geiste*, i. 187.

whereby he achieves success within the legitimist upper stratum. He is representative of the smart, fashionable physician patronized by the aristocracy and the rich, much the same as Axel Munthe, the Swedish physician, depicts him for the twentieth century in his autobiography, *The Story of San Michele.* Without any outstanding medical knowledge, but allopath and homeopath at the same time, he concentrates on the soul of his patients, a formula which wins for him all the ladies of society. For the leisured lady, untouched by the economic struggle for existence, this interest in her own misunderstood soul is fascinating. The less seriously the ladies of the leisured class take life, the more seriously do they want to be taken by these therapeutists skilled in the knowledge of human beings.

Next to the polished lawyer and the fashionable physician comes Probst Gelbsattel, as the type of the political cleric. From about 1848 till 1853, clerical reaction was predominant at the court of Frederick-William IV, and after the repulse of 1849 the liberal teachers in the government schools, especially, were subjected to the power of protestant orthodoxy.[1]

The influence of leading politicians of the Church was far-reaching. Contemporaries thought they saw in Probst Gelbsattel such theologians as the warlike Professor Hengstenberg (editor of the *Lutherische Kirchenzeitung*),[2] or Bishop Eylert.[3] Probst Gelbsattel is de-

[1] See K. Biedermann, *1840–1870, 30 Jahre Deutscher Geschichte*, Breslau, 1896, ii. 99–105.

[2] E. W. Hengstenberg (1802–68) was the leader of Prussian orthodox protestantism between 1835 and 1859. As professor of theology at the University of Berlin and as a publicist he exercised a great influence, especially on appointments to theological lectureships and to ecclesiastical livings. He was married to the daughter of a strongly religious Pomeranian aristocrat. For further information about him see article "*Hengstenberg,*" *Allgemeine Deutsche Biographie*, xi. 737–47, by O. v. Ranke; also Max Lenz, *Geschichte der Friedrich Wilhelm Universität zu Berlin*, Berlin, 1910–18, ii (1), 327 and ii (2), 107. On the restoration theology with its tendency to be a state-conserving Church, cf. E. Tröltsch, *Protestantisches Christentum und Kirche in der Neuzeit* in *Die Geschichte der Christlichen Religionen* (*Die Kultur der Gegenwart*), 2nd Ed., 1909, part I, sect. ii, pp. 731–5.

[3] For Eylert, cf. *Allg. Deutsche Biographie*, vi. 494.

scribed as a powerful nature, the true rock of the Protestant church. He is skilful in reconciling the various
theological tendencies and bending them to his own
purpose, and manages to use his connections with the
court to consolidate his prestige as a preacher. The
court "gives the tone" in all spheres, i.e. it has the function of selecting what is fashionable to suit the taste and
edification of its adherents. Through the example of
the court-circles therefore, it becomes universally fashionable within the strata of the rich and the aristocracy to
have one's Christian conscience awakened and moved by
Probst Gelbsattel. He is not merely a preacher, he is
also the cultural adviser of the court, the leading stylist in
the country, and even an urban politician.[1] As a member
of the Consistory Council he has, further, a powerful
influence on the choice of candidates for the ministry.

The conservative fighting élite which we have just
been analysing, and whose members occupied distinguished positions in society, is contrasted by Gutzkow
with a picture of a counter-élite of young idealists that
is more fanciful than realistic. Whilst his sketch of the
conservative circle agrees in essentials with historical
facts, his description of the progressive circles is rather
the expression of what he wanted it to be than what it
actually was—and as such it has some significance for
our purpose. In the conservative salon and in the
Treubund an amalgamation of aristocracy and middle-
class ensues from a common interest in reaction, but in
the secret society of the *Ritter vom Geiste* the amalgamation is not one arising from common interests, but due
to an idea. It is a club of youthful universal reformers
without concrete or fixed aims, and with a vague liberal
doctrine of opposition to the encroachments of state and
princes.

---

[1] O. v. Ranke, *op. cit.*, p. 746: "However much Hengstenberg may have
made the impression in outward appearance of belonging completely to the
learned world of the present, he yet knew all the claims of active life, followed
with great interest all the movements of the state and the social and political
world; he possessed an immense knowledge of persons and circumstances of
all kinds and criticized conditions from the standpoint of a practical realist."

The state, society, [says one of them] is feelingless and cruel; the princes treat their people like inherited chattels. How can one protect oneself against it, otherwise than by writing and agreeing to strengthen the individual with the power of the whole community?[1]

For this secret society the typical structure of the small group with esoteric tendencies, mutual obligations and responsibility of the members for its common aims and objects is characteristic. Certain circles of the twentieth-century German youth movement, before and after the Great War, had a similar structure and similar romantic tendencies. The "secret society" is frequently to be found in the German novel, from Goethe's *Wilhelm Meister* and Jean Paul's *Unsichtbare Loge* to Gutzkow's *Ritter vom Geiste*. The important part played by it at that time in the imagination of contemporaries had in reality two sociological roots: (i) *Freemasonic lodges*, which were usually exclusive, and (ii) *political secret societies* which were formed everywhere in Europe by the persecuted liberal-democratic youth. After the prohibition of 1819 there existed in Germany secret student-associations.[2]

To return to the *Ritter vom Geiste*, this circle consisted of two brothers (the sons of a parson, one being a lawyer and the other a painter), an artisan of Latin origin, a liberal officer who was the son of a field-marshal, and Prince Egon von Hohenberg. The last-named is the most important and later also the most influential member. He brings with him from Paris the doctrines of Saint Simon, which had stirred Gutzkow himself so much in his youth.[3]

For industrial development and against bureaucracy [ran his slogan]. As long as labour does not itself approach the throne

---

[1] *Die Ritter vom Geiste*, v. 282 ff.

[2] Cf. O. Schuster, *Die Geheimen Gesellschaften, Verbindungen und Orden*, Leipzig, 1906, ii. 324, and E. Manheim, *Die Träger der Öffentlichen Meinung*, Brünn, 1933, pp. 97 ff. and 124 ff.

[3] Cf. the valuable book by E. M. Butler, *The Saint-Simonian Religion in Germany, A Study of the Young German Movement*, Cambridge, 1926, part V, pp. 258–319.

to act as its own spokesman, and as long as bureaucracy acts as mediator for the interests of labour, things cannot improve; we need statesmen who have been trained amongst the people.[1]

The antipathy against bureaucracy is typical of the aristocrat (it was shared by Bismarck as a young man),[2] whilst the demand for rapprochement between people and throne is characteristic of the democrat. This circle develops a spiritual code of honour through its aversion to the growing reaction and through its aloofness to a revolution the imperfections of which were recognized; it is a liberal intellectual élite in the midst of a counter-revolution.

We must preach [the young lawyer explains] an equality different, for instance, from that of public assemblies. Equality with the common people is no longer the desire of thinking men. Equality of claims to the great honour which lies in a common purpose that binds us all together, an honour that is reflected on all of us from a single idea that deserves honours, that is an ideal worth striving for, something that will rescue us from a relapse into barbarism, from sinking into a worship of existing order through fear of revolution.[3]

What is characteristic here is the seeking for a new idea of honour which we have already noted in Immermann. Now that the specific code of honour springing from status has lost its meaning, a democratic code of honour is sought for that will be valid for everybody and which will yet satisfy the special demands of the intellectuals.

But as soon as concrete problems of society come into question, there appears a discrepancy between the views of the commoners and of Prince von Hohenberg. A conversation that takes place between them on seeing the insolvent estate of a prince which has been entrusted to middle-class creditors clearly reveals the difference in

---

[1] *Die Ritter vom Geiste*, i. 239.

[2] This aristocratic antipathy against bureaucracy, which is mainly of middle-class origin, is also strongly expressed in Fürst Pückler's *Briefe eines Verstorbenen*, Stuttgart, 1831, 1st Ed., pp. 33 ff., and in Countess Hahn-Hahn's *Aus der Gesellschaft*, Berlin, 1838, pp. 120 ff.

[3] *Die Ritter vom Geiste*, loc. cit.

their points of view. Prince Egon defends the private
ownership of land and expresses resentment against
burdensome ground-rent and against the state's prefer-
ential treatment of Industry and Commerce. The
burghers, however, sharply oppose the precedence of
aristocratic estates and condemn aristocratic institutions
in general. They uphold the definitely middle-class
principle of a division of human beings, not according
to birth, but according to different grades of property
and culture.

Thus two groups within this circle can be found, one
advocating *reform of the aristocracy*, the other *abolition of
the aristocracy*. For the prince is convinced of the absolute
necessity of the aristocracy for the state; it is not to be
destroyed, but ennobled. He welcomes as a solution
the English practice whereby only the eldest-born belongs
to the aristocracy, but he repudiates the prevailing German practice of ennobling middle-class financiers and
civil servants.

III

Gutzkow described the building-up of the conservative front from the standpoint of a democrat writer, and
contrasted it with the idealized picture of the *Ritter vom
Geiste*. An aristocratic and royalist writer of the same
period sought, conversely, to "expose" the liberal and
democratic party and to confront it with his idealized
picture of a patriarchal Prussianism. Alexander von
Ungern-Sternberg gives us in his story *Die Royalisten* a
work of little artistic merit, but of great symptomatic
significance.[1] This book, half leading article, half novel,
is a very significant pamphlet of the ultra-conservative
section of the aristocracy, directed against the destruction of the state by the victorious democratic revolution.
It presents a picture of society as seen from the standpoint of the hard-pressed feudal stratum. The documentary significance of *Die Royalisten* is by no means
lessened by the disavowal which the author published

---

[1] *Die Royalisten*, Bremen, 1848. This book has not hitherto been noticed
in research.

a few years later.[1]   It is precisely the lack of understanding that Ungern-Sternberg, as an aristocrat, has
for the liberal bourgeois period of 1848, that makes his
book a sociological source.   As we analyse the development of this aristocratic writer elsewhere in this work,[2]
we shall endeavour to reveal here only the social content
of the counter-revolutionary *Die Royalisten.*

In crude black-and-white colours, the motives of the
revolutionaries are here condemned, whilst those of the
royalists are idealized.   It is always the method of a
political ideology to assign to the existence and actions
of its own group a positive valuation, and to the existence and actions of hostile groups a negative valuation.
The prestige of its own cause and its own adherents is
exaggerated as much as possible, that of its opponents
correspondingly belittled and despised.   An ideology is
an expression of this attitude in principle.   Its peculiarity is shared by the political or military legend, with
the difference that the latter confines itself to perverting
some particular historical event, twisting it for a special
purpose without any regard to the actual facts.   After
the events of March 1848, the aristocracy and officer-
circles set about constructing a military legend.   The
part played by the army in the March revolution had
not been exactly heroic.   After the happenings of the
18th March, the King had ordered it to withdraw from
Berlin without fighting.   It was the democratic middle-
class, and not the army led by the aristocracy, that
won the day.   Such being the state of things, it was
to the interest of royalist circles, by a kind of political
metaphysics, to see behind the events secretive and
hidden destructive revolutionary powers.   One saw and

[1] A. von Ungern-Sternberg, *Erinnerungsblätter*, Berlin, 1855, i. 11: "I was
not able to recognize the more deeply rooted ideas of our times which strove
magnificently to introduce a bold idea of justice into the world.   I have to
apologize very much to the young generation whom heaven has called to
struggle.   If I could, I would buy back with years of my life these unfortunate
books which I have written in a blind zeal against a tendency of our time
of which I only heard the extremely shrill voice, but of which I did not
recognize the wonderful inner contents."

[2] See chap. viii, p. 296 f.

scented secret societies everywhere in the opponent's camp. The instigators and wire-pullers of the revolution were "exposed" as aliens (especially Frenchmen and Poles), Jews and morally inferior subjects.[1]

In dealing with this "exposure," the *Royalisten* concerns itself closely with the events of the 16th, 17th, 18th and 19th March, devoting a chapter to each of these days respectively. The occurrences without and within the castle on the 18th and 19th March, and the attitude of Frederick-William IV, are presented so as to harmonize with the legend. Ungern-Sternberg describes sketchily four main groups:—

(i) The loyal military aristocracy.
(ii) The propertied middle-class.
(iii) The "common" people, the petty-bourgeoisie, who form the *Bürgerwache* (civic guard).
(iv) The political and organizing élite of the revolutionary literati.

(i) *The royalist aristocracy* has been thoroughly embittered by the events of March, especially by the King's capitulation to the people, and is filled with a keen resentment against the revolution.[2] One of the chief characters of the book—an old retired colonel—considers the political development to be such a disgrace to his Estate that he will no longer accept a pension from a king who has proved so weak. This man of honour, impoverished by his action, secretly sells his valuables and makes a living with wood-carvings which his former batman, a faithful peasant from the provinces, sells for

[1] Characteristic of the military legend born of the resentment of the defeated, is a speech made by Major-General Webern in the Berlin *Landwehrkasino* on 24 May, 1849: "Comrades, whom have we really to thank for the revolution? None else but Polish and French emissaries and the corrupt literati who all deserve to be hanged. I really don't know how to describe these scoundrels [after a pause for thought]—they are just *Scheisskerle*." The speaker repeated this last term (which will not bear translation into English) twice and earned a thundering round of applause. (Cited in V. Valentin, *op. cit.*, ii. 231 ff.)

[2] For the tension between aristocracy and people, see also the interesting letters of Caroline von Rochow, *Vom Leben am Preussischen Hofe, 1815–52*, ed. L. v. d. Marwitz, Berlin, 1908, p. 469.

him. The colonel's daughter adapts herself bravely to
their new economic circumstances and takes a position as governess in the family of a finance-councillor
(*Finanzrat*).[1]

The young aristocrats in the novel feel the loss of
honour, which they have suffered through the revolution, to such a degree that they long for the honour
of a soldier's death. They discuss amongst themselves
the attacks of the revolutionaries against their class, and
especially the accusation that they have lost all touch
with the people. It is characteristic of their soldier's
mentality that they try to repudiate this accusation by
pointing to the common struggle waged by the people
and aristocracy in the wars of liberation (1813–15).

At the King's call to arms, aristocrat and peasant formed *one*
line. The noblest families sought honour in fighting for the
Fatherland side by side with the brave men of the people. Such
was the Prussian aristocracy. And these robbers, these empty
phrase-mongers, dare to deny the capacity and superiority of the
aristocracy and to slander it before the people. And all this has
to be endured—endured by a soldier! [2]

(ii) *The propertied middle-class* has the typical attitude
of the *juste milieu*; in accordance with its class structure,
it holds a position midway between the conservative
upper strata and the democratic mass-movement. The
home of the finance-councillor, as depicted by Ungern-
Sternberg, serves therefore as a meeting-place of representatives of the various political and social groups.
Here we find an old widow of a minister and a royalist
colonel, as well as a blasé banker and a middle-class
landowner of progressive views, and last but not least,
the leader of the revolutionary group of literati, Dr.
Weldt.[3]

[1] Her new employers exhibit no class-haughtiness towards her, but feel
themselves visibly honoured by the symbiosis with a companion of blue-blood!

[2] *Die Royalisten*, p. 176.

[3] The name Weldt is supposed to cover the identity of the revolutionary
leader and club-politician, *F. W. A. Held*, for whom see A. Buchholtz, *Die
Literatur der Berliner Märztage* (*Deutsche Rundschau*, vol. xciv, p. 428) and
Allg. Deutsche Biographie, xi. 679.

The ambiguity of the bourgeois financier is also revealed, for his son is, on the one hand, an officer in the democratic militia (*Bürgerwehr*), but on the other hand seeks the affection of an aristocratic lady and sees his ideal in the aristocrat. Whilst he deems nobility, bought and paid for, to be ignoble, he does yet strive for an inner ennoblement, for the uplifting of the distinguished burgher to an aristocratic bearing, and wishes to show "that a burgher can also be an aristocrat just as, to-day, many aristocrats wish to show that they can also be burghers." [1]

(iii) *The petty-bourgeois masses* are only superficially described, and then very disdainfully, for they provide the men for the *Bürgerwehr*, where they exhibit, by their narrow egoism, their self-indulgence, and their lack of discipline, a complete absence of military virtues, those very qualities which, from the royalist's point of view, alone give one the right to rule. Just as vulgar as these democratic members of the *Bürgerwehr* are the milliners who maintain liaisons with them.

(iv) *The revolutionary literati and their followers* are, in the opinion of the royalists, much more dangerous than the rude petty-bourgeoisie. With them lies the centre of revolutionary action. Just as the Left exposed the connection between the conservative cliques and the common people whom they paid, so did the Right believe that it could detect a similar relationship between foreign emissaries and the revolutionary circles on the one hand, and with a corrupted and incited mob on the other. Both parties were convinced that the enemy was always supported by a "political clique" which used and misused the people for their sinister purposes.

What is the structure and function of the literary clique according to the view of the royalists?

It is a loose union of failures in life who have not succeeded in attaining their objective of an academic career. These young men had originally prepared themselves for academic posts, or had intended to take up

---

[1] *Die Royalisten,* p. 133.

the legal profession; they became neither professors nor lawyers but, missing their goal through lack of patience, industry, or money, they gave themselves up to the easy-going life of a journalist and were ever at the disposal of any paper that paid them well.[1] Amongst these bohemian and proletarian literati was to be found a considerable percentage of Jews.[2] The description shows the distinct contempt which royalist circles had for the "ignoble trade" of mercenary journalism and for the insecure existence of the literati. (Ungern-Sternberg himself, however, soon entered into the service of the newly-founded, ultra-conservative *Kreuzzeitung!*)

These literati are just as much the tools of foreign powers, thinks Ungern-Sternberg, as they in their turn make use of the dregs of the people as their tools. Like Gutzkow, Ungern-Sternberg also stresses the significance for Germany's development of Saint-Simonism with its gospel of the equal distribution of work and pleasure. But he confuses intellectual influence and actual political participation; the latter was a pure invention of counter-revolutionary ideology.[3] Yet the secret society imported from France again plays its part in his book in bringing together the Saint-Simonists and the literati.

[1] *Die Royalisten,* p. 220. This professional mobility is characteristic especially of Held. Held was one of those versatile natures such as often snatch leadership for themselves in times of revolution. He had first served as officer in the army; then became an actor, later an author and journalist, until he achieved a position of leadership in the democratic club in 1848. In 1850 he probably made a pact with the reactionaries and suddenly became a royal inspector of moors in the provinces. (See Jordan, *op. cit.,* p. 290.)

[2] Amongst these literati there was, in fact, as can be seen from their names, a large proportion of Jews. The Jewish intelligentsia was at that time still excluded from various professions and fought therefore at the same time for their emancipation. The literati did indeed propagate democratic demands amongst workers, students, professional men and petty-bourgeois, especially in the so-called reading-rooms (*Lese-Kabinetten*) and newspaper-rooms. In these were displayed the foreign newspapers in which the public was passionately interested on account of the strict censorship on the Berlin newspapers. On the other hand, these propagandists later disappeared completely into the background, even before the beginning of the battle between people and army. (See Lenz, *op. cit.,* ii (2). 191 ff.)

[3] The reactionary legend that the Berlin March Revolution had been predominantly inspired by foreigners is wrong. (See V. Valentin, *op. cit.,* i. 419.)

The function of the literati is twofold: to canvass various middle-class groups and to organize the populace as revolutionary fighting-troops. The literati exploit the discontent which they find in the upper- and petty-bourgeoisie. They form the extreme wing of the Left whose moderate elements consist of Industrialists, factory-owners, professors, doctors, etc.[1] Their revolutionary agitation finds an echo, principally, amongst three middle-class groups:

The petty-bourgeois craftsmen.—Many of the older artisans are unemployed or economically ruined, whilst the younger ones show youth's desire for an upheaval and a change of conditions.[2]

The students, who reveal the ideological effect aimed at by the literati "through impractical systems and philosophies." The influence is particularly strong amongst students of philosophy and of law.[3]

The young business-men, who are cultured, with minds broadened by study and travel abroad, and who often have a far better view of the real state of affairs than the students.[4]

Whilst these groups form the object of the revolutionaries' intellectual propaganda, the latter find in the mob their paid auxiliaries. The literati are supposed to sow the seeds of revolution amongst the dregs of the population in public-houses.

Their efforts were unceasing, their perseverance never faltered, their patience was inexhaustible. They had to deal with brutality

[1] For the separation of liberal and radical elements see R. Griewank, *Vulgärer Radikalismus und demokratische Bewegung in Berlin, 1842–1848, Forschungen zur Brandenburg. und Preussischen Geschichte,* 1924, xxxvi. 14–38.

[2] Whilst the bakers and butchers in Berlin at that time represented the prosperous artisans, the condition of the shoe-makers and tailors was essentially bad. Two-thirds of the Berlin tailors were not adequately employed. (See Valentin, *op. cit.,* i. 84 ff.)

[3] For the students' share in the Berlin Revolution, see Valentin, *op. cit.,* i. 433; and for the connection between literati and students, see Max Lenz, *op. cit.,* ii (2). 191. Many students appeared as leaders in the days of March; cf. also A. Wolff, *op. cit.,* i. 87.

[4] "The students, artists, merchants, the artisans' union and the machine-builders formed a mobile corps, usually armed in the same way and wearing as far as possible the same uniform" (R. Springer, *op. cit.,* p. 54).

and vileness—it was their task to arm them both. . . .   They let
loose the devil wherever they found him. . . .   The most unre-
strained vices, the most abominable excesses and crudest indulgence
alternated with a sort of vagabond's politics such as is pursued in
the dens of the plague-sufferers of our civilization.[1]

Such, according to their opponents, was the function
of these literati in the planning and rationalizing of the
revolutionary fight.   It is they who are erroneously [2]
accused of having provoked the conflict of the 18th
March, and in particular the two momentous shots of
that day before the royal castle.

The actual details of the story are unimportant for
our purpose.   Only one more fact need be mentioned,
because it accentuates the intermediary status of the
middle-class landowner.   A rich non-aristocratic landowner joins the salon of the finance-councillor as the
patron of the leader of the literati.   As a moderate liberal,
convinced of the necessity of reform from his observation of real defects in the state and its administration,
he is impressed by the oratorical talent of this literateur
and even gives him his daughter in marriage.   Other
needy and hungry literati also profit by his protection.

After the events of March, however, the noble man
(so runs the story) sees through the immorality and
seditious agitation of the literati and turns his back on
these "criminals."   "Bowed down and shattered," this
patriot becomes, after the 18th March, the founder of
one of the royalist Prussian movements that we have
analysed above; they uphold "the virtue of the true
burgher, loyally devoted to his king" as the only means
wherewith the monarchy may be saved.[3]

This conversion is symptomatic, for it clearly shows
how much the threatened aristocracy desired at that

[1] *Die Royalisten,* p. 216.
[2] An organized, deliberate procedure was completely lacking in the March
Revolution.   Even the literati were merely exponents, not leaders, of the
March Revolution.   "Not a single one of these men was a real leader who
supervised the actions of the whole and followed a fixed plan" (Valentin, *op.
cit.,* i. 434).
[3] *Die Royalisten,* p. 288.

time to win over middle-class allies in order to regain its authority.   As a matter of fact, the propertied middle-class, influenced by the proletarian outbreak in France, turned not so much against the counter-revolution from the right as against the danger of "anarchy" from the left.   The dynastic "International" of the counter-revolution, supported by army, bureaucracy and church, succeeded in France and Austria, as well as in Prussia, in diverting the capitalist bourgeoisie from revolutionary democratic politics during the next ten years and in confining its interests to economic prosperity; it thereby was successful in creating an enmity between liberalism and democracy.[1]

[1] See H. Rosenberg, *Die Weltwirtschaftskrise 1857–59*, Stuttgart, 1934, pp. 13–32.   Also H. v. Srbik, *Deutsche Einheit*, i. 319.

CHAPTER IV

MIDDLE-CLASS SUPERIORITY, 1850–1870

THE year 1848 constitutes a turning-point in the economic development of Germany. It is only then that the actual capitalistic development of Germany takes firm hold, with an intensity increased by the delay in its coming. The decade between 1850 and 1860 reveals an impetuous advance of middle-class individualistic enterprise and an unfolding of hitherto undreamed-of industrial energy.[1] Rapid technical development facilitated economic expansion; railways and steamships made their appearance, and there arose great machine factories and spinning mills, sugar refineries and chemical works.

In all this, capitalist development and political reaction maintained a characteristic alliance. The spirit of enterprise which had been repressed by the fear of political unrest in the revolutionary period could thenceforth pursue its development unchecked in the era of Prussian reaction. A new form of capital organization, the joint-stock company, appears on the scene, and the whole German banking system from now on receives its characteristic shape. If the sixth decade of the nineteenth century is a period of impetuous expansion which suffered a sharp setback through the economic crisis of 1857–9, the seventh decade represents a period of quiet consolidation and uniformity of labour. As an example of the increased activity on the money-market, we instance here the number of newly-founded joint-stock companies for one branch of industry only—namely, the mines and

[1] Cf. W. Sombart, *Die Deutsche Volkswirtschaft im 19. Jahrhundert*, 7th Ed., pp. 80 ff.; H. Rosenberg, *op. cit.*, p. 13, and H. v. Srbik, *op. cit.*, ii. 161.

foundries of the Kingdom of Prussia. This amounted
to fourteen in the years 1834–51, with a capital of 23·29
million Taler. On the other hand, in the six years from
1852 to 1857 the number was 59 with a capital of 70·69
million Taler. The share-capital of the banks founded
in Germany in 1853–7 alone amounted to 200 million
Taler, and the share-capital of the new railways amounted
to 140 million Taler.[1] Correspondingly there was an
increase in, above all, great private fortunes. For instance, the income-tax on fortunes of over 1,000 Taler
in Prussia increased as follows:[2]

		Relative increase % in:	
		1852–5	1855–60
A. Class-tax:			
up to 400 Taler		4·0	5·8
from 400 to 1,000 Taler		20·6	28·8
up to 1,000 Taler		4·4	6·3
B. Income-tax:			
from 1,000 to 1,600 Taler . .		14·0	20·7
„ 1,600 „ 3,200 „ . .		14·8	25·2
„ 3,200 „ 6,000 „ . .		14·6	22·7
„ 6,000 „ 12,000 „ . .		17·4	40·9
„ 12,000 „ 24,000 „ . .		32·3	34·4
„ 24,000 „ 52,000 „ . .		33·8	41·2
„ 52,000 „ 100,000 „ . .		5·3	52·6
„ 100,000 „ 200,000 „ . .		— 16·8	60·8
over 200,000 Taler		300·0	— 100·0
from 1,000 up to over 200,000 Taler .		15·0	22·7

If the great fortunes increased much more than the
small ones and the mass of the small artisans and merchants in no way improved their conditions of life, the
new industrial opportunities and the possibility of an
economic advancement did, however, have an encourag-
ing effect. Periods of economic prosperity and development give rise, in the nature of things, to an optimistic
view of the world in the classes affected, just as, conversely, periods of political depression, political unrest,

[1] W. Sombart, *op. cit.*, p. 84.
[2] H. Rosenberg, *op. cit.*, p. 77. Further statistical proof of the wave of
prosperity is to be found in G. Hermes, *Statistische Studien zur wirtschaftlichen und gesellschaftlichen Struktur des zollvereinten Deutschland. Archiv für
Sozialwissenschaft und Sozialpolitik*, 1930, vol. lxiii, pp. 121–60.

and widespread unemployment result in a pessimistic outlook on life. The dominant feature in German literature in the period after 1848 is therefore an outspoken feeling of satisfaction with the expected rise to power and the efficiency of the German middle-class. It is the feeling of a moral and intellectual superiority in this class that permeates the works of Freytag, Spielhagen, Auerbach, Keller, etc. These works reflect the new pride of the well-to-do middle-class which arose, on the one hand, because of the economic dilettantism of aristocratic agriculturalists, and, on the other, because of the alleged morally questionable business-conduct of the increasingly powerful Jewish competitors. If, in what follows, we intend to present the middle-class consciousness of superiority in its different variations, then we must first of all examine the ideology in which it expresses itself, the ideology of the gospel of labour.

The literary trend of so-called "poetical realism" found one of its most important impulses in the *gospel of labour*. It shared in the positive appreciation of middle-class labour as contained in the philosophy of the Manchester School, which was so influential in Germany; it shared its sympathy also, to a certain degree, with the doctrines of St. Simon, which had made their appearance a little earlier. However different the doctrines of the Manchester School and St. Simon may otherwise be,[1] they both postulate productive labour as a moral ideal, they both condemn idlers of all kinds and praise an unceasing devotion to labour as the highest aim of an independent earthly existence. Middle-class self-reliance and the glorification of the idea of labour are inseparably bound together both in philosophy and in literature between 1850 and 1870. The stories of Gustav Freytag, Spielhagen, Auerbach and G. Keller present, in literature, the artistic expression of middle-class liberalism; they describe in different ways the positive and negative aspects

---

[1] Cf. H. Freyer, *Die Bewertung der Wirtschaft im philosophischen Denken des 19. Jahrhunderts*, Leipzig, 1921, pp. 68 and 109.

of the doctrine that the individual can only attain to his proper place in society through his own labour and achievements.

The industrial and commercial middle-class in the middle of the nineteenth century was conscious of its economic power and regarded this power as existing not only in possessions, but far more in the ability to acquire possessions and to employ them in the service of some work. In a prospering society, labour yields simultaneously an immanent satisfaction as well as an opportunity for advancement. Even the son of the petty-bourgeois believes that a commercial or industrial occupation is the certain guarantee of future activity as a captain of industry, as certain as if it were already in his knapsack. In the circle in which he lives, possessions and efficiency are the chief virtues, and one wins the respect of one's fellow-citizens above all by achievement. The ideology of labour is not a specifically German manifestation, it is rather a collective European reaction to the rise of the middle-class in the modern world.[1] This ideology had already found its representatives in the early period of capitalism: at the beginning in the widely-known writings of the Italian Alberti, in the middle in those of the Englishman Daniel Defoe, and at the end in those of the American Benjamin Franklin. The virtues that Franklin preached are the specific virtues of labour of the European middle-class. Moderation, order, sufficiency, diligence, determination, calmness, etc., form those qualities that have assisted the merchant and the entrepreneur to victory in the modern competitive struggle. It is significant that the later development of capitalism in Germany is accompanied also by a later reception of Franklin's doctrines of labour and virtue. In the liberal moral catechism in Auerbach's novel *Das Landhaus am Rhein* (1869) a direct reference to Franklin's model is to be found, whilst the description of modern large-scale commerce and the virtues of the diligent merchant in Freytag's *Soll und*

[1] See W. Sombart, *Der Bourgeois*, pp. 135–69.

Haben, although not mentioning his name, testify at least to the spirit of Franklin's doctrines.

As regards realistic observation and clarity of form, Auerbach's novel cannot be compared with Freytag, for Auerbach prefers to reflect rather than to describe, to construct rather than portray social events. Auerbach had definite pedagogical intentions. His novel wants to educate the reader. The positive doctrine of the fullness of meaning of labour is developed out of the folly of the negative types that have no proper relationship to labour. The aristocrats are lacking in a comprehension of labour, the *nouveaux riches*—represented by an American millionaire—misuse and pervert it. The millionaire's son obtains an ideal instructor in the person of an ex-captain. The latter finds some notes left behind by his father, a professor, in which Franklin is described as the model for the education of a true man and a good citizen. Franklin appears here as "a real man, a genius of healthy understanding and steadfast mind." [1] The distinguishing excellence in Franklin's life is the success produced by his own efforts, the master's rules of conduct prevent carelessness and enable the individual to lead his own life in a society that is no longer bound by tradition. Middle-class liberalism sees in Franklin "the first modern self-made man." Franklin, as the representative son of the century, recognizes only innate, and not hereditary, qualities. The poet in Auerbach may pity the soberness of the calculating citizen, Franklin, but the liberal *Bürger* in him welcomes the industrious virtues of a progressive epoch:

The world would not have overmuch beauty if all men were like Franklin, the latter's own way of life is completely lacking in any romantic fragrance, but the world would live in integrity, truthfulness, labour and achievement. . . . Franklin is good prose, sensible, transparent, enduring.[2]

Auerbach had already laid down similar ideas at an earlier period, without directly mentioning Franklin,

[1] B. Auerbach, *Das Landhaus am Rhein*, ii. 111–12.   [2] B. Auerbach, *ibid*.

in a popular educational treatise, *Der gebildete Bürger*
(1843). In this little book, which appeals to the artisan
class and to the petty-bourgeoisie, the correlation between
love of labour and middle-class becomes completely
visible. As a litterateur, Auerbach emphasizes more the
function of education rather than that of property in
middle-class prestige. The middle-class is called the
"kernel and mark of every healthy state and national life";
and "the free and cultured middle-class," corresponding
to liberal consciousness of progress, is represented as the
highest achievement of the peaceful development of
mankind.[1]

The educational ideal, which Herder and Wilhelm
von Humboldt proclaimed only for a small élite, had
in the meantime become an evident good, common to
officials, scholars, and large-scale merchants, and was to
be imparted now to the lower strata of the middle Estate
through the didactic efforts of Auerbach in the period
of the first national-education unions.[2] Culture could
now appear as general culture because its foundation,
labour, is recognized as a quality valid for everybody.
"We have advanced," says Auerbach, "beyond the
honour and rights of Estates to the honour and rights
of human beings." But the honour and rights of human
beings only possess their general validity through the
new common bond of labour. "The whole of humanity
is one great guild of workers, we have all been born and
brought up to labour, some in this way, others in that."[3]
Industry must be the central virtue not only of the
middle-class, but also of modern society as a whole, which
was silently identified with it by the liberal publicists:
"It is the chief virtue, whose possession brings with it
automatically, as it were, all the subsidiary virtues."
The one-sidedness of a life of ceaseless labour is overlooked by Auerbach. For him labour is the *summum*

[1] B. Auerbach, *Der gebildete Bürger*, Karlsruhe, 1843, p. 2.
[2] The three fundamental principles of this middle-class educational doctrine
sound somewhat scholastic: Learn to know thyself! Learn to appreciate
thyself! Learn to educate thyself!
[3] B. Auerbach, *op. cit.*, p. 76.

bonum, being "not only the school of justice, but also of goodness and kindness." Correspondingly, the worst vice in the eyes of this pedagogic liberalism is idleness. "Idlers or such like, who live purely on inherited wealth, are usually selfish, hard-hearted, without mildness of disposition and without helpful beneficence." It is characteristic of the life of man that he alone can be industrious or indolent. He prepares his own fate by his attitude to labour—"Life's Hell is the wishing of the idler, he can do nothing but wish; but life's Paradise is opened to labour." [1]

At that time in England too, we find this didactic doctrine of labour as the touchstone of human existence. But we find it in a writer who rejected completely the liberal utilitarianism of the Manchester School, and who passionately maintained the dignity of labour from quite another tradition, that of Puritanism. The passionate praise of labour is as absolute in Carlyle as in Auerbach, but it is, in addition, heroic; for according to Carlyle man has everywhere to pay for his existence, he has to do his work "as a soldier does, at the expense of life." Labour for him is not only grand; it is much more: it is holy. [2]

The ethic of middle-class labour stands out more clearly in Freytag's novel of commerce, *Soll und Haben*, than in Auerbach's, for here it is not only preached but also described; middle-class industriousness is not only postulated but also illustrated by symbolic examples.

If *Soll und Haben* has been rightly called a "contribution to the renascence of middle-class self-confidence," [3] we must add that this middle-class pride takes root in the

[1] B. Auerbach, *Schatzkästlein des Gevattermanns*, quoted in M. I. Zwick, *Berthold Auerbachs sozialpolitischer und ethischer Liberalismus*, Stuttgart, 1933, p. 71.

[2] We might almost believe sometimes that we hear Auerbach in Carlyle: "In idleness alone is their perpetual despair. Work, never so Mammonish, mean, is in communication with Nature." "It has been written, 'an endless significance lies in Work'; a man perfects himself by working." " Blessed is he, who has found his work; let him ask no other blessedness." (Thomas Carlyle, *Past and Present*, book iii, chap. xi.)

[3] H. Bieber, *Der Kampf um die Tradition*, Stuttgart, 1931, p. 466.

optimism of a period which, in spite of all setbacks and crises, vouchsafed to the efficient an almost unhampered career in the economic world.[1] Middle-class standards, customs, modes of thought, and feelings are centred in this novel, too, around the gospel of labour. The motto of the book, borrowed from Julian Schmidt, Freytag's friend and co-editor of the *Grenzboten*,[2] most aptly characterizes this ideology: "The novel should seek the German people where it is to be found exercising its diligence, namely at work."

In contrast with the conservatism which, as we saw in Immermann, identifies the *Volk* chiefly with the peasantry, moderate liberalism here identifies *Volk* with the bourgeoisie, both great and small. Freytag's novel is a companion-piece, a kind of literary supplement to Prussian liberal historiography, to the school of the "political historians." This school combined liberal and conservative elements: its historical spirit, which measured man by history, was conservative; its active tendency to a political reformation of Germany under middle-class leadership was liberal.[3] Freytag, in a characteristic appreciation[4] of a representative work of this group of historians, once criticized the false objectivity of Ranke's approach to history, and in contrast observed in the political historians "a moral dignity and inner constancy

---

[1] Freytag's life is partly analysed in chap. ix of this work.

[2] Julian Schmidt, through his periodical *Die Grenzboten*, and through his popular history of literature, exercised a widespread influence on the formation of taste in the sense of a national Prussian liberalism. Like Freytag, he was definitely a Protestant, emphatically a Prussian, and a representative of middle-class interests. "Prussianism and middle-class, the State and the Estate of duty and labour were the poles which his compass fixedly followed" (*Allg. Deutsche Biographie*, vol. 31, p. 754). Lassalle directed a vigorous attack against the dragging of German idealism down to middle-class standards by J. Schmidt, in his *Herr Julian Schmidt, der "Literarhistoriker,"* 1852.

[3] One of these political historians pointed in 1853 "to the direction taken by our literature in history, in recent history, and in Prussian history," and "to the undeniable participation of the public in those things." Cf. H. v. Srbik, *Deutsche Einheit*, ii. 301.

[4] Review of H. v. Sybel's *Geschichte der Revolutionszeit*, 1856; separately printed in G. Freytag, *Vermischte Aufsätze aus den Jahren 1848–1894*, ed. E. Elster, Leipzig, 1903, ii. 222 ff.

in their judgment of persons and events." Filled with
pride, he confessed his adherence to them and cried out:
"We know what we want." The same desire and moral
aim found its artistic expression in the novels *Soll und
Haben* and *Die verlorene Handschrift*. It is this middle-
class of merchants and scholars, such as was politically
represented in the *Deutscher Nationalverein*,[1] whose
qualities Freytag propagated and for whose coming
political domination within the framework of the Prussian state he hoped.

Although in *Soll und Haben* only certain types of
the middle-class, namely the wholesale merchant and
his employees, are described, in these types there is
reflected, as if representative of the whole, that middle-
class self-confidence and feeling of superiority. In
Freytag, the industrious middle-class is designated by
the merchant Schroeder as the first Estate of the State.

> In primeval times [he argues] individuals were free and more
> or less equal; then came semi-barbarism with its privileged free
> men and serfs. Only since our cities have grown up have there
> been civilized states in the world, only since that time has the
> secret been revealed that free labour alone makes the life of the
> peoples great and sure and enduring.[2]

Free labour constitutes the specific middle-class concept
of honour, and the correlation of the conceptions of
labour and honour is illustrated in Freytag through
a toast which the aristocrat von Finkh proposes to the
success "of a German business where work is a joy,
where honour has its home." [3]

In Freytag's *Soll und Haben*, the background of a
wholesale warehouse is sketched for the first time in
exact detail, and the division of labour in this kind of
commercial undertaking is described with the minutest

[1] On the *Deutscher Nationalverein*, see the biography by H. Oncken, *Rudolf von Bennigsen*, Berlin, 1910, 2 vols. Wilhelm Raabe, in *Guthmanns Reisen* (1892), describes later the philistine aspect of the members of its congress for German unity from the point of view of a participant.
[2] G. Freytag, *Gesammelte Werke*, Leipzig, 1887, iv. 383.
[3] *Ibid.*, iv. 315.

precision.[1] The different functions of individual employees, the activities of the foreign and provincial
departments, the duties and specialized knowledge of
the book-keeper, cashier, customs clerk, agents, corre-
spondents, and even of the cleaners are humorously
described with an intimate knowledge. The typical
rise of a clerk from apprentice to correspondent and
manager, and finally to partner, is demonstrated by an
imaginary picture of the opportunities open to middle-
class industriousness. A network of interdependence
and subordination is represented. The relationship
between employee and employer is still patriarchal
and kept within proper bounds. The bachelor employees still live on the premises and eat their midday
meal with the employer—a last relic of the mediæval
family relationships of master and apprentice [2]—but
apart from this a proper distance is maintained between
the employer, who associates with the cream of the city
society in his club, and his employees who, with the
exception of the aristocrat von Finkh, only associate
amongst themselves.

Freytag has not exemplified the middle-class labour
ethic through a modern wholesale house or through a
banking business of the period after 1850; he has selected
rather the older type of wholesale house as known to
him from immediate personal knowledge. Breslau,
where the action takes place, played an important part
in the earliest period of railway-construction in Silesia
as a frontier capital and as a commercial centre. Besides
the marketing of its own provincial products, it flourished
as an intermediary on its own account on the extended
trade-routes stretching from America, England and the
German coast-towns through Silesia, and over Galicia
and the Bukovina, as far as the Turkish border—an
activity which the author himself has described in an

[1] On Freytag's experiences, which form the basis of the novel, see his *Erinnerungen aus meinem Leben*, Leipzig, 1887, p. 266.

[2] Examples of such a patriarchal relationship are given in the German book-
trade of the nineteenth century by J. Goldfriedrich, *Geschichte des deutschen
Buchhandels*, Leipzig, 1913, iv. 495.

essay.[1]   The broad view which commerce of this kind gave to the merchant, the large scale on which it was carried on, played no small part, in Freytag's firm opinion, in giving the merchant class of Breslau self-confidence, stability and respect.[2]   The firm F. T. O. Schröter is described in his novel as the kind of trading establishment

that is becoming ever scarcer nowadays when railway and telegraph link up coast and interior, when every merchant in the seaport towns sells his goods far inland through his agents almost before they have reached harbour; it is becoming so scarce, that our descendants will find this sort of commerce hardly less strange than we the trafficking in a Timbuctoo market or a Kaffir kraal.[3]

These words of Freytag indicate a contrast between two types of commerce in the nineteenth century, which modern economic historians distinguish as local trade (*Lokohandel*), that is trade in so-called prompt or ready-to-hand, visible goods, and as contract trade (*Lieferungshandel nach Probe*).[4]   In the latter type of trade the goods are no longer examined in bulk by the merchant in the warehouse of the middle-man, but are ordered directly from small samples.

In local trade, which lasted far into the 'fifties, the power of the provincial wholesale merchant was made obvious through the huge storehouses which were to be seen in his business.

The importance of such a mercantile house as this depended upon the quantity of stores it bought with its own money and at its own risk.   Of these a great part lay in long rows of ware-

---

[1] *Vermischte Aufsätze*, ii. 322.

[2] A small élite of leading merchants, liberal aristocrats and publicists joined together at that time in Breslau in the interests of a national and liberal policy. They included Th. Molinari, head of a big trading house and President of the Breslau Chamber of Commerce. Freytag described him in a letter to Duke Ernst of Coburg-Gotha, the later President of the German National Union, as an enlightened Catholic who was known in the whole province as a man of honour and was able to prove his qualities as a leader in 1848 in the command of the citizen army. (*G. Freytag und Herzog Ernst von Coburg im Briefwechsel, 1853–1893*, Leipzig, 1904, p. 7.)

[3] G. Freytag, *Ges. Werke*, iv. 58.

[4] Cf. W. Sombart, *Die Deutsche Volkswirtschaft im 19. Jahrhundert*, pp. 202 ff.

houses along the river, some in the vaults of the old house itself, and some in the warehouses and stores of those around. Trades-men of the province provided themselves with colonial products from the warehouse of the firm, whose agents were spread to east and south and carried on even as far as the Turkish frontier.[1]

Although Freytag has here chosen an establishment of the older type for presentation, the manner in which he describes it and its several functions is completely filled with that sober and optimistic realism that char-acterizes the period after 1848. Here are no longer the hazy and confused events and endless dialogues of the Young Germans, nor the pedagogic maxims of Auerbach, but it is the earthly temporal world in its immediate aspect and palpable comprehensibility which is here made alive and illustrated, in accordance with the changed consciousness of the middle-class.[2]

When an individual becomes conscious of himself, it does not only mean that he becomes conscious of his power, but that he feels a superiority over others; he has a more or less strong consciousness of the fact that there are individuals in his immediate surroundings who, as regards general or specific capabilities, as regards social position, property, cleverness, etc., are inferior to him. The consciousness of superiority of the individual may, in modern society, be more individualistic or more collective, may relate more to the specific advantages of the individual or to the superiority of the group or class to which he belongs. In the first case we can speak of an *individual consciousness of superiority*, in the second of a *collective consciousness of superiority*.

Collective self-confidence, arising from membership of a group or class, can again be either institutionalized and legitimized through the social structure handed down by history, as for example the self-confidence of the nobility and higher clergy in a society of Estates, in which case we speak of an *established collective con-sciousness*; or the self-confidence may be within a chang-ing social structure, one still questioned by counter-

[1] G. Freytag, *op. cit.*, iv. 58.   [2] Cf. H. Rosenberg, *op. cit.*, p. 31.

forces and not legitimized by tradition; in the second case the self-confidence of the class or group is only recognized by the group itself, but not yet established in society as a whole, and here we speak of an *aspiring collective consciousness*.

The self-confidence of the German middle-class round about 1850 was in this sense not yet established, but potential. The German bourgeoisie of 1850–70 based its self-confidence on its power of property and education. This—as manifested in literature—was a consciousness of superiority over two different social strata: over the nobility as a stratum which had hitherto enjoyed a precedence over the middle-class in the social scale, and over the Jewish merchant and trading element which had hitherto had in public estimation a rank beneath its Christian competitors. The Christian middle-class emphasized with self-complaisance, as against both these strata, the dignity of righteous labour as represented by the merchants as well as by the petty-bourgeoisie, but in each case the emphasis is different; as against the nobility the contrast is: acquired wealth is better than inherited wealth; as against Jewry: honourably acquired wealth is better than wealth dishonourably begotten. In a similar way the middle-class insinuated its superiority as regards education over the rival strata. The nobility was reproached with being uneducated, Jewry with being half or wrongly educated. The "Christian" burgher alone possessed the real key, be it to just wealth or to true education.

In what follows we shall describe the superiority-consciousness of the merchant and academic middle-class over the noble and court society as it appears in Freytag's novels, and shall then go on to analyse its consciousness of superiority over the Jews as illustrated by Freytag and Raabe.

1. MIDDLE-CLASS SUPERIORITY TOWARDS THE NOBILITY

In Immermann, the middle-class capitalist is the grave-digger of aristocratic power. In Freytag, the wholesale merchant Schröter, the representative of middle-class industriousness, watches with indifference the rural nobility becoming a prey to Jewish calculation and intrigue owing to carelessness and economic inexperience. The Christian merchant is too honest to ruin the aristocracy economically, but he has no objection if Jewish commercial enterprise brings about the destruction. As a patrician, he shows to a certain extent an understanding for the traditionalism of the country-nobility and also for the institution of the *Fideikommis*.

> True, every man [he affirms] must allow it to be desirable that the culture of the same soil should be handed down from father to son. We all prize what our forefathers have possessed before us, and Sabine would unlock every room in this house with pride, because her great-great-grandmother turned the same keys before her.[1]

With the aristocracy, however, the belief in tradition becomes a numbing superstition. If tradition is to retain its meaning, it must be continually adjusted to suit new conditions. "You must labour in order really to possess what you have inherited from your fathers!" —thus might be expressed the watchword of this middle-class stand between traditionalism and radical innovation. The outlook of the wholesale merchant who shares in the revolution in real-estate is not static, but dynamic. Not the inheritance in itself, but the power to maintain and increase it, is a middle-class ideal. Liberalism values achievement rather than the enjoyment of one's achievement, acquisition rather than consumption.

> Where energy dies in families or individuals [says the merchant in *Soll und Haben*] then it is well that their means die too, that their money should circulate through other hands, and their ploughs should pass to those who can guide them better. A family that has become effete through luxury, ought to sink down into common life to make room for the rise of fresh energy and faculties.[2]

---

[1] G. Freytag, *op. cit.*, iv. 561.   [2] *Ibid.*

The ideological appreciation of mobile trading capital and labour power as superior to mere traditionally inherited goods, is more clearly expressed at the end of the work. "Neither wealth nor position have any value for the individual or the community without the healthy energy which keeps the dead metal in life-producing action." [1]

The superiority of the Christian merchant over the aristocrat is more sharply revealed here than in Immermann. What Goethe still admired in the aristocrat— that he is active in the totality of his being and not in a one-sided efficiency in a specialized subject—is for Freytag a serious reproach. The superiority of middle-class knowledge stands out all the more strongly in Freytag, in that he does not caricature the country-nobility like Spielhagen, but seeks to describe it as true to nature as possible. According to Freytag's observation, the Silesian nobility is not lacking in amiable qualities, but very much in energetic concentration; it is not lacking in intellectual limitations, but very much in common sense.

The Silesian Freiherr von Rothsattel is described far more indulgently in the novel than was consonant with the politically hostile attitude of Freytag, the liberal publicist. As a publicist and politician, Freytag opposed the nobility much more than the Jews at the time he was writing his novel; yet as a novelist who wanted to gain a wider circle, he the depicted merely the weaknesses of the aristocracy, but the vices of the Jews.

In a letter to his liberal patron and sharer of his ideas, Duke Ernst of Saxe-Coburg, he has, with a consciousness of middle-class integrity, sharply illuminated the economic and moral decline of the Silesian country-nobility.[2] He here reproaches the aristocracy with not being able to shake off its negative Prusso-Polish habits: it is distinguished by overmuch pretension and unstable land speculation: the aristocratic estates, which constitute

[1] *Op. cit.*, v. 403 f.
[2] *G. Freytag und Herzog Ernst von Coburg im Briefwechsel, 1853–1893*, pp. 4 ff.

in Silesia over 50 per cent of the whole land-area, are for the most part—two-thirds—burdened with debts.

The last ten years have still more demoralized the Silesian aristocrat in many respects, not in his family life, but in his industrial life. The exorbitant sums obtainable for estates there means for many families the beginning of the end, estates pass from hand to hand at huge prices, and in some circles there is hardly a family that is seriously intent on preserving its paternal inheritance. It is a remarkable fact that the noble estate-owner, as soon as he becomes a speculator, is in great danger of sinking as low as the worst Jew.[1]

With the malicious joy of a representative of a rival class, Freytag prophesies in the near future a great fall in estates, with an accompanying "disclosure to the world of the weaknesses of our country-nobility," and this fall, so he hopes, will have political consequences, upsetting for ever the gentlemen of the conservative party in Silesia. This prophecy arising from resentment was, in any case, biassed, and if in the novel the rapid industrial prosperity in Silesia means the destruction of the aristocracy, then this does not completely coincide with the historical facts. For whilst the aristocracy of the Rhine cut itself off from industrialism, the Silesian nobility largely, and with success, took advantage of it.[2] The desire to see the enemy class destroyed caused Freytag, like most other middle-class writers, to generalize hastily from a few cases of economic ruin amongst the Junkers.

[1] *G. Freytag und Herzog Ernst von Coburg im Briefwechsel, 1853–1893,* p. 4 f.

[2] See F. Schnabel, *Deutsche Geschichte im Neunzehnten Jahrhundert,* iii. 277. The enterprises of Prince Pless, Count Henckel zu Donnersmark and other aristocrats were throughout crowned with success. The industrialization of agriculture is discussed by Freytag in the following words: "It was just the time when a crowd of new industrial enterprises sprang up out of the fields, when large sums had been acquired and still greater wealth was hoped for from the tall chimneys of the steam-engines, from the newly-discovered coal and iron-mines, and from the new methods of agriculture. The most aristocratic landowners of the country stood at the head of extensive financial enterprises which were based on a combination of modern industry and ancient agriculture" (Freytag, *Ges. Werke,* iv. 33 f.). See also R. Lewinsohn, *Das Geld in der Politik,* p. 32 f., and G. Hermes, *Statistische Studien zur wirtschaftlichen und gesellschaftlichen Struktur des zollvereinten Deutschland,* p. 135.

The Freiherr von Rothsattel, used as an example, is at the beginning of the story a solvent Silesian country aristocrat. After withdrawing from service in the Guards, he retired with his wife, a poor lady of society, into the country. He is honourable, knows how to live and let live; in short, he has the reputation of "a complete aristocrat." But lacking independence in economic matters, he becomes only too easily susceptible to the promptings of a sly Jewish dealer. The latter urges him to indulge in speculation, involves him in the most difficult undertakings, and deliberately makes trouble for him.[1] He first suggests mortgaging the Freiherr's property to the *Landschaft*, a credit institution for the provincial estate-owners, which lent cash on the security of estates. The dealer later borrows money from his victim and permits him, in order to lull him into security, to make a profit of 2,000 Talers on the loan.[2] When social obligations and expenditure for his children rapidly increase the aristocrat's debts, the dealer advises him to sell his mortgage deeds for a second mortgage and causes him by underhand methods to negotiate a bad one. In a similar way the idea of a beet-sugar factory is suggested to the aristocrat. An advance of capital is obtained, and the Freiherr combines manufacturing and agriculture in an unhappy and unprofitable manner. He concentrates wholly on the factory, agriculture becoming hateful to him because the estate is now encumbered with mortgages.[3] The formerly cringing Jewish dealer gradually

---

[1] "He must give him anxieties—the anxieties of business, ceaseless activity, daily cares; that's what the Baron could not stand. That class is accustomed to little work and much enjoyment. Everything is made too easy to them from their childhood. There are few of them who may not be ruined by having some great care boring always at their brains" (*Ges. Werke*, iv. 258).

[2] See Freytag's essay *Die Juden in Breslau*, pp. 192 ff. "The Jewish dealer pretends an appearance of certainty and reliability, with persistence and success, until it pays him to do something shady" (*Vermischte Aufsätze*, ii. 341 ff.).

[3] The attitude of the Freiherr von Tucher in Spielhagen's novel *In Reih und Glied* (1866) is very similar. The calculating superiority of the Jewish dealer and estate-spoliator towards the careless and economically inexperienced aristocracy is already to be found in Schücking's novel *Die Ritterbürtigen* (1846), and even still at the end of the century in W. v. Polenz, *Die Grabenhäger* (1898). The following sentence in *Die Leute aus dem Walde* by W. Raabe

reveals himself as the relentless enemy of the aristocracy and a destroyer of estates: Anton Wohlfahrt, however, the representative of middle-class respectability, as employee and later attorney of the aristocratic family, passes through a typical process of disillusionment in his attitude to the aristocracy.   Disillusionment occurs very frequently when one changes the distant view of a group, family, or institution as a spectator "from outside" for the view of it as a member "from inside."   Many imagined ideals are shattered with decrease in distance.   Therefore, the intimate contact in which Wohlfahrt lives with the aristocratic family after its economic collapse changes the shy admiration of the social inferior into the critical appraisal of the successful man on the up-grade.

The economic circumstances of the family deteriorate, but its pretensions remain.   Its snobbery, as the middle-class guest sees from close contact, is in inverse proportion to the degree of its education.   The standards by which it measures men and things have not changed, it still continues to judge everything from a class-standpoint.

Unconsciously they measured all the things by the scale of their own class-interests.   Whatever ministered to these found favour, however unbearable to mankind at large; whatever militated against them was rejected, or at least brushed aside.   Their opinions were often mild, sometimes even liberal, but they always seemed to wear an invisible helmet, visor up, and to look through the narrow space on the doings of common mortals, and whenever they saw anything in these that was displeasing but unalterable, they silently shut down the visor and isolated themselves.[1]

(1865) is representative of the description of the decline of the aristocracy and the cold acquisitiveness of the Jew: "The fortunes of the dynasties of v. Poppenhof and v. Poppenhagen had considerably melted away in the course of the nineteenth century.   Poppenhof was encumbered with mortgages and completely in the hands of a rascally steward, since the young Baron considered it completely beneath his dignity to plough with his own oxen the field inherited from his fathers.   More than one black-haired, hook-nosed business man has his sharp Semitic eyes on the house in town; many a considerable debt has piled up on its bricks" (W. Raabe, *Sämtliche Werke*, 1st series, vol. v, p. 182).

[1] *Ges. Werke*, v. 56.

If this exclusiveness and onesided aristocratic consciousness amuse rather than vex the burgher, he cannot, however, pardon the lack of education which is rapidly revealed on closer association with them. He soon discovers
that the aristocrats possess an education completely different from his own, and indeed by no means a better one.
Their geographical and historical knowledge is small,
and of their political crassness it is said: "When they
discussed the newspapers—the usual topic of conversation
—he marvelled at their ignorance of foreign politics." [1]

This charge of lack of education is a typical middle-
class criticism at that period, for in the middle-class
strata of all countries property and education are the
leading qualities. Throughout Europe the circles of
"property and education" show, under the leadership
of the intelligentsia —in this case, of the liberal historians and publicists—an increasing interest in the rules
of the game of international politics, which were formerly
arcana imperii, accessible only to a small circle of court
politicians and officials.

Now that we have analysed the self-confidence of the
wholesale merchant (based predominantly on property)
as against the aristocracy, let us examine the consciousness of superiority of another section of the middle-class,
namely the university intelligentsia, as against the court
and society; for this purpose we shall use the description
in Freytag's novel *Die verlorene Handschrift*.

The German academic intelligentsia between 1830
and 1870 felt itself to a large extent to be the advance-
guard of the middle-class, from which it almost completely originated; it very often identified itself, as a
glance at the composition of the 1848 parliament shows,
with middle-class demands and represented them, literature and science becoming largely "finger-posts" for the
national and liberal movement.[2] It was especially the
demand for a constitution, for middle-class participation

[1] *Op. cit.*, p. 55.
[2] Cf. Friedrich Paulsen, *Geschichte des gelehrten Unterrichts*, ii, 3rd Ed.,
Berlin, 1919, pp. 447 ff., and H. v. Srbik, *Deutsche Einheit*, i. 236–56.

in government, that was for the most part urged by professors. In some cases, as for example in the Göttingen conflict of 1837, the Princes stepped into the arena against the liberal tendencies of certain professors. The principle of freedom of instruction was represented by liberal groups and parties, and was expressly recognized in the constitution of 1848. But the demand for freedom of instruction was, in practice, not fulfilled, for the feudal-clerical governments after 1848 exercised a strong influence through the pressure of nominations and dismissals, and through the distribution of decorations and titles.[1]   Further, it was the aim of the reactionaries to console the professors and students for their loss of political freedom and to divert them from politics by the encouragement of "true science," i.e. by increasing specialization.

One consequence of the professorial class-consciousness was the restraint of the majority of the university intelligentsia towards the aristocratic world of court and society. To show "manly pride before princely thrones" was an unwritten law for the majority of academicians in face of the arbitrariness of the small and insignificant rulers who occupied the thrones of the numberless German states. How far this principle was applied in practice is difficult to discover.[2]   In any case, there were scholars in every state who stood on an intimate footing with the court and the ruling aristocratic stratum and who more or less consciously represented their ideology.[3] Prussia, for example, had in Ranke and Treitschke its court historiographers, whilst in Bavaria the conservative sociologist W. R. Riehl was appointed at the express desire of the king.

The majority of German scholars in the nineteenth century were of humble origin, many of them coming

---

[1] Cf. F. Paulsen, *op. cit.*, p. 463.

[2] In 1848 Lassalle found bitter words for the liberal professors' pride of freedom: "The freedom that our German liberals mean consists in their bowing and scraping to his Highness the Prince in order to be able to increase his Civil List" (quoted in M. v. Boehn, *Biedermeier. Deutschland von 1815–1848*, p. 238).

[3] Cf. F. Schnabel, *Deutsche Geschichte im 19. Jahrhundert*, ii. 208.

from the peasantry or petty-bourgeoisie; they had often
had slow, hard careers, which had led to the professorial
chair along a path beginning with the giving of lessons
whilst they were schoolboys and students and passing
through activities as secondary school teachers, as in the
case of Ranke and Droysen.   They were, for the most
part, indefatigable workers without worldly experience,
filled with the defiant self-reliance of the self-made man.
Individualism and application to work formed their
guiding stars. "In all these men," says Schnabel,
"there lived a desire to develop their own personality
which was immediately and closely allied with the middle-
class conception of service by labour."[1]

The mentality of this professorial type, as well as its
attitude to court and society, is a dominant theme in
Freytag's novel *Die verlorene Handschrift*. Although
the novel suffers largely from over-emphasis and is not
free from exaggeration,[2] it possesses for our purpose a
documentary importance, for Freytag knew both the
professorial circles and the petty courts of central Germany from personal observation.[3]

The book has a definite middle-class anti-court bias.
Its aim, in Freytag's own words, was to throw light on
the conditions of the old courts and on the damage
caused by the gulf between the throne and the people.
Liberalism here criticized the princely domination, but
mildly, and with a fear of a real political overthrow that
was peculiar to it in contrast with democracy.   Freytag
wanted to delineate in this book "our masters" as they
are judged by the people, but in doing it he was conscious as the friend of an enlightened prince, "of having
expressed this judgment mildly and sparingly."[4]

[1] Cf. F. Schnabel, *op. cit.*, iii. 131.
[2] Cf. Mielke-Homann, *Der deutsche Roman des 19. und 20. Jahrhunderts*,
Dresden, 1920, 7th Ed., p. 189.
[3] Through his friendship with Duke Ernst of Coburg-Gotha, Freytag was
acquainted with the court and society, and with the university world through
his university lectureship in Breslau and through his later association with
professors in Leipzig.
[4] *G. Freytag und Herzog Ernst von Coburg im Briefwechsel, 1853–1893*, p. 200.

The world of the court and the academic world are brought into contact, in Freytag's novel, in two ways: the heir of a Central German prince, rather ignorant of life, is sent with an attendant to a university to be educated —whilst later, the chief representative of the academic class, the classical philologist Professor Werner, goes with his wife to the court of the Prince to arrange the latter's collection of plaster-casts and to pursue the object dearest to his heart, the search for a lost manuscript.

The scholars in Freytag are filled with the same "ethical idealism of learning" which at that time was characteristic particularly of the representatives of the humanist studies.[1]   They possess a strong belief in the mission of learning.   There is no scepticism in this optimistic period concerning the meaning and significance of knowledge for life.   Realism and universalism still go hand in hand.[2]   The passion for learning is indeed no longer so lofty as expressed some fifty years before in Fichte's *Die Bestimmung des Gelehrten*.   But knowledge, as an intellectual process in which many successive generations take part, is characterized in Freytag, the one-time university lecturer, by a specific dignity, by the earnestness of sobriety and abstinence. Knowledge is never finite, especially in the branches of philology and history which stand in the forefront of the novel, if it is understood as an endless process of positivistic research.[3]

The consciousness of belonging to a cultural élite gives the idealistically militant university scholar a specific

---

[1] Cf. H. v. Srbik, *Deutsche Einheit*, i. 254 ff.   [2] *Ibid.*, p. 235.

[3] The same dynamic consciousness of history which fills *Soll und Haben* appears in the *Verlorene Handschrift* as the expression of the infinite process of knowledge: "For it is the lot of the scholar that few look with sympathy upon his trouble, his struggle, and the value of his work.   The world regards him as an unyielding labourer.   What he has formed, with enduring strength, henceforth becomes a building-stone in the immeasurable house of learning in which all the races of the earth have been working for thousands of years. Hundreds of others make of it a foundation to advance their own work; thousands of new blocks are piled upon it, and there are few to inquire who has chiselled the separate columns, and still more seldom does a stranger grasp the hand of the workman" (cf. *Die verlorene Handschrift*, English translation, *The Lost Manuscript*, London, 1887, i. 265).

pride which rather impresses the representatives of Society. At one point it is said of the classical philologist in *Die verlorene Handschrift*: "The energetic dignity and proud frank character of the scholar attracted the courtiers, and Werner soon became a valued acquaintance to him." [1]

On the whole, the scholar wavers between his own self-respect and devotion to the court of the strange Prince. As long as he is in his own kingdom, the university, he shows a democratic pride towards all the special claims raised by his princely students; if it were still usual in North German universities at the end of the eighteenth century for aristocratic students to have their own benches and to be honoured at every lecture by a special address from the lecturer, the liberal professor in the nineteenth century opposed with vigour any such presumptions which might give expression to the class differences amongst his hearers. It is not an aristocracy of birth that he recognizes, but an aristocracy of learning.

The professional cultural élite fought indeed for the same ends as the capitalist middle-class, namely, for a constitutional state based on property and culture,[2] but it did so—as was recently shown in the characteristic example of Rudolf Haym [3]—from a different motive, an "idealist" motive, and not like the new economic leaders, from a "capitalist outlook." This liberal aristocracy of learning hated the servility of the court just as much as it did the democratic demands for the rise of the masses by means of universal, equal and direct suffrage.

In the novel, the rector of the university conveys to the professor the wish from "above" that he shall give the heir-apparent special tuition in his room. The professor curtly refuses the request to deliver a special course of lectures to the Prince. He will only instruct

[1] G. Freytag, *Ges. Werke*, vii. 41.
[2] H. v. Srbik, *Deutsche Einheit*, i. 246.
[3] Cf. H. Rosenberg, *Rudolf Haym und die Anfänge des klassischen Liberalismus*, München, 1933, pp. 123 and 163.

the student as a listener with others in the college, and rejects any kind of favouritism. It is the court's desire, on the other hand, that the distance between the Prince and the masses shall be preserved. In the end a compromise is found.

Whilst the university sphere, in spite of all the failings and peculiarities of its scholars, represents a sphere of diligence, sincerity and proficiency, the court is a centre of caprice, deceit and intrigue.[1] The Prince and the heir-apparent, in accordance with Freytag's purpose, are supposed to be types; the Prince shows the "perverted education of an old family which had survived the ruins of the Napoleonic period," and the heir-apparent "the repression and narrowness of the provincial life of that time." [2] The Prince is tyrannical and autocratic through lack of a decisive democratic impulse in his subjects, or of a public opinion.[3] The consciousness of superiority of the middle-class bases itself precisely on the fact that it has long ago overcome the formalism of the court.

A century ago there was the same tormenting eagerness about rank and social precedence among the citizens. With us it has become different, since our life has been pervaded with a strong intellectual element. In the future, even at Court, people will laugh at these things as antiquated frippery.[4]

The dualism between the courtly and middle-class virtues, as well as the superiority of the rising class towards the declining one, is characteristically expressed in a conversation between the professor and an old Lord High Steward. The Lord High Steward here embodies the cultured *grand seigneur*, regarded by the middle-class

---

[1] We have a similar picture sketched by Raabe in *Abu Telfan*, 1870, and by Spielhagen in *In Reih und Glied*, 1866. In contrast to the democrat Spielhagen, Freytag does not consider court and society as bad in themselves, but only backward and injurious through their defective understanding of middle-class aims.

[2] Freytag, *Erinnerungen aus meinem Leben*, Leipzig, 1887, pp. 296 ff.

[3] Freytag, *Ges. Werke*, vii. 155.

[4] *Ibid.*, vii. 175. Very realistic, also, is the description of the degree of expressions of thanks with which the court acknowledges the receipt of a learned work.

as the exception which alone does not come under the negative criticism of the aristocracy.[1]   He is, so to speak, the last representative of the alliance between cultural élite and courtly refinement on the model of Weimar. He lives completely under the cultural idea that "the princes and the aristocracy are the born leaders of the nation."   But now he senses with discomfort the incongruity between what ought to be and what is, between the mission of the Court and its actual decline.[2]   The *grand seigneur* acknowledges with painful regret that the supreme value of court and society—elegance—is no longer being realized, whilst the professor emphasizes with pride that the supreme value of the rising classes —middle-class proficiency—is to be seen everywhere. Indeed, this politically-minded professor, drawn after the type of Gervinus and Droysen, himself admits the cultural leadership of the German courts round about 1800 as only a conditional one:

There was a short period during which the courts became the home of the most liberal culture of the time, and it was only through the strange political circumstances of our nation that this leadership was possible.   Now it has passed into other circles, and for the distinguished culture of individuals we have exchanged the increased capacity of many.[3]

The superiority which the professor feels towards the Lord High Steward is fundamentally the same as that which the merchant in *Soll und Haben* exhibits towards the impoverished country-nobility.   The aristocracy appears to be incapable, the court unfair, and in contrast the merchant and the professor are equally efficient, strong, and conscious of the rise of the class to which they both belong.   The merchant as the trusted guardian of material things, the scholar as the trusted guardian of

[1] See the 2nd bk., chap. xi, "The Lord High Steward."

[2] "A secure feeling of superiority, and a gracious rule over others, was general at Courts and in business; of this we were deprived . . . an uncertain pettiness, a grumbling, irritable, reserved character has gained the upper hand at Courts, and in diplomacy ill-bred frivolity, without knowledge and without masculine will" (Freytag, *Ges. Werke*, vii. 398).

[3] *Ibid.*, vii. 399.

the nation's intellectual goods, embody in Freytag an importance which the country-nobility lacks and which the court-nobility has lost. A strong consciousness of progress, which is not frightened by difficulties, fills this middle-class. The idea of progress is allied in it with the idea of the nation, the consciousness of the rise of the middle-classes is amalgamated with the conception of nationalism. This combination comes out clearly in a christening speech delivered in the professorial circle:

> But we wish that you too will help preserve for a future generation the proud and lofty spirit with which your fathers have dedicated their lives to science, to thought and to creative activity. You too, be you man or woman, must become the faithful guardians of the ideals of our people. You will find a national spirit that has higher aims and makes greater demands on its intellectual leaders.[1]

The same idea of the *Volkstum* of the historical school which Immermann acknowledged only for the peasantry in a period of political stagnation, is here twenty years later, in a period of economic development and optimistic progressiveness, attributed by Freytag to all middle-class strata, that is to say, to the non-aristocratic and non-proletarian strata including the merchant as well as scholar, and even the peasant. The nation, according to this ideology, is indestructible as long as optimism is able to predominate in the middle-class.

2. Middle-class Superiority towards the Jews

Still stronger than the pride of the Christian burgher towards the aristocracy (for it was continually crossed by feelings of inferiority, which we shall analyse in the next chapter) was the feeling of superiority in a wide circle of upper as well as lower middle-class towards the Jews, who had been emancipated only since 1848. In contrast with the aristocracy, we are concerned here not with a stratum that was for centuries socially and politically superior and which was now being forced on to

[1] Freytag, *Ges. Werke*, vii. 499.

the defensive, but with a group related in its class structure to the middle-class, a group which was for a long
time regarded as socially inferior, but which now presented a not undangerous competitor in the struggle
of professions. "He who cannot be an aristocrat so
that he may look down on the burghers," L. Börne
once shrewdly remarked, "wishes at least to be a
Christian so that he can have the Jews to look down
upon." [1]

The Jews undoubtedly profited in the middle of the
nineteenth century from the middle-class liberal ideas of
tolerance and from the practice of political equality.   On
the other hand, there was always a latent movement of
hostility in the German upper- and petty-bourgeoisie
against the complete social equality of the Jews.   In this,
motives of competition and the traditional consciousness
of their own social superiority went hand in hand.[2]   The
Christian merchant circle of the lower middle-class as
well as the Christian intellectual strata were filled between 1848 and 1870 with a hidden anti-semitism which
first developed in the new empire into the open anti-
semitism of the artisan and petty-merchant (in the Christian Social Movement of the court preacher Stöcker) and
of the *Verein Deutscher Studenten* (under the influence of
H. von Treitschke).   For a long time large sections of
the middle-class, especially the officials [3] and those
practising free professions, found it difficult to treat "the
helot of yesterday as the equal of to-day."

In two characteristic and effective books, the novel
acted as a trumpet for the prejudices and hostility of a
large section of the Christian bourgeoisie against the
Jews: the Polish-Jewish dealer in Freytag's *Soll und
Haben* and the Jewish intellectual in Raabe's *Hunger-*

---

[1] L. Börne, *Gesammelte Schriften (Reklam)*, ii. 351.

[2] Cf. A. Ruppin, *Soziologie der Juden*, Berlin, 1931, ii. 37 ff. See also
B. Lazar, *L'Antisémitisme*, Paris, 1934, vol. ii, chap. xiv.

[3] A special case is the traditional dislike of the German bureaucracy and
judiciary shown towards the Jewish intellectuals, especially towards the
numerous Jewish lawyers to whom the higher official careers were closed. See
S. Feuchtwanger, *Die freien Berufe*, Munich, 1922, pp. 165 ff. and 599.

pastor are both compared with their Christian competitors and found to be morally wanting.

(a) *The Contrast between Christian and Jewish Merchants*

Freytag describes exclusively the Jewish dealers of Silesia as they appeared to him shortly after their immigration from Poland. He knew them from personal observation in rather unfavourable circumstances, for he had represented the interests of relations in court against Jewish usurers.[1]

In an essay which Freytag wrote a few years before his novel, he gives a realistic picture of the Jewish traders in Breslau.[2] Through the revolution of 1848 the Jews were for the first time admitted to the Chamber of Commerce, a semi-official organization controlling the merchant profession. This professional equality between Jewish and Christian merchant by no means signified a social equality. The contempt with which the Christian merchant looked down on the Jewish merchant as an unfair competitor, was by no means extinguished.

> The Jewish merchant [affirmed Freytag] is not so well reputed as he is, for example, in Frankfort or Leipzig, partly through his own fault. The position of Silesia on the frontier of Poland and Galicia favours a continual influx of Polish huckstering Jews, and this Jewish element that comes from the East begins its process of development in the first generation with us. The second generation goes to Berlin, the third to Frankfort. Since it is here that the distillation begins, it follows that most of the filth remains with us.[3]

These dealers, in their lack of personal requirements, of restraint and culture, are, according to Freytag, still primitive. The intercourse of the Christian merchants with the Polish-Jewish dealers is an intercourse "as with children or savages; and it is as children and savages that they are treated."[4]

The Jews, objects this middle-class Prussian publicist, with their own moral code and their own ritual, are a

---

[1] G. Freytag, *Erinnerungen aus meinem Leben*, p. 266.
[2] *Die Juden in Breslau* (1849), *Vermischte Aufsätze*, ii. 339–47.
[3] *Ibid.*, p. 340.   [4] *Ibid.*, p. 373.

separate community in the State, cut off from the majority
of the citizens; they create a gulf through their own
religious usages and holidays, through their dislike of
non-Jews and through their refusal to intermarry.[1]
Because of its primitive moral and intellectual level,
Freytag believes that "the Jewish element is a disease
in the life of the Eastern portion of Prussia, which can
be cured only by rigorous means."[2]   Of course, in
judging them, the repressed social position of the Eastern
Jews supplies some extenuating circumstances.   It is
certainly understandable if the Christian merchant
despises the Jewish huckster for his lack of business
honour, but on the other hand he is unjust in scorning
the bigger Jewish merchant because of his nervous rest-
lessness and hastiness.   Also his lack of genteel nonchalance in negotiating a business deal and his lack of
the finer feelings of honour (which the merchant can
distinguish perfectly from legal honesty) are unjustly
reckoned as a crime in the Jew.[3]   These failings are, for
the author of *Soll und Haben*, to be explained by the uncertain position of the Jew in society, by his inferiority
in his associations with Gentiles.[4]   Throughout his
criticism of their haggling business conduct in this essay,
Freytag reveals a definite sociological understanding of
the conditions of the Eastern Jews.

On the other hand, there is little of it in his novel
Soll und Haben.   But whilst the essay was only accessible
to readers of the journal *Die Grenzboten*, this novel was
for several decades one of the most widely-read books

[1] The same objections against the Jews as a state within the state, as a community of exaggerated exclusiveness and cohesion, were also developed at that
time by Schopenhauer in his *Parerga und Paralipomena*, vol. ii, § 132.

[2] Freytag, *op. cit.*, p. 346.   Freytag recommends as a cure the abolition of
all the barriers raised by the Jewish community itself against its non-Jewish
surroundings.

[3] Freytag, *op. cit.*, p. 373.

[4] Freytag's understanding of the Jewish position is also revealed in a later
essay *Der Streit über das Judentum* (1869), *Gesammelte Aufsätze*, ii. 321–6;
here his former criticism has completely given way to a sympathy for the
Jews and he stresses their achievements in science and art.   He is especially
satisfied that in comparison with 1848, the participation of the Jews in the
leadership of the radical Left had in the meantime greatly decreased.

in the whole of German literature.[1]   The strikingly
virtuous figure of a private Jewish scholar, which he did
introduce, could not outweigh the negative impression
made by the Jewish merchant stratum as a whole.   The
Christian reader without any special critical faculty was
therefore only too easily inclined to identify the attitude
of the Polish-Jewish hucksters of Breslau with the whole
of Jewry.   Since the parallel careers of a Christian and
a Jew from apprentice to independent business-man are
drawn in this novel in contrasting colours of black and
white, of good and evil, then it would be very easy for
the reader to come to damaging conclusions as to the
tactics of Jewish competitors.[2]

The fundamentally important question in the sociology of literature, as to whether a writer describes a
social group with a strong negative bias in order to
please his public or with the purpose of influencing
the public against this group, is here difficult to determine.   It is probable that Freytag took into account
the traditional anti-semitism of the majority of his
public, i.e. the educated middle-class, and that he presented the figure of the private teacher, inspired by
the model of a Jewish acquaintance, as a concession
to the free-thinking minority of his readers.[3]   What is

[1] See the article *Gustav Freytag* by A. Dove in *Allg. Deutsche Biographie*,
vol. 48, pp. 749–67.
[2] In his black-and-white delineation Freytag has a strong affinity with
Dickens, who influenced him.   Both are representatives of a moral liberalism,
both describe the triumph of honesty and goodness over dishonesty and egoism.
Undoubtedly, Fagin in *Oliver Twist* and the aristocrats in *Nicholas Nickleby*
show also a certain antipathy against Jewry and nobility in Dickens.   (Cf.
L. M. Price, *The Reception of English Literature in Germany*, Berkeley, 1932,
pp. 413–14.)
[3] This opinion has already been expressed, significantly, at the end of the
nineteenth century in an anonymous anti-semitic pamphlet: "What purpose
had this figure, if not the very practical one of protecting the author from
the reputation of an over-zealous anti-semitism.   A book like *Soll und Haben*
must have placed the author on a hostile footing with Jewry, if only such
scamps as Itzig, Ehrenthal, Pinkus and Tinkeles represent the chosen people.
If, however, at least one ideal Jew were portrayed, then the Jewish liberal
press critics might concentrate on him and praise the writer for his sake.   The
others would then get away half or totally ignored" (anonymous brochure,
Fritz Reuter und die Juden, Dresden, 1895, p. 5).

the picture of the Jewish dealer as portrayed in *Soll und Haben?*

Regarded from the standpoint of the middle-class, the aristocracy has a different code of honour, whilst the Jewish merchant has none at all. The Jewish dealer, as pictured by Freytag, betrays not only the gentiles, but also the members of his own race and religion. He is made to appear crafty, unscrupulous, abstract and miserly. *His* characteristics anticipate, as it were, the very questionable generalization made sixty years later by Sombart on *the* Jewish character.[1] The novelist of 1850 and the economist of 1910 thereby only systematized opinions which had become widespread in both the middle-class and the educated bourgeoisie under the stress of competitive relationships. The Jewish merchants and dealers in Freytag possess the three distinguishing characteristics that Sombart ascribes to the Jewish type: strength of will, unswerving selfishness, and an abstract way of thinking.

The tenacity with which *the* Jew, according to Sombart, pursues a plan and accomplishes his economic success, and which underlies also his ability to assimilate quickly, is illustrated by Freytag in the figure of Veitel Itzig: Veitel Itzig, the dark antithesis to his honest Christian school comrade Anton Wohlfahrt, who only achieves success in the long run because of his probity, begins his business career in a very humble position with a Jewish dealer who is as uneducated as himself. He fulfils there not only business functions, but is at the same time a kind of servant and errand-boy for the whole family. But he soon learns how to exploit the weaknesses of the. individual members of the family, does business on his own account, takes lessons in law from a broken-down lawyer, exchanges his jargon for proper German and learns how to write correctly. He soon becomes so indispensable to his employer that he is made book-keeper and is permitted to dine at his employer's

[1] Cf. W. Sombart, *Die Deutsche Volkswirtschaft im 19. Jahrhundert*, 7th Ed., pp. 113–17.

table. Through tenacity and cunning he finally works himself up to being an independent business-man who moves about in elegantly furnished rooms under the glitter of chandeliers and keeps a fashionably dressed servant. "He became quite a gentleman and had the negligent airs of the successful man."

In him and his erstwhile employer, Ehrenthal, we find further a relentless *egoism*, both figures thereby appearing as an illustration of Sombart's dictum that "the Jew is usually not too fastidious in choosing the means that will lead him to his ends." [1] The dealers in Freytag subscribe tacitly to the principle that one can do anything that one can get away with. Ehrenthal systematically plans the economic ruin of the Freiherr whose business adviser he is, intentionally giving him false information on mortgages or making him fraudulent offers through intermediaries. In the systematic exploitation of the unsuspecting aristòcrat, the dealer views his victim with that intimate interest that the persecutor shows towards the persecuted, and the betrayer towards the betrayed.

The lord had been for a long time the object of his pre-occupation, of his work, of his jealous watchfulness. He had become for the scoundrel what his fields are to the farmer, what her pet is to the housewife. There was a very nice touch of sympathy. [2]

The attitude of *abstract calculation*, which Sombart ascribes to the Jew, is also to be seen in the dealers in Freytag These figures have no appreciation for æsthetic qualities. They assess houses, people, nature purely according to the economic value that they represent and for which they can be acquired and exploited. The capitalistic frame of mind, the tendency to acquire property for the sake of property, develops in the primitive Jew from his very childhood a shrewd acquisitive instinct, a presence of mind in matters of profit-calculation, which day and night acts as the driving force in

[1] W. Sombart, *op. cit.*, p. 114.
[2] G. Freytag, *Ges. Werke*, iv. 346.

the life of these people.[1]   In contrast to the Christian merchant, the Jewish dealer is no honest representative of creative capital, but a dishonest representative of rapacious capital.

The Jews are lacking in middle-class business morality which is to a large extent identical with the middle-class idea of honour.   The honourable merchant develops the virtues of business solidity, of reliability in the making of agreements, correctness in social intercourse, indeed a certain narrow-mindedness in his way of life.   His morality is just as much a morality in business as morality for business.[2]   An honourable way of life benefits business reputation; if one is thought to be a good citizen in the eyes of those around, then one's credit rises.

In contrast to him, the Jews appear to the bourgeois middle-class to be as unfathomable as they are uncitizen-like.   They are not reliable in regard to mercantile solidity, their behaviour is queer, and their lack of philistinism arouses suspicion.   It is especially the petty-bourgeois circles that combine these critical observations with traditional prejudices, despising and fearing the Jews at the same time.   The contacts that they make with the Jews are determined by stereotyped prejudices. Contemporary observers were astonished how rough the categories of the public in general used to be.[3]

[1] Freytag has already remarked on this speculative capitalist mentality in his essay *Die Juden in Breslau*.   "The foreign Jew has left his heart in his homeland; he thinks of nothing, he dreams of nothing, he wants nothing but speculation, and his imagination broods for days on end not only over large sums, but over petty halfpence" (*Vermischte Aufsätze*, ii. 341).   The psychological basis of the Jewish preference for trade has been recently better described by A. Ruppin: "The hope of a chance and luck and big profits in the future keeps him happy and in a way supplements the actual takings of the day" (A. Ruppin, *The Jews in the Modern World*, London, 1934, p. 206).

[2] Cf. W. Sombart, *Der Bourgeois*, p. 160.

[3] This is the opinion, for example, of a higher Prussian official on the Jewish question (1844): "The public in general does not go into particulars.   It loves and hates, praises and condemns, according to categories, and only in the rarest cases do individuals who belong to a hated category gain public estimation for themselves.   It is in this that the Jews feel its injustice.   *For it* (public opinion) *the Jew is a Jew*.   He may be one of the noblest, the most upright, the most cultured of men, but from the very beginning he has prejudice against him.   The journeyman, the common labourer, will be more

If the Christian burgher emphasizes his superiority in intellectual culture over the aristocracy, towards the Jew he feels the superiority of complete culture over semi-culture. The distance which the aristocracy assumes towards the middle-class parvenu, is repeated here in a different degree in the relationship of the Christian merchant rooted in tradition towards the immigrant, mobile Jewish dealer. The wholesale merchant in Freytag belongs to people of rank and to the national upper stratum which, in common with the aristocratic landed-proprietors, defends the nation against the encroachments of foreign nations—in this case the Poles.[1] He is filled with a consciousness of patriotism, whilst the Jewish dealers regard the struggle against the Poles only from the point of view of their own advantage with the inner indifference of foreigners. The city patrician therefore looks down with contempt on the rootless, unstable dealers who regard money as an end in itself and not as a means for the cultivation of life.

The semi-education in the house of the Jewish dealer is sharply revealed by means of a contrast effect during a visit of the Herr von Finkh and his honest friend the clerk Wohlfahrt. The clever aristocrat is amused at the vulgarity of the old usurer, at the affected luxury of his wife and the superficiality of their beautiful daughter. He relates stories about society, which is closed to these circles, thereby delighting the socially ambitious mother. The relation of the city patrician to the successful Jewish dealers presents a defensiveness similar to the relationship of the old aristocrat to the *arriviste* Christian industrialist. Both recognize a par-

cautious than usual in concluding an agreement with the richest Jewish banker —he will take off his hat to him more slowly and bow less deeply, than for the Christian; and if he meets with the same politeness there, then it must be only because they want to make certain of a good customer. If he is justly, or even well and generously paid, he will be amazed, and will ascribe to Jewish vanity that which he owes to goodwill." (K. Preuss, *Wirkl. Geh. Oberregie-rungsrat a. D. A. F. C. Streckfuss, Über das Verhältnis der Juden zu den christ-lichen Staaten*, ii. *Schrift*, 1844, p. 12.)

[1] Cf. *Soll und Haben*, bk. iii, chap. i.

venu in the intruder and react with the weapon of mockery against a stratum which may sooner or later shatter their prestige.

(b) The Contrast between Christian and Jewish Intellectuals

In Freytag's merchant novel, the fates of the Christian clerk and the Jewish dealer run parallel from beginning to end. Both come simultaneously from the provincial town to the capital to begin their careers; both later are intermediaries in the affairs of the careless aristocrat, the one as a fraudulent criminal, the other as a good-natured helper; both succeed in business, the one in a respected wholesale firm, the other with a usurious dealer. The contrast between black and white, between good and evil, is thereby distributed sociologically in an unequivocal manner between Jewish merchant parvenus and Christian middle-class.

Similar, if not more marked, is the contrast between the Jewish and Christian intellectual in Raabe's *Der Hungerpastor* (1864). This book, also, enjoyed the widest popularity of all its author's works, although it is by no means the best nor artistically most finished work of Raabe.[1] Whilst Freytag represented the joyful optimism of upper middle-class prosperity, in Raabe it is a petty-bourgeois provincial pietism that finds its outlet.

Raabe belongs, from the point of view of intellectual history, to a conservative German tradition which is characterized by the line, Lutheranism-Pietism-Storm and Stress-Romanticism. As the son of an official and as a provincial intellectual, he is dominated by the old Lutheran antithesis between religious subjectivity and passive obedience to the secular ruler, between emotional irrationalism and rejection of the "harlot reason," between belief in the value of genuine emotions and pessimism as regards the way of the world. The sociological basis of this old, conservative German attitude is determined by the pluralism of German territorial states

---

[1] The book was often treated in the literature course of German secondary schools from 1880 to 1914 and praised as a masterpiece of German literature.

as well as by the political weakness of the German middle-class. It is throughout a secularized pietism which is represented in Raabe's contrast of petty-bourgeois subjectivity and semitic cunning, between middle-class appreciation of the soul and Jewish knowledge of the ways of the world.

Raabe is a step in the long path from German pietism of the seventeenth and eighteenth centuries to the nationalism of the nineteenth and twentieth centuries, a development which had remained unnoticed until recently described by Pinson.[1] The emphasis on the emotions as the real basis of life is with him still half religious, but has already a semi-nationalist accent. The resentment against reason which already character-ized early pietism, is not only shown in Raabe in a sharper form,[2] but also finds there a definite type in society as the object of its hatred, namely the Jewish intellectual. Pietism has not yet completely disappeared in him, but is rather combined with a deep pessimism of a Schopenhauerian kind and provided with an em-phatic national colouring. German subjectivity on a petty-bourgeois basis is "good," Jewish worldly greed and lust "bad," a synthesis between subjectivity and activity in the world outside receives here just as little recognition or value as a harmony between form and content, such as is represented perhaps by the English Gentleman-ideal.

Poor but honest, lacking in influence but conscien-tious—such are therefore the characteristics of the pietistic hero in Raabe's *Hungerpastor*, the student Hans Unwirrsch. Very probably, the widespread success of this book amongst the middle-classes is to be attributed not only to the black and white contours, but to the idealization of this dreamy theologian from the lower

[1] K. L. Pinson, *Pietism as a Factor in the Rise of German Nationalism*, New York, 1934.

[2] A characteristic example of the specific ideology of the German Protestant middle-class, which considered reason as destructive and emotion as positive, is the chapter *"Gemüt"* in the apologetic work by Raabe's friend, the "Ober-schulrat" W. Brandes, *Wilhelm Raabe*, Wolfenbüttel, 1901.

middle-classes and to the condemnation of his antagonist who comes from the class of old-clothes Jew dealers.

The moral condemnation of the Jewish intellectual type might console some readers for the unpleasant fact of the existence of successful competitors of a strange race. As in Freytag, the superiority of the Christian burgher which is here expressed, is an ethical one. If, in contrast to Freytag, the son of the Jewish second-hand clothes dealer gets on better than the son of the Christian shoemaker from the same provincial town, the one becoming only a poor parson in the country whilst the other achieves office as a privy councillor, then this corresponds to the pietistic antithesis of corrupting worldly success and good conscience. In addition to this, the worldly success of the Jewish intellectual is only apparent; the moral superiority of the Christian, on the other hand, complete.

Raabe is a representative of the German provincial middle-class before 1870, which this writer is always describing with a simultaneous affection and mockery. Brought up in a backward German provincial town as the son of a higher administrative official, he lived only relatively few years outside Brunswick, and it is noteworthy that his first and last educational tour, which he undertook in his youth, did not lead him beyond the German-speaking frontier.[1]

Let us examine briefly the antithesis between the Jewish and Christian hero and their respective destinies. The father of the hero is a ruminating cobbler on the model of Hans Sachs and Jakob Böhme and the uncle is also a master cobbler, embodying the typical German worthy of the middle-class such as Keller painted him in the person of Meister Hediger of *Das Fähnlein der*

---

[1] The original objective of the journey was Italy, but Raabe did not get to this country. Nor did he heed the patriotic advice of his colleague Freytag: "What is it that German artists are always seeking in Italy! They should go rather to the Netherlands. There is the praised land of German art, it is there they ought to *adjourn* if they want to learn something useful." (See A. Krüger, *Der junge Raabe*, Leipzig, 1911, p. 54.)

sieben Aufrechten.   He is the purveyor of political gossip
and opinions who is not untouched by the liberal popular
enlightenment.[1]   His aunt Schlotterbeck similarly represents the petty-bourgeois qualities of honesty and warmth
of feeling.   The *milieu* of the cobbler's son is already in
contrast with that of the Jewish old-clothes merchant's
son.   Both grow to manhood in the same provincial
town of 10,000 inhabitants, round about the year 1820.
Here already there is a characteristic difference: the
family of the shoemaker has been long established in the
place, that of the Jewish dealer is still strange.   The
father of the latter had for many years led a peripatetic
existence as a dealer in skins and furs in Prussia and
Turkey, and after many tribulations had settled in the
German country town, marrying there the daughter of
a co-religionist.   The Jews and Christians live here as
two distinct communities, separated indeed no longer
in space, but socially.   At that time—Raabe himself
reports—the Jews were widely despised, especially in
the smaller cities and districts.

Both the old and the young of God's chosen people have certainly had much to endure from their Christian neighbours, and
only very slowly has that terrible cry of "Hepp—hepp!", which
has been the cause of such endless mischief, ceased to be heard
in our streets.   Especially the children of Jews had to endure a
great deal of annoyance; and sickly little Moses certainly led no
pleasant existence in Kröppel Street, for whenever he appeared,
the worthless little scamps fell on him like birds of prey. . . .   His
hair torn out, abused and beaten, as he was sure of being; it was
not surprising if he kept indoors as much as possible, and led a
dark, miserable existence in his father's semi-subterraneous
dwelling.[2]

Throughout his childhood the Jewish youth felt himself persecuted and developed a protective armour of

---

[1] This German worthy was, in accordance with the liberal fashion of his
time, an eager reader of newspapers, had his liberal political principles, and
behaved mostly in a doctrinaire way.

[2] *Der Hungerpastor*, 55th Ed., p. 40, English translation, London, 1885, i. 50.

hostility.[1]   The child of Christian as well as of Jew attended the Gymnasium of the provincial town.   If the cobbler's son inherited a genuine desire for learning from his father, knowledge for the Jewish boy is merely a means to an end, a means to domination.   The Jewish child studies only through motives of revenge, in the hope of revenging himself later on his persecutors through intellectual superiority.   Whilst Hans, the idealist, has a hunger for intellectual things in themselves, Moses, the grim realist, has a hunger for power and property. The imagination of the Christian and the intellect of the Jew are sharply contrasted.   If the future theologian entertains illusions about the friendship with his Jewish contemporary, the latter only clings to it through calculation.

The different mentalities and dispositions of the two representatives are clearly revealed at the university. Hans Unwirrsch studies theology, Moritz Freudenstein philosophy; the Christian is filled with a seeking for the cardinal principle of religion, the Jew with a sophistic joy in destructive dialectic.   The one regards the university authorities with a respectful shyness, the other deliberately undermines this belief in them.   He builds up for himself a "rather original system of objective logic."   For this he employs Hegel and fashions a political philosophy which is characterized by the principles of Macchiavelli and of Reynard the Fox.   With cold objectivity, he subordinates his friend and everything that he had with him to "some atrocious category or other."   In his heart of hearts he is a materialist, and he is able, by means of adroit sophism in his doctoral thesis "Matter as momentum of the Divine," to stir up a great deal of dust, making himself famous with some, notorious with others, but in any case, well-

---

[1] Raabe has before his eyes the anti-semitic riots that occurred between 1815 and 1819. Cf. S. Dubnow, *Weltgeschichte des jüdischen Volkes*, Berlin, 1929, Bd. ix, pp. 16–26.   We have a similar mocking of the old second-hand clothes-dealing Jew in Westphalia by schoolboys in Schücking's novel *Die Ritterbürtigen* (1846), and of Jewish children in a provincial town east of the Elbe in W. von Polenz's *Die Grabenhäger* (1898).

known.[1] Whilst the theologian clings inwardly to
the provincial town and to the "small narrow circle of
loyal, limited men," the free spirit of the Jew knows no
such bonds with a surrounding that only hindered and
despised him. With the characteristic mobility of
Jewish literary men, like Heine and Börne, he leaves the
narrow confines of Germany in order to breathe more
freely in Paris. In reproaching the Jews here with
a lack of German national consciousness, Raabe raises
an objection that is typical at that time amongst the
conservative intelligentsia in regard to their Jewish
competitors. Treitschke explains the preference and
affinity of the German-Jewish intelligentsia of the nineteenth century for Western Europe by their defective
historical sense and by their rational outlook.[2] If the
representative of the lower middle-class naturally thinks
"nationally" and identifies himself emotionally with the
German fatherland, the Jews, according to Raabe, feel
themselves to be "true cosmopolitans," "through the
grace of God . . . or through His displeasure."[3] The
Jew in Raabe is morally disintegrated and unpatriotic.
He exploits to his advantage the enlightened, liberal
currents of the time and sophistically changes the nega-

---

[1] The competitive motive, i.e. envy towards the successful Jewish rival, is
clearly indicated in the following sentence: "From the incense of the Aula, Moses,
however, came forth Doctor Philosophiæ; during the last part of his university
career he had acquired decided celebrity, and where he was not famous he was
at least notorious. Of Hans Unwirrsch no one spoke, and no one felt either
relieved or depressed at his departure. *Der Hungerpastor*, English translation,
i. 174 ff.

[2] Raabe represented the same conservative nationalist attitude towards the
Jewish intelligentsia, such as H. von Treitschke always passionately upheld.
"In so far as the Jewish cosmopolitan was competent to understand western
nations, he was chiefly attracted towards the French, not merely from reasonable
gratitude, but also from a sense of inner kinship. For a nation which for
centuries had ceased to possess a political history nothing seemed so alien as
the historic sense. To the Jews, German veneration for the past appeared
ludicrous, but modern France had broken with her history. Here they feel
more at home in this new state, created, as it were, by pure reason" (H. von
Treitschke, *History of Germany in the Nineteenth Century*, London, 1918, iv. 556).
Already W. Menzel used similar arguments in his *Deutsche Dichtung von der
ältesten bis auf die neueste Zeit*, Stuttgart, 1859, iii. 464–84.

[3] *Op. cit.*, i. 167.

tive exceptional position of earlier times, which excluded the Jews from all the rights of their co-citizens, into a positive exceptional position of the present, by means of which he frees himself from all the duties of his co-citizens.   The reproach of lack of national loyalty, which was repeatedly raised in the conservative national literature of the nineteenth century, is, in Raabe, cynically acknowledged by the Jewish dialectician.   He regards the German fatherland just as objectively as everything else that lends itself to discussion.   He is devoted to the eudaemonism of the sentiment *ubi bene, ibi patria* and claims for himself the right of being a German only where he wishes, and of resigning his German citizenship whenever he wishes.[1]   The Jew is the voluntary outsider in regard to a community whose advantages he enjoys without sharing its burdens.   Moritz Freudenstein embodies the falsity and characterlessness which, in the opinion of this pietistic irrationalism, are inevitably bound up with a sharp and shrewd intellect.   Through his sinister power of assimilation this Jew is just as treacherous to his faith as he is to his fatherland; whilst abroad, he goes over to Catholicism,[2] changes his name, achieves a certain reputation as a writer, and does not shrink from serving the Prussian secret State-police by spying on and betraying German fellow-countrymen

[1] It is not argued by Raabe that the Jews, as mobile elements, cannot declare themselves for the German nation, but indeed that they are not inwardly bound, remaining free at all times in their attitude. They play the rôle of a stranger in a community (*ibid.*, i. 168 ff.). "Since we are no longer struck dead or burned alive as poisoners of springs and murderers of children, we are better off than any of you Aryans—German, French, English, or whatever you may call yourselves." . . . "If any important issue is at stake, such as the fate, honour, or happiness of the German nation, we can descend into the arena and undergo suffering or death for the cause in question. On the contrary, our advantage consists precisely in the fact that we take part in such distress or death with an unbiassed and Platonic *animus*. You struggle and suffer *pro domo*; we sacrifice ourselves for pure principle."

[2] A German university career still remained closed to the Jewish scholar for a long time in the nineteenth century, or at least it was difficult of entrance. He was nearly always faced with the choice: baptism or resignation. (See S. Dubnow, *op. cit.*, ix. 38 ff. and 325.) Moritz Freudenstein chooses the first course in Raabe because he has hopes of a professorship; the Jewish private scholar in Freytag's *Soll und Haben* chooses the second.

abroad.[1]   Whilst the Jewish writer causes himself to be
noticed and is able to insinuate himself through calculation into the family of a Prussian Geheimrat, his dreamy
Christian counterpart passes through the various stages
in the life of a private tutor.   The hero of Raabe
becomes successively tutor in three different social strata:
first in the house of a patriarchal country Junker who
understands more about agriculture than education, then
in the house of a manufacturer who represents, as it were,
the prosperity of the age and feels himself to be a "very
useful member of the great human society"—he greets
capitalist expansion in a manner similar to Freytag's
merchant: "Time makes rapid progress and we merchants and manufacturers cannot complain of it, for it
is ready enough to take us along with the current, if we
want to go."[2]   The third stage is in the house of a privy
councillor who is completely dominated by his aristocratic wife.   The servants here despise the unworldly
tutor just as much as they respect the elegant man of
letters.   The Jew finally advances to the position of a
privy councillor, the Christian becomes only a parson
in a village on the Baltic where he associates with estate-
owners and retired officers.   The Jew has attained
worldly honours, but has been morally destroyed; the
Christian holds a modest office and enjoys complete
respect in a rural, conservative, circle of life.   "The Jew
is overtaken by the fate of traitors, being despised by
those who use him as well as by those against whom he
is used; an outcast in the most terrible sense of the

---

[1] The figure of Moses Freudenstein is modelled, according to Raabe's own
admission, on Joel Jacoby, a Jewish man of letters who began with writing
sentimental, plaintive songs on the disabilities of the Jews, then went over to
Catholicism and performed important services for the Prussian State through
his secret work during the demagogue-persecution. Anyhow, as far as the
sociological interpretation is concerned, the question of who was the model
is of minor importance. Despite the whitewashing endeavours of H. Spiero
(*Raabe*, Darmstadt, 1924, p. 139), it is justified to see in Freudenstein not merely
the type of a renegade, but *the* Jewish intellectual. The type of the Jewish
dialectician and renegade has been portrayed with much finer psychological
insight by Thomas Mann in the figure of Naphta in the *Magic Mountain*.

[2] *Der Hungerpastor* (Transl.), i. 228.

word." [1]   Hunger for worldly goods has corrupted
Moses Freudenstein, hunger for spiritual goods has
made the theologian productive for the world. The
young parson is soon reckoned amongst men of rank,
but this honourable membership is closed to the Jew;
he remains an outsider and carries on his activities in
the darkness of society.

---

[1] How tendencious this black-and-white approach is, that is so effective
amongst large classes of readers, is stated by the self-complacent words of the
young theologian: "Evil genii surrounded Moses' crib while none but good
and beneficent spirits were gathered around me" (*Ibid.*, ii. 113).

CHAPTER V

ARISTOCRATIC AND MIDDLE-CLASS PRESTIGE

I

In the foregoing chapters we have examined the phenomena of the economic and political antithesis between
aristocracy and middle-class. This has revealed clearly
the defensive attitude of the one and the progressive
attitude of the other. We proceed now to analyse more
in detail the aristocratic and middle-class consciousness
of prestige as it was to be found in the second half of
the nineteenth century.

What was the psychological reaction of the aristocrat
to the middle-class way of life, and what was the reaction of the burgher to that of the aristocrat? How did
the aristocracy behave socially when confronted with the
fact of growing middle-class prosperity, and what was
the attitude of the middle-class to the precedence of an
aristocracy which, although indeed forced on to the
defensive, was still politically influential and socially
predominant?

It would be an error to seek the answer in a simple
formula or according to some ready-made scheme. An
inductive analysis shows rather that the psychological
attitude in both camps was a complex one, and that
there were various reactions to the existence of the rival
class.

We shall analyse first the types of aristocratic attitudes to the middle-class and democratization, and then
examine conversely the different middle-class attitudes
to the aristocracy.

In both German social history and the literature of the nineteenth century we meet with *two different aristocratic attitudes* towards the progressive middle-class: *the exclusive and the conciliatory*.

The exclusive attitude is characteristic of the majority of the aristocrats; for them, of course, it is the "natural" one, whilst the more unbiassed attitude is characteristic only of a "liberal," enlightened minority. The exclusive aristocrat rejects the burgher and opposes him as an intruder: the conciliatory aristocrat, on the other hand, assimilates middle-class forces, is open to progressive ideas and shows a decided interest in the fundamentally urban middle-class domain of art and science. The exclusive aristocrat adheres to his Estate and continually pursues an Estate policy, whilst the liberal moves away from his hereditary caste and approaches voluntarily those intellectual groups of middle-class origin that have themselves attained to a certain position outside the middle-class.

A. *The Exclusive Attitude.*—This had been the characteristic attitude of the continental aristocracy for centuries, and is the distinguishing feature of the "Junker." The claim to exclusiveness is not only based on superiority of blood (which the aristocrat believes he possesses), but also on the specific modes of life in his Estate which permeate every phase of aristocratic existence. These modes of life are handed down from generation to generation, forming the foundations of a spiritual home in which every member of this Estate must live. Even in other Estates and strata of society the power of tradition is of a significance not to be underrated. Despite this, the bond the aristocrat feels with fixed modes of life, through his membership of a privileged stratum, is much more intense than that of the burgher. For the class-norms, the unwritten laws of *esprit de corps* are for him much stronger than for the burgher who has smaller obstacles to overcome with his individual power of determination. The middle-class of the nineteenth century was not, moreover, a relatively closed group like the aristocracy. It was, rather, a class to which anyone could belong by reason of the ownership of property. Of course there existed still within this class—as we saw—a special aristocracy, the patriciate of old imperial cities, as for example Augsburg, Frankfort-on-Main, Hamburg, Bremen, Lübeck, whose structure and way of life was similar to that of the aristocracy and which closed itself as far as possible to new-comers. But this patriciate, from the middle of the nineteenth century, was no longer the leading stratum in Germany, being supplanted by the self-made men of the richer bourgeoisie who did not owe their importance to inherited wealth and tradition, but to their own rise through success within the capitalist order of society.

In comparison with the aristocracy, the middle-class does not offer a positively defined and limited unity: it was purely the aggregation of all non-nobles. The aristocracy, on the other hand, was still in the nineteenth century (down to the rise of the New Empire) an Estate to which entry was not accessible to anyone possessed of nothing but mere wealth.[1]

The sentiment "noblesse oblige" characterized the constraint placed on aristocratic existence by the standards of "what was worthy of the Estate." For only in this stratum did all the forms and content of life, such as education, marriage, occupation and social display, have to conform to an unwritten law and be judged "worthy of the Estate" or not, according to a definite, traditional principle.[2] The law of an Estate-worthy way of life had, from of old, a double significance for the aristocrat, a negative and a positive one: (1) it *forbade to the aristocrat what was allowed to other groups in society* (e.g. pursuit of commerce, the exercise of "degrading" functions such as those of lackey, servant, etc.); (2) it

---

[1] A strong tendency to ennoble burghers began in Prussia after the death of William I. (See R. Lewinsohn, *Das Geld in der Politik*, Berlin, 1930, p. 19.)

[2] See the excellent excursus on the aristocracy in G. Simmel's *Soziologie*, Munich, 1908, p. 550.

demanded of him what was not allowed to other groups in consequence of their smaller prestige (e.g. a definite kind of public representation, of conduct, often of clothes; also readiness for war-service, the obligation of representing the State).

For a long time the aristocracy had been a closed group, and as such was outwardly characterized, in contrast with relatively open groups (e.g. a modern professional organization or an ordinary glee-club), by exclusiveness and solidarity. These criteria become, then, especially obvious when the prestige and power of the closed group is threatened by the rivalry of other groups. Under the pressure of incipient liberalism, the German aristocracy, which had split into many regional and religious groups, combined together after 1815 to form the so-called "aristocratic chain," a union which maintained a religious and political neutrality in order to concentrate on the protection of common class interests.

The exclusiveness of a group is expressed in the distance preserved by its members between themselves and outsiders. Distance is a category of space-measurement;[1] e.g. objects, animals, men exist in space at a definite distance from each other. But when taken over into the domain of sociology, "distance" indicates the degree of social disparity between men, especially between the members of different strata. Just as the individual can lessen or increase the physical distance between himself and others, can approach or withdraw from them in space, so can the relationship between members of different Estates and classes be subject to greater or lesser distance. The tendency to decrease the distance in society is one of the main social features of the nineteenth century.

The aristocrat in the eighteenth century still expressed the distance between himself and other Estates by sym-

---

[1] I am indebted to the London University lectures of Prof. K. Mannheim for the indication of the significance of distance as a physical and sociological category.

bols. He associated but little, and then reluctantly, with non-nobles; he "kept them away from his body." Distance between noble and non-noble had already made its definite appearance in space in the society of Estates.[1] In the seventeenth and eighteenth centuries a rope separated the aristocrat from the middle-class at dances, operatic performances, and garden-parties, and this separating-rope was preserved in the small courts right into the nineteenth century—in Bavaria until just before the last war.[2] At festivities where entry was permitted both to aristocrat and burgher, the exclusiveness of the aristocrat was exhibited by his privilege of wearing special dress. He alone had the right in the eighteenth century of sporting a dagger and a hat decorated with white ostrich-feathers.[3]

Distance was also expressed at church. In *Soll und Haben* (1853) the middle-class business magnate was much incensed by the fact that, even in Polish exile, his noble lordship does not attend service at the German church because in a church without choir and loge he would have to sit in the nave next to his middle-class countrymen. The Freiherr, instead, installs a chapel in his own house and occasionally has the priest visit him there. In a contemporary English novel, Trollope's *Doctor Thorne* (1858), distance at church is shown by the privilege of a special entry which prevents the aristocracy from coming "into unseemly community with the village multitude."[4]

From the nineteenth century we see the exclusiveness of the group threatened more vigorously than before by the increase of intruders of middle-class origin. The conflict between these antagonists is a favourite theme

---

[1] This is also true of the relationship of the urban patriciate towards the "plebs."

[2] G. Steinhausen, *Geschichte der deutschen Kultur*, Leipzig, 1929, 3rd Ed., p. 500.

[3] The aristocracy only could appear in dominos of pink material at the ball in the Berlin Opera House in the eighteenth century. (See Th. Mundt, *Geschichte der deutschen Stände nach ihrer gesellschaftlichen Entwicklung und politischen Vertretung*, Berlin, 1854, p. 454.)

[4] See A. N. Monkhouse, *Society and Fiction*, The Aryan Path, 1935, vi. 313.

of the middle-class novel. We may distinguish two types of intruder:

(*a*) *The educated burgher paid for his work by the heredi-tary aristocracy.*

(*b*) *The parvenu economically independent of the aristo-cracy.*

In the German novel, we are often shown the contact made through his employment by an intelligent young burgher with a noble family or aristocratic circle.[1] As tutor, architect, estate-administrator, the young burghers show superior intelligence and execute usually very responsible tasks for the aristocracy. The aristocrat is, in such cases, often ready to acknowledge the sterling achievements, the excellent knowledge of these middle-class experts, but never to recognize them as individuals. He merely employs the services of burghers, without favouring them with social intercourse on an equal foot-ing.[2] The burgher, who is only required by the aristo-cratic estate-owner for a job of work, often wins the sympathy of aristocratic ladies through his personal qualities and charm, a fact which occasionally gives rise to serious conflicts between the burgher and the male aristocrat. The "intruder" is reminded of his position as a mere employee and is hurt by the open or hidden reference to his social inferiority.

In the novel it is chiefly the tutor who attracts now the interest of bored ladies, now the rebuke of proud aristocrats. In point of fact, the old institution of the house-tutor still existed in the middle of the nineteenth century amongst the country-nobility. The aristocrat clung to it as long as possible, because he rejected and opposed the association of his sons with burghers on

---

[1] E.g. in the novels *Von Geschlecht zu Geschlecht*, by Fanny Lewald; *Proble-matische Naturen* and *Sturmflut*, by Spielhagen; and in Freytag's *Soll und Haben*.

[2] The same, of course, also applied to the relationship between the head of a trading or business concern and his employees, in contrast, for example, with America as Max Weber has pointed out in his *Religionssoziologie*, Munich, 1920, i. 216.

the benches of high schools, as was desired by the State.[1]

The actual, if not the intended, function of the tutor was that of a middle-man. The tutor brought new political ideas and cultural fashions from the capitals and university towns to the remote seats of the country-nobility. Thus round about 1830—as especially the writings of Laube show—he introduced liberal ideals to the Silesian aristocracy, whilst at the same time he acquainted the aristocratic ladies of Mecklenburg with the latest fashions of mesmerism and somnambulism.

> Tutors [says a contemporary feminine observer in retrospect] were then the sunbeams in the sombre lives of noble ladies. They were an olive-branch sent to them in the desert by the new times, and whilst their lords and husbands amused themselves away from home or conversed in their smoking rooms with the gentlemen of their acquaintance, the tutor passed the time with madame.[2]

The tutor, as the type of intellectual intruder in the Pomeranian nobility, has found significant shape in Spielhagen's early work, *Problematische Naturen* (1864).

---

[1] The Prussian noble was, after 1835, finally compelled to send his sons, if they intended to become officers, to the high schools, at least for a few years, as a Sixth Form report was necessary for this career. The dislike of the aristocrat for this educating of his offspring in common with members of the middle-class was strong, as was also his dislike of over-emphasis on academic knowledge; he suspected the headmaster-class as a whole, finding it to be fundamentally hostile to the "better classes" and filled with the destructive rationalistic tendencies of the time. (K. Demeter, *Das deutsche Offizierscorps*, Berlin, 1930, p. 93.)

The attitude of the English aristocracy towards public schools in the nineteenth century was, on the other hand, quite different. It was precisely the aristocrat who gave the public schools in the eighteenth and nineteenth centuries their particular stamp; and even if the sons of the wealthy middle-class were stronger from point of numbers, they yet stood completely under the sway of the "gentleman" ideal which had its origin in the aristocracy. (See W. Dibelius, *England*, Stuttgart, 1923, ii. 144 ff.; also R. H. Tawney, *Equality*, London, 1931, pp. 93 ff.)

[2] *Erinnerungsblätter aus dem Leben Luise Mühlbachs*, ed. Th. Ebersberger, 1902, p. 67. A comprehensive history of the institution of the private house-tutor in Europe is still lacking. Information on the position of the German house-tutor in the eighteenth century will be found in Fr. Neumann, *Der Hofmeister*, Halle, 1930; (see also my review of it in *Zeitschrift der Geschichte*

Spielhagen himself had for a long time been a tutor in an aristocratic family in Rügen, and if one cannot accept the story as an absolutely true description of facts, it does yet reveal the resentment felt on both sides.[1]

In his novel a young graduate, Dr. Oswald Stein, comes as tutor to the castle of a baron on the Baltic Sea, a few years before the revolution of 1848. He soon notices that tutoring is regarded in these circles as an inferior, middle-class function. It is placed on a level with the work of governesses and servants. Such people have, in the opinion of the aristocracy, an office to perform, but no opinion to express, they have a duty but no importance, they are, as says the daughter of the lord of the castle on one occasion, mere supernumeraries. "They are only seen when the persons of consequence have withdrawn."[2]

But Dr. Oswald Stein is not a petty, maladroit tutor such as is elsewhere portrayed. With scholarly knowledge he combines excellent manners and the air of a man of the world, he is an adept at pistol-shooting and dancing, which are specifically aristocratic virtues, and as a man of intellect he gains the sympathy of Baron Oldenburg, an enlightened aristocrat belonging to this

der Erziehung und des Unterrichts, Bd. 1931, xxi. 243 ff.). The house-tutor as a character in literature at the end of the eighteenth century is described by Clara Stockmeyer in *Soziale Probleme im Drama des Sturm und Drang*.

Whilst in the eighteenth century even personalities like Hamann, Kant, Fichte, Hegel, Schleiermacher, Jean Paul, Hölderlin had been house-tutors for a long period in aristocratic families after the completion of their studies, the numbers of tutors decreased in the nineteenth century as a result of the re-organization of the high-school system as well as of the now independent occupation of high-school teacher. Yet writers like Laube (*c.* 1830) and Spielhagen (*c.* 1855) were still house-tutors with the country-nobility after completing their studies at the university. If the position of the house-tutor was partly a very oppressive one and sensitive natures like Hölderlin had to suffer a great deal under it, there are yet counter-examples of a harmonious relationship between a highly-intellectual house-tutor and a cultivated aristocrat. This applies especially to the activities of the young Schleiermacher in the house of Count Dohna-Schlobitten. Cf. W. Dilthey, *Das Leben Schleiermachers*, Berlin, 1870, i. 44–61.

[1] Cf. the memoirs of Spielhagen, *Finder und Erfinder*, ii. 106 and 440 ff., and of L. Mühlbach, *op. cit.*, p. 68.

[2] *Problematische Naturen, Sämtliche Werke*, Leipzig, 1872, i. 397.

circle.   But it is precisely because of his social qualities
that the position of this "problematic nature" becomes
doubly problematic.   Oswald, the aristocracy-hater, lives
within the circle of an aristocratic family, "half the friend
and half the servant."   The profession of tutor invokes
little enough regard in these circles.   "There must be
tutors," states one of these aristocrats, "just as there
must be labourers in the arsenic-mines, although I, for
my part, would like to be neither one nor the other." [1]

What is the picture of the Pomeranian country-nobility
that is offered to the intruder?   The intense contempt
for all socially-inferior strata is here allied with an astonishing ignorance and narrow-mindedness.   Spielhagen
makes his hero observe the "thin veneer of outward
culture which formed the whole of the so-called education of this privileged class."   It is a "leisure-class" [2]
par excellence that is here seen through bourgeois eyes.
Hunting-exploits, horse-racing and gambling, ambiguous gossip and boastfulness supply the topics of conversation   at   visits   and   parties.[3]   Its   solidarity   from
without only conceals the looseness of morality within.
Marital infidelity offers not rarely an interesting change
in a life of boredom.   The wife of B., for example, has
an aristocratic lover, whilst her husband keeps mistresses.
The aristocratic lack of concern in *rebus eroticis* gives the

[1] *Problematische Naturen, Sämtliche Werke*, Leipzig, 1872, i. 164.

[2] For the "leisure class" idea see Th. Veblen, *The Theory of the Leisure
Class*, London, 1924.

[3] An example of this feudalistic mode of life is to be found at that time
in Count O. F. Hahn-Basedow, the husband of the authoress, Countess Ida
Hahn-Hahn, who later divorced him.   One of the wealthiest landowners of
Mecklenburg, he kept his horses in stables fitted out with prodigality, establish-
ing himself as the leader of horse-racing in Germany.   As for intellectual
interests, the pleasure-seeking Junker had not the slightest capacity for appre-
ciating them.   (See E. I. Schmid-Jürgens, *Ida Gräfin Hahn-Hahn*, Berlin,
1933, pp. 13 ff.)

Fritz Reuter's novel, *Ut mine Stromtied*, the original draft of which was
written in High German, describes from intimate experience the glaring contrast between the carousing Junker always steeped in pleasure and the distress
of his tenants and labourers.   The Junkers are naturally interested in hunting-
dogs and thoroughbred stallions, but have not the slightest thought for their
servants.   Cf. R. Bender, *Manuscript eines Romans—die hochdeutsche Urgestalt
der "Stromtied*," Halle, 1930.

adroit tutor, Oswald, also his opportunities amongst the
ladies.   Perhaps besides his handsome face, it is precisely the charm of "social distance" that makes an adven-
ture with him interesting for the women of this circle.[1]
After various affairs with aristocratic girls and women,
the tutor attracts the interest of his employer's young
daughter who is to be married off by her parents to a
decadent, aristocratic heir, Felix von Grenwitz.   This
arouses jealousy in the heart of the injured fiancé who
organizes, in an impressive scene, a counterbloc by the
aristocratic clique that feels its class pride to be insulted
by the impertinence of the intruder.   Strengthened by
the support of this clique, the offended rival orders the
tutor with coarse words to perform a service for him
that is demanded only of inferior servants.   When the
tutor hesitates to carry out this order, the clique supplement Baron Felix's insults,[2] and a scuffle starts which
is stopped by the intervention of the "liberal" baron.
The logical consequence of such an affair of honour is,
according to the unwritten law of the aristocratic stratum,
a duel; and in this Baron Felix is seriously wounded,
but the tutor loses his position and has to shake the
aristocratic dust from his feet.   The intruder has been
shown his place and the aristocrats have acted according
to the maxim:

> These burghers are all alike.   As soon as they see that we
> want to be what we are of right—masters in the State and in
> the house—they humble themselves.   They only become pre-
> sumptuous through our own fault.   They must be continually
> reminded of their position.[3]

Conversely, the burgher observes, in the working of a
general law of social psychology, that the "esprit de
corps" of the aristocracy—as the specific attitude of a
group—is stronger if several aristocrats come into contact with a burgher than if one does.   "The aristocrat,"

---

[1] It is in the nature of that which is strange, owing to the charm the new
and the unknown has, to create a particular effect in which shyness, mistrust,
curiosity and readiness to open oneself to the new-comer are curiously mingled.

[2] Spielhagen, *Sämtliche Werke*, i. 547 ff.   [3] *Ibid.*, 1. 415.

affirms Oswald, "is only polite and genial to the burgher so long as he is alone with him, but if several are together, they coalesce as swiftly as quicksilver and bring out against the burgher their 'esprit de corps.' " [1]

Spielhagen traces the antithesis between aristocracy and burgher to the tendency shown by members of one social group to undervalue members of rival groups. "Never will the Catholic truly see his equal in the Protestant, nor the aristocrat his in the burgher, nor the Christian his equal in the Jew, and vice-versa." [2]

Besides the tutor, it is frequently the building-contractor and architect who are the non-nobles brought into contact with the country-nobility by their employment.   In the many-volumed novel of the Königsberg Jewess, Fanny Lewald, *Von Geschlecht zu Geschlecht* (1857), the building-contractor Herbert has to construct a chapel for the castle of an East Prussian Freiherr and, just like Dr. Oswald in *Problematische Naturen*, he proves himself efficient and adroit in his aristocratic surroundings.   At first the burgher is warmly received as a welcome change in the castle's monotony: he soon wins the goodwill of the lady of the castle, who compares him favourably with aristocrats: "For he possesses indeed—in the judgment of the baroness—the elegance of a man of our class and has more spirit, more heart, more energy, than many of our men."   Through this success, however, he—like the tutor in Spielhagen—arouses the jealousy of the baron, who now makes him feel the full sharpness of the difference in their social standing.[3]   The building-contractor is reminded that duty is the sole honour of the burgher, and that he comes under consideration only as a worker, but not as a cavalier. The contractor later avenges himself for this humiliation by sequestering, along with other burghers, the family's debt-ridden estate.

[1] Spielhagen, *Sämtliche Werke,* i. 149.   [2] *Ibid.,* i. 151.

[3] As a Jewess who is strongly sensible of the limitation of her racial group, as a woman who advocates equality of the sexes, Fanny Lewald took the part of all socially repressed groups. Cf. her memoirs, *Gefühltes und Gedachtes,* (1838–88), ed. L. Geiger, Dresden, 1900.

Whilst the contractor is at first accepted socially in the castle and then dropped, the relation between Baron and steward is a very distant one from the start. The steward is an official in the service of the nobleman and as such carries out the orders of his master. He stands socially between the nobleman and the contractor, but he and the contractor find strong points of contact in their common preference for burgher political ideas. And if the contractor at first feels himself honoured by his social intercourse with the socially superior aristocracy, so does the steward feel that association with the contractor is an honour for him.[1]

It was relatively easy for the aristocrat to use the middle-class skilled artisan and expert as a means to an end, and to remind him of his proper place if he should overstep the distance between them. But it was, in the nature of things, more difficult for him to subdue the *second type of intruder, the parvenu.* Him he usually regarded with the contemptuous hatred of rivalry, encountered him outwardly with cool reserve and was easily amused at the strenuous efforts of the newly ennobled who at one stroke wanted to give themselves a noble air and assimilate the ways of life of a strange tradition. But since one could only attain to the new nobility by reason of property and achievement, there was mingled in his contempt a secret envy.

We can best understand the essence of the parvenu by a comparison with the snob. It is common to both types to display flamboyantly any acquired social or economic position because they wish to belong, at any price, to a leading group or stratum in society. It is only the direction of their gaze that differs; the parvenu

---

[1] "The bailiff who knew himself to be superior in knowledge, efficiency and material wealth to some of the aristocrats who acted the great lord in the neighbourhood, and sometimes also in the castle, and before whom he had to bow and humble himself however much he might despise them, always felt himself exalted by contact and conversation with the architect, whom the Freiherr honoured as his guest and social equal whilst the former placed himself as an equal by the side of the steward" (*Von Geschlecht zu Geschlecht,* iv. 327).

looks up to the superior ones, to the stratum that is his model and aim, for he wants to prove that he belongs to it inwardly and outwardly; the snob, on the other hand, looks down to the inferior ones, for the distance between them and him is a source of pleasure and dignity. The parvenu wants to show that he now has and can do what others have long had and been able to do; the snob, however, wants to show that he has and can do what others have not and cannot do. The former lays stress on the assimilation, the latter on the exclusiveness of privileged qualities.

The parvenu wishes to be regarded as a member of an élite, the snob hates to be considered as a member of the masses. The parvenu assimilates himself, the snob draws himself away, but both are concerned with outward effects, with the effect on the world, and not with the real essence of the thing. In nineteenth-century Germany the striving parvenu type was dominant, but in nineteenth-century England the snob type prevailed.

Parvenuism usually occurs in a society where a rising stratum controls economic power, whilst political and social power still rests with the old leading classes. Snobbery, on the other hand, is more to be found in a society where the public privileges of a ruling stratum are unshakably valid and not questioned.

The social privileges of the aristocracy in nineteenth-century Germany were never so quiescently acknowledged as those of the aristocracy in England. The reason lies in the opportunity of rising possessed by the greater part of the middle-class in England, so that the appearance of this upper stratum could never signify a degrading of the socially lower-placed strata. The *nouveau riche*, the successful politician, the lawyer who was much sought after, could obtain a peerage in England and had thereby for themselves and their children the right, nay even the duty, to display the snobbery of the privileged. It is Thackeray who has best realized this connection between a comparatively easy access to

the nobility and snobbery in England.[1]   Snobbery is
here a phenomenon of public life which is just as much
liked and demanded by the spectators as by the actors,
that is by those who wish to see and often secretly
admire snobbery, as well as by those who display it.   In
such a society, nearly everyone wants at least to have
the possible chance of a future right to snobbery, he
is, so-to-speak, a latent snob and is therefore also ready
to vouchsafe it to the actual snobs.   In this sense
could Thackeray say: "It is impossible, in our condition
of society, not to be sometimes a snob." [2]

What was the attitude of the hereditary aristocracy
towards the plutocratic parvenu?

In the novel *In Reih und Glied* by Spielhagen (1866)
there is described the relationship between the hereditary nobility and the parvenu monied-nobility of semitic
origin.   The Freiherr von Tuchheim had helped the
banker Sonnenstein to acquire ennoblement after the
latter had gone over to Christianity.[3]   The rich banker,
on his part, had rendered the Baron financial services,
and the result of this connection was a marriage between
the children of the two families.   On neither side was
there any need to repent the bond thus made.   The
money and credit of the banking house proved their
usefulness more than once for the baronial relatives, and
the son of the newly-ennobled banker was, conversely,
proud of the honour of his alliance with a Fräulein von
Tuchheim.   The different situations of three genera-

---

[1] W. M. Thackeray, *The Book of Snobs*, chap. iii, "The Influence of the
Aristocracy on Snobs."

[2] *Ibid.*   Also Meredith has shrewdly recognized the function of snobbery
in Victorian England.   (See B. Alberts-Arndt, *Die englische Gesellschaft im
Spiegel der Romane von Meredith*, Karlsruhe, 1931, i. 16–23.)

[3] This method of achieving social success for the merchant is typical for
the years between 1820 and 1830.   It is also confirmed by the following
observation of Prince Pückler: "The merchant, whether of Christian or pre-
Christian persuasion, finds his credit, and if he knows how to manage, useful
protection also; indeed, a lot of money is almost worth as much as being a
real privy councillor, and if the rich bankers live in a good style they will be
counted as belonging to the privileged Estates, and will even sometimes be
raised to the aristocracy" (*Briefe eines Verstorbenen*, 1831, i. 35).

tions of this parvenu family are sketched in the novel.
The newly-ennobled banker remains, in spite of his
Christianity and the arms on his carriage-door, a butt
of mockery: "When one needed his money, one made
him reverences and told him the nicest things; but
behind his back one shrugged one's shoulders, and in
the street the boys shouted 'Hep!'—'Hep!' after him." [1]
The son, who inherited his father's business, is still
stained with the blemish of work as far as society is
concerned, and he himself clearly feels this blemish.
On the other hand, he is filled with the demon of capitalism, and urges the inexperienced Freiherr to indus-
trialize his estates.   He whispers into his ear that a poor
aristocrat is no aristocrat, and if the aristocrat does not
want to yield to the striving burgher, then he must keep
pace with him in the acquisition of wealth.

The Freiherr does indeed follow his advice, but the
rationalist ways of the parvenu disgust him.   The
banker is too positive and calculates too well.   A feeling of strangeness between the old aristocrat and the
capitalist *arriviste*, between a leisured dignity and an
actively calculating frame of mind, also emerges.   We
are concerned here with a typical conflict between a
traditional and a rationalist outlook.   The Freiherr
thinks of his relative as a natural force that has no
inner contact with him and his like.

> I believe that he is fond of me [is the feeling of the Freiherr]
> so far as that is possible for him: but I am convinced that he
> would cold-bloodedly reckon me out of his life, if I no longer
> fitted into his calculations in some way or other.[2]

It is not until the third generation of the newly-ennobled family that the traces of parvenuism, the uncertain attitude of transition, are obliterated.   Not till
then does the luxury of the elegant attitude replace
sober work.   The banker has two children, a son and
a daughter.

[1] *In Reih und Glied*, Leipzig, 1872, 3rd Ed., ii. 212.
[2] *Ibid.*, ii. 212–14.

You have [he tells them with satisfaction] ancient noble blood in your veins; your position in society is quite different from mine. *Alfred does not know what work is:* it is my pride, that he does not need to know it, that he can live his life of enjoyment like any cavalier. I have never held a card in my hand; Alfred has already lost more at cards than ten such aristocratic starvelings are worth taken together. It is my pride.[1]

The decadent son copies the elegant ways of the man of the world as he had seen them in the house of his aristocratic cousin. He associates only with Counts, Barons, officers, ambassadorial attachés, he rides the best horses, gives the finest suppers and plays a part in the *demi-monde.*

Gambling and nonchalance are here aptly observed by Spielhagen to be the essential attributes of the feudal way of life, of the really "elegant" existence. One of the most important demands that the European aristocracy made for the recognition of the parvenu was that the latter should show a serious interest in gambling. For, as Max Weber once expressed it, "gambling inevitably has, in the life of the feudal strata, the rôle of a highly serious and important business: a counter-weight to the whole rational economic behaviour which lies as an obstacle in its path." [2]

Thus the development of this family in the novel is a statement of the sociological observation that the bourgeois who grows rich seeks as quickly as possible to forget his origin and to rise into the country-nobility or at least into the feudal landowner-class.[3]

The scorn felt for the parvenu has various roots: firstly, a feeling of defence against the *homo novus,* the intruder into an exclusive sphere whose balance of power it threatens: secondly, a snobbish feeling of superiority in the hereditary aristocracy, because it has cultivated its ways of life "organically" and is therefore certain of

[1] *Ibid.*
[2] Max Weber, *Wirtschaft und Gesellschaft*, chap. viii, p. 750.
[3] Cf. for England the remarks of Disraeli in *Sybil*, 1845, chap. vi.

them, whilst the parvenu must suddenly assimilate these forms "inorganically" and, because of his lack of experience and tradition, appear with them like a man in ill-fitting clothes.

The defamation of the *homo novus* through the weapon of satire and caricature has been, since the time of the Romans, a common feature in the upper stratum threatened by intruders. Even the "aristocratic" wealth of the industrialists and merchants who have "arrived" a long time before turns voluntarily against the pressing display of upward striving strata. Their style of life is that of an intermediate station: it corresponds *no longer* to that of the *original stratum* from which the parvenu comes, and it does *not yet* correspond to the *stratum at which it aims* and whose attitude of life the parvenu wants to assimilate.

B. *The Conciliatory Attitude.*—The Junker—as we have seen—regarded the rising burghers with mistrust, displeasure and contempt: he sought to preserve his exclusiveness even whilst the decrease of distance was in progress. *The attitude of the unbiassed aristocratic type*, of the *enlightened "liberal" aristocrat*, is of quite a different character, however: and it is this that we shall now proceed to describe.

The enlightened aristocrat is reserved towards his own Estate, as well as possessing insight into the changing structure of society in the period of incipient industrialism: he therefore accepts the changing equilibrium of society with that calmness which springs from a realization of the inevitable. He is usually an individualist and has broadened his horizon partly by his inclination for art and science, partly by his schooling in the world through travel or through the exercise of high office. In contrast with the Junker, he has not only trained his desires, but has also educated and refined his intellect.

The independent outlook that is peculiar to him expressed itself in various ways in the course of the nineteenth century. The "liberalism" of his attitude

could, according to his individuality, be more passive
or more active, more unpolitical or more political, more
that of a literary world-citizen or more that of a national
parliamentarian.   *Between 1800 and 1840 it is very often
the type of the intellectual nobleman educated in philosophy
and literature* that stands out; *between 1840 and 1900*, on
the other hand, corresponding to the change in the
political and cultural structure of society, it is *the aristocratic leader of the liberal parties in Parliament, possessed
of a juristic and administrative training.*   The part that
the enlightened aristocrat first played was that of an
interested spectator in the social and political tension
within society.   Later, however, he came down on the
side of the middle-classes and took over the leadership
of the middle-class opposition.

The *intellectual aristocrat* plays a significant part in
the literature of the first half of the nineteenth century.
He is to be found in the writings of the young Germans
(Laube, Heine, Gutzkow) as well as in the books of
political liberals after 1848 (Spielhagen, Freytag).   He
is regarded by them all as a typical "modern being."
The high appreciation shown for him betokens the secret
admiration of the middle-class writer for the man of the
world, the hope of being read and being taken seriously
by him.

Otto von Dystra in Gutzkow's *Ritter vom Geiste*, Baron
Oldenburg in Spielhagen's *Problematische Naturen* and
Herr von Fink in Freytag's *Soll und Haben* personify
this aristocratic man of the world.   He belongs either
to the diplomatic aristocracy or to the newly ennobled
patriciate.   He combines the characteristics of the
cavaliers (bearing, good manners, inner independence
as a consequence of outward independence) with knowledge of the world and literary culture.   In contrast with
the provincial outlook of the Junker, he knows all sorts
of men, classes and countries.   He is blasé, yet not
narrow; does not cling to any clique, but is not without
solidarity with congenial spirits in all camps.   In Otto
von Dystra or Baron Oldenburg, contemporaries saw

this type deftly portrayed.[1] Otto von Dystra appears
as a much-travelled diplomat who, like Prince Pückler,
returns home from his roving expeditions with niggers
and monkeys. He is "interested" in all progressive
movements and is therefore also brought close to the
circle of the *Ritter vom Geiste* (described above), less on
account of their ideas, than because of the secret character of this organization which exerts a peculiar charm
on the blasé men of the world.[2]

To such a modern sort of person belong [thus runs a contemporary comment of Gutzkow on Otto von Dystra] noble descent, rank, wealth, possibly an estate, experience of the world
and the gift of elegant conversation, independence and freedom
of thought. Such brilliant capabilities result continually from
world-wide relationships and are bewildered by nothing.[3]

This type, as we hear later, is culturally productive: both
as stimulator and as a creator of his own ideas, he has
won a significant place in the history of literature and
culture. Count Bückeburg, Count Schlabrendorf, the
"apostle of the French Revolution in Paris,"[4] the
scientist Count Buquoy, the philosopher Franz von
Baader and the writer Prince Pückler-Muskau are
quoted as examples.[5]

Of these, Prince Pückler-Muskau has a special importance in our connection as an enlightened, seigneurial
writer.[6] One of the foremost nobles of Prussia's First
Estate, former officer, and married to the daughter of
the Chancellor von Hardenberg, Prince Pückler was at

[1] See A. Jung, *Briefe über Gutzkows "Ritter vom Geiste,"* Leipzig, 1856,
p. 200. " The actual originals will be easily recognized by everyone, for the
copies are true to the smallest hair."

[2] A. Jung, *op. cit.,* p. 197. These modern aristocrats "are as a rule greatly
attracted, often indeed greatly enthused, by every sort of secret organization,
like free-masonry."

[3] A. Jung, *ibid.*

[4] For him see also Eichendorff, *Sämtliche Werke,* x. 397.

[5] It is significant that three of them spent a long period abroad: Count
Schlabrendorf in France, Count Bückeburg in England and Prince Pückler-
Muskau in England, France, North Africa, Egypt, Greece and Asia Minor.

[6] For Prince Pückler cf. *Allg. Deutsche Biographie,* 1888, Bd. 25, pp. 692–5;
E. M. Butler, *The Tempestuous Prince,* Cambridge, 1929; A. Erhard, *Le Prince
Pückler,* Paris, 1927, vol. i.

the same time an extensive traveller, a peculiar and self-willed contrast to the more-or-less stay-at-home majority of members of his own class. He combined an extraordinary imagination with an original personality, and took joy in intellectual experiments in a way peculiar only to an aristocrat. But mere rank based on blood and Estate was for Pückler no longer the sole criterion: his modest attitude towards a Goethe shows that he acknowledged the primacy of the mind over blood and rank.

In the famous *Briefe eines Verstorbenen*, a fragmentary diary concerning England, Wales, Ireland and France, written in the years 1828 and 1829, Prince Pückler illuminates sharply, and with wit, the social relations in Germany and Western Europe, comparing the situation and ways of life of the German and English aristocracy. The writer allows himself no illusions about the increasing impoverishment and decline in power of the German aristocracy. The aristocracy, he maintains, is now merely tolerated: the stronger forces of the bureaucracy and plutocracy claim the field.[1] Quite different is the position of the English aristocracy. Here he distinguishes between the town- and court-nobility on one side, and the landed-gentry on the other. For the looseness of manners, the dandyism [2] and intellectual emptiness of the English court-nobility, the foreign observer finds sharp words. He prophesies the decline of this branch of the English aristocracy within the next half-century unless it completely reforms itself. This rather independent mind admires, however, the healthiness and self-sufficiency of the English gentry whose circumstances of life are so much more favourable than those of the German Junker.[3]

---

[1] Cf. *Briefe eines Verstorbenen*, i. 34–7.

[2] For dandyism in the nineteenth century and the forms it assumed in life, see the interesting study by O. Mann, *Der Dandy*, Berlin, 1925.

[3] Pückler's criticism of the English court-nobility is, of course, biassed, since the object of his journey, which was to marry the daughter of a wealthy English lord in order to repair his fortunes, came to nought. He, himself a dandy, although more than a dandy, finds at court only blasé hedonists

The extraordinary success that the *Briefe* met with is largely to be explained by the social position of the author, for through this work literature became actually "aristocratic" and the aristocracy, conversely, fitted for literature. Even amongst the provincial nobility it was considered good tone to read the *Briefe*.[1] The middle-class, however, was attracted by the unconcerned frankness and the social criticism of the highly-placed anonymous. Amongst the middle-class writers, sympathy with the interesting aristocrat (shown by Heine, Laube, Menzel) outweighed the immovable hatred of the aristocracy (represented by Börne) and the jealousy of competition (shown by Gutzkow and Immermann). Varnhagen von Ense observed well the connection between the intellectual aristocrat and a section of the Young German writers. Pückler, he declared, possessed in common with the Young Germans complete freedom of spirit. *In German literature he represented the Upper House just as Heine represented the Lower House.*[2] Varnhagen described at the same time the astonishing success of the writer who was simultaneously seigneurial and enlightened.

The name of Prince Pückler acts on men like magic. The whole universe listens when anyone speaks of him. He has an overwhelming reputation, and the cleverer the people the more they value him. His literary qualities are raised by his social station, and vice versa. Since we have no war and therefore no outstanding warriors, then literary fame is all the more important.[3]

There can be no doubt as to the function of this princely literature for the middle-class. It was the function of a substitute, of a makeshift of imagination,

and dandies. The English dandy, according to Pückler, lacks feeling, is unmoral and arrogant, and the only thing to which he is capable of devoting himself is fashion. He might, finally, even become virtuous, if virtue were fashionable. *Briefe eines Verstorbenen*, iv. 397 ff.

[1] Cf. for Silesia the observations of H. Laube in *Moderne Charakteristiken,* Mannheim, 1835, ii, chap. 18, pp. 305–19.

[2] Cf. George Brandes, *Die Literatur des 19. Jahrhunderts in ihren Hauptströmungen,* Leipzig, 1891, vi. 379 f.

[3] K. A. Varnhagen von Ense, *Tagebücher,* Leipzig, 1861, i. 142.

for strata to whom the desired access to the wide world, to international society, still remained for the most part closed.[1]   Heine dedicated his letters of travel to Prince Pückler and was proud of his friendship with him; and Laube, who imitated some of the Prince's literary forms in his travel pictures, found protection with him against persecution by the Prussian police.

It is worthy of note in our connection to see how Prince Pückler, as an enlightened aristocrat, in contrast with Goethe,[2] the *arriviste* Patrician's son, maintained the necessity of a constitution.   He did so with the reference to the English model.[3]   Goethe, however, held firmly to a quietist, conservative standpoint and was of the opinion that if every man "would concern himself only with labouring with loyalty and love in his special sphere, be it a great or small, then general blessedness would not be lacking whatever the form of government."   In contrast, Prince Pückler saw in the constitutional form of government just those necessary conditions of Goethe's

[1] Gutzkow on one occasion describes this interest of non-aristocratic circles in aristocratic cultural production from the point of view of the middle-class author fearing the threat of literary competition: "Strange also was the effect produced by each venture of a princely person into the sphere of art or literature; that Prince Radziwill composed, that Duke Karl of Mecklenburg-Strelitz acted comedies or rather, as was believed, wrote comedies under the name of Karl Weishaupt, was a piece of news received with delight and hawked around *as if it meant that one knew something quite special and that one almost belonged to the circles of the exclusive oneself*" (K. Gutzkow, *Rückblicke auf mein Leben*, Berlin, 1875, p. 68 f.).

[2] How very much Goethe admired Prince Pückler as a cultural aristocrat, is shown by a paragraph in his review of the *Briefe eines Verstorbenen*.   "A work significant for the literature of Germany.   Here we make the acquaintance of an eminent man in his best years, the forties, a man *born in a higher Estate where one does not need to wear oneself out before reaching a certain level,* where one early finds opportunity to be the smith fashioning one's own happiness—and if the work misses its mark, we have ourselves to blame for it. The writer appears as an experienced man of the world possessed of spirit and vivid comprehension, as a man who has been educated in the higher relationships by a life of travel and changing society, and furthermore also, as a persevering, enlightened German, who is at home in literature and art" (S. v. Arnim, *Goethe und Fürst Pückler*, Dresden, 1932, p. 23 f.).

[3] Goethe turned precisely against England as the classical land of liberalism in action and example of a constitutional state.   He claimed: ". . . in no land is egoism more predominant, no people perhaps fundamentally more inhuman in its political and private relationships" (S. v. Arnim, *ibid.*, p. 14).

principle "because it obviously confirms in every individual the conviction of greater security for person and
property, resulting in cheerful activity, thereby giving
rise at the same time to the most reliable patriotism."[1]
But the liberalism of Prince Pückler remained in the
period that followed, a purely theoretical one; he took
no part in the later struggle between the old and new
powers, middle-class and aristocracy, in 1848.

The figure of the intellectual, liberal Grandseigneur
after the fashion of Pückler has been best preserved in
Baron Oldenburg in Spielhagen's *Problematische Naturen*
(1864). Widely travelled, well-read and cultured, the
baron is considered by the Junker of his homeland as
an unpleasant outsider. Being really lonely he is nearly
always travelling, and only appears from time to time
on his Pomeranian estates. To the annoyance of the
country-nobility, he parades as a typically free spirit
and, in the opinion of the members of his own Estate,
so far forgets himself at district diets (*Kreistage*) and
provincial diets (*Landtage*) as to support the party of
innovation at every opportunity. His position outside
the aristocratic circle is expressed in the superior mockery
with which he reduces the prejudices and backwardness of
the aristocratic caste *ad absurdum*. He delivers grotesque
reports of his travels amongst foreign peoples to the
ignorant Junkers, and he renders the ideology of the
aristocratic privilege ridiculous in a delicious persiflage.[2]

Baron Oldenburg, as we have already seen, is drawn
towards the middle-class tutor, Dr. Stein, and feels a
common bond with him in their ideal of the cultured
and pleasure-loving man of the world. Both are por-

---

[1] S. v. Arnim, *Goethe und Fürst Pückler*, Dresden, 1932, p. 13 f.

[2] The baron tells, for example, at an aristocrats' party, of a document which
he found on his travels in the library of a monastery. According to it, God
divided mankind from the beginning, creating it as an aristocratic and a
middle-class couple. The aristocratic gentleman and his lady possessed the
country-estate "Paradise," and their servants Adam and Eve proved themselves
such good-for-nothings that at last the gentleman took his whip and drove
them both from the court. In the servants-register, however, he inscribed it
as "dismissed for dishonesty, love of finery, and work-shyness" (*Problematische
Naturen, Sämtliche Werke*, i. 172–7).

trayed as "problematic natures" in Goethe's sense of the
word, i.e. as characters who cannot cope with any situation in which they happen to be and who are themselves
not satisfied with any situation.[1]   Both are to be found
in the end fighting side by side on the barricades of 1848
against the aristocratic caste and its arbitrariness.

Baron Oldenburg preserves his individuality in the
midst of the backward Junker world; the figure of the
young Herr von Fink in Freytag's *Soll und Haben*, on
the other hand, stands out through contrast with the
world of an honest, sober trading house wherein Herr
von Fink moves as a volunteer worker.   Herr von Fink
possesses, indeed, all the nature of the lordly aristocrat,
but his origin and eventful life have completely freed
him from the narrowness and provincialism of the
average Junker; for he is the son of an aristocratic
merchant and as such has already led an exotic life in
America.   From America he returns to his father in
Germany, gives up for the time being his ambition to
become a farmer and enters a wholesale firm as a volunteer.   Here he leads a double life, by day the negligent
businessman, secretly admired by the rest of the per-
sonnel, by night the elegant cavalier.   Indicative of this
medial existence, there is to be found in his room a book-
case next to a gun-cabinet: he seems to be just as interested in horses as in music.   Amongst the elegant,
chiefly aristocratic, youth of the town he is regarded as
an authority in the domain of seigneurial pleasure, such
as horse-riding and hunting-parties.

He was young, adroit, of noble birth, passed as immeasurably
wealthy and possessed a mastery in all things which could possibly be thought of in connection with a horse's hoof, a gun-

---

[1] Spielhagen himself later admitted that he had not succeeded in piercing
the peculiar private spheres of his characters and in explaining the mode of
existence of these problematic natures by the wretchedness of public life before
1848, for "the insufficiency of public conditions could then," as he said retro-
spectively in a self-criticism, "excuse men if they, for their part, showed themselves to be without joy and hope and no longer properly able to cope with
their special occupations and tasks" (*Finder und Erfinder*, Leipzig, 1890,
ii. 440).

barrel and a gold-plated tea-spoon—and what stood out above everything was that he treated everyone who came into contact with him with the easy self-assurance that has always passed amongst the great majority of men who lack independence as a sign of superiority.[1]

We are not interested here in the ultimate fate and adventures of this crazy Junker, but content ourselves with two observations. Firstly, the fact that, at bottom, sober commercial work does not quite suit even this lordly and lively person, with the result that he finally prefers the freer and more generous life of a landowner and farmer; secondly, the noticeably small regard shown for the ennoblement which Herr von Fink achieved by his knowledge of the world and especially by his experiences in America.[2]

The share of aristocrats in the leadership of the liberal German middle-class between 1847 and 1900 has hitherto scarcely been examined and assessed by sociological and historical research.[3] In this place only a

[1] G. Freytag, *Gesammelte Werke*, iv. 115.

[2] In the same way as between the baron and the house-tutor in Spielhagen, there develops also in *Soll und Haben* a friendship between the self-willed aristocrat and the worthy middle-class employee, Anton Wohlfahrt. This friendship arises characteristically from a quarrel, when the burgher refuses to allow his aristocratic colleague to use him as a servant. Later the aristocrat prepares for himself the great satisfaction of smuggling his friend into an exclusively aristocratic circle by all sorts of secretive references to his high descent, and at the same time plays the "devil's advocate" for the middle-class against the aristocracy. He continually strengthens the middle-class self-confidence of his modest friend, and in doing so symbolically helps towards the decrease of class-differences, towards the closer co-operation of aristocracy and middle-class, which was dear to the heart of Freytag himself: "It is just you and the people like you who have more right to carry their heads high," he observes on one occasion to Anton Wohlfahrt, "being the largest section of the society that will foregather there. Anton, it is just you who now through awkward conduct, now through servility, preserve the pretensions of the country Junker families. How can you therefore think yourself inferior to anybody else?" (*loc. cit.*, iv. 164 f.).

[3] The social phenomenon of the leadership of a class by personalities who derive from another class can be deeply observed for the nineteenth century in the leaders of the German middle-classes and the proletariat. The fact that numerous liberal aristocrats appeared at the head of the middle-class opposition is mentioned by H. Oncken in his biography of *Rudolf von Bennigsen*, Berlin, 1910, i. 20, without, however, inquiring into the sociological causes of this fact.

few sentences can be devoted to it.   A considerable percentage of the liberal leaders in the German parliaments
between 1847 and 1890 were aristocrats.   For instance,
the president of the German national assembly of 1848 in
Frankfort was a Franconian noble, Heinrich von Gagern,
whilst at the same time the presidency of the Prussian
National Assembly in Berlin was filled by the son of a
Prussian general, H. V. von Unruh.   The old aristocracy
produced, further, the liberal opposition leaders von
Vincke, von Auerswald, and Count Schwerin, the last
two of whom later became liberal ministers.   The leader
of the *Deutscher Nationalverein* (founded 1851), and later
of the national-liberal party, was the Hanoverian aristocrat R. von Bennigsen, and there stood with him at the
head of the national-liberal party the deputies von
Stauffenberg and von Forchenbeck.

We can sum up matters by saying that for the intellectual aristocrat, individualism is the real root of his
liberal attitude.   Because he desires to live his life as
an individual in the sense of the Renaissance, he turns
against the restrictive limits of his Estate; because he
strives for wider fields, he finds congenial natures in
other strata and classes.   He is interested rather in
individual people of the middle-class, than in the middle-
class as a whole; he nearly always prefers enjoyment
rather than work, interesting dilettantism rather than
serious devotion to any one thing.

It is significant of the characteristic difference of *the
aristocratic liberal politician* from the intellectual aristocrat,
that the former not only displays a liberal trend of
thought, but completely identifies himself with liberal
policy, becoming indeed often its parliamentary standard-
bearer against the members of his own Estate.   In the
novel it is nearly always the intellectual aristocrat who
plays the greater rôle; in historical actuality, however,
it is the type of the aristocratic liberal politician.   If
we glance at the evolution of these aristocrats, it will
be seen that they had not all originally been officers or
farmers, but academically educated jurists and officials

who had already come into close contact with burghers at school and university.   They possessed an intimate acquaintance with the administration, and consequently were often filled with the specific aristocratic resentment against the bureaucratic machine which was also not foreign to the conservative Bismarck.   As liberals, they placed little value on their descent, but a great deal on practical knowledge and general culture.   They were "renegades to the lower regions." [1]

Most of them gave up their posts in the government service after a few years, partly out of dislike for the "job," partly as a result of conflicts between them and their superiors arising out of their opposition views. After surrendering their official posts they became, like Gagern or Bennigsen,[2] professional politicians, possessing as such the advantage over the burghers of a better economic basis in their family estates.   Both their experience in government service, as well as their social origin which impressed the liberal voters not a little,[3] were of benefit to them in their parliamentary activities. This liberal aristocratic parliamentarian, whose historical importance cannot be over-emphasized, has, remarkably, been scarcely described in the German novel. Although writers like Spielhagen and Freytag were intimately acquainted with eminent representatives of this

[1] Cf. A. Meusel, *Die Abtrünnigen, Kölner Vierteljahrsschrift für Soziologie,* iii. 152–69.

[2] The typical development of the liberal aristocratic parliamentarian can be particularly analysed in the examples afforded by v. Gagern and Bennigsen. A brief reference must suffice in connection with our theme.   For H. v. Gagern see the article in the *Allg. Deutsche Biographie,* Bd. 49, pp. 654 ff; further, P. Wentzke, *Zur Geschichte H. v. Gagerns* in *Quellen und Darstellungen zur Geschichte der deutschen Burschenschaft und der deutschen Einheitsbewegung,* Heidelberg, 1910.

[3] Cf., for example, the valuation of Bennigsen as leader of liberal opposition in the Hanoverian Parliament in a newspaper report of 1858: "Free from all aristocratic pride and free in his innermost spirit, having early descended, indeed, to the lowest strata of society, he yet does at least hold fast to the social privileges and differences of culture.   His inability to lower himself without noticeable effort is accounted a decisive defect in the leader by a party consisting for the most part of peasants, but it is the only one" (quoted in Oncken, *op. cit.,* i. 290).   This type of "renegade" has therefore gone over to the lower classes only ideologically, not socially.

type,[1] we do not find them reflected in their works. Contemporary critics of these writers have already felt this omission to be damaging.[2]

Only once did Spielhagen, in whose works numerous reactionary aristocratic figures are to be found, portray a liberal aristocratic politician: and even this one, State-Councillor Arthur von Hohenstein in the novel *Die von Hohenstein* (1863), is negatively and contemptuously described. Arthur von Hohenstein is a parasitical beneficiary of his medial position between aristocracy and middle-class in the period round about 1848, which he, the son of a lord-lieutenant, occupies through his misalliance with the sister of an aspiring printer and inventor. Because of this misalliance, he gives up his class and his officer's career and enters as a partner into the book-printing business of his brother-in-law. But the elegant aristocrat cannot reconcile himself to the sober middle-class everyday life and prefers to exercise the adventurous urge of the former officer in speculation on the Stock Exchange. He succeeds through fortunate dealings in a period of prosperity and becomes one of the most respected men in the Rhineland town. The aristocracy indeed rejects him, as before, but he is wel-

---

[1] Gustav Freytag, for example, was for decades friendly with Duke Ernst of Saxe-Coburg-Gotha, the leader of the German National Union; and Spielhagen came into close contact with R. v. Bennigsen during his activity as an editor in Hannover (1861). Th. Fontane alone planned to portray the character of a liberal aristocrat modelled on Bennigsen, in an unfinished political novel (cf. J. Petersen, *Fontanes Altersromane, Euphorion*, vol. 29, 1928, p. 65). The reason for this omission lies perhaps in the polemical attitude of those liberals for whom, in the heat of battle, the branding of the average aristocratic enemy seemed more important than the praising of a few renegade exceptions.

[2] The question is postulated in this way, for example, by J. L. Hoffmann in his critical appreciation of Gutzkow's *Ritter vom Geiste*. "Does he believe that the independent aristocracy has died out? The aristocracy which, loyal, self-sacrificing, cultured and ethical even in a time like ours so unfavourable to this institution, still produces amongst both men and women many a powerful, courageous, blossoming shoot? Should the debt-ridden, immoral, crude old prince alone be the representative of the aristocracy, or his bastard, now sentimental now blasé, self-willed and stubborn with the possession of power, physically and mentally broken before his time? Should these latter be the representatives of the aristocracy in the country of Schwerin and Vincke, in the period of a Gagern reviled only by party-hatred?" (*Album des literarischen Vereins in Nürnberg*, 1854, p. 221).

comed all the more by the bourgeoisie with open arms.
Herr von Hohenstein understands how to make a virtue
of necessity in his border-line position.

Liberalism was then the order of the day, and by assiduously
displaying a cheap freemindedness, Arthur von Hohenstein, provoked by the inexorable hardness of members of his class and
especially by the consequent contempt he had to suffer from his
own brothers, created for himself in the easiest way in the world the
reputation of a well-meaning, true-hearted man. . . .   It flattered
the broad-shouldered, well-to-do burgher that the slender white
hand of a "von So-and-so" should place itself with a slight pressure in his clumsy, rough hands.[1]

The burghers therefore elected the aristocrat a town-
councillor and the government confirmed the election
since it well knew the disposition of Herr von Hohenstein's "liberalism." [2]

Whilst we seek vainly in the German novel for the
figure of the aristocratic leader of the liberal opposition,
we do find there a kind of related type, the *liberal
aristocratic officer*. The liberal officer is a border-line
figure; he stands in sharp contradiction to the ideology
and unwritten standards of his group, the officers' corps.
The Prussian officers' corps in the nineteenth century
formed a closed, elegantly aristocratic group in which
especially the younger sons of landed-proprietors found
their livelihood and profession. Its members constituted only a small number, for promotion in the long
years of peace was very slow and the surrender of personal
freedom demanded of every officer was very strict.   The
officer was therefore privileged like no other class.   He
enjoyed a public reward for the most valuable activity
in the State. Whilst the importance of the agrarian
function of the aristocracy waned, that of the military
function remained and its high prestige was now even
carried over to those officers who came from the middle-
classes. The principle prevailed that the sword ennobles.

[1] *Die von Hohenstein, Sämtliche Werke,* iv. 91.
[2] A case of this kind is reported in the civic history of Berlin (1808) by
H. Preuss, *Die Entwicklung des Deutschen Städtewesens,* i. 287.

The officer was allowed to introduce into the middle-class life of the nineteenth century the tone of master towards subordinate, taken from the barracks and manor-house; no businessman and no village-magistrate would have dared to demand satisfaction from him for so doing.[1]

The army was an institution of the State, i.e. of the stratum exercising and controlling political power; it had the function of protecting this stratum without and within, and of embodying its power. Originating almost wholly from the dominating feudal stratum, the officers' corps remained conservative and naturally regarded with hostility any currents and tendencies that threatened the power of the feudal stratum in the State.

The liberal officer, on the other hand, largely identified himself with liberal-democratic views and ideas propagated by the middle-class. He therefore supported, above everything, the reorganization of the feudal army as a national army in which the reserve officers, who were almost exclusively from the middle-class, would not have a lower standing than the usually aristocratic professional officers.[2] The democratic current of 1848 wished further to bridge the huge gulf between the officers' corps and the non-commissioned officer, and strove for the possibility of promotion for capable non-commissioned officers (i.e. for soldiers of simple origin and without higher education) to the rank of officer. The officers' corps, however, saw in these plans a threat to its prestige. The liberal aristocratic professional officer who sympathized with the 1848 revolution was a very rare exception in Prussia. In Bavaria, however (which, with a different social structure, had already progressed further on the road to parliamentarianism), he was more fre-

[1] F. Schnabel, *Deutsche Geschichte im 19. Jahrhundert*, ii. 330.
[2] The tension existing in Prussia between the active officers of the line and the reserve-officers of the territorial army had (up to 1860) social causes. The territorial officer was of middle-class origin, often from a petty-bourgeois milieu, and was therefore looked down upon by the, mainly, aristocratic officers' corps of the line. (See K. Demeter, *Das Deutsche Offizierskorps in seinen historisch-soziologischen Grundlagen*, Berlin, 1930, p. 22.)

quently to be met with.[1]   It happened there that gifted
and independent natures, seized by the liberal currents
of the time, saw through the mistakes and faults of
the military institutions.   Much more cultured than
the majority of their class and profession, they were
more than mere military specialists and creatures of
routine.

The liberal officer of noble origin, who was subject
to a sharp conflict between *esprit de corps* and his own
convictions, has been fully described by Gutzkow in *Die
Ritter vom Geiste* and by Spielhagen in his tendencious
novel *Die von Hohenstein*.   Both writers show an unmistakable sympathy for this—one might say—tragic
type.   With both authors the conflict between officers'
corps and liberal outsider in the revolutionary period
of 1848–9 comes to a head, and ends with the expulsion
of the liberal officer who then either joins the ranks of
a progressive élite (as in Gutzkow), or a democratic
revolutionary army (as in Spielhagen).[2]

The gradual process of the estrangement of the independent outsiders from the officers' corps, and its accompanying tension, are well observed by both authors.   On
one occasion the guards-major von Bredow bitterly
explains his isolated position to the circle of the *Ritter
vom Geiste*.   He stands, as he knows, at a forlorn post
and gives hurtful offence on all sides.   The threatening
atmosphere of this situation makes him feel isolated, and
he envies the burghers who can find support in the

[1] The revolution had only a negative effect on the Prussian officers' corps;
it crowded all the more strongly than before around king and throne under
the impulse of the rejection of all liberal tendencies.   In Bavaria, on the other
hand, a number of liberal officers, including Count Bothmer the later Chief
of General Staff, caused themselves to be suspected of liberal tendencies.   (See
K. Demeter, *op. cit.*, pp. 158 and 338 f.)

[2] Gutzkow perceives sharply the levelling effect of the revolution: "A
major of the guards, an aristocrat, Herr v. Werdeck, taking part in such
a debate with an advocate, a technician!   That is, indeed, a picture of a
disturbed time!   All had plunged into public affairs.   Every restriction had,
for a time at least, fallen to the ground.   There was soon, indeed, a return
to the old stations of life, but many a man still maintained himself in his
advanced position and actually burnt the boats which could take him back
to his earlier way of life" (*Die Ritter vom Geiste*, vi. 268 ff.).

sympathy of the members of their class and of their friends. The major finds himself torn between devotion to his soldierly profession and his reformative convictions, between professional honour and rejection by the officers' corps.

Now one may say: Get out of the ranks of fighters who recognize only the aristocrat as commander, get out!—[this is how the guard-officer states the extremes of his position]. But this, for him who has once chosen the profession of soldier, is just the same position as for a priest who may no longer mount the pulpit where he has preached in contradiction to the will of the consistory: the priest who feels himself to be a Christian will strive his utmost against leaving the community. The career which one chooses can harmonize completely with one's nature. I am a soldier . . . why should I fly the field? [1]

Major von Degenfeld also, in Spielhagen, feels his medial position to be full of tension. Contrasted with his colleague in Gutzkow, he is more scholar than soldier, more man-of-the-world than fighter. He loses the favour of his superior officer and the sympathy of his comrades when he produces a book on the reform of the army. In it he not only sharply criticizes weapons and tactics, parades and garrison-service, but demands the gradual reorganization of the army as a national army with promotion for non-commissioned officers. The fact alone that an officer had engaged in literary activity, arouses suspicion and dislike in the corps at that time, it being considered a breach of discipline.

For since the counter-revolution of 1849, the Prussian officer could have only one conviction—a monarchist, anti-liberal one. This was taken "for granted" through his loyalty to the crown and needed no apologia or exegesis. "To become a representative of the people was regarded as not indecent only if one did it as a champion of the conservative party." [2] Therefore the

---

[1] *Die Ritter vom Geiste*, vi. 269.

[2] F. C. Endres, *Soziologische Struktur und dazugehörige Ideologien des deutschen Offizierscorps vor dem Weltkriege, Archiv für Sozialwissenschaft und Sozialpolitik*, 1927, vol. 58, p. 309.

politically-minded officer, the political writer in uniform, was disliked in the feudal stratum.   The anti-rationalist mentality of the soldier, which had for centuries placed little value on the handiwork of writers and the arguments of intellectuals, still predominated amongst the overwhelming majority of the Prussian officers' corps in the nineteenth century.[1]   It found its classical expression in the admonition of a Prussian commander : "A Prussian general dies—but he leaves behind no memoirs." [2]

II

If we study the psychological attitude of the middle-class towards the aristocracy as expressed in literature, we find an ambiguity of emotions.   We mean by ambiguity of emotions an attitude in which are present simultaneously the possibility of a positively acknowledging and a negatively rejecting reaction towards individuals or groups.   According to Freud, such an emotional ambiguity which has its origin in the subconscious, is especially characteristic of the masses.[3]   The ambiguous attitude is to be found to some degree in intimate relationships such as marriage, friendship, the relationship between parents and children and, still more strongly, in the relationship of two business-partners, in that of subordinate and superior, etc.

We find this double tendency (of a desire for identification, and a rejection of it expressed in hostile

[1] An amusing proof of the contempt for knowledge is afforded by the following conversation (in Fontane) between two officers in a casino. They are discussing a colleague who will be summoned to the great general staff which included the intellectual officers' élite:

"Moltke has great expectations of him, and he is said to have produced a fine work." "Doesn't impress me. It's all stuff copied from libraries. Anyone who is at all resourceful can produce books like Humboldt or Ranke" (Theodor Fontane, *Irrungen Wirrungen, Ausgewählte Werke*, Leipzig, n.d., iv. 133).

[2] K. Demeter, *op. cit.*, p. 160.

[3] The concept of ambivalence (in German *Ambivalenz*) was first employed by psychoanalysis for mass-psychology. (See S. Freud, *Group Psychology and the Analysis of the Ego*, London, 1922, pp. 55–56.)

independence) also in the psychological attitude of men of a socially inferior class towards a socially superior one. Even if in individual cases now the one, now the other tendency predominates, both tendencies, the positive and the negative, always exist side by side. In the social framework of society, one and the same class can acknowledge the higher prestige that another possesses, through imitation of the higher ways of life, and at the same time resist the pressure of this prestige, seeking indeed to suppress and destroy it. Whilst ambiguity continually (without those subject to it always being aware of the fact) determines the psychological attitude of the inferior group towards the superior, the preponderance of the positive or negative tendency in the individual is dependent, on the one hand, on his individual make-up, on the other upon the attitude of the superior group. Where, for example, an aristocratic class segregates itself and makes access difficult (as with the feudal aristocracy in Prussia before 1870), the animosity in the inferior stratum will stand out more strongly; where, on the other hand (as with the aristocracy in England), the upper class does not resist reinforcement from the inferior stratum and the difference between old and new nobility is not sharply stressed, the animosity is weaker.

The dualism of economic strength and relative political weakness in the German upper middle-class after 1866, resulted psychologically in a strong lack of equilibrium between the contrary tendencies of acknowledgment and imitation of the aristocracy as a social superior on the one hand, and scorn and contempt for it as an economic and cultural inferior on the other.

Just as the middle-class in the German Reichstag after 1866 was split into two different liberal parties, one of which supported the policy of the feudal military state whilst the other stood in sharp opposition to the Junker-caste, so was the collective psychological attitude of the upper and lower middle-class strata towards the aristocracy one that swayed between resentment and imitation.[1] When an individual feels himself inferior to another in the competitive struggle, two possibilities emerge— either, goaded by animosity, he will attempt to avenge himself, or will discover the reason for the superiority and equalize matters by imitation. What is valid for the relationship between individuals as such is also valid for the relationship between different classes. One can seek to bridge class-differences by destruction or by equalization, by powerless resentment or by successful imitation. We shall first analyse here examples of middle-class resentment, and then go on to the pheno-menon of its imitation of the superior class.

(*a*) *Resentment.*—By resentment we mean a psycho-logical attitude that combines feelings of powerlessness with the impulse of hatred. In every society wherever a social group or stratum is repressed, stifled or restricted in the development of its powers by another, there are to be found specific dispositions making for resentment. Resentment can fill the worker who feels himself ex-ploited by the entrepreneur, as well as the researcher who sees his work unappreciated and scorned by other scholars. The younger generation that believes itself repressed by parental authority can display resentment, as well as the older generation that sees itself pushed aside by the eager pressure of youth. M. Scheler, in a penetrating, if at the same time one-sided essay, has designated resentment as the moral attitude of the man who has been handicapped in life.[2] Scheler's discussion on resentment has immediate import in our connection,

---

[1] This uncertain swaying between resentment and imitation has been clearly observed by a decided advocate of the rise of the middle-class. Gustav Freytag, in *Die Verlorene Handschrift*, makes the mild and wise High Court Steward say: "I am ready to acknowledge the great progress made by the middle-class in the last 50 years. But the efficiency which the people develop in trade and industry is allied too seldom with firm self-confidence, too seldom, indeed, with the firmly founded position which a political power requires. Too frequent is the swaying between unsatisfied pride and over-great submissiveness; inordinate desire flies too high, the spirit of sacrifice is too small" (bk. iv, chap. ii).

[2] M. Scheler, *Das Ressentiment in Aufbau der Moralen* in *Abhandlungen und Aufsätze*, Leipzig, 1915, i. 39–274. The essay is chiefly concerned with a criticism of Nietzsche's well-known interpretation of Christianity as a pheno-menon of resentment.

for he maintains the thesis that the psychological root of middle-class culture from the thirteenth to the nineteenth century is to be sought in anti-aristocratic resentment. Scheler, who in writing his book was himself clearly filled with a romantic resentment against the burgher, has failed to prove such a sweeping statement. Anti-seigneurial resentment undoubtedly played an important part in connection with the middle-class moralization of modern times. Members of every class, indeed of every profession, are disposed to consider their specific class or professional values as generally binding primary values. The aristocracy for a long time only recognized as valid its own specific class virtues, such as bravery, fine manners; whilst the middle-class, conversely, was disposed to consider its peculiar virtues of diligence, thrift, sobriety, as generally binding for society as a whole. So long as the aristocracy possessed a social precedence in society, the repressed middle-class was only too easily disposed by its resentment to pronounce the lack of middle-class virtues in the aristocracy as a moral minus.

This middle-class resentment is extensively reflected in literature. Although it is difficult to determine here whether it is only observed by the author or is shared by him, the appearance of such a psychological motive in several realistic writers gives always an indication of its importance to society, for a resentment that is only accidental and not typical, but in spite of that repeatedly reappeared in literature, could, in the long run, find no echo in the public. If, for instance, the characters of Dostoievsky, Gogol and Tolstoi in the Russian literature of the pre-war period are filled with resentment, then this is undoubtedly due to repression by the autocratic Czarist system and to lack of means for publicly ventilating grievances. If, on the other hand, anti-aristocratic resentment in German nineteenth-century literature did not assume such definite sharpness as anti-authoritarian resentment in Russian literature, then this is to be explained by the concession of a pseudoparliamentarianism which the aristocracy and bureaucracy were forced to yield after 1848.

Middle-class resentment against the arbitrariness of the feudal régime and the unscrupulousness of the aristo- cratic castes found expression throughout German litera- ture, from the dramas of Lessing and Schiller to the novels of Spielhagen and Wolzogen. The uneasiness of the indeed socially inferior, but self-confident, middle- class was expressed either as (1) discontent with its own social weakness, as (2) contempt for the now weakened aristocratic position, or as (3) moral denunciation of the class enemy. The *discontent* with their weakness was expressed by the burghers more strongly before (in accordance with their political position) than after 1848. The resentment of the youthful Laube illustrates this:

> But I wonder if there is any middle-class canaille who does not mind always being disadvantageously compared with the aristocracy if that should mean he is considered as belonging to the same species as the latter: will you, nay can you, deny that in a so-called unbiassed consideration the old race takes the lead in the nature of things? Are not the most important offices of state still accessible only to aristocrats, e.g. all the diplomatic and consular posts—the officials of which haggle over us in war and peace as if we were goods in a market.—Is not the middle-class creature always only legitimized by a "von," when it is sensible and enters on a high post, and does it not admit thereby that that pertains to full validity? [1]

If the unwillingness of the burgher to be an *object of aristocratic scorn* speaks here, the tables are turned after 1848 and it is the aristocrat who not seldom becomes the *object of middle-class scorn*. This is shown, for example, in Freytag's merchant in *Soll und Haben*. He notes with cool placidness the economic and moral decay of the nobility, the inferiority of the incapable.

> He who has a traditional claim to enjoyment in life and to a privileged position on account of his ancestors, will generally not conserve the full energy that is deserving of such a position.

[1] H. Laube, *Politische Briefe*, Leipzig, 1833, p. 25 f.

Very many of our old, settled families have fallen a prey to decline, and it will be no misfortune for the state if they perish. Their family memories make them supercilious without justification, limit their vision, confuse their judgment.[1]

Moral denunciation of the aristocracy is expressed in a variety of accusations. The aristocracy is said to have taken a sadistic pleasure in the way it displayed its domination so as to humiliate the member of the middle-class. It is Heine who gives a drastic example of this sadistic attitude, which he claims to have observed with his own eyes. Some aristocratic students in Hanover offered a few Taler to an exhausted runner who had just reached the finishing-post, so as to make him run the race over again: "Close behind him, accompanied by whirling clouds of dust, galloped the well-fed, aristocratic youths on their noble steeds whose hoofs every now and again struck the exhausted, panting man—and he was a man."[2]

This perverted aristocracy is also work-shy: the aristocrat, so say the fault-finding burghers, allows his talents to atrophy because an intensive development of his powers would interfere with his inclination for doing nothing. The repugnance to real, serious work is clearly exposed by the genuine democratic writers. Not only is contempt for manual labour branded, but also dilettantism in the higher arts which does not allow of the production of a real master.

An aristocrat, a Herr von Arten, can become a painter [it is said in one of Fanny Lewald's novels mentioned above[3]]. He can paint, if he has time and inclination, as much as he likes, but a Herr von Arten cannot live by the works of his hands, he cannot paint for Tom, Dick and Harry in order to get money. An aristocrat lives for himself on his estate, on his revenues or in the service of the King.

The middle-class writers, who have to struggle hard for their success, find it amoral that a Freiherr does not

[1] G. Freytag, *Soll und Haben*, see *Gesammelte Werke*, iv. 560.
[2] H. Heine, *Reisebilder*, 1826, ii. 73.
[3] F. Lewald, *Von Geschlecht zu Geschlecht, Gesammelte Werke*, ii. 339.

live from the proceeds of his personal talents, that he will not sell pictures or make music for money.[1]

The contrast between the idle aristocratic daughter and the diligent homely middle-class girl is similarly exposed in literature with harsh moralization. In the tendencious novel *Die von Hohenstein* by Fr. Spielhagen (1865)—which distorts nearly all the aristocratic types into devils—this is fully demonstrated. The young, unspoilt Wolfgang von Hohenstein, the son of an inter-marriage, feels the complete difference between aristocratic and middle-class womanhood. He admires the diligence of a poor middle-class embroidery-girl:

What a wonderful play of expression and above all what application to labour! How different was this picture from that which Wolfgang so often observed in the salon of his future mother-in-law! How brightly shone there the double-bracketed lamp on the costly cover of the sofa-table! How luxuriously Madame President leaned back in the swelling cushions, how lazily her satiated, white hands played with the long ears of the lap-dog, how often the work of the young lady paused, if one could call her frivolous tinkling on the piano, work.[2]

The nobility is said to be prodigal. Rational conduct of economic affairs was lacking in the greater part of the aristocracy. To incur debts was the *bon ton* of the aristocratic officers,[3] and irrational management a characteristic of aristocratic estate-owners. Therefore the charge of defective rationality occurs again and again in the novel—from Immermann and Freytag, up to Ernst von Wolzogen. We give only a few examples. The dislike of the capitalist for the drones in Immermann's *Epigonen* has already been mentioned in another part of this work.[4] The reaction of the burgher-hero

[1] F. Lewald, *Von Geschlecht zu Geschlecht, Gesammelte Werke*, ii. 255.

[2] Spielhagen, *Die von Hohenstein*, p. 438.

[3] Debt-ridden officers appear, for instance, in Spielhagen's *Die von Hohenstein*, Freytag's *Soll und Haben*, Ernst von Wolzogen's *Ecce Homo*, and Fontane's *Poggenpuhls*.

[4] Cf. *Die Epigonen*, iii. 245. "It is now, at last, time for a better order to be established in the world. One's heart bleeds to see how they mismanage their economic affairs; because they never had to make an effort for anything

in Fanny Lewald's *Von Geschlecht zu Geschlecht* is similar when, after some years, he sees the dilapidated estate of an aristocrat.

He would have liked to lend a hand, to help, so that such a fine, large property should not decay entirely, so that, through diligence and care, welfare and prosperity would be achieved where foolish prodigality, ignorance and carelessness had resulted in decay.[1]

One of the fundamental charges of middle-class resentment against the aristocracy was, further, its overweening pretension to possess true courage, aristocratic courage. In essence, it was only the aristocracy—according to its own point of view—that could be heroic, only the aristocrat had true courage, only *his* death on the field was a hero's death. This silent arrogance which presumed to have an option on genuine courage was often regarded critically by the simple burgher. Fontane has aptly recorded the resistance of the simple man to this contention. In *Irrungen Wirrungen,* Count Haldern extols to a petty-bourgeois widow the heroic courage of his young nephew as being the natural and traditional devotion to duty of the aristocrat in the last war. Because he was a Haldern, so runs the argument, he was the first of his company to reach the enemy and he collapsed over his horse, covered in wounds. The brusque middle-class woman reminds him, however, that the common infantrymen of the people also did their duty. "But that is just another of your silly ideas, you're always thinking that we understand nothing and know nothing of the Fatherland, and only little of courage."[2] It is interesting to note here that this petty-bourgeois voice is not directed against the aristocrat as such, but only

they therefore do not think of increasing their wealth, hardly of preserving it." The resentment of the capitalist is also expressed in the following words: "We middle-class people have an indescribably short memory. It is not so long ago that we were being called 'burgher canaille,' although it already sounds a bit old-fashioned."

[1] *Von Geschlecht zu Geschlecht, Gesammelte Werke,* v. 77.

[2] Th. Fontane, *Ausgewählte Werke* (Reclam), iv. 72.

against his disposition to identify himself alone with true national feeling.   For the middle-class claims the national idea completely for itself.   Indeed, it feels that it is the source of it.[1]   The middle-class heroes in Freytag and Spielhagen prove their worth not only in their specifically middle-class virtues such as intelligence, endurance and diligence, but also through the qualities, once monopolized by the aristocracy—courage, presence of mind and patriotism.

(*b*) *Imitation and Admiration.   Aristocratic Way of Life as Secret Ideal.*—Imitation of a privileged stratum by a socially inferior one plays a part in every society.   As long as the socially-superior class does not possess exclusive privileges of dress, uniform and conduct of life, the lower stratum is free to imitate it.   The ruling class in most cases will not recognize this imitation as complete, it will regard and scorn it as a makeshift, but will at the same time feel the attempt as belonging to its prestige, believing that its class should be worthy of imitation and give the lead in tone.   In any society, mode of life, appearance, erudition, piety, martial bearing or flight from the world, are respectively imitated according to the one which happens to be stressed by the ruling élite.   As G. Tarde has expressed it in reference to Latin countries, there is imitation respectively of patrician by plebeian, of aristocrat by commoner, of clerk by layman, of Parisian by provincial, of townsman by peasant.[2]

Hostility, however, does not exclude imitation of a superior class on the part of a socially-inferior one.[3] One can distinguish between conscious and unconscious imitation of the higher modes of life, or to put it otherwise, between secret and open, partial and complete imitation.   Imitation can relate either to a stratum's

---

[1] This was especially the case after 1871.   Cf. A. Rosenberg, *The Birth of the German Republic, 1871–1918*, London, 1931, chap. i.

[2] G. Tarde, *Les Lois de l'Imitation*, Paris, 1907, p. 233.

[3] A good example of this is to be seen in the manner of life of the socialist trade-union officials in the German republic, amongst whom could be observed an extensive assimilation and imitation of petty-bourgeois ways of living.

customs of life as a whole, or only to certain features of them.

The secret imitation and admiration of the aristocratic style of life has been repeatedly confirmed by skilled observers between 1850 and 1914 in Germany. As long as the aristocracy remained the politically dominant stratum, it acted as a model of conduct of life and tone for the wealthy middle-class. Often though the middle-class strove against the tendency to imitation, it was still partly or unconsciously filled by it.

This imitation arose very frequently from the desire for release from the pressure of the superior caste. As a burgher, one did not indeed belong to it, but one acted in certain habits of life *as if* one did belong to it: in other words, one sought refuge in a social fiction.

The public [Gutzkow observed in Vienna in 1845 [1]] feels the burden of this social prerogative, and attempts to help itself by aristocracizing everyone, by raising everyone to an aristocratic status. It is not politeness that causes people in Austria to address the whole world as "Herr von So-and-so," but self-defence. It is too oppressing, too humiliating, to appear as a burgher in the midst of this general nobility of birth.[2]

If the aristocracy's lack of a *raison d'être* detracted from its value in the eyes of the German middle-class in the nineteenth century, the court- and city-nobility did, however, remain for the latter the teacher of fine manners. After the revolution of 1848, W. H. Riehl stressed the fact that the general politeness of social intercourse in Germany was due largely to the influence of the aristocracy.[3] Sixty years later Walter Rathenau, in a critical review of the Wilhelmine period, revealed the marked tendency of the feudal upper stratum to

---

[1] K. Gutzkow, *Gesammelte Werke*, Frankfort-on-Main, 1845, iii. 329 f.

[2] On the other hand, Bogumil Golz mentions an aristocratic lady who introduces the wife of a merchant (to whom she is indebted) as Frau *von* "So-and-so" to her aristocratic acquaintances, in order to avoid being despised for having middle-class friends. (See Bog. Golz, *Typen der Gesellschaft*, Berlin, 1864, 3rd Ed., ii. 153.)

[3] W. H. Riehl, *Die bürgerliche Gesellschaft*, Stuttgart, 1858, 5th Ed., chap. iii.

rouse the wealthy middle-class to imitation. Just as
Louis XVI tamed his aristocracy by directing its energies
to a new end, so did the Prussian feudal system act
towards the ambitious middle-class:

> At the price of conviction [or, as we would prefer to say, at
> the price of its political fidelity], a new avenue of ascent was
> opened to the middle-class. The imitation of the feudal attitude
> was more successful in its result than in its appearance. For,
> lacking the slight intermixture of scepticism that is characteristic
> of the aristocrat exempted from being tested, because he is genuine,
> it strides about a little too mistrustfully, and a little too splendidly.[1]

We can distinguish in German literature three types
that are motivated by a positively imitative relationship
to the aristocracy:

(i) The burgher from petty surroundings who lacks
experience of life.

(ii) The admirer of the aristocracy against his will.

(iii) The rich parvenu who openly displays imitation
of aristocratic magnificence.

The attitude of the first type is naïve; of the second,
equivocal; of the third, calculating. The first takes the
glamour of the aristocratic world for a complete reality,
the second allows himself to be dazzled by it only
occasionally, the third seeks to endow himself with it.

(i) Naïve admiration of aristocratic glamour (such as
undoubtedly filled thousands of burghers of the most
varying social standards, especially in the small towns
of Middle and Western Germany) is well reflected in
the bearing of one of the chief characters in Freytag's
Soll und Haben. Anton Wohlfahrt is, as the son of a
petty official grown-up in a provincial town, filled with
the respect of his class for the powers that be. Whilst
the upper middle-class exhibits simultaneous contempt
and imitation of the aristocracy, the petty-bourgeoisie and
the lower officialdom are conscious of the unbridgeable
gulf, which fills them with a mixture of worship and

[1] W. Rathenau, *Von kommenden Dingen*, Berlin, 1917, p. 273 f.

envy for the great. When the young Anton Wohlfahrt tarries in the park of an aristocratic manor, he is
enchanted by its elegant splendour. Everything is beautiful for him because it is of elegant origin, and everything is elegant because it is beautiful. His surroundings touch the reflex of his social inferiority-complex:

> Respect for everything that walked the world with dignity,
> certainty and self-assurance was innate in him, the son of the
> poor arithmetician, and when he now, in the midst of his over-
> whelming delight in the surrounding splendour, thought of him-
> self, he appeared to himself as utterly insignificant, as nothing
> worth speaking about, as a kind of social Tom Thumb, tiny,
> hardly visible in the grass.[1]

(ii) The secret or involuntary admiration of the aristocratic attitude, of the æsthetic qualities of the feudal
upper stratum, amongst some of its political opponents,
is exhibited especially by intellectuals and writers:[2] and
it is especially in publicistic æsthetes who waver between
joy in word and joy in battle, that a secret admiration
of the aristocratic way of life, and an effort to adopt it,
are to be observed.

This twofold attitude is particularly well expressed
in Laube's early work, *Die Poeten* (1833). The hot-
blooded poet Valerius represents the mobile Young
German intelligentsia. His watchword is, democracy
of social rights but aristocracy of splendour. Already
Immermann, as we noted, had seen through the aristocratic ideology of a caste summoned to rule, but at the
same time he had expressed his admiration of its æsthetic
ideals in his character of the lawyer. Laube also displays the double tendency of acknowledgment and rejection, of imitation and destruction. In the opinion of
Valerius the historic hour of the aristocracy was past,
the superior claims of the aristocrat had been revealed

[1] G. Freytag, *Soll und Haben*, bk. i, chap. ii.

[2] Lassalle, for example, had undoubtedly a stronger feeling against the
bourgeois than against the aristocrat—at any rate he was not unwilling to
associate with conservative Junkers like Prince Bismarck or with liberal aristocrats like Prince Pückler; his long-standing relationship with the emancipated
Countess Hatzfeld is well known.

as pure ideologies unrelated to reality. If it was for a long time impossible for property as such to represent a higher class, now the political primacy of the aristocracy was crumbling—but the primacy of its customs remained firm.[1] Valerius admires the elegant ways of life of the aristocracy, the aristocratic *savoir-vivre*, no less than did Wilhelm Meister. But whilst in society based on status the aristocratic way of life was unattainable and aristocratic existence could in no way be bridged with middle-class achievement, the adoption of the ideal ways of life of the feudal stratum by a middle-class conscious of victory is now proclaimed. "What the aristocracy has preserved from the period of its domination," says Valerius-Laube, "and what we have still not been able to copy from it, is its easy way of living." The easy manner of living is a merit, but a merit that is to be understood only by the social position of this class. What Goethe's *Wilhelm Meister* admires without explaining it, is still admired by Laube, but explained at the same time and thereby overcome:

> The aristocracy was unacquainted with effort, therefore its ways are easier, therefore it escapes the error of regarding business as an end, as, for instance, our merchant does. The aristocrat lives more easily because he has been without a care from his youth onwards.[2]

The assimilation of an aristocratic style is only a question of time. "The victory has long been decided and the stress of battle will soon be forgotten. We shall then acquire this merit also." [3] In Valerius-Laube a symptomatic struggle ensues between the anti-aristocratic principles of the democratic writer and his half-conscious partiality for the aristocracy. The seemingly superior culture of feudalism leaves behind, even amongst its opponents, strong feelings of inferiority.[4] It is the suspicion of secret admiration of the aristocracy that

---

[1] H. Laube, *Die Poeten, Gesammelte Schriften*, Wien, 1876, vi. 107 ff.
[2] *Ibid.*, p. 109.   [3] *Ibid.*
[4] Laube, who wrote *Die Krieger* shortly after a period spent in the house of a Silesian country noble as a tutor, experienced this discord in himself.

torments men of insight like Laube. When Valerius believes himself to be loved by a princess, he scrupulously tests himself as to whether this distinction flatters him merely because it comes from a lady of the aristocracy.

His whole democratic pride [it is stated [1]] rebelled against it, but of what use were principles against traditional weaknesses! In our time of great differences of Estate, there grows up with a large part of the low-born a hidden earthly heaven in which the higher Estates move, for which his spirit strives without knowing it.

The feudal stratum is invincible as long as it assumes a prominent place in the desires of the socially ambitious burgher. The idealization of the Estate next above

passes from peasant to burgher, from aristocrat to prince and through all the members of this Estate. Nothing is of use against this but an inconsolable indifference that knows no susceptibilities, and poetic men are the soonest to fall into this illusion. [2]

It is interesting to notice how the higher stratum is idealized here only until it has been attained, at which point disillusionment sets in. The motive for the idealization of a higher stratum by a lower one seems, moreover, to correspond to the motive for the idealization of one individual by another. One loves the favoured individual, the object of love, "because of the perfections which one has aimed at for one's own ego, and which one should like now to procure by satisfying one's narcissism in this roundabout way." [3]

[1] H. Laube, *Die Krieger, Gesammelte Schriften*, vi. 270.   [2] *Ibid.*

[3] S. Freud, *op. cit.*, p. 66. Whilst Valerius has an inferiority-complex as regards the aristocracy, another character from the circle of the poets wishes, on the other hand, to accomplish the democracy of love. Hyppolith defiantly parades his humble origins and his democratic views before the Princess Constantine and then enjoys making her belong to him sexually as to the "sunny Hercules." There is here combined with sexual desire the reaction of a resentment which satisfies itself in the subjection of the hitherto socially unattainable object of passion. After such an act all social restrictions in the conqueror are set aside. He who was hitherto repressed can now do the repressing on his side. Laube represented, moreover, apart from the general demand of democratization, a special democratization of literature, i.e. he desired that the heroes of novels should themselves no longer pine for unattainable princesses. (Cf. P. Przygodda, *H. Laubes literarische Frühzeit*, Berlin, 1910, p. 70.)

(iii) We have already mentioned, in the first part of this chapter, the repulse of the parvenu by the old stratum threatened in its prestige. Now we are concerned with the imitation that is to be observed in the attitude of the parvenu. Its forms of expression are by no means limited to one country, they are to be found in almost every stratified society. They have always furnished a subject for the satires of cultured or envious writers, and have been recorded in periods of threatening middle-class rivalry, starting with the *Banquet of Trimalchio* by Petronius, and continuing through Molière's *Bourgeois-Gentilhomme*, up to the society novels of Balzac and Fontane.

The imitation of the style of life of an old stratum by a new one can be accomplished in a threefold manner. It can express itself in fitting out the home, in form and style of sociability, in the attempt to win persons of the idealized sphere as social companions. The style of life of the parvenu is of a medial kind. It corresponds *no longer* to the *original stratum* from which the parvenu comes, and it does *not yet* correspond to the *desired stratum*, whose way of life the parvenu wants to make his own.

The furnishing of his house, his style of life, and sociability are characterized by a peculiar transitional aspect. A sentence from a novel of A. von Ungern-Sternberg [1] is applicable to the furnishing of the parvenu's home: "Here prevails the hapless middle kingdom where the elements of domestic organization range from the placid, solid stability of a good burgher home to the frivolity of an upper-class, elegant mode of housekeeping." Fontane's *Frau Jenny Treibel* gives us significant glimpses of the imitation of the sociability of the leading stratum. The factory-owner and *Kommerzienrat* Treibel, who had become rapidly rich in the period of wild speculation after 1870, is an uneducated pusher. He not only welcomes the visits of friends of his own class, but is proud

---

[1] A. v. Ungern-Sternberg, *Palmyra oder das Tagebuch eines Papageis,* Stuttgart, 1838, p. 96.

to see in his home, also, an old-fashioned retired lieutenant and canvasser of conservative votes and two
aristocratic court-ladies.   The two old ladies have to be
treated by the servants with quite special ceremonious-
ness, for they have some contact with the court and
consequently with a stratum which is still closed above
all to the parvenu.   The social ambitions of the parvenu are realistically illuminated in a conversation between him and one of the court-ladies.   She is surprised
at the industrialist's political change of front, for he
wants to stand as a conservative candidate.   "You are
an industrialist and live in the Köpnicker Strasse?" she
asks him doubtfully, and then goes on to say, "To every
station in life there correspond definite political principles.   Aristocratic estate-owners are agricultural conservatives, Professors are national middle party, and
industrialists are progressives.   Do be a progressive!" [1]

It is indicative of the parvenu that he disdains the
average class-attitude of his stratum or occupational group
in order to receive that of a higher one: he attempts by
calculation to become familiar with the modes of thought
and feeling of the higher stratum.   The *Kommerzienrat*
by no means tries to hide the fact that calculation is
the motive of his adhesion to the courtly aristocratic
stratum.

You know, people of our kind reckon and reason and can no
longer get away from the rule of three: the statement, "if this
and this brings in so much, how much will that and that bring
in" is always with them.   And look you, my friends and patron-
esses, I have weighed up progressiveness and conservatism according to the same statement, and I have come to the conclusion
that conservatism—I will not say is more profitable for that
would of course be false—but suits me better, fits me better.[2]

Here we have the typical attitude of the section of
the wealthy middle-class that wants to feudalize itself;
whilst before 1870 a large part of the prosperous middle-
class had shown a strong dislike for the spendthrift and

---

[1] Th. Fontane, *Ausgewählte Werke*, iv. 270.   [2] *Ibid.*

irrational aristocracy, this attitude had changed with the victory of the Prussian militarist monarchy. A large part of the middle-class now sought to fit itself for the aristocratic feudal style and to gain connections with the court and ruling bureaucracy by upholding prescribed, conservative convictions.[1]

The parvenu wishes to hide his social shortcomings as well as his aims by holding the right kind of opinions. "Housekeeping in a big style," wrote Rathenau,[2] "demands elegant guests. Apart from that, there remain small faults of culture and education to be covered up: nothing covers them more suitably than a thick coating of prescribed opinions." The feeling of "not yet, but soon," still prevails in the strata of high finance, of rich merchants. They have not yet quite fitted themselves to the aristocratic model, but soon they were to be superior to it. In spite of all pertinent mockery and all sharp criticism, these strata circulated strongly around the aristocratic models.

An unconscious interest [as an experienced cicerone of the Wilhelminian court society formulated it[3]] was present. They looked with curious eyes at the other classes to which they were already superior—with the exception of one or two extremely big lords—in money and standards of living. They wanted to learn, from them, from their manners, from their equipages, from their ways, how to be, have, and manage with sociability.

Herein, the wealthy aristocracy was still superior through its older customs, older culture, and closer contact with the court which the newcomers lacked (with the exception of a few *Geheime Kommerzienräte* who

---

[1] Significant of this is the lively interest taken by the family of the *Kommerzienrat* in every event in the courtly sphere. The *Kommerzienrat's* wife says on one occasion to one of the court ladies: "I have always been extremely interested in this young princess, yes, in the whole line of the house. She is said to be happily married. I do so like to hear of happy marriages—in the higher circles of society, of course: and if I may be allowed to say so, I think it is very foolish to assume that conjugal happiness should be excluded in the high regions of mankind" (*ibid.*, p. 265).

[2] W. Rathenau, *op. cit.*, p. 273.

[3] G. v. Ompteda, *Deutscher Adel um 1900*, Berlin, 1900, ii. 196.

enjoyed a personal invitation to court), but which was at the disposal of the Counts and Barons.

If the aristocracy mocked this tendency to assimilation that was characteristic of large circles of the bourgeoisie, an alliance was welcome to the feudal ruling class at a time when the organized proletariat threatened equally both the aristocratic position of domination and middle-class capitalism. The menacing of both groups by the lowest class resulted in a rapprochement which facilitated the imitation of society for the burgher and which made it much less ridiculous than in the days made it much less ridiculous than in the days of the unbroken rule of the court in the seventeenth century.

CHAPTER VI

POPULAR LITERATURE AND PHILISTINISM

1. The Family Journal

In the previous chapter we analysed the ambiguous attitude of the middle-class towards the aristocracy, using as our source for this purpose the "higher" type of fiction, i.e. those authors who in their time were taken seriously and discussed by literary critics because of their form and content. But our investigation would remain very one-sided if we did not also glance at the so-called "lower" type of literature. We can call this "lower" type of fiction, which existed in the nineteenth century in all Western European countries, "mass-literature," at the same time distinguishing between a better and a worse type of mass-literature according to the æsthetic and intellectual level. These two groups correspond in the nineteenth century to two types of periodical which appeared in Germany after 1848 and which rapidly became indispensable in the life of the masses through technical developments in the way of illustration and distribution: they were the middle-class family journal, read by all sections of the middle-class, and the sensational mass-journal that was read by the lower classes. If the middle-class family journal answered the intellectual needs of the educated middle-class (which means, chiefly, the intellectual needs of the female dependants of artisans, merchants, officials, teachers, etc.), the primitive mass-journal pandered to the curiosity and lust for sensation of unskilled and uneducated workmen and peasants.

Both the middle-class family journal and the primitive

mass-journal had their models in English periodicals, such as Dickens' *Household Words* on the one hand, and the *Penny Magazine* on the other. The prototype of the family journal made its appearance with the *Gartenlaube* whose subscribers rose from 5,000 in 1853 and 100,000 in 1860, to 225,000 in 1867, reaching 378,000 in 1881. Its success encouraged the foundation of rival periodicals with the result that the *family journal became a permanent institution*.[1]

In contrast with the primitive mass-journal, the family journal was—at least in the period up to 1870—not merely a pure business enterprise, but also the advocate of certain political and cultural tendencies: it represented a journal of principles. Its character was determined by the particular reading-public to which it was addressed, viz. the middle-class family. Unlike the æsthetic periodicals of the first half of the nineteenth century, the family journal did not consider its public to be individual intellectuals, cultural groups or circles of literary amateurs, but the family which, in accordance with a quite definite ideology, was regarded as an organic cell of the nation, as a living emotional unity. It is not, however, the proletarian family, which was already beginning to disintegrate in this period of advancing industrialization, that is here exalted and defended in its respectability, but the family of the upper and lower middle-classes in town and country. Whilst this middle-class periodical proclaims decidedly liberal ideas in politics and condemns traditional institutions like the Church and the feudal régime as obsolete, it emphasizes all the more strongly the moral value of the family and of private property.[2]

[1] See H. Wuttke, *Die deutschen Zeitschriften und die Entstehung der öffentlichen Meinung*, Leipzig, 1875, 3rd Ed.; also, the article *Familienblatt*, by F. Kainz, *Reallexikon der deutschen Literaturgeschichte*, i. 344–8.)

[2] A remark made by the publisher of the *Gartenlaube*, 1848, in connection with the Paris Commune, is typical of this stress on private property and of the middle-class anxiety for security: "May the Lord of Heaven be merciful to those who have inherited the hard-earned savings of their fathers or who have acquired property through diligence and orderliness." (See K. Feisskohl, *Ernst Keils publizistische Wirksamkeit und Bedeutung*, Leipzig, 1914, p. 44.)

It is striking to see how strongly every section of the nineteenth-century German middle-class stressed the idea of the family. The individualism of the economic struggle was counterbalanced by the social collectivism of the family. Whilst literature of the classical and romantic periods sharply underlines the contrast between genius and philistine, between the aristocracy of culture and the conventional respectability of the family, both the higher and lower literature of poetical realism after 1830 emphasize unceasingly the virtues of the middle-class family.[1] The conservative sociologist, W. H. Riehl, affirmed at that time with much satisfaction the actuality of the family in literature and science. The new science of the family was for him an instrument for its preservation.

How completely different [he said] is the attitude of science now towards the home, from what it was a hundred years ago! The family has earned an infinitely deeper recognition from science, and at the same time it has become once again a matter of public interest in our nation. Recognition is already half an improvement.[2]

The concentration of the middle-class periodical on the family meant in practice a specific selection in its contents. All its articles laid stress on the moral aspect of things; if social realities were not completely concealed, good care was taken not to probe them too thoroughly. The discussion of sexual problems was completely taboo. Divorces and suicides did not exist.[3] Since wives and daughters formed the major contingent of its readers, and since their interests were concentrated mainly on the family or on the rearing of families in the future, the family-journal had to adapt itself to their mentality. The result is to be seen in the story-pages of the family journal.

[1] The counterpart in plastic art is to be found in the family-idyll of Schwind and Ludwig Richter.

[2] W. H. Riehl, *Die Familie*, 1882, 9th Ed., p. 212.

[3] Cf. R. Mayreder, *Family Literature* in *A Survey of the Woman-Problem*, English translation, London, 1913, pp. 172–82.

The stories printed therein catered for the average woman-reader whose mental capabilities had not been over-developed in the girls' high-schools and who, in accordance with prevailing custom, rarely took up a professional career. They were written for the most part by women, for women. They were discussed in family circles and amongst the ladies, and formed just as much an intimate bond between the authoress and her feminine readers as did the political article between its author and the male readers.

We shall now attempt to present the attitude assumed in the family-journal novel towards the aristocracy and middle-class; and for this purpose have chosen the *Gartenlaube* and *Daheim*, two periodicals of opposed political tendencies. We therefore have to distinguish between the novel of liberal protest and the conservative novel of loyalty.

a. *The "Gartenlaube" and the Change in Middle-Class Political Opinion*

The most widely-spread and most representative family-journal of the liberal bourgeoisie between 1850 and 1900 was the *Gartenlaube*. Its contents, taken as a whole, reflect characteristically the intellectual and political changes within this class. The political and social ideologies of a broad stratum of merchants, officials, artisans, teachers, in short of the non-professional middle-class are just as faithfully reflected in it as is the attitude of the Prussian national-liberal university intelligentsia in the *Preussische Jahrbücher*. The *Gartenlaube* is a gold-mine for research into the thoughts and feelings of the so-called middle-class.[1] Its founder, Ernst Keil,

---

[1] Recently two studies of the *Gartenlaube* have appeared: H. Zang, *Die Gartenlaube als politisches Organ* (Ph.D. Thesis, Coburg, 1935), is not a scientific analysis, but a very biased denunciation of the liberalism of that periodical and of its Jewish contributors. The careful treatise of R. Horovitz, *Vom Roman des Jungen Deutschland zum Roman der Gartenlaube. Ein Beitrag zur Geschichte des deutschen Liberalismus*, Breslau, 1937, which has only just been published as this book goes to press, confirms on the whole the above interpretation of the *Gartenlaube*, although using another approach.

was a self-taught man, and he embodied the self-reliant, industrious, German merchant who was able to recognize and skilfully exploit in the middle of the century the new possibilities offered by technical progress and improved communications.   He was born in a small town of central Germany, the son of a petty official, became first a bookseller, and firmly favoured both the writings of the Young Germans and a democratic policy.   Later on he founded several periodicals which all fell foul of the censor, before and after 1848, and then in 1853 he started the *Gartenlaube* which, as we have already seen, soon achieved an extraordinary success.   Keil's intention was to produce a popular journal whose chief aim should be to popularize the achievements of science. In other words, the periodical wanted to be the organ of a middle-class, liberal enlightenment.   Its readers were to be informed about the human body and its functions, as well as about the significance of a liberal middle-class in a united Fatherland.   The paper fought against superstition of all shape and form, against the political pressure of feudalism as well as against the intellectual pressure of·tyrannical clericalism.   It combined at one and the same time two tendencies that were later to prove mutually exclusive; for it advocated on the one hand an enlightened humanitarianism, and on the other, a nationalism in the sense of an integration of a rent and torn Germany under the leadership of the middle-class.   Its slogans were "Down with German reaction!" and "Up with German unity!"

But the attitude of this middle-class organ underwent an astonishing change in the period between 1866 and 1880.   We can best realize the extent of this change if we examine and compare the contents of different volumes.   For this purpose we shall take those for 1866, the year of the German civil-war, for 1871, the year of the unification of Germany, and for 1887, the year which saw the ninetieth birthday of William I.

In the volume for 1866, the double tendency of the paper, humanity and enlightenment on the one hand,

nationalism on the other, is curiously illustrated by the
juxtaposition of an unprejudiced essay, "Poet and Jew,"
with one on the young historian Heinrich von Treitschke.
The first shows the harm caused by religious prejudice;
it cites as an example an unfortunate Jewish doctor and
poet whose marriage to a Christian girl is forbidden by
her parents out of prejudice, whereupon the girl dies
of a broken heart (a sentimental engraving shows the
Jew at the bier of his bride). In the second, the young
von Treitschke, who blossomed later as a nationalist and
an anti-semite, is exalted as a champion of German unity,
as a representative of patriotic and liberal convictions.

Other articles, also, reveal the double tendency of
German liberalism: biographical sketches sing the praises,
with a fervour of enlightenment, of free-thinking religious rationalists like the former Protestant priests,
Uhlich and Balzer. These two were the leaders of the
so-called *Lichtfreunde*, who at that time proclaimed in
congregations of their own the religion of scientific progress instead of orthodox Christian doctrine.[1] In these
articles they are glorified as knights of a modern Round
Table who wished not only to investigate the world,
but to improve it, and there prevails throughout an
idealistic optimism, even a chiliasm, which is based on
the belief in the possibility of creating by means of
science a world of truth and betterment.[2]

The increasing pride of the burgher, which we have
already found on a higher literary plane in Freytag, is
proclaimed with similar high-sounding phrases. The
harm caused by the feudal régime and the arbitrariness
of princes is denounced in essays like "Fr. Chr. Daniel

[1] See H. Rosenberg, *Theologischer Rationalismus und vormärzlicher Vulgärliberalismus, Historische Zeitschrift*, 1929, cxli. 529 ff.

[2] The following passage is characteristic: "These people, standing on the
firm unshakable ground of science which they have themselves built up on
the foundation of nature with cool scientific spirit, with remarkable zeal and
industry and with glowing enthusiasm, place a lever beneath the world as it
has hitherto appeared in order to lift it out of its socket with Archimedean
strength, and put in its place a new world truth that has resulted from scientific
discovery, being born in an enlightened spirit and baptized with the fire of
an inspired poetical enthusiasm" (*Die Gartenlaube*, 1866, p. 171).

Schubart. A victim of the arbitrariness of German princes," or "Heinrich the 72nd Prince of Reuss-Lobenstein-Ebersdorf, ruler of a petty state." On the other hand, inventors and entrepreneurs are lauded as representatives of middle-class efficiency and solidarity. Thus an essay entitled "Prussia's Military Luther" praises Dreyse, the inventor of the needle-gun, and an idyllistic account of this ennobled arms-manufacturer, who supplied weapons to all the German states, declares with satisfaction that in spite of his social and economic success he has still remained a simple man of the people. The work of Krupp, the cannon-king, is treated in the same way; and acknowledgment is given to the importance of the Prussian bank, as "the greatest business-house of Prussia," for the development of trade and industry. The support of capitalist development does not preclude the democrats from an interest in the social problem. Schulze-Delitzsch, the well-known founder of the German co-operative associations (*Genossenschaften*), analyses the serious social consequences of the division of labour.[1]

The connection of this radical journal with the refugees of 1848, who lived scattered abroad, can still be clearly seen. A poem is dedicated to Freiligrath's silver wedding in exile in London, some articles are devoted to German associations in London and Baltimore, and the often instructive reports on English conditions and customs usually come from the pens of German emigrants. Taken all in all, the attitude of the periodical appears decidedly liberal and filled with the optimism of a prosperous stratum wishing to employ the power of science, technology and industry to attain its desired domination in a free and united German Empire.

A totally different attitude is assumed by the *Gartenlaube* under the impress of the German victory of

---

[1] In a notice appealing for a Schulze-Delitzsch fund, the committee reveals the influence of middle-class dignitaries in the liberal camp: it is composed of the President of the German National Union, von Bennigsen, a publisher, a book-dealer, a titled merchant (*Kommerzienrat*), a lawyer, a law-court proctor, and a business chief.

1871. A few commemorative articles in appreciation of liberal leaders like Prince Pückler, Gustav Freytag and Jacob Venedey show its traditional liberal sympathies; a rather cutting article on the "victims of railway-capitalism," dealing with the exploitation of subordinate railway employees, reveals an understanding of the seamy side of capitalism; but in addition there begins the glorification of the military leaders of 1870–1, of Kaiser Wilhelm and his paladins, in pictures, poems and articles. The success of Bismarck can also no longer be overlooked by the democrats, but his feudal, inner aloofness from the people fills them with mistrust. "Bismarck," they say anxiously, "is the most popular man of the time, but is he really the favourite of the people? Will Bismarck, in whose aristocratic veins middle-class blood flows and who remains in spite of it always the great man aloof from the people, will he become the founder of German freedom as he has become the founder of German unity?"

But national feeling, identification with the victorious feudal ruling stratum, is becoming stronger than bourgeois class-consciousness. A poem, *Deutschlands Siegesdank*, proudly extols German courage:

> The Franks' proud armies
> were thrown to the ground by German fury.
> And, in truth, those who fell
> bore their wounds in front.[1]

The old democratic burgher pride was still alive, but an adjustment to the victorious Prussian monarchy and to the new prestige of the feudal stratum was found to be absolutely necessary if the sales of the periodical within a bourgeoisie fast becoming nationalist were to

[1] Vol. 1871, p. 187. Perhaps the true feeling of the middle-class entrepreneur and merchant class is expressed in a poem on the war, with an opposite tendency, that appears in the same volume:

> "Ein Handel ist's, bei dem der Krämer
> Im Leben keine Seide spinnt;
> Ein Lotto, wo der Unternehmer,
> Sowie der Spieler nichts gewinnt."

(*loc. cit.*, p. 186).

be maintained. Whereas hitherto the political struggle
of middle-class liberalism had been chiefly directed
against the alliance of throne and altar, against the
feudal stratum and Protestant orthodoxy, it is the Roman
Church that is now proclaimed the enemy, a change of
front which indicates the willingness of the North German Protestant middle-class to support the later *Kultur-
kampf* of Bismarck.[1]

The volume for 1888 reflects with astonishing clarity
how large sections of the middle-class have accepted
their due place within the social order of the imperial-
istic Reich. Both upper- and lower-class feel themselves
to be an indispensable component of the Empire and
now express an admiration for the court circle, Emperor
and royal family. The celebration of the ninetieth birthday of Kaiser Wilhelm I takes up considerable space in
this volume: a large picture shows the Kaiser riding
over the battlefield of Sedan, and accounts of his childhood and of the birthday celebrations in Berlin follow.
Prince Wilhelm's bear-hunting expeditions are reported
and illustrated, and also the summer holiday of Moltke.
Previously it had been exceptional to have aristocratic
contributors, but now a whole string of aristocratic
writers were able to make their appearance in the pages
of this middle-class periodical.[2] Aristocratic titles no
longer sounded degrading in middle-class ears, but
flattering. The accounts written by aristocrats gave
readers the illusion of knowing the feudal places of
amusement and the court world still closed to them.
The antipathy towards flunkeyism that the once very
independent and democratic middle-class had, has disappeared. The same stratum that twenty years before
had read with keen approval the descriptions of princely
arbitrariness and democratic courage, now submitted
under a changed sky to a bombastic servility such

[1] See the typical aggressive poem, "*In Jesuitas,*" vol. 1871, p. 544.

[2] For instance, Anton Freiherr von Perfall contributes a tale of the Bavarian
mountains and an account of the carnival on the Riviera; Alex. Baron von
Roberts writes the novel *Götzendienst*, and Georg von Amyntor acts as reporter
of Society News.

as is expressed in an article entitled "In the Marble Palace of Potsdam." The author of this, Georg von Amyntor, was allowed to inscribe a congratulatory poem of ostentatious devotion on the occasion of the birth of an heir to the later Kaiser Wilhelm II, and his wife Victoria "in the autograph book of the high lady." His last verse runs:

> Such an imperial four-leaf has never been seen,
> So long as the stars have circled round the sun!
> An Emperor, a Crown Prince speedy in victory,
> A smart grandson, a greatgrandson child!
> Lift up your hearts! We bow our knees!
> Such a May miracle never happened before!
> Preserve the four-leaf, O mighty Lord,
> And put all its enemies to shame![1]

b. *The Liberal Novel of Protest*

The large circulation of the *Gartenlaube* is very closely connected with its publication of the novels of E. Marlitt. How thoroughly they appealed to the taste, thoughts and emotions of the petty-bourgeois feminine reader is attested by the fact that after the appearance of Marlitt's first novel the paper experienced an astonishing increase in circulation, and the publisher therefore decided to make this type of story a permanent feature.[2]

This kind of novel represented with only slight variations by E. Marlitt, E. Heimburg and E. Werner is distinguished neither by æsthetic qualities of form nor by artistic descriptions; its psychology is crude, being either tendencious or sentimental, its treatment is arbitrary and full of blatant sensationalism. But its distortions still reflect clearly a class-consciousness and class-conflict, whether it be in the obstinate middle-class hostility of Marlitt or in the more conciliatory sentimentalism of Heimburg.[3] We must not regard their description of

---

[1] *Die Gartenlaube*, vol. 1887, p. 571.

[2] See the article *Zur Geschichte der Gartenlaube* in *Die Gartenlaube*, 1902, vol. 50, pp. 9 ff. ; also the article *E. Marlitt* in *Allg. Deutsche Biographie*, lii. 213–16.

[3] For the women writers of the *Gartenlaube* see R. von Gottschall, *Die deutsche Nationalliteratur des 19. Jahrhunderts*, Breslau, 1892, 6th Ed., iv. 593 ff.

the aristocracy as a result of realistic observation, but as the typical middle-class conventional picture of it.

E. Marlitt, whose real name was E. John, was acquainted through the course of her life with the aristocratic as well as with the bourgeois milieu. She was the daughter of a merchant in a Thuringian petty state who found a patron for her talents—like Gustav Freytag and Fanny Lewald—in one of the petty princelings of Thuringia. With the assistance of the reigning Princess von Schwarzenburg-Sondershausen, she was able to take up a stage career and soon obtained the title of Court-singer (*Fürstliche Kammersängerin*). She later became reader to the court. As the only commoner in these exclusive surroundings, she soon found herself forced into the defensive position peculiar to the isolated, and had the opportunity of experiencing aristocratic class prejudices as exercised on her own person. In spite of this, the fact that after her departure from court she wrote anti-aristocratic novels is not to be explained solely by her individual experiences. Fifty years before a middle-class woman with the same experiences would have kept quiet about them, or would have toned them down. The liberal tendencies of the time, the example of "higher" literature, formed probably an important factor in urging this authoress to write as she did.

Her novels were in any case interpreted as challenges to the aristocracy and they made a powerful impression on ladies of the upper middle-class, and also on readers of the lower middle-class and proletariat.[1] The middle-class novel of protest stressed more strongly than did the "higher literature" the identification of moral good with the middle-class and of moral evil with the aristocracy. There are occasional exceptions, but these only serve to emphasize the general rule. The figure of the noble-minded aristocrat or of the aristocrat who joined with the middle-class to achieve there the "happy end" of intermarriage with its resultant moral reward for the middle-class hero or heroine, was indeed by no

---

[1] Cf., for instance, *Die Gartenlaube*, 1887, p. 476.

means infrequent.[1] The "happy end" of inter-marriage doubtless appealed to the secret wish-dreams of the petty-bourgeois feminine reader. Nevertheless, it is an error to maintain with Proelss that the first novels of Marlitt were the poetical expression of a growing rapprochement between aristocracy and middle-class, between prince and people, under the banner of liberal ideas.[2] They reveal rather the intention of exhibiting the superior moral qualities of the middle-class and of protesting against the arbitrariness of an institution destined for destruction. In them, aristocratic titles are no longer striven for as distinctions, but are sometimes even emphatically rejected.

According to these novels the gulf between middle-class and aristocracy is no longer unbridgeable, but this is due to the victorious economic and moral power of the middle-class which vitiates all the ranks and falsities of the feudal stratum and of the clergy that is allied to it. The same black-and-white colouring, which we have already observed in the "higher" liberal novel, appears here on a lower scale in greater distortion. The aristocrats are presented as "scoundrels, nonentities and fools" and their legacy-hunting, lust for domination, religious hypocrisy and bigotry, pride, brutality, arbitrariness against individuals as well as against the lower classes, are crudely elaborated. Life at the petty courts has only a superficial brilliance, in reality it is empty and arid. The aristocracy, as is the way of primitive communities, has developed a double ethical standard: an inner morality and an outward morality; its unwritten maxim is responsibility to members of its own estate and unbounded arbitrariness towards the middle-class. In *Gold Else*, for instance, the landowner, Baron Wolf von Gnadewitz, is described as a gourmet of vice. His twenty-year-old son strikes down a beater on a hunting expedition because the man had hurt one of his hounds.

---

[1] Several of Marlitt's novels end with intermarriage, e.g. *Gold Else, Reichsgräfin Gisela, Die Zwölf Apostel*, etc.

[2] *Zur Geschichte der Gartenlaube*, 1902, vol. 50, 137.

The latter avenges himself by hanging the baron. "By this event," says the novel, with outspoken resentment against the aristocracy, "the long tale of robber barons, wild excesses, hunting orgies and horse-races came to an end." [1]   In *Reichsgräfin Gisela*, a young lady of aristocratic birth breaks her engagement with a middle-class foundry overseer in a despicable manner, so that her career at court might not be endangered.[2]   The young Countess herself, in accordance with a custom prevailing in Prussia at that time, is brought up with the parson's children at the parsonage.   She is treated here on an equality with the parson's children, and her former aristocratic governess protests against this degrading democratic procedure.   The class-pride of the aristocracy is thus stressed in all aspects of life.

As the story proceeds, the disillusionment that is brought by intimate contact with aristocratic and court society is illustrated in the experiences of the Countess. The motive of disillusionment that we have already found in "higher" literature is repeated also in "lower" literature with moralizing importunity.

It is a sociological law that an intimate glimpse into the life of a group or stratum usually gives a more negative impression than does a distant one from outside.   In other words the "view from inside" is more sober and less glamorous than the view from outside.   The young Countess in Marlitt's novel had formed an idealized picture of the exalted life at court and of princes, but it was completely destroyed on her first contact with this sphere: "This, then, was the court circle," the anti-aristocratic authoress makes her say, "the quintessence of the nobility of the land, and amongst them was the mighty one who should have the greatest wisdom in his mind and the greatest self-control in his soul."

[1] See English translation of *Gold Else*, London, 1873, p. 7.

[2] The generalizing, anti-aristocratic tendency is in this case especially sharply stressed. "The age-old tragedy for which this noble line of hunters had supplied actors enough, was once again performed: once again love was betrayed by aristocratic pride" (*Reichsgräfin Gisela*, i. 206—English translation, *The Countess Gisela*, London, 1870, p. 110).

The Prince ruled by the grace of God and embodied the highest juridical and political power in the country.

> How she had been deceived. The court circle yonder was only exclusive because of the strict adherence to laws of etiquette, not from any innate superiority. There was nothing to choose between a rustic party of ordinary mortals and that miniature picture on the meadow.[1]

Disillusionment signifies here at the same time an inner *feeling of equality*: the highest dignitaries and those possessed of power are not only brought down to the level of ordinary mortals, but are also inwardly degraded as bad mortals. It is the age-old theme of the fairy-tale *Cinderella*, of the slaving and suppressed woman, that reappears in realistic and blatant form in these novels at a time when the idea of the emancipation of woman was beginning to take effect. The woman who has been abused and humiliated by aristocratic pride and priestly arbitrariness maintains herself successfully in spite of the arrogance of the old powers, and in doing so experiences the sincerity of middle-class life.[2] Faithfulness or faithlessness in sex relationships are again completely identified with certain classes. Faithful and sincere are the men and women of the middle-class, faithless and deceitful usually the men and women of the aristocracy. The protest against the repression and exploitation of the presumed inferiority of the woman is always successful as a result of her superior inner qualities: in Marlitt's *Gold Else* the middle-class heroine who gives pianoforte lessons is regarded by the Baroness von Lersen as a paid servant and is socially humiliated; in *Die Zweite Frau*, a poor aristocratic lady is the plaything of the polite indifference of her husband, and the object of the cunning and desire of the court chaplain and court steward. In *Reichsgräfin Gisela* the defence-

---

[1] *The Countess Gisela*, pp. 227 ff.

[2] The suppressed women in Marlitt's novels are partly middle-class women, as in *Gold Else* or in *Die Zwölf Apostel*, partly déclassé members of the aristocracy, as in *Reichsgräfin Gisela* and *Die Zweite Frau*.

less aristocratic lady is again the victim of the intrigues of her courtly surroundings. In *Lumpenmüllers Lieschen* by E. Heimburg, a proud aristocratic grandmother humiliates cruelly a mill-owner's daughter who is deeply in love with her grandson.

Aristocratic wickedness is contrasted with a bourgeois or petty-bourgeois world of idyllic and honest loyalty, a world of petty towns and villages. Parsonage, forester's lodge, and village-mill are the homes of middle-class respectability and idyllic family life. Whilst the aristocrats regard each other coldly and contemptuously behind their class conventions, there prevails in the simple burgher's house a tone of heartiness and sincerity. Warmth of feeling is the sign of a sincere mind. Sentimentality, perseverance and respectability are correlative values in the middle-class novel of virtue and protest.[1] They represent at the same time the specific virtues that were then stressed in the upbringing of middle-class girls.[2]

This type of novel exposes the hypocrisy of pietist court circles and clerical cabals,[3] but on the other hand it is precisely the liberal parson's house that is the model and representative of all middle-class virtues. We are presented with an idealization not of the orthodox hypocrite, but of the liberal parson who preaches practical Christianity instead of dogma. The protestant parsonage is described as being exactly in accordance with Luther's idea of it—a pattern of Christian and middle-class virtues: life in it consists of the Bible, cooking-pot, mending of stockings and breeding of children: and its inhabitants are healthy, upright, cheerful people who

---

[1] This correlation is always a characteristic feature of the outspoken middle-class novel. It is therefore to be found in eighteenth-century England in, for instance, the works of Richardson.

[2] An article entitled *Französische Salondame und deutsche Hausfrau* (*Daheim*, 1866, pp. 751–4) is typical of this.

[3] For this reason the *Gartenlaube* had to face a strong resistance and boycott amongst the orthodox priesthood of both Christian religions: see for example the extremely polemical brochure from the Catholic side, L. Deibel, *Die Gartenlaube*, Munich, 1879.

know how to manage life.[1]   In the same way foresters and
mill-owners are typical honest Germans.   One of them is
portrayed thus: "The master of the house with his handsome, benevolent face framed in a full, luxuriant beard." [2]

The strong response evoked by the liberal novel of
protest between 1866 and 1880 resulted in the production of a whole string of similar efforts; but the middle-
class novel of protest, since it corresponded more to the
experiences and day-dreams of middle-class strata, had
a bigger public than its rival, *the conservative novel of
loyalty*.   The latter found its most significant expression
in the pages of the Christian conservative periodical,
Daheim.   The readers of this periodical consisted chiefly
of officials, clergymen, and artisans who supported the
conservative ideology with its stress on union between
throne and altar, between Prussian feudalism and orthodox protestant piety.   Loyalty to the King and Church
was the distinguishing mark of this periodical.   For
instance, the volume for 1866 has, besides war-com-
muniqués written from the Prussian standpoint, edifying
essays from the pens of Protestant theologians: a caustic
article defends the "most slandered house," the well-
known pietistic educational institution in Hamburg
called *Rauhes Haus*, against attacks of the *Gartenlaube*.
Literature is judged in this periodical completely from
a national and ecclesiastical viewpoint.   Christian novels
and religious tales are recommended, whereas a free-
thinking democratic poet like F. Freiligrath—a typical
hero of the *Gartenlaube*—is sharply censured because of

---

[1] Thus, for instance, is it said of the parson's wife in *Lumpenmüllers Lieschen*:
"She was always joyful, although she had a whole row of little children at
home who followed one another like the pipes of an organ and for whom
she often never knew where to get a new coat or jacket" (p. 88). It might
be added here that the much praised tendency of the Protestant clergy to live
a simple life is sociologically speaking only the result of a somewhat modest
social position. The clergy was drawn for the most part from the lower
middle-class and the students of theology were the poorest amongst their
academic colleagues. Although the prestige of the clergy was higher than
in the eighteenth century, their income remained, compared with that of
other professions, very small. (E. Heimburg, *Lumpenmüllers Lieschen*, 45th
Ed., Stuttgart, 1928.)   [2] *Op. cit.*

his political attitude and unbelief, and rejected as a German poet who has fallen from grace.[1] Conversely, aristocratic poets like Graf M. Strachwitz and Annette von Droste-Hülshoff are placed on a religious and patriotic pedestal.

The conservative novel of loyalty, which sometimes approached submissiveness, differs from the liberal novel of protest chiefly through its positive attitude to the aristocracy and Court circle. This attitude is expressed in the identification of aristocracy of birth with aristocracy of soul, and in the humble subordination of the middle-class girl to the superiority of the aristocratic lady. The princess, for example, in a story in the volume for 1866,[2] to whom the middle-class heroine is brought by a trick to act as reader, is noble, pious and resolute. Her authority is presented as a salutary one, and Johanna recognizes completely her goodness and superiority. The middle-class girl looks up to the princess as her model and guide, and transfers to her all her mother-longing.[3] The princess fulfils the function of a mother, of a higher being that understands and pardons everything. She is at the same time a kindly mediating authority between God and people. Submission to the will of God and submission to the existing semi-feudal social order is the moral that is preached uninterruptedly by the novels of this periodical from 1866 to the end of the century.

[1] The clerical authoritarian attitude is expressed for instance in the following sentence: "Like a swaying cane he (Freiligrath) surrendered to the demoniac powers of our time, to those who sowed the storm of 1848. . . . A nature without a peaceful and organic culture, without home and rest, more at home in a physical than in an ethical cultural element, without belief, wherefrom could his inner powers of resistance come?" (*Daheim*, 1866, ii. 26).

[2] *Führe mich nicht in Versuchung*, by A. von Auer (*Daheim*, vol. 1866).

[3] For this see the following remark: "With a cry of joy and delight she rushed to the arms of the princess, to the motherly heart of the noble lady." The tendency to try and adapt the aristocracy to the middle-class and to the idyll of the honest burgher is expressed in a sentence describing the princess: "A kindly smile played about her lips, a look of indescribable sincerity shone from her dark eyes, when she extended her hand to the girl and said with winning friendliness . . ." (vol. 1866, p. 233).

2. The Philistines in Germany and England

Now that we have examined middle-class self-confidence as reflected in literature, we shall attempt briefly in the following excursus to analyse the attack of middle-class writers on the self-satisfaction of the philistine who is regarded as a caricature of the bourgeois.

The essence of philistinism is conceited self-satisfaction, indifference, hostility to intellectualism, a limited horizon, such as were to be found throughout politically disunited Germany and the numerous residential and petty towns. The prevalence of disintegrating individualism in towns was the result of the eighteenth century. The lack of a central power and the tardy development of a public opinion supplied the fertile soil for German philistinism. Philistinism as a distinguishing characteristic of a certain bourgeois mentality is—as W. H. Riehl had already recognized [1]—a thoroughly modern phenomenon.

To German classicism the philistine is already the counterpart to genius, to the philosophical mind, incapable of understanding or creating the beautiful and the significant. The philistine is the literary scribbler, the embodiment of mediocrity, who hates everything significant and noble because he fails to understand it and fears its competition; he is the Wagner type in Goethe's *Faust*—a pedant without taste and depth, a type that seeks only security and a comfortable position in life. For the classicists the philistine is dull, slow and cowardly. It is in this sense that he is referred to in one of the Xenien written by Goethe and Schiller together:[2]

> Only the fiery horse, the courageous, falls on the race-course,
> With cautious step proceeds the ass.

For romanticism, also, the philistine signified simply the prosaic dullard. He is the enemy of the fresh,

---

[1] W. H. Riehl, *Die bürgerliche Gesellschaft*, Stuttgart, 1858, 5th Ed., p. 220.
[2] *Xenien, 1796*, ed. E. Schmidt and B. Suphan, *Schriften der Goethegesellschaft*, viii. 27.

cheerful, and natural life such as is embodied in both students and poets. He is old, self-satisfied, has seen and knows everything, and remains for ever a stranger to great passions. The philistines form a compact majority; they have, according to Brentano, "an invisible, unconscious bond with each other." [1] They are the born opponents of all ideas, of all enthusiasm, of all God's free creations.

Eichendorff, especially, never tires of illustrating in humour and satire the eternal and fundamental difference between the philistine anxious for security and the unconcerned, migrant poet. In his dramatic fairy-tale, *Krieg den Philistern* (1824), he pointedly satirizes the mentality of a sober young civil-servant, who considers all relationships and situations from the point of view of advantage to his career. The young man reflects with self-satisfaction on the approval he has won from his superiors and tries to meet them even at places of amusement and recreation. He stresses pharisaically his superiority over a school-comrade who has become a poet and praises the advantages of well-paid professions over the wayward muses.[2]

In Heinrich Heine the fight against the philistines takes a political turn; the philistine is also for him, to begin with, the prosaic man who thinks only of utility and lacks intellectuality:

The number of the Göttingen *philistines* [he says with biting scorn in his *Harzreise*] must be as plentiful as the sands (or, more correctly speaking, as the mud) of the sea; indeed, when I beheld

---

[1] Cl. Brentano, *Der Philister vor, in und nach der Geschichte* (*Gesammelte Werke*, Frankfort-on-Main, 1852, v. 379).

[2] "One meets here curious strangers, distinguished and influential men; one modestly begins a sensible conversation so that whilst having recreation one can also gather useful information. How I thank my God that I have not become as so many of my former schoolfellows have! That one there, for instance, who, with good society all around him, sits alone on a bench and reads a book, has nothing but verses in his head. Oh, I also do not mind, after the day's work is done, sometimes taking up a good classical poet for recreation or composing a few verses for the birthday or marriage of a superior —but, give me a sure occupation—solid bread" (Eichendorff, *Krieg den Philistern*, Berlin, 1824, p. 138).

them of a morning, with their dirty faces and clean bills, planted before the gate of the collegiate court of justice, I wondered greatly that such an innumerable pack of rascals should ever have been created.[1]

The philistine has a shallow, utilitarian conception of nature and art, and appears especially ridiculous when travelling because he understands nothing of either. In *Die Reise von München nach Genua*, the typical professions of the philistine are also suggested, for the representative philistines there are a councillor of commerce (*Kommerzienrat*) and a cheese-monger.[2] But Heine's philistine is by no means so harmless as that of the romantics. He is rather the cowardly burgher who hinders progress and acknowledges every existing authority, nay more, identifies himself with it. The philistine for Heine is not only the representative of a class, but even of a nation. He represents the non-political German who patiently allows himself to be controlled and ruled by numberless governments.[3] This great mocker in exile holds that it is typical of Germans that they have, besides great and profound thinkers, a large intermixture of astonishingly narrow philistinism.[4]

Heine [one of his friends remarked of the last period of his life [5]] often laughed at the Germans. That widely-spread philistinism which felt itself so secure and comfortable behind its high mud walls, the lack of temperament which poses as moral superiority, the pedantry which would like to set up as school-teacher of the nation, the belief in being able to rule the world

[1] H. Heine, *Works*, translated by Ch. O. Leland, London, 1891, ii. 60 f.

[2] For Heine's satire on Philistines in *Reisebilder* see E. Löwenthal, *Studien zu Heines Reisebildern*, Berlin, 1924, pp. 38–48.

[3] See J. A. Hess, *Heine's Views on German Traits of Character*, New York, 1929, p. 60.

[4] Heine expresses the antithesis between the philosophical mind and the philistine very much like the authors of the *Xenien*: "Beside the thinker there stands a prosaic man peacefully carrying on his business, beside the crib wherein is born a saviour, a world-redeeming idea, there stands also an ox quietly eating" (*Gesammelte Werke*, ed. O. Walzel, vol. x; *Gedanken und Einfälle*, Leipzig, 1915, p. 285).

[5] Alfred Meissner, see H. H. Houben, *Gespräche mit Heine*, Frankfort-on-Main, 1925, p. 641.

with ideas whilst one grovelled before petty despots,—all this was
the object of his most searing scorn and wildest mockery.

The same political conception of the philistine as the
drag-chain on intellect and progress is to be found in
liberal poets before and after 1848 (like Hoffmann von
Fallersleben and G. Herwegh). A lampoon by Hoffmann von Fallersleben, *Das Lied vom deutschen Philister*,
has the following lines:

> The German philistine, he should remain the man
> in whom the Government can still put their trust.
> He fits in with their ideas of making everyone happy,
> And good-naturedly allows anything to be done with him.[1]

The philistine hinders the progress of the age, destroys
everything good and positive, is the enemy of the beautiful and the sublime, and ignores "honour, virtue and
right." He is not only content with the existing order
of society, but he does nothing to prevent himself from
being diverted by the government's tricks and intrigues;
of this mentality Georg Herwegh was at that time able
to say:

> And should they forbid you everything,
> Don't you worry too much!
> You still have your Schiller and Goethe,
> Sleep! what more do you want?[2]

The attitude of Wilhelm Raabe differs in a singular
way from this outspoken denunciation of philistinism
by Heine and the political lyricists.

Raabe was typical of the German provincial and
Heimat-writers; he spent most of his life in central
German provincial towns like Brunswick and Wolfenbüttel and was never able to rid himself of the atmosphere of *Niedersachsen*. The mingling of a pessimistic
pietism with a semi-realistic art gives to his description
of petty-bourgeois philistinism, as represented by un-
intellectual dignitaries and notabilities, a peculiar note.

---

[1] See B. von Wiese's anthology *Politische Lyrik 1756–1871*, Berlin, 1933,
pp. 85 ff.

[2] G. Herwegh, *Wiegenlied*; cf. *Politische Lyrik 1756–1871*, pp. 88 ff.

Just as Raabe himself is a true German combination of the philosophically-minded and the philistine, so we find also in his works that the bourgeois philistine is now tenderly caressed, now remorselessly revealed in his limitations.

Raabe, too, works with the antithesis between original, profound and worldly-wise individuality, and philistinism that takes the existing moral and social order for granted. In *Abu Telfan*, the shrewd-minded adventurer who returns home unexpectedly from Africa to the German petty town is contrasted with the dull-witted petty-bourgeoisie which judges a man's worth only by his outward success. The dignitaries' desire for security and their inability to understand the returned prodigal are caustically caricatured.

The German philistines [says Raabe mockingly in his baroque style] *vis-à-vis* of this problematic, unsettled, unhinged, uprooted existence, felt themselves to be living in a glorious security of tax and rate-payments, of pew-holding, police protection and princely supervision, and they expressed their opinions accordingly.[1]

The world-traveller delivers a lecture to the upper stratum of a residential town, and its reactions are similar to those of the petty-town dignitaries. Here the notables and higher officials set the tone.

Councillors of State and Major-Generals, Presidents of the High Court and Consistory Court, Directors, Ministerial Councillors, War-Councillors, and Board-Councillors, State-Directors, Customs-Inspectors and State-Treasurers, Prelates, Medical-Councillors, Archivists and Librarians, these display here the triumph of civilization at its highest.[2]

But according to Raabe this bureaucracy is mechanized, is unfree, and lives a life that is so much a "rationally ordered vulgar habit" that it feels itself repelled by the impulse of freedom embodied in the impoverished world-traveller, and as a result its self-confidence begins

---

[1] W. Raabe, *Abu Telfan, oder die Heimkehr vom Mondgebirge*, Stuttgart, 1870, 2nd Ed., p. 61.

[2] W. Raabe, *op. cit.*, ii. 2 ff.

to waver. Although the philistinism depicted here is vulgar and conventional, it has yet for Raabe a positive function. Its way of life he regards as a necessary counterpoise and counterpart to the way of life of the philosophers and artists, of the cultural élite which in Germany was so much inclined to forget the "rationally ordered vulgar habit" of everyday life.

The genius and the philistine, the superior worldly writer and the normal tax-paying citizen were for German Classicism and Romanticism mutually exclusive contradictions, but for Raabe they are elements that necessarily postulate each other. The more the German character inclines to philosophical speculation, the more is there necessity for this philistinism that settles itself comfortably in the world.

> Wherever we look [says Raabe] we see that German genius everywhere and always draws a third of its vigour from philistinism, and it is hugged and swept into the air by that old giant, Thought, with which it struggles . . . if it does not manage at the same time to keep in touch with the soil from which it grew.[1]

Genius and philistinism are for Raabe products of the same social origin, viz. of the German middle-class.

> Luther, Goethe and Jean Paul are also by no means ashamed of their origin; they readily show a homely understanding for the workshop, office and council chamber, and even Friedrich Schiller, who of all our intellectual heroes perhaps broke the most sharply with Nippenburg and Bumsdorf, feels from time to time the hearty need to be reminded of all natural and intimate relationships by the greeting of an official and a relative, and by an honest "hallo."[2]

It is the stratum of petty bourgeois and dignitaries, of teachers, tax-officials and state-inspectors from which the German cultural élite originates, and which it can never completely renounce.

It might be instructive to compare with the two types of German critics, as embodied by Heine and

---

[1] W. Raabe, *op. cit.*, iii. 172 f.   [2] *Ibid.*

Raabe, the great critic of English philistinism in the middle of the nineteenth century. Matthew Arnold received an important stimulus from German literature in his vigorous struggle against the English philistine. This is clearly revealed in his famous essay on Heinrich Heine.[1] The great German satirist is for him a pioneer in the fight against philistinism, his whole being "a life and death battle with philistinism." If Matthew Arnold did not take over from Heine the word philistine, he very probably took over from him the conception of philistinism.[2] For Matthew Arnold, Philistinism is the enemy of a cultural aristocracy, "a strong dogged unenlightened opponent of the chosen people, of the children of the light." His viewpoint is not that of the politician, nor that of the poet, but that of the reformer and critic of culture. In the dramatic struggle of modern society there stand on the one side the innovators, "the party of change, the would-be remodellers of the old traditional European order, the invokers of reason against custom, the representatives of the modern spirit in every sphere where it is applicable," and on the other side, the philistines, that "humdrum people, slaves to routine, enemies to light; stupid and oppressive, but at the same time very strong." [3]

He therefore understands quite easily that Heine, the "born lover of ideas and hater of commonplaces," should have a strong antipathy against England. For the distinguishing feature of English philistinism which strikes the foreigner so much is its want of, and its inaccessibility to, ideas.

If the philistine for the German classicists and romantics was the prosaic man, if he was for Heine the embodiment of German national failings, he was identified

[1] *Essays in Criticism*, 1865, Oxford, 1918, pp. 116–42.

[2] See his biting remark: "Philistinism!—we have not the expression in English. Perhaps we have not the word because we have so much of the thing" (*loc. cit.*, p. 120).

[3] *Ibid.*, p. 121; for Arnold's criticism of contemporary German philistinism see J. R. Renwanz, *Matthew Arnold und Deutschland*, Thesis Greifswald, 1927, chap. iii, pp. 16–38.

briefly by Arnold with a whole class, the English middle-class. The German writers were too closely bound up with the middle-class in its political struggle to identify the middle-class completely with philistinism. *Bürger* (citizen) and *Spiessbürger* (philistine) are therefore by no means identical for them. In any case, their hatred of the aristocracy was not less than their hostility to the philistines. But Arnold, the English æsthete, had no antipathy against the aristocracy, against the Leisure Class, but a bitter feeling against the bourgeoisie, the Ruling Class.

In his essays on social criticism he distinguishes between three classes, aristocracy, middle-class and proletariat—or as he calls them, Barbarians, Philistines and Populace.[1] Of these the middle-class is the most important. In Germany the aristocracy still rules, whilst the bureaucracy of middle-class origin administers. In England, however, the position is reversed. There, according to Arnold, the middle-class rules, whilst the aristocracy merely administers. "The Philistines take their doings and manners absolutely for granted." They have only two interests, which are in no way connected—making money and saving their souls. "They are children of the established fact and therefore inaccessible to ideas." Their life is also determined—to quote Raabe—by "rationally ordered vulgar habit," or to use the words of Arnold—by "that sort of machinery of business, chapels, tea-meetings, and addresses by Mr. Murphy and the Rev. W. Cattle." [2] The philistines' life-interests are acquisition of money and church-going piety, and the synthesis of them is best typified by the Methodist grocer. The æsthetic Arnold attacks especially the empty crudeness of their amusements.

It has an enjoyment in its business and in a narrow unintelligent repulsive religion. What else makes up their life? Eating and drinking, reading of newspapers and of religious or semi-

[1] Cf. M. Arnold, *Culture and Anarchy*, London, 1869, chap. iii.
[2] *Ibid.*, p. 99.

religious books that are completely lacking in culture; and then a lecture in the evening on abstinence or nunneries.[1]

Arnold intensifies his attack on the middle-class by a twofold contrast: he compares middle-class and aristocracy and English middle-class with continental middle-class. The nobility is no longer what it once was: it has surrendered its domination and is lacking in guiding principles and impulses. It still sets the social tone, is rich, indolent and satisfied with itself. The old English aristocracy of 1800, by contrast, was still great and important and the feeling of greatness gave it "force to endure labours, anxiety, danger, disappointment, loss, restrictions of liberty."[2]

The "Barbarians" no longer have an intellectual life, but they still possess to-day a behaviour of their own, "a kind of image or shadow of sweetness." Arnold bestows a compliment on the aristocracy when he admits that it possesses guiding ideals, "Gods." The Gods of the aristocracy are "exterior Gods, but in a way they are Gods." These Gods appear as worldly glitter, security, power and amusement. Seduction by them is not perverse like the attitude of the philistines, but natural. The extenuating circumstances which this severe critic grants the aristocracy are by no means allowed by him to the middle-class; for it is not the aristocracy, but the middle-class that now represents England in the eyes of other countries.

The typical failings for which the English are blamed by foreigners are not so much the failings of the aristocracy, but rather those of the middle-class. The aristocracy always preserves its dignity. Long tradition has made it adept in social intercourse, reserved, dignified, and sensitive on points of honour. The middle-class in this period, however, is "testy, absolute, ill-acquainted with foreign matters, a little ignoble, very dull to perceive when it is making itself ridiculous."[3]

[1] See M. Arnold, *Friendship's Garland*, London, 1871, p. 142 f.
[2] *Ibid.*, p. 81.   [3] *Ibid.*, p. 128.

If, as we saw, German middle-class liberal writers always hold up the qualities of the English aristocracy as an example to the backward German aristocracy, the English critic of culture, for his part, praises the continental middle-class (especially that of Germany) as an example for the English middle-class. The continental middle-class has an understanding both of work and of the enjoyment of life.[1] The English middle-class, however, is accustomed only to work, but not to enjoy life. The philistine in Germany is servile, has a love for titles, and betrays no independence at all towards the aristocracy and bureaucracy that govern him; the philistine in England, by contrast, governs himself, but without charm and without dignity, devoted only to money and to conventional piety; for six days a week he worships at the Bank of England, and the seventh day in Church.[2]

Raabe stressed the interdependence of genius and philistinism, but Arnold, very much like the German classicists, emphasizes the gulf between the autonomous cultural élite and the dull mass of philistines. He speaks distinctly of the intellectual élite, of "a certain number of *aliens*" in society, as "persons who are mainly led not by their class spirit, but by a general *humane* spirit, by the love of human perfection."[3] This cultural élite is the true repository of Arnold's ideals of "sweetness and light."

The German critics of philistinism fight chiefly against its political backwardness, the English critic, however, against its complete lack of æstheticism. The Germans attacked a combination of utilitarianism and political servility, the Englishman, however, a mixture of the capitalist acquisitive instinct with empty, formal piety. The philistine appears to his German opponents as

---

[1] "The world of enjoyment, so liberalizing and civilizing, belongs to the middle-classes there, as well as the world of business; the whole world is theirs, they possess life" (*ibid.*, p. 143).

[2] Similar views were expressed from the German point of view by Th. Fontane in his essay *Ein Sommer in England*, Berlin, 1854, esp. pp. 263–71.

[3] *Culture and Anarchy*, p. 110.

stupid, to his English adversary, as ugly; the German philistine is narrow in obedience, the English philistine is narrow in governing; but both varieties of the same phenomenon are regarded as being in implacable opposition to the eternal struggle of a select minority for human dignity and intellectual freedom.

CHAPTER VII

POLITICAL ALLIANCE AND SOCIAL FUSION
1871–1900

1. Aristocracy and Upper Middle-Class in the New Empire

The period after 1870 is characterized by a marked rapprochement between the feudal stratum and considerable sections of the upper middle-class. In Germany, as in France, the heavy industries and agriculture joined together under the banner of protective duties. They were further brought into close relation by their common dependence on the soil, for, like agriculture, heavy industry was bound to the soil and localized in its need of coal and iron.

The modern captain of industry, "through the fact that he lives for the most part outside the towns and through his economic position in the social whole," has become "increasingly the sharer of the convictions of the aristocratic landowner, and is possibly therefore more a member of this class than of the class of bourgeois merchants and bankers." [1] He seeks to gain contact with the feudal tradition by the purchase of estates in the form of a *Fideikommiss* and by ennoblement. The old aristocracy was being replaced more and more by a ruling class of feudal and bourgeois, agricultural and industrial entrepreneurs, who were the real upholders of German nationalism and imperialism. The aristocracy was less directly connected with the commercial

---

[1] C. Brinkmann, *Die Umformung der kapitalistischen Gesellschaft, Grundriss der Sozialökonomik,* 1926, Abt. ix, i. 19 f.

and banking world, for the latter's free-trade principles stood in opposition to its nationalist ideology.

If the fusion of aristocracy and upper middle-class had become a fact in many countries in the last three decades of the nineteenth century (especially in England and France), the prestige of the aristocracy remained nowhere so politically important as in pseudo-constitutional Germany. Even if the economic strength of the aristocracy had declined, its social prestige remained itself unchanged. The feudal tradition still set the tone in Germany more than in any other country. If the decisive factor in America was money, in Italy education, in Germany, as in England, it was the power of tradition alone which could lend prestige to the successful *arriviste* families. In England the aristocracy maintained an organic contact with the other strata of the nation by sending its younger sons into the business world,[1] and also by the bestowal of knighthood or peerages on successful middle-class business magnates. In Germany, however, the process was one-sided, for although a number of wealthy industrialists, bankers and leading civil servants ascended into the feudal stratum, the aristocracy, for its part, adjusted itself only slightly to the new economic structure and often disdained to engage in middle-class occupations. And only in Germany did the uneducated and impoverished section of the aristocracy, also, still enjoy social importance. This can be seen by the fact that whereas in Vienna only the higher aristocracy belonged to court society, in Berlin the pettiest and most insignificant aristocrat did. Between 1870 and 1914, Germany—as R. Michels has expressed it[2] —"was not ruled by a class of culture and economic power, but by hussars and Ulan officers of noble blood, by *assessors* (judges) and diplomats who possessed coronets." In short, the aristocracy in Germany re-

[1] For the rôle of the English aristocracy in industry and trade see S. D. Stirk, *Die Aristokratie und die industrielle Entwicklung in England vom 16. bis zum 18. Jahrhundert*, Breslau, 1933.

[2] R. Michels, *Zum Problem der internationalen Bourgeoisie* in *Probleme der Sozialphilosophie*, Leipzig, 1914, pp. 158–88.

mained, on the one hand, a country-nobility of struggling agriculturalists whose members could be called
true aristocrats only with an effort,[1] and, on the other
hand, a military, court and diplomatic nobility that was
the exclusive representative of the German military
monarchy.

Despite this there was, as we have already pointed out,
a certain amount of contact and amalgamation between
upper middle-class and aristocracy. Practically every
section of the middle-class acknowledged for the most
part the deeply-rooted political privileges of the Junkers,
ensuring for themselves thereby, in return, the assistance
of the state-machinery against the newly organized proletariat and against foreign competition. The rapprochement between aristocracy and large-scale industry was
greatly strengthened by *commercium* and *connubium*, i.e.
by their common participation in the boom-period following the Franco-Prussian war, and further by inter-
marriages that relieved the financial necessities of the
aristocracy and satisfied the social ambition of the
enriched bourgeoisie.

We shall endeavour, first, to describe the rapprochement brought about between these two strata by the
economic situation in town and country, and shall then
proceed to the question of intermarriage; finally, we shall
illustrate the relationship between aristocracy and middle-
class as experienced by Fontane, who was perhaps the
finest social observer of his time.

International capitalist expansion after 1870 resulted
in Germany, under the influence of French reparations,
in a wave of new enterprises and undertakings. After a
long period of placidness in economic life there occurred
a boom which was accompanied by a marked disintegra-
tion of commercial morality. Business-ventures sprang
up overnight to build streets, parks, galleries and baths
for which there was no real need, and swindling activities flourished, especially in the founding of private

[1] See the analysis of the situation of the Junker in Max Weber, *Wahlrecht
und Demokratie in Deutschland*, Berlin, 1918, p. 33.

railways.[1] We are not concerned here with the disreput-
able methods employed by the promoters in pushing their
shares on the Stock Exchange and in advertising their
prosperity by a corrupt press, so that they could unload
them quickly when prices rose; we are only considering
here the fact that this financial epidemic had to a certain
degree a levelling influence on social distinctions; for all
sections of the population joined in this chase after the
easily-won profits of speculation; there arose a kind of
economic symbiosis between aristocrats and privy councillors and cab drivers and porters, between bankers and
postmen.[2] One of the cleverest charlatans of the boom-
period, Dr. Strousberg, attracted the public with a
display of dukes and counts as company-directors; in
these companies the aristocrats performed the function
of ornamental figure-heads.[3]

The description and criticism in the novel of this over-
rapid capitalist expansion varies according to the standpoint of the author. A democratic writer like Spielhagen singles out for caustic criticism the part played
by the thoughtless country-nobility; an aristocratic
writer like von Polenz, however, brings out the activities
of the *arriviste* plutocracy. But both authors observe
keenly the contact and amalgamation between aristocracy
and middle-class; both condemn the shaky alliance between insolvent country-nobles and middle-class stock-
jobbers. Whilst the basis of Spielhagen's *Sturmflut* is
formed by a definite historical event—the economic
crisis of 1875—and the manœuvrings on the Berlin
Stock Exchange are described in connection with the
speculations of the Pomeranian country-nobility, Polenz'
realistic novel, *Die Grabenhäger*, gives a detailed picture
based on intimate knowledge of the economic and social
position of the East Elbian country-nobility.

The rapprochement between aristocracy and middle-

---

[1] Cf. Sartorius von Waltershausen, *Deutsche Wirtschaftsgeschichte 1815–1914*,
pp. 261–80.

[2] Sartorius von Waltershausen, *op. cit.*, p. 271.

[3] Cf. W. Hallgarten, *Vorkriegsimperialismus*, Paris, 1935, p. 102.

class is revealed in the fact that middle-class writers no longer paint the aristocracy with the crude bias of twenty years before and, on the other hand, by the fact that aristocratic writers like W. von Polenz or Ernst von Wolzogen now indulge in a detailed criticism of the behaviour of the Junker. A democrat like Spielhagen, who could never completely suppress his hatred of the aristocracy since 1848, depicts for the first time, in *Sturmflut*, honourable and capable representatives of the aristocratic stratum. Vice versa, the narrowness and cunning of the Junkers is either satirically con-demned (as in Wolzogen's outspoken novel *Ecce ego. Erst komm' ich*, 1895), or at least subjected to criticism (as in von Polenz' *Die Grabenhäger*, 1893) by authors of noble origin. In any case, the gulf between aristo-cracy and middle-class was no longer absolute; it could be bridged by representatives of both classes.[1] Yet it was just the positive natures on both sides who conducted themselves with reserve and who for a long time strove against a rapprochement with the other stratum, whilst the frivolous and unscrupulous elements of the middle-class and country-nobility united under the common banner of easy speculative profits.

The contrast now remains not so much one of aris-tocrat versus commoner, but rather of character versus rascality. The attitude of middle-class literature, as represented by Spielhagen, was indeed still sermonic, but not so much filled with class-hatred and resentment. The founding of the Empire had strengthened the pre-cedence enjoyed by aristocracy, army and bureaucracy, and stressed still further the non-political nature of the German middle-class. The bourgeoisie still grumbled at times against the hegemony of the feudal stratum, but it grew resigned to it and sought to enter into it by means of the reserve-officer corps and the student corps.

---

[1] The new amalgamation of Junkers, officers, merchants and higher officials formed also the social background of the Swiss writer C. F. Meyer, and of his heroic interpretation of history. Cf. the interesting essay by L. Löwenthal, *C. F. Meyers heroische Geschichtsauffassung* in *Zeitschrift für Sozialforschung*, vol. ii, Frankfort-on-Main, 1933.

On the other hand, aristocratic men of letters found it no longer necessary to defend the aristocracy, since it was now more firmly than before entrenched in political power.   Such aristocratic writers as von Polenz and von Wolzogen, or M. von Ebner-Eschenbach, suffered much more from the tension existing between the lack of culture of the class of their origin and the level of the free intelligentsia to which they considered themselves to belong.   For them, the new movement of Naturalism was a means of casting light on the aristocracy from which they came, but from which they held themselves aloof without completely surrendering their membership. We shall first deal with Spielhagen's *Sturmflut* and W. von Polenz' *Die Grabenhäger* as the literary expressions of a middle course which did not, indeed, find social conditions to be ideal.   But they also did not wish to introduce fundamental changes, merely desiring to make improvements in certain details.   The aim of these two literary representatives of the democratic and aristocratic camps was not political revolution as in 1848, but moral reform.

In Spielhagen's impressive picture of society, *Sturm-flut*, the central theme is furnished by a private railway project launched by unscrupulous promoters, such as was typical of the bubble-period.   A former *Geheimrat* with influential government connections,[1] a young manufacturer and a banker draw up the scheme and obtain as a figurehead a heavily-indebted Pomeranian landowner, a count.   The count is swept into the net because he hopes to clear off his debts—the old motive of aristocratic insolvency and foolishness again coming into play, except that the aristocratic foolishness is here not so much morally condemned as sociologically explained. The aristocrat is on the defensive, but not so much now through his own fault as through the rules of his caste

---

[1] This character is supposed to be based on the *Geheimer Oberregierungsrat* H. Wagner, an influential, conservative politician and speculator. Cf. J. Ziekursch, *Geschichte des neuen deutschen Kaiserreichs*, Frankfort-on-Main, ii. 301.

which make impossible for him a complete participation in the capitalist struggle for profit, especially in trade. One would seek vainly before 1870 for such an understanding of the aristocrat's obstacles where capitalism is concerned.

For a long time [explains an aristocratic bureaucrat in *Sturmflut*] in this levelling century of ours, we have been standing on the same level, in the same dusty arena where the struggle for existence is being fought out, with the classes which are pressing behind, or rather which are already forcing themselves against us; but the sun and the wind are not equally distributed—a host of weapons which the middle-class employs with tremendous success is forbidden us, for: *Noblesse oblige!* Very fine! *Privileges* we no longer have! God forbid! But *duties*! We are expected to maintain our position in State and Society and yet still preserve our moral qualities! That is very often a difficult business, and sometimes an impossible one: we might as well try to square the circle.[1]

Such restrictions undoubtedly did exist within the nobility in regard to capitalism, but in the long run they were usually relaxed. In reality the large estate-owners, the possessors of the *Fideikommiss*, participated more strongly in the "dance around the Golden Calf" in the boom years than any other class in the nation.[2]

In Spielhagen's novel the usual tactics of the company-promoters are shown. They secure the count by giving him money, for "it is imperative for them to have an aristocratic name to attract both high as well as low," to interest both Pomeranian aristocracy and middle-class in their enterprise.[3] The rapprochement between aris-

[1] F. Spielhagen, *Sturmflut*, Leipzig, 1877, i. 59.

[2] Cf. Max Weber, *Gesammelte Aufsätze zur Soziologie und Sozialpolitik*, Tübingen, 1924, p. 386. The statement of the aristocratic economic historian, Sartorius, in defence of the aristocracy, that the Jews were the chief promoters of the companies and the aristocrats merely their figureheads, is true only in a certain sense; the aristocrats were usually inferior to the bourgeois in the exercise of cunning.

[3] "The aristocratic company-promoters from the country, however, who conceal their greed beneath patriotic words, are at bottom only swindled swindlers; they are the marionettes dancing on the wires manipulated by the city stock-exchange speculators" (V. Klemperer, *Die Zeitromane Friedrich Spielhagens und ihre Wurzeln*, Weimar, 1913, p. 124).

tocrats and commoners through the general speculative
fever is symbolically illustrated at a party arranged by
a bold city businessman. Here we see unfolded not
only the signs of a rapidly and recently acquired luxury
in an elegant palace modelled on that of the Emperor,
but also a revelation of the typical connection between
proud aristocrats and bankers, between guards-officers
and commoners who, inspired by common interests, find
here a meeting-place. The parvenu makes the aristocrats feel at home by cleverly flattering the aristocratic
ladies and respectfully emphasizing the distance between
nouvelle-richesse and ancient nobility, and just because of
this the aristocrats tend to relax their detachment.

Whilst economic necessity and greed of gain thus
unite the "light" characters on both sides, the profit-
seekers and parvenus, the old class-contrast is embodied
by two men of honour, a strict Prussian general of the
old school and a democratic factory owner. In the
verbal duel in which the two engage during the course of
a conversation, the hereditary virtues and hereditary
failings of the penurious, tradition-conscious, devotedly
loyal, military aristocracy and of the obstinate middle-
class, always mindful of its capability, are effectively
contrasted. The vassal's fidelity to his feudal lord,
devotion to the reigning house, pride in tradition, form
the virtues of the military aristocracy; consciousness of
his own capacities, courage in facing the tasks of daily
life, tenacity in the struggle for advancement, are those
of the middle-class. The son of a boatman who has
succeeded in achieving wealth is here filled with the
hatred of the democrats of 1848 for the repressive institutions of monarchy and aristocracy, and he protests
against the unjustified repression "that does not proceed
of necessity from the nature of men, like sickness and
death, or from the nature of society, like law and order." [1]

This strong-charactered, self-made man, who detests
Bismarck as much as the socialists, is the idealized
type of the free-thinking middle-class opposition which

[1] *Sturmflut*, ii. 170.

resisted in Parliament, after 1870, the autocracy of the Iron Chancellor. The opposition was composed of small merchants, Jewish tradesmen, ordinary officials and elementary school-teachers.[1] This type played some part in the civic administration of a few big cities like Berlin and the Hansa-towns, but it did not really make German history; it had in the long run to give way to the other type of national-liberal bourgeois who resigned himself to the domination of the army and the bureaucracy and put up with the fact of his subjection.

The literary ideal of the progressive burgher as here portrayed in Spielhagen, but which had already appeared earlier in Gutzkow and also occasionally in Keller, is the defiant *Biedermann*.[2] For him conviction meant more than appearances, the ethical content of life more than the form of life. As an ideal type the *Biedermann* stood in complete contrast to the "man of the world," for the latter cared not so much for principles as for appearances, not so much for a permanent point of view as for one suiting present circumstances. The man of the world was possessed less of constancy of aim than of broadmindedness, less of character than of understanding of the world and its ways. The *Biedermann*, however, regarded family, profession and party as "absolute" and instinctively rejected anything that might cut across them. The consciousness of the relativity of things appeared foreign to him.

The class-contrast of aristocracy and middle-class was crossed in Germany by a type-contrast of *Biedermann* and man of the world. In Germany, unlike England, the man of the world remained almost completely restricted to the court circle, because of the lack of an earlier cultural fusion between aristocracy and middle-class, owing to the want of a gentleman-ideal.

[1] Cf. Joh. Ziekursch, *Politische Geschichte des neuen deutschen Kaiserreiches*, i. 201.

[2] There is no term in English equivalent to *Biedermann*. It implies a man of honesty, sobriety, worthiness, although not necessarily of intellectual brilliance—in short, the embodiment of the ideal middle-class citizen—what the French call *honnête homme*.

(Certain groups of the aristocracy, especially the court- and diplomat-aristocracy, were, indeed, a favourable breeding-ground for him, but he was to be sought for in vain amongst the country-nobility, amongst the true Junkers.)

It is highly characteristic of German conditions, there- fore, that Spielhagen should present the mutually hostile characters of the defiant middle-class manufacturer and the Prussian general as two different forms of the same *Biedermann* type, and that he should finally find a syn- thesis between the two in a lay-sermon on the fight against Mammon and on the love of the national com- munity. For, from the sociological point of view, the petty-officer and official aristocracy is really to be ranked with the respectable middle-class in so far as its economic and moral position is concerned.

The old officer families [according to Max Weber], which in often extremely necessitous circumstances honourably keep alive the tradition of the Prussian army, and the official families which are akin to them, are, whether aristocratic or not, economically and socially and in their intellectual outlook a middle-class people.[1]

If Spielhagen stresses above all the drift of the Pomeranian country-nobility to the city, von Polenz, on the other hand, deals chiefly with the life of the East Elbian Junkers on their estates, and their attitude to non-aristocrats. His novel, *Die Grabenhäger*, is especi- ally valuable in our connection because of both the aristocratic author's intimate acquaintance with his subject matter and the naturalistic treatment to which he inclines. Of all the naturalist writers of the nine- teenth century, von Polenz is the only one who has adequately described the economic, political and social conditions of the aristocracy.[2] His novel gives us not only a detailed picture of its mode of life as a whole, of the ideologies and types of the East Elbian aristocracy, of its peasants and pastors, he also describes the function

---

[1] Max Weber, *Wahlrecht und Demokratie in Deutschland*, p. 34.
[2] L. Niemann, *Soziologie des naturalistischen Romans*, Berlin, 1934, p. 28.

of church and school, of *Landrat*—office and agricultural union as the instruments of the power of Junkerdom; all this he does without any attempt at extenuation, but also without exaggeration. The Junkers, as he portrays them for us, are engaged in a hard struggle for existence. They are for the most part domineering and authoritarian, imbued with the desire to keep their peasants and labourers in servile restriction.

Polenz also now contrasts both the egotistical, domineering Junker and middle-class parvenu with the honourable outstanding type of impoverished but high-minded aristocrat on the one hand, and with the capable, sterling middle-class landowner on the other. According to Polenz the new community of (financial) interests of aristocracy and middle-class signifies the final intrusion of the capitalist spirit into agriculture and the destruction of all the patriarchal relationships between landowner and day-labourers.[1]

The ruthless country Junker and the moneyed parvenu both regard peasants and workmen purely as instruments of labour and objects of exploitation, and oppose with pitiless vigour any attempt made by the workers to organize themselves in a social-democratic sense. "The men must obey"—thus runs a malcontent clergyman's description of this authoritarian attitude— "work hard, learn as little as possible, be pious and vote conservative." [2]

---

[1] Capitalist exploitation is opposed by the type of Christian Socialist pastor who, in contrast to the orthodox country parson, no longer supports the alliance between throne and altar, but finds sharp words for the arbitrariness of the large landowner. The essay of a Pomeranian pastor, *Die Landarbeiterfrage und die evangelische Geistlichkeit in Ostelbien* (*Soziale Praxis*, Berlin, 1895, vol. iv), is characteristic of this; it blames the increasing indifference towards the Church in country districts on the Junker policy towards the agricultural labourers. The author makes an interesting suggestion as to the connection between the agricultural labourer and the country priest, in that they are the strata which may hope for emancipation from the domination of the Junker through an economic revolution. Pastor Lorenzen in Fontane's *Stechlin* also comes close to the type of the critical country parson. Cf. J. Petersen, *Fontanes Altersromane*, *Euphorion*, 1928, xxix. 40 ff.

[2] *Die Grabenhäger*, i. 110.

The spirit of the authoritarian vigour of the ruling class is most strongly embodied in the figure of a government official (*Regierungsassessor*) who later becomes a county squire. He belongs to a very rich industrialist family and wishes to make up for his upstart ennoblement by out-Junkering the Junker. His family seeks to win greater esteem by purchasing an estate in its home county. This squire (*Landrat*) is a typical representative of that socially ambitious *Assessorismus* which, together with its connection with the student-corps and official patronage, Max Weber has described as one of the most characteristic features of the second empire.[1] His father, the Kommerzienrat von Katzenberg, behaves in the same way as the son by arousing feeling among the landowners against the workers; he argues that landed-estates and heavy industry belong together in their common resistance to the enemy from below.[2]   He declares at a meeting of landowners that

the heavy industrialist, every entrepreneur, has to fight against the greed and insubordination of the lower classes, just as has the owner of an estate or a tenant. This is the calamity that we have to suffer, we who belong to the upper ten thousand in town and country. The interests of all of us who are better situated are fundamentally allied.[3]   In face of the revolution that threatens us from that direction, all professional differences between us property-owners ought to cease.

[1] Max Weber, *Wahlrecht und Demokratie in Deutschland,* pp. 34–40.

[2] *Die Grabenhäger,* i. 190.

[3] It is also worth noticing, from the point of view of this co-operation, the composition of the conservative electoral committee in a rural constituency, of the Mark, as it is described by Fontane in *Stechlin.* There, a personally very popular country-noble opposes a socialist workman and progressive lawyer as candidate for the Reichstag. In the conservative electoral committee we find chiefly country-nobles together with their directly or indirectly dependent auxiliary troops, viz. tenants and officials. The latter embrace domainal tenants, judicial councillors or *Gerichtsräte* (who were so happy to be able to inscribe "Captain of the Reserve" on their visiting cards), forest and tax inspectors, stewards, clergymen and school-teachers (cf. Fontane, *Stechlin,* *Ausgewählte Werke* (Reklam), vi. 187). But here also, it is interesting to note, there comes a parvenu upon the scene, the owner of a mill and timber-yard, who is despised by the aristocrats because of his origin (he is supposed to be the son of a mid-wife) and who seeks to make up for this shortcoming by particularly vituperative speeches against the socialist candidate.

The *Kommerzienrat's* aristocratic counterpart is a
vigorous Junker, coarse and energetic, who is possessed
of a by no means scrupulous business morality.   When
this Major von Pantin deals in horses with other aristocrats, the cheating of his fellow-aristocrats is quite permissible according to the unwritten laws of his class.[1]
The same type of the naïve, robust Junker has been
portrayed still more caustically and with biting scorn in
Wolzogen's *Ecce ego. Erst komm' ich*; here, not only is
the Don Quixotic character of the Junker exposed, but
also the ruthlessness and cunning with which he manages to escape imminent economic bankruptcy.

The ruthless Junker and his kindred spirit, the parvenu, are contrasted with two kinds of outsider, the refined, enlightened aristocrat and the capable middle-class
landowner.   Herr von Klaven in Polenz' novel represents the positive *grand seigneur*.   He is no longer, as
Prince Pückler once was, purely an interesting man of
the world, but is also a social realist; because of his
critical attitude towards society, he opposes the older
generation's watchword of "Authority" with the younger
one's watchword of "Justice."   He learns to understand
the perils of his caste through the economic decline of
his own family and wishes to remove them.   For self-
critical reflection usually only begins in an individual,
as with a class, after failures have occurred or if danger
of collapse threatens.   His family, like all the distinguished families in East Elbia, lost most of its former
wealth, and on account of its erroneous class scruples
failed to adjust itself properly to its new situation.   The
family disintegrates, a brother perishes because of his
thoughtlessness, the sisters have to accept posts as
governesses or companions, only one being able to
marry and even then beneath her class.

The aristocratic author expresses through the mouth
of Herr von Klaven a criticism of the stratum of his
origin.   Whilst he sharply condemns the defects of the

[1] This is affirmed also by Max Weber in *Gesammelte Aufsätze zur Soziologie
und Sozialpolitik,* p. 386.

aristocracy as it is, he yet retains a belief in the aristocracy as it ought to be. The aristocracy does not merely exist, it also has a social significance. It must eliminate its diseased elements, then the healthy elements will succeed, and it will survive the struggle for existence. It is enlightening that this aristocratic critic of the aristocracy employs a completely middle-class ideology when he demands of the aristocracy that it shall legitimize itself by achievement—"But one thing is necessary above all else: we must work." [1]

His criticism of the aristocracy is most bitter in its opposition to the alliance of insolvent country-nobility and urban capitalists, yet it acknowledges the capability of a simple middle-class farmer. The career of the latter, the landowner Merten, symbolizes a kind of compensatory justice, for his grandparents were peasants who had fallen victims to the so-called "peasants' ordinances." His father was a small tenant, and the son succeeds through economy and shrewdness in becoming one of the largest landowners in the county.

Free from the petty hatred of the aristocracy such as the capitalist displayed in Immermann's *Epigonen*, he yet shares with him a healthy utilitarianism and a dislike of the pleasures of the leisured class. He replaces the æsthetic hobbies of his aristocratic predecessor on the estate with achievements of a practical nature; instead of statues he erects workmen's houses, instead of breeding race-horses he wants to beautify the dwellings of his employees, and, finally, the Christian-socialist author makes him conceive the idea of parcelling out his estate,

---

[1] The adjustment of the aristocracy to the new conditions such as the author advocates, is expressed, for instance, in the following: "All classes and Estates work in order to rise; it is a struggle such as perhaps has never before existed. In point of fact our heritage is at stake; whether we are to retain it or whether it is to be irretrievably torn from us. In spite of all the unexampled blindness and criminal indifference which smothers many of our compeers, I cannot give up the hope that we Junkers still have a great future before us. I believe in it as firmly as I believe in the Gospel. The country without us is a thing not to be thought of. We are too deeply rooted in the soil which we have cultivated for centuries for us to be so easily torn up and thrown aside" (*Die Grabenhäger*, ii. 258).

thereby achieving in his own way the demand for the democratization of the East Elbian estates which remains unsatisfied to the present day. This doctrine of the reconciliation of aristocratic tradition with middle-class efficiency does not aim at eliminating the Junkers, but only at reforming them. The ideal Junker of the future shall no longer proudly hold himself aloof, but shall live "in the midst of the people, and none the less elegantly for that. Thus will he fulfil his obligation of being the first in the community through capacity." [1]

But the history of Germany travelled a different path. The Junkers remained concerned almost exclusively with the interests of their Estate and not with those of the nation. They pursued them as egotistically in the Empire as in the Weimar Republic. Before the war they prevented parliamentary reform in Prussia and after the war they prevented the stabilization of German democracy. [2] Although some remarkable exceptions must be admitted, on the whole they were utterly lacking in an understanding of foreign affairs, in political common sense, in the consciousness of responsibility that an intelligent aristocracy bears, and must bear, for the nation as a whole.

MISALLIANCES. The old aristocracy—as we have repeatedly seen in the course of our exposition—still regarded itself as an Estate far into the nineteenth century, although the legal recognition of its caste-privileges had long since disappeared. The unwritten privileges that it still claimed were upheld by the Crown, but were, on the other hand, often resented by public opinion. As long as the North German aristocracy remained in an impoverished condition, the typical characteristics of its position as an Estate were threatened, viz. its *connubium* and its avoidance of professions branded as degrading. The ideology of a specific aristocratic conduct of life was endangered from the moment that

---

[1] *Die Grabenhäger*, ii. 337.

[2] For the part played by the Junkers after the war, see K. Brandt, *Junkers to the Fore Again, Foreign Affairs*, New York, 1935, xiv. 120–34.

other strata of society became important factors in the
State and claimed a special prestige on the grounds of
economic power. An antithesis began to appear in
society between the principle of Estate-stratification and
class-stratification. Estate-stratification—to quote Max
Weber—is based on a specific prestige, class-stratification
on the possession of a certain amount of money.

> *Possession of money* and being an entrepreneur are not as yet,
> *in themselves*, qualifications for membership of an Estate—although
> they may prepare the way, and lack of wealth is not as yet in
> itself a disqualification for membership of an Estate, although it
> may lead to it.[1]

Contrasting examples of the antithesis between position
as an Estate and position as a class are afforded on the
one hand by the parvenu, who is not accepted by the
older aristocracy on account of his lack of tradition and
because of his different mode of life, on the other hand
by the poverty-stricken girl of aristocratic rank who,
although she has but slight prospect of marrying, does
mix in the highest circles of society where she is accepted
as an equal.[2] This distinction between position as an
Estate and position as a class, however, was rarely very
pronounced after 1870. As a result of the political and
economic rapprochement between aristocracy and upper
middle-class, there took place a social amalgamation, a
union of *commercium* and *connubium*. From a very strictly
aristocratic point of view, indeed, the traditional antithesis
between marriages that were and were not consonant with
the dignity of the Estate, between honourable marriages
and misalliances, still held good; but the pressure of
new social conditions brought about a definite modifica-
tion in practice. Intermarriage between aristocrats and
wealthy middle-class families was an established fact in
many European countries at the end of the nineteenth
century, the tendency being especially strong in France,
but also to be noted in Germany, Hungary and Eng-

---

[1] Max Weber, *Wirtschaft und Gesellschaft*, p. 180.

[2] An excellent example of the impoverished but class-conscious aristocratic
spinster is Therese von Poggenpuhl in Fontane's tale *Die Poggenpuhls*.

land. "The mothers of a large part of the aristocracy have, for several generations, been no longer coming from the aristocratic, but from the democratic spheres of society." [1]

With regard to the growing laxity in the aristocracy's feelings of prestige, we can distinguish at the end of the century three types of marriage:

    (i) Marriage consonant with the dignity of the Estate, according to the principle of *social equality*.

    (ii) Marriage not consonant with the dignity of the Estate, but according to the principle of *social compensation*.

    (iii) Marriage not consonant with the dignity of the Estate, but according to the principle of individual choice *without social compensation*.

The outstanding feature of the second and third types is inequality of blood and tradition. This inequality is in no wise compensated for if, for example, an aristocrat marries the daughter of a small peasant or a factory hand, that is, if there is an absolute discrepancy in class-position as well as in Estate-position. The inequality, however, is compensated for to some extent in the case of an impoverished aristocrat marrying the daughter of a wealthy industrialist, for then the superior Estate-position of the aristocratic family is compensated by the superior class-position of the bourgeois family. Such compensation is usually only possible in a society where the separation of Estates has already broken down. The possibility of compensation means, then, the acknowledgment of a pluralism in the principles governing validity in society. Apart from blood, such a principle is afforded in modern society by property and, in a lesser degree, by education.

As regards his social situation, an individual can be represented in the novel more as a type or more as an individual. If, for instance, an aristocratic estate-owner

[1] R. Michels, *Zum Problem der zeitlichen Widerstandsfähigkeit des Adels* in *Probleme der Sozialphilosophie*, pp. 132–57.

strives to avoid impending poverty by marrying the daughter of a wealthy industrialist, then his behaviour is socially typical and is to be explained by the particular economic position of his Estate. If, on the other hand, an aristocrat marries a poor working girl, then it is clear that his motives are necessarily individual. In the first case fiction describes rather types and typical behaviour, and in the second individuals and individual behaviour.[1]

We shall proceed to analyse a few examples of these three types of marriage contracted by aristocrats, taking them from novels which appeared between 1870 and 1900.[2] Most useful to us for this purpose is Fontane who, as a realistic observer mixing with both middle-class and aristocratic circles, was able to illustrate the phenomena of intermarriage and amalgamation with an almost scientific precision.

(i) Marriage between Aristocrats, conforming to the Dignity of the Estate

The terms: *marriage of equal birth* and *marriage of unequal birth* were originally applied by the aristocracy not only to mark the difference between aristocrat and commoner, but also to mark the difference between members of the higher and lower nobility. Whilst much legal subtlety was still being exercised on the problem of misalliance between the various aristocratic groups in the eighteenth and the first half of the nineteenth century, this particular problem receded into the background as the nineteenth century advanced, on account of the increasingly defensive attitude that the

---

[1] The break-away from convention and from the norms of caste and class, the nineteenth-century tendency towards individualism, is also of course a typical phenomenon of modern society. Cf. the article *Intermarriage, Encycl. of Social Sciences*, viii. 151–6.

[2] The problem of misalliances was already being discussed in German literature in the eighteenth century: at that time it was the aristocratic dramatists who turned against mixed marriages. See C. Stockmeyer, *Soziale Probleme im Drama des Sturm und Drang*, p. 132.

In England, the problem of a compensation between aristocratic blood and middle-class wealth was excellently presented in Trollope's novel, *Dr. Thorne*, 1858.

aristocracy as a whole was compelled to assume.[1] The community of feeling, springing from their common mode of life, which united the higher and lower nobility in spite of their differences, became more and more significant through their joint defence against the upward-pressing middle-class. In any case, neither middle-class nor aristocratic writers treat this inequality of birth within the aristocracy as a social problem. Whenever purely aristocratic marriages are dealt with, only local or professional differences play any part, as in, perhaps, a marriage between a member of a diplomat's family and a member of the country-nobility. But even in such a case, the differences between the two families are so slight that they quickly disappear. Only assimilation, but no compensation, is needed. The partner coming from the higher aristocracy does, indeed, occasionally make the aristocrats of lower birth feel his or her superiority.[2] But the rule of equality of birth is only seriously involved when it is a matter of intermarriage between noble and non-noble blood.

(ii) *Misalliance with Social Compensation*

The compensation to be obtained from combining aristocratic title with middle-class wealth in marriage, may be sought for from both sides: either on the part of aristocrats who wished to mend their fortunes by marrying into the wealthy middle-class, thus enabling

---

[1] See, for example, Chr. G. Göhrum, *Geschichtliche Darstellung der Lehre von der Ebenbürtigkeit nach gemeinem deutschem Rechte*, Tübingen, 1846, and H. Zöpfel, *Über Missheiraten in den deutschen regierenden Fürstenhäusern überhaupt*, etc., Heidelberg, 1853.

[2] This applies to the mother of Count Haldern, who, in Fontane's *Stine*, wants to marry a girl from the lower-classes: "She was far and away the proudest of women, a Kurland lady filled with Petersburg memories; the Halderns themselves could only stand up to her with difficulty, and for her, a daughter-in-law of the type of Stine Rehbein would simply mean death and shame. She imagined, just because a prince had once written her a tender note, nothing less than that she had contracted a misalliance" (Th. Fontane, *Ausgew. Werke*, iv. 68 f.). The struggle between marriages of convenience and marriages of choice plays some part, of course, also within the aristocracy. It will be found described from personal observation in M. v. Ebner-Eschenbach, *Zwei Komtessen*, Berlin, 1894.

themselves to get rid of their debts and open up an opportunity of entering the diplomatic service, or by rich bourgeois who, as industrialists or bankers, wished to gain an entry into society, into the leisure-class, for themselves and their children. For the former, material luxury was the main motive for such an unequal marriage, for the latter, acceptance in society.[1] In the one case an old but now threatened position was to be maintained, in the other, a newly-created one to be extended. Such a marriage had often to overcome prejudices in both social spheres, for it was not only two people who were here united, but two families of different origin and tradition brought into contact. Both sides had to traverse a path from strangeness to familiarity, but a certain distance usually remained. Reservations in acknowledging the family from the other social stratum persisted according to the age, worldly experience and open-mindedness of the individual members. The aristocratic writer Georg von Ompteda, especially, although without any artistic pretensions, has portrayed in the novel the marrying of a successful industrialist into an impoverished aristocratic family.[2] The commoner wants to gain an entry into society, and to this end acquires not only an aristocratic estate, but also takes to wife the daughter of the former impoverished owner.[3] He is the son of a Berlin machine-manufacturer, but he gets himself ennobled by paying the huge sum of 30,000 marks, and then climbs the social ladder, step by step. The different degrees of the typical ascent

---

[1] See R. Michels, *op. cit.*, pp. 150 ff.

[2] See his novel *Deutscher Adel um 1900*, vol. ii, "Eysen," Berlin, 1901, where such intermarriage is approvingly portrayed. Here it is used to demonstrate the idea of a national synthesis between the social forces which have to acquire a tradition and those which have to preserve one. The new amalgamation forming the upper-class shall, according to Ompteda, have but one common aim: to rear strong healthy men in the nation.

[3] By marrying the daughter of the former aristocratic owner of his estate, the recently-ennobled baron meets with less opposition from his neighbours than before: for he now appears almost as a continuation of the aristocratic tradition. For the increase of ennoblement in the new Empire see R. Lewinsohn, *Das Geld in der Politik*, p. 19 f.

into the leisured-class of the second empire are strikingly conveyed by the different visiting-cards the parvenu successively uses.

On the first he describes himself as:

Dr. Jur. et phil. Heinrich Gideon
Leutnant der Reserve im Dragonerregiment Graf Schwerin.

On the second as:

Heinrich Freiherr von Gideon
Leutnant der Reserve.

On the third:

Heinrich Freiherr von Gideon auf Pölze.

This gradual rise ending in the purchase of an estate (like Pölze) is typical of the *arriviste* tendencies of the Prussian bourgeoisie after 1870. For purposes of social recognition the lieutenancy of the Reserve was just as important as the academic degree, since military prestige was just as high in society, if not higher, than that of the university.

Whilst Ompteda's hero is characteristic of the middle-class intruder into aristocratic circles, the hero of a caustically satirical novel by E. von Wolzogen [1] personifies, conversely, the typical aristocratic intruder into a wealthy middle-class family. He becomes friendly (not without some cunning), with the intention of acquiring economic stability by marrying one of the daughters. After he has finally won her, he still uses her as a means to an end and immediately after her early death he concludes a second marriage with the daughter of a rich recently-ennobled baron. The ruthless and vigorous pursuit of self-interest, untroubled by any self-criticism, is bluntly portrayed here, although overstressed by the author's bias as a renegade.[2]

[1] E. v. Wolzogen, *Ecce ego. Erst komm' ich*, Berlin, 1895.
[2] The haughtiness of the impoverished Junker family towards its new middle-class relatives is very sharply pointed out. "As individuals they may perhaps be very refined and cultured, and all the rest of it, but there are always troublesome elements in their family. Such a thing just can't happen with us. We are landed-proprietors, or officers, or officials and therefore all right!" (*Ecce ego. Erst komm' ich*, p. 339).

The tendency of the petty and impoverished military aristocracy towards misalliance has been depicted less crudely, and with finer touch, by Fontane in his tale *Die Poggenpuhls*. Here the father, a major, has fallen in the war of 1870 whilst leading his battalion; the mother, a woman of the middle-class, lives with her five children in straitened circumstances. The story vividly recounts how differently brothers and sisters react to the same social situation—in this case, impoverishment within the circle of an honourable tradition. The eldest daughter is filled with pride in her Estate, mixes with the social circle of generals and ministers and gratifies them by her caustic criticism of the relations maintained by her younger sister with the upstart plutocracy.[1] The second sister, however, prefers the homes of bankers, especially non-Christian ones, where she succeeds in making herself popular. The youngest is gifted with a variety of talents which she secretly employs to earn money; a part of the family regards such activities as degrading and undignified. The son, an amiable but thoughtless lieutenant, could put the family on its feet by marrying into the Jewish upper-class. We are not concerned here with the unsatisfactory treatment of the story, but with the striking portrayal of the crisis in the position of the déclassé petty-nobility and its border-line situation. One member still strives assiduously to maintain appearances which could be dropped in a democratic society, and one wavers inwardly between relying on the generosity of a rich relation and a solution of the problem by a misalliance.[2]

[1] A subtle observation of the renegade type is revealed by the following passage: "The friend of the general's family, an under-secretary of state who lived opposite, although himself of the newest aristocracy (or perhaps because of it), showed himself always entranced by the subtle malice of the poor, but caste-conscious girl" (*Die Poggenpuhls*, Berlin, 1896, p. 8).

[2] The following passage shows Fontane's keen observation as regards the socially-ambitious banking circles; it is taken from a letter written to an aristocratic lieutenant by one of his sisters: "The wishes of both parents, also of Flora herself, incline undoubtedly in the direction of the nobility, but yet with much eclecticism; and if, for instance, the choice should lie with Frau Melanie—who is very well aware of the advantages of herself and her family—

There are, in the main, three categories of women who come into consideration as regards a marriage for money with impoverished aristocrats:[1]

(*a*) The illegitimate daughter.
(*b*) The rich Jewess.
(*c*) The successful artiste.

The illegitimate daughter was usually of royal or princely blood; she was especially in demand since she often enjoyed, apart from a large fortune, special connections with court-circles, and thus offered to ambitious men excellent opportunities of advancement.

The religious and social scruples, which thirty years previously had still offered serious obstacles to a marriage between an aristocrat and a Jewess, had long since broken down. Now—as a contemporary has put it—"the union of penniless aristocrats and wealthy Jewesses seems to be a process demanded by nature." The aristocrat was attracted by the money, the Jewess by the prospect of mingling at court with the circles of the ruling caste.

Likewise, the successful artiste (actress or dancer) sought to obtain the splendour of an aristocratic name, whilst her husband mended his fortunes with the rich revenues of the stage.[2] If the aristocrat was an officer, then he very often had to face the loss of his career, for marriage with an artiste was still besmirched with a slight social blemish. We still have an echo here of the old prejudice against jugglers and actors as outsiders of society.

I know for certain that she would not be content with less than an Arnim or a Bülow. And now just reckon out the chances of us Poggenpuhls! They are, in spite of Therese, not exactly overpowering, and your personal charm would in the end be of much more consequence in turning the scale than the measure of our historical eminence. For that also is a factor to be reckoned with, especially as regards Flora, who, in contrast to her parents, has a definitely romantic strain and assured me again only yesterday that when she recently saw the grenadier caps of the 1st Guards Regiment in Potsdam, tears came into her eyes" (*Die Poggenpuhls*, p. 125 f.).

[1] *Briefe eines Wissenden, Die Gartenlaube*, Jahrgang, 1887. 3. Brief, *Hoher Adel*, pp. 832–5.

[2] A good example is the marriage of the celebrated actress Henriette Sontag with an impoverished Italian count and diplomatist. See the *Memoirs* of A. F. von Schack, *Ein halbes Jahrhundert*, Stuttgart, 1894, i. 109.

(iii) Misalliance (or Liaison) without Social Compensation

Marriage between aristocrats and persons of the petty-bourgeois, peasant or working-classes was—as we have seen—still forbidden by the State in accordance with the common-law code of 1794. Although this prohibition was officially removed after 1848, it still exercised a powerful influence on the feudal stratum. On the other hand, it was fashionable and permissible for young aristocratic officers and Junkers to indulge in temporary relationships, in erotic liaisons unhallowed by the marriage-tie. Dancers and actresses, especially, were favoured for such liaisons—partly, of course, through the display of their charms, partly because of their free way of life.[1] The man from the higher stratum compensated the devotion of his lady-love from the lower stratum with money, expensive presents, and so on. Marriage was often, if not always, neither desired nor expected. The difference in social origin did not come into consideration. Nothing more than the satisfaction of the sexual instinct was wanted. The misalliance without social compensation differed from these, however, in that it was characterized by an individual affection. In it the inner bond with one's partner was stronger than the bond with people of one's own class. The individual tie was more important here for the aristocrat than his attachment to the code of his group. Whilst the liaison entailed no social conflict (for, according to the unwritten laws of the ruling-class it was quite compatible with the dignity of the Estate so long as it was kept more or less hidden), the misalliance without social compensation always implied a conflict. This conflict was one between individual affection and the pressure of Estate-norms, between individual and group-morals. In all ages the ruling-classes have sought to preserve their prestige and property by the denunciation of marriages with persons of inferior rank and lower income.[2] Whilst inequality

---

[1] Even the wealthy city patricians preferred them sometimes, as is shown by the affairs of Christian Buddenbrook in Thomas Mann's novel *Buddenbrooks*.

[2] See the article *Intermarriage, Encl. of the Social Sciences*, vol. 8, pp. 151–5.

of blood could be compensated for by money, a marriage without any social compensation at all is banned by the aristocracy.

Fontane strikingly brings out in two stories, *Stine* and *Irrungen Wirrungen*, the contrast between the usual liaison and the conflict of a deep affection between aristocrats and girls from the lower-class.

In *Stine* an old, decrepit Count maintains a liaison with a coarse, resolute widow of the lower middle-classes living in small circumstances. The Count furnishes a flat for his mistress in a manner that is abundant rather than elegant.[1] What he does for amusement, the widow does out of sheer economic necessity. Because she is compelled to enter into this liaison by force of circumstances, she is not troubled by the gossip of her neighbours. Her situation reveals a certain relativity of morals:

> To be upright and behave properly is all very nice and good, but really it is only a luxury for the aristocrats and the well-to-do. Those who suffer distress want, above everything, to escape from their distress and misery, and they plan and think of nothing but how it is to be done.[2]

We have a similar description of a whole string of liaisons between superficial officers and pleasure-loving courtesans of humble origin in *Irrungen Wirrungen*, where they are strongly contrasted with the profoundly human romance of Lieutenant von Rienäcker and the gardener's daughter, Lene Nimbsch. Whilst the officers are mainly concerned with sexual satisfaction, their mistresses are chiefly out for cash, or regard the love-affair somewhat calculatingly as a halting-place on the road to a solid marriage later with a partner from their own class.

Quite different is the situation in the case of real indi-

---

[1] "A sideboard, a sofa and a piano," says Fontane, "would also not have been out of place in a privy-councillor's house, but some of the pictures are trashy, and on the book-shelves luxurious editions of Hume and Frederick the Great stand side by side with the primitive popular journal *Berliner Pfennigmagazin*" (Fontane, *Ausg. Werke*, iv. 19).

[2] *Ibid.*, iv. 39.

vidual affection, for here we have a deeper bond which causes all class differences to be forgotten. Lieutenant von Rienäcker sees embodied in the laundry-girl, Lene, the qualities of simplicity, naturalness, and emotional sincerity which he misses so much in the Countesses of his own world. He spends a happy summer with her, and he shows a great deal of understanding, one might even say sympathy, for the simple people of her petty-bourgeois world. It is charming when the officer, who is simultaneously to be seen in the officers' club, in society and amongst the humble petty-bourgeois people of his sweetheart, gives the latter glimpses into the ways of the elegant world which otherwise remained closed to them. But conflict does not fail to appear—a conflict between individual affection and group-morality which has but two courses open to it: renunciation of the beloved one, or renunciation of membership of the group (and for an officer the latter often involves renunciation of his career).

It is intended that Lieutenant von Rienäcker shall marry a rich cousin in his home-town, whereby he shall free his family from all economic difficulties. Crushed by the pressure of circumstances, he yields with a heavy heart and severs his relations with the simple girl. He sees no other way out, as he is little inclined to do what one of his regimental comrades did in a similar situation, give up the service and become a cowboy or a waiter in America for the sake of a romantic love.

Who am I? [he ponders under the strain of the conflict]: An average person from the so-called upper stratum of society. And what am I able to do? I can handle a horse, carve a capon and deal a card. That is all, and so I have the choice of becoming a trick-rider, a head-waiter, or a croupier.[1]

He shrinks with fear from these primitive solutions, just like his comrade. He had hoped to hide his happy love-affair from the world, expecting later the silent approval of society for sparing it an affront; but the economic

---

[1] Fontane, *op. cit.*, iv. 175.

position of his family shatters this hope. He puts an end to the conflict, strengthened by a traditionalistic conception of order. Order implies marriage, and only a marriage between people of equal rank appertains to order. Marriage within one's own class indicates the place to which one belongs within society as a whole.[1]

The pressure of his caste and the jeopardy to his career decide the lieutenant to renounce his love. In the less typical case of the story *Stine*, the young suffering Count Haldern wants to emigrate to America with his poor sweetheart, but in this instance it is she who is afraid that the class-gulf can never be bridged; "It might work for a certain time, perhaps a year or two—but then it would become impossible, even over there." [2] The ailing Count solves the problem by suicide, whilst Lieutenant von Rienäcker resigns himself to a marriage of convenience.

In spite of being taboo, misalliances without social compensation occurred with increasing frequency in the second half of the nineteenth century. Therefore, whilst repudiating them as far as his own family was concerned, the average aristocrat did not mind them so much for rival aristocratic families. Indeed, the benefits of a biological admixture from other strata were admitted, but this acknowledgment remained practically a passive one; the principle might be applied by other aristocratic families but never by one's own. Fontane, who was intimately acquainted with the aristocracy, gives a striking example of this peculiar attitude. The caste-views of the old Count von Haldern in *Stine* have become lax through his residence in the capital. When a member of his aristocratic club becomes engaged to a ballet-dancer and the club ballots for his expulsion on account of this offence against caste-standards, he alone

---

[1] "When our people of the Mark marry, they don't speak of love and passion, they just say: 'I have got to fit into the order of things.' And that is a fine feature in the life of our people, and by no means a prosaic one. For order is a great deal, and sometimes everything" (*op. cit.*, iv. 178).

[2] *Op. cit.*, iv. 77.

votes in the man's favour, for he sees that continual in-breeding within the aristocracy produces nothing but mediocrities, and that only two means of regeneration exist: illegitimate children or misalliances; he prefers the latter.[1]   Yet later on, when the nephew of the Count declares to him that he wants to marry a poor middle-class girl, he sharply distinguishes theory from practice.

He has no objection to misalliance on the part of others, but this is not due to his deep, social insight; it is due to the malicious feeling of superiority which such an event would give him.   One likes one's rivals to behave in an "enlightened" manner, so that one can become conscious of a superiority towards them.   A shrewd aristocrat in Fontane gives sharp expression to this state of things:

Always the other, the other!   Because a thing is all right for the Schwielows, it doesn't mean that it is all right for the Halderns. Every individual thinks that it does not matter what happens to "someone else," so long as it does not happen to himself.   It is remarkable to see with what indifference old families pass judgment on each other and what an arsenal of mockery is expended on ridiculing competitors who pretend to be equal.   But this mockery, I must repeat, is always only for the other.   What does my uncle care about the Schwielows?   The more ballet-dancers the better; for with every new ballet-dancer he not only has a new topic for malicious gossip at the Club, but also a con-tinually renewed cause for being conscious with ever-increasing pride of the immense difference between the Schwielows who have stooped to marrying a Duperré and the Sarastro-Halderns who have maintained their high-priestly purity.   The same thing is to be seen throughout the history of the nobility, it is repeated in every family.   The freer they are in theory, the more pre-

[1] The contrast between in-breeding and regeneration through misalliance is very bluntly put by the Count: "But I tell you this—this ballet-dancer will put the whole tribe on its feet again; the whole family-tree, which is so barren for us and for mankind just because it flowers and blossoms so wonder-fully of itself, will acquire a new reputation, and where hitherto only squires or petty captains stood, there will be from 1900 onwards young geniuses, field-marshals and statesmen" (*op. cit.*, iv. 56).

judiced they are in practice, and the narrower and more anxious concerning its application to themselves.[1]

On the whole, however, as the conversations in Fontane show, the male members of the aristocracy are always more inclined to compromise than the elderly female members. The former have at least occasional contact with people of the middle-class in the course of their military or diplomatic duties, whilst the aristocratically-conscious ladies mix almost always only with the narrow circles of their family and of their caste, and in pursuance of their conservative function of preserving the existing order, they keep themselves more rigidly apart from the non-aristocratic world.

2. THEODOR FONTANE: IDEAL PUBLIC AND ACTUAL PUBLIC

Theodor Fontane is the subtlest interpreter of the rapprochement between the aristocracy and the middle-classes in the new Empire. Although he came from the middle-classes, he had an intimate knowledge of the nobility and was therefore able to describe the sociological structure of the Berlin upper strata, with a realism tempered with profound human understanding. His development shows in a unique way the peculiar attitude of a conservative writer oscillating between nobility and bourgeoisie. We shall first briefly analyse Fontane's career and then deal with the peculiar character of his public.[2]

Fontane's family were notabilities of French extraction. The grandfather, a court painter and secretary to the Queen, had already proved his devotion to the Prussian Court. His father was an apothecary, a cheerful man, full of *joie de vivre*; his mother was the daughter of a Huguenot manufacturer. Fontane grew up at

---

[1] *Op. cit.*, p. 56. The social function of mockery is clearly revealed in this behaviour; by showing up the lapses of rival families from caste-standards one reduces their value and feels superior to them.

[2] For Fontane's life, see his autobiographies: *Meine Kinderjahre*, Berlin, 1894, 2nd Ed., and *Von Zwanzig bis Dreissig*, Berlin, 1925, 19th Ed., and also the biographies of Fontane by K. Wandrey, München, 1919, and H. Spiero, Wittenberg, 1928.

Swinemünde, a Baltic holiday resort of the upper-class, which consisted of a mixture of feudal and well-to-do bourgeois elements. His family was one of the twenty ruling families which constituted the society of the town. This relatively high standing of Fontane's family is perhaps responsible for the author's later sensitiveness to the lack of prestige enjoyed by his profession. The Swinemünde notabilities formed, together with some of the aristocrats, an exclusive club called "Die Ressource," which included amongst its members the aristocratic squire (*Landrat*), the inspector of taxes, the major, the physician (*Hofrat*) and the vicar. The three wealthiest merchant families took the lead in this club. The most distinguished merchant was, indeed, called "King of Swinemünde." He possessed those gentlemanly manners which are usually the result of social position, extensive travel and wide reading. The Swinemünde society had two typical features: the accepted precedence of the aristocracy and an antipathy towards intellectualism. To these merchants a private tutor was no more than a mere servant. "The Swinemünde merchants, who were fond of the grotesque, spared no effort to try and make the representatives of so-called intellectual refinement feel that the spiritual factor or even ideals did not count for much." [1]

A symptomatic incident related by Fontane shows how much the aristocratic members of this club were aware of their superiority. The Landrat von Fleming, the large estate-owner von Borke and Fontane's father, the apothecary, formed an intimate circle within the "Ressource."

They had met at Fleming's and on going in to dinner old von Fleming gave his arm to the beautiful Frau von Borke and Herr von Borke took in Frau von Fleming. My father and my mother were left. "*Eh bien, Madame, Dieu le veut,*" said my father, and both followed as the third couple. The next day the sincerest apologies were given, but they could not resuscitate this *circle intime.*[2]

[1] Th. Fontane, *Meine Kinderjahre*, p. 129.   [2] *Ibid.*, p. 92.

Fontane suffered in his youth from the differences between his parents, as well as from the irregularity of his education. He attended a "*Gymnasium*" for three years only, then became a pupil of a technical college in Berlin, and in 1836 he entered an apothecary's shop as an apprentice, for he was intended to follow his father's profession. In 1840 he was employed as an assistant in Berlin and Leipzig. Having up till now secretly written poems and essays, he undertook in 1849 a very important step, when he gave up the security of the apothecary's profession for the unstable career of journalism and writing.

To a certain extent Fontane's career is typical of the difficulties with which a German novelist had to contend. It was haunted by continuous insecurity and by a hard struggle which brought him fame only when he was old. In 1850 he married, although his income, which was derived from a temporary engagement in a government press office, did not amount to more than 40 Taler a month. In 1852 he was sent for a few months by his office to London. Afterwards he managed to make ends meet by giving lessons and lectures on literature and history in certain circles of Berlin Society. From 1860 to 1870 Fontane was an editor of the conservative *Kreuzzeitung*, where he dealt especially with English politics. In 1870, however, he gave up this position for that of dramatic critic of the Liberal *Vossische Zeitung*. His real artistic work began only after his sixtieth birthday. Fontane, who declined to accept a position in the civil service or any cramping occupation, has stressed emphatically the dangers of the career of a free writer in comparison with the security of an official.

My wife [he said, on one occasion] would have made an excellent wife for a clergyman or an official with a fixed, well-paid post, but she is not fitted for the life of a writer, which I admit can never be undertaken without considerable risk. Yet I cannot do anything for her. In marrying me she has married a writer and she must reconcile herself to the fact that I prefer this free-lance kind of life, in spite of its risk of destitution to the usual professions with their pressure, their narrowness and their pretentious boredom, especially now that I have gained still more intimate knowledge of them.[1]

As a mediator between different social worlds, Fontane is characterized by a peculiar combination of mobility and of traditionalism, of liberal and of conservative elements. The parental tradition had already brought about his inner contact with the Prussian spirit. It had been undermined but not eliminated by the relations of the young Fontane with some free literary circles. There an independent and critical attitude was shown which produced, for instance, in the Herwegh Club, hymns of liberty in the style of Herwegh.[2] The frequent ambiguity and vacillation of the man of letters were strikingly revealed in Fontane in 1848. Whilst taking quite an active part in the revolution and contributing to a democratic paper, he became at the same time conscious of the importance of a well-disciplined army and the inefficiency of the so-called will of the mass.

I could not help feeling [he said later] that the so-called victory was nothing more than a thing which could only have occurred with the tacit approval of the authorities and which was quite unnecessarily turned into a triumph of the masses. I was more than ever convinced of the complete invincibility of a well-disciplined force in opposition to any formation of the masses, however brave. The will of the masses was nothing, royal power was everything. I have maintained this view for forty years.[3]

In 1849 Fontane became for a short time Liberal delegate for the indirect election of deputies, but at the same time he was instructing nurses in pharmacy in a pietistic conservative circle. This is significant in view of the fact that his political and his æsthetic humanitarian sympathies were often separated. He disagreed with the opinions but sympathized with the people. Curiously enough, he said later himself: "It always happened to me that I have spent my most pleasant days—in any

---

[1] Th. Fontane, *Briefe, Zweite Sammlung*, Berlin, 1910, i. 369.
[2] Cf. *Von Zwanzig bis Dreissig*, p. 115.   [3] *Ibid.*, p. 404.

case no unpleasant ones—amongst 'Pharisees,' the Orthodox and Pietists, as well as amongst aristocrats of the Junker type." Although Fontane had changed his political views, his sympathy for the conservative ruler type never faded.

From the standpoint of this Prussianism, he keenly criticized England during his visit there, whilst in turn his comparative knowledge of the English and the German aristocracy gave later a particular charm to his *Wanderungen durch die Mark Brandenburg.* In his writings of 1854 he compared England and Germany in form and content or in appearance and essence. England, he argued,[1] is aristocratic, Germany is democratic, England is selfish to the last degree, Germany unselfish to the almost complete surrender of herself. England resembles a college of cadets, which allows only one uniform; Germany a class at a "*Gymnasium*" with people of differing peculiarities. In England only the prestige of noble blood is valid, but in Germany much more the prestige of culture. And only in Germany can the clever son of a peasant outdo the less intelligent offspring of noble birth.

Later on Fontane gave up his biased interpretation of the world and displayed that broad-mindedness of a true world-citizen which in his novel *Stechlin* is embodied in the family of the diplomat Barby. But his characters, his wisdom, his social criticism, remained always deeply rooted in the world of the Mark and of Prussia.

A good social novelist needs an intimate knowledge of the different strata of a society. Fontane was a thorough connoisseur of the different groups of Berlin society between 1840 and 1900. His social connections reached from the court-nobility to Jewish scholars and from conservative country clergymen to radical journalists. Through the literary club *Der Tunnel über der Spree*, he came into contact with the high ministerial bureaucracy; as a tutor and lecturer in the families of

---

[1] Th. Fontane, *Ein Sommer in England*, Berlin, 1854, chap. "Parallelen," pp. 263–71.

cultivated officers, he met generals, court-preachers, secretaries of state, catholic politicians, musicians, painters and ladies of society.[1]   A social sense and a feeling of loneliness are closely intermingled in Fontane.

I went through life absolutely lonely [he said, in looking back on his past], without belonging to any party, clique, coterie, club, beer and skittle circle, bridge club, or freemason's lodge, looking neither to the right nor to the left. . . .   I have had the disadvantage of this, but also the advantage, and if I should have to live my life again, I should take the same course.   One loses much by it, but one gains more.[2]

Yet this statement is only partly correct.   For Fontane owed some useful contacts to his membership of the *Tunnel*.   There he met a high official, who later appointed him to the press department of the Government.   There he also became acquainted with the conservative journalist Hesekiel, who later procured him the position of editor of the *Kreuzzeitung*.

Ideal Public and Actual Public.—To understand Fontane's position as an author swaying between nobility and bourgeoisie, a distinction must be made between two types of literary public.   It is proposed to call them "Ideal Public" and "Actual Public."   By the "ideal public" of an author, we understand those strata or groups to which he appeals and which he probably had in mind when writing and planning his work.   The "actual public" may be a circle of friends, the readers of a periodical, one particular profession, a class, or even a whole nation.

The ideal public is always that public whose feelings and ideology are completely or partly shared by the author.   On the other hand, the actual public represents the public which one might say really consumes his works, which reads, buys, borrows and discusses them. It accepts or criticizes their contents and sometimes even imitates their ideas and characters.

[1] Cf. the list of persons Fontane met at the home of Freiherr von Wangenheim in *Das Fontanebuch*, Berlin, 1919, p. 118.
[2] Th. Fontane, *Briefe an seine Familie*, Berlin, 1905, ii. 34.

The ideal public and the actual public can be identical or different.   An example of an identical public is the public of Tennyson in England, because the taste of the author and that of his favourite readers—the English aristocracy and upper-classes—coincided.[1]   Between the two World Wars, to mention only one example, the Danish writer M. Andersen-Nexö appealed to the class from which he came—the proletariat—and was widely accepted as its writer.

If there is a difference between the ideal public and the actual public, either the class or group which the author concerned has in mind is not interested at all in literature, or it is not able to accept his valuations and ideologies.   In Germany a disharmony between the ideal public and the actual public was brought about by the negative attitude of the bulk of the aristocracy towards literature.

The desire of many authors to be read by the nobility was not fulfilled.   The taste, for instance, of the feudal Prussian ministers of state and of their families, which was displayed by their choice of books or by their judgment of pictures and plays, showed remarkably little refinement.[2]   For the feudal military caste, culture was neither an inner need nor, what is perhaps more important, was it necessary for the maintenance of its power. Even after 1870, the aristocracy could afford to be indifferent to art and scholarship.

At the end of the century, middle-class and aristocratic authors like Fontane, von Wolzogen, von Polenz, protested in vain against the cultural indifference of the aristocracy, which they regarded as their ideal public, and had to be satisfied with an actual public composed from the middle-class, especially from Jewish circles. Again and again some of these writers have reflected on the striking contrast between the literary apathy of the nobility and the outspoken cultural interests of the Jewish plutocracy.

[1] Cf. H. Taine, *History of English Literature*, Edinburgh, 1870, ii. 535–41.
[2] See R. Michels, *Probleme der Sozialphilosophie*, p. 143 f.

Unlike the aristocracy, the Jews needed a counter-balance to their still second-rate, if not inferior, social position. The characteristics of their race—intellectuality and versatility—could be developed particularly in this field. The Jews were regarded by these writers as a vital factor in all cultural movements. They were the first to recognize the significance of new ideas and tendencies in art and science and to propagate them. Not only property, but also a high cultural level, are passed on from one Jewish generation to another.

The recent great development in literature [says Ernst von Wolzogen, probably with reference to Naturalism] [1] owes to them an extraordinary amount. It was nearly always the Jews who started, or at least supported, the literary unions, the free theatres, the ethical societies, as well as the periodicals devoted to the spiritual revolution.

In discussing a book on Henriette Herz, the hostess of a literary salon in Berlin about 1800, Fontane states somewhat reluctantly that

the higher cultivated life in Berlin Society was always a life of Jews or rather of Jewesses. The wife or daughter of a (Christian) bourgeois has never in this country said anything worth while discussing, and the nobility, having taken to religion among other things, also fails. [2]

Fontane has illustrated the cultural attitude of the wealthy Jewish stratum in his story, *Die Poggenpuhls*. In this the daughter of an impoverished but distinguished noble family points out to her brother the advantages of these cultivated and well-to-do Jews. She says about the family of a Jewish banker:

The Crown Prince has visited the Bartensteins. Bartenstein is a Roumanian Consul-General; that means more than *Kommerzienrat*; Droysen and Mommsen were there [and] once even Leopold von Ranke shortly before his death. They have in

[1] E. v. Wolzogen, *Linksum kehrt schwenk Trab! Ein ernstes Mahnwort an die herrschenden Klassen und den deutschen Adel insbesondere*, 6th Ed., Berlin, 1895, p. 27.

[2] Th. Fontane, *Briefe, Zweite Sammlung*, ii. 432.

their galleries several pictures by Menzel, showing, I believe, a Court Ball and a sketch of a picture for a coronation. Dear Leo, who else has that? [1]

Fontane's ideal public consisted of the Prussian aristocracy, but his actual public was composed mainly of officials, teachers, professional men and Jews. Already the young journalist, who lived in modest circumstances, admired the non-bourgeois attitude which was embodied, in his view, especially in the nobility. He once pointed out [2] that he did not possess a middle-class outlook and that he was only interested in the aristocracy.

But I solemnly protest against the fact that what I call noble is confined only to that class which is known as nobility. It is to be found in all classes. It means a sense of the common good, of the ideal, and an antipathy towards the triflings of a narrow and petty circle.[3]

Later on, during his activities with the feudal Conservative Press, he explains his predilection for the nobility by his social position.

It is true that I have more contact with the aristocracy than with the middle-classes, but that is partly a consequence of my profession as a poet and as the author of the *Wanderungen* and partly a result of my political opinions. Poets and artists have always confined themselves almost exclusively to intercourse with princes. That is quite natural, too. But to-day it is no longer necessary for this to be so. The middle-classes (in the widest sense of the word) have now an outstanding importance and are at the present time partly in possession of social advantages which were formerly confined to the aristocracy and to the clergy. But everyone who is fighting in the camp of the feudalists has to be content with the old elements.[4]

---

[1] Th. Fontane, *Die Poggenpuhls*, 1896, p. 124 f.

[2] Th. Fontane, *Briefe an seine Familie*, i. 130.

[3] Cf. also the following characteristic sentence in one of Fontane's letters: "Ten generations of 500 Schulzes and Lehmanns are by no means as interesting as three generations of a single branch of the von Marwitz family. Who would abolish the nobility would abolish the last vestige of poetry in our world" (*loc. cit.*, i. 112).

[4] Th. Fontane, *Briefe an seine Familie*, i. 121.

Indeed, the former relation of the poet to, and his dependence on, the aristocracy had nearly vanished. It only existed for those men of letters who, like Adam Müller, Gentz, Hesekiel and Fontane, supported the Conservative feudal party. After his separation from the *Kreuzzeitung*, a conflict arose in Fontane between political antipathy to and human sympathy with the nobility. In his *Wanderungen durch die Mark Brandenburg* (1892), which gave a geographical and historical survey of the peculiarities of this province, Fontane attempts to maintain a middle course between

independent thought and deference, between acknowledgment of the personal and social aristocratic charm on the one hand and doubts as to the political ability of our country aristocracy on the other. Unfortunately, an imitation of the English Tories, in which aristocrats and bourgeois notabilities co-operate, miscarries in Germany through the intolerant character of the Junkers, through the naïve conviction of their exclusive right and capability to rule. The pseudo-conservatism of our aristocracy, which in the long run is only based on egoism and on all that which is subservient to it, embarrasses the conservative middle-class notabilities considerably and makes them feel extremely desperate.[1]

These mixed feelings of Fontane towards the aristocracy found their best expression in the sentence: "These fellows are intolerable and charming at the same time." [2] The burgher had to fight the aristocrat as a ruthless enemy, but the contemplative writer knows the aristocrat's more pleasant features which appear in his home life. Fontane observed both the inflexible rigidity of the nobility in public affairs and the *jeu d'esprit* attitude of the "Grand Seigneur" in his private life.

He realizes on his journeys that at home the Junker of the Mark "is able to change from the inflexibility of his *non possumus* to a *laissez-passer* which wins every-

[1] Th. Fontane, *Wanderungen durch die Mark Brandenburg*, Berlin, 1892, iv. 454.
[2] *Ibid.*

one's sympathy."[1]   The aristocracy is by no means stupid or blind to the natural claims of its opponents.

It does not fight its life struggle so hardly and bitterly because it misunderstands the rights of its opponents, but on the contrary, because it recognizes them.   It is only not prepared to take the last step from recognition to acknowledgment of these rights.[2]

Owing to his vacillating attitude between the two classes, Fontane could not satisfy either.   After the publication of *Wanderungen*, the middle-class liberals accused him of having written the book to the order of the Conservative party and denounced his servile pandering to the aristocracy.[3]

In its turn the story *Die Poggenpuhls*, owing to its realistic description of impoverished officer-nobility, met with violent opposition from aristocratic circles.   The poet himself defended his work as a glorification of the aristocracy, which unfortunately was too petty and stupid to realize the flattery in it.[4]   Almost until his death, Fontane was engaged in the history and literary portrayal of the aristocracy.   At the age of seventy he proposed writing a history of one of the great aristocratic families of the Mark;[5] and for this purpose visited the family estates, but felt keenly the literary indifference of these people in spite of all their good manners.   Eventually the old man found staying on estates intolerable and gave up the projected work.[6]

Whilst this country-nobility only reluctantly reacted to the literary ideas of Fontane, it sometimes happened that the court-aristocrats would ask him to write a biography but were not prepared to pay much for it.

---

[1] *Ibid.*   The rest is also characteristic: "No longer on the defensive, no longer forming a circle of besieged people, who, owing to old tactics, think that attack is the best defence, it divests itself of its spiked armour and dresses itself in a weft of its virtues, made up of a large amount of good nature, a still larger one of common sense and largest of criticism.   And this criticism is the best part of it."

[2] *Ibid.*   [3] K. Wandrey, *Th. Fontane*, p. 70.

[4] See the note in his Diary, *Das Fontanebuch*, p. 192.

[5] The title was to be "Die Bredows, ihre Geschichte und ihr Besitz."

[6] See *Das Fontanebuch*, pp. 178 and 184.

"I have found something unpleasant," Fontane re-marked rather bitterly, "in my association with courts and courtiers. They pay only by 'honour,' but as this honour has not the slightest value for me, I have no difficulty in refusing it." [1]

To sum up, we have seen the permanent discrepancy between the ideal and the actual public of Fontane. If, according to him, the aristocrat, although a bully in the world, was a charming person at home, he was, how-ever, not so charming when it came to reading and buying the books of refined Conservative writers. But what the nobility failed to do, other sections of the nation, especially the Jews, did to a considerable extent.

The whole tension between Fontane's aristocratic ideal public and his largely Jewish actual public is masterly expressed in an ironical poem, which he wrote on the occasion of his seventy-fifth birthday. [2]

Hundreds of letters have arrived.
I was quite numbed from joy,
only a little astonished by the names and places
from which they came.
Filled with vanity, I thought:

You are the man of the *"Wanderungen"*
You are the man of the poems on the *Mark*
You are the man of the history of the *Mark*
You are the man of old *Fritz*
and of those who shared his table,
some chattering, others silent,
first in Sans souci, later in Elysium.

You are the man of the Jagows and Lochows,
the Stechows and Bredows,
the Quitzows and Rochows.
There marched from Uckermarck,
Havelland, Barnim,
the Ribbecks and Kattes,
the Bülows and Arnims,
and on all of them have I written.

But those who came to my jubilee,
had far, far different names;
"Sans peur et reproche", too,

without any fear and blame,
but of nearly prehistoric nobility.
The names ending in "*berf*" and "*heim*"—
they are countless.
Whole masses of them invade me.
There are entire battalions
of Meyers and of Pollacks,
and of those who live further out,
in an easterly direction.

Abram, Isaac, Israel,
all the patriarchs have arrived,
putting me kindly at their head;
what use have I now for the Itzenplitzes?

To each of them I have meant something,
All have read me,
All have known me
for a long time,
And that's the main thing . . .,
"Come along, Cohn."

PART II

THE PLACE OF THE WRITER IN GERMAN
SOCIETY

1830–1900

CHAPTER VIII

PUBLIC AND PATRONS

In the course of the previous chapters we have touched upon the careers of individual authors and their attitude towards the relations between the aristocracy and the bourgeoisie. It is the task of this and of the final chapter to endeavour to give a more detailed contribution to the sociology of the German writers of the nineteenth century. Only a few observations can be made on a problem so far rather overlooked both in research into social history and into the history of literature.[1]

We must begin by asking: what was the social situation of the writers as part of the intelligentsia in a century characterized by development from an agricultural to an industrial state, from benevolent absolutism to parliamentary constitutionalism, from the political hegemony of the aristocracy to its fusion with the bourgeoisie? Were the writers at that time dependent on or independent of social forces? Were they favoured or hindered or only tolerated? Did they themselves advance or hinder the social and political issues of their time, or did they as pure æsthetes seclude themselves and remain indifferent?

And further: Was the social intercourse of writers mainly restricted to their own circle, or did it extend to members of the two classes: the aristocracy and the

[1] But the sociology of knowledge has done some pioneer work in stressing the co-relation of the intellectuals and society. Cf. nearly all the works of Prof. K. Mannheim mentioned in the bibliographical Appendix and his unpublished work on the *Sociology of the Intelligentsia*; further the stimulating book of A. Guérard, *Literature and Society*, Boston, 1935, parts ii and iii; see also H. Gerth, *Die sozialgeschichtliche Lage der bürgerlichen Intelligenz um die Wende des 18. Jahrhunderts*, Berlin, 1935; and C. P. Magill, "The German Author and His Public in the Mid-Nineteenth Century," *Modern Language Review*, October, 1948.

bourgeoisie? What was their income, their prestige, the peculiar situation of their different groups? What was the connection between their literary production and their position in society?

An exhaustive answer to all these questions is beyond the scope of this study. A general sociology of writers would subsume these questions under two groups of problems:

1. The man of letters as a professional type.
2. Forms of association of writers and their significance for literary production.

In the following analysis we shall confine ourselves to illustrating, by examples of the period between 1830 and 1900, the characteristics and the importance of these two problems.

1. INCOME AND PRESTIGE

When we regard the man of letters in relation to the society of the nineteenth century, we at once realize that he is a kind of luxury.[1] Merchants and officials, artisans and labourers are needed in every society based on division of labour as also are certain groups of the intelligentsia such as doctors, judges and teachers. But the existence of artists always presupposes at least a certain degree of culture in the stratum which provides the main demand for artistic products. The artistic professions have, in Germany, always been in sharp contrast to the civic professions (*bürgerliche Berufe*). The truth of the dictum *Primum vivere deinde philosophari* expresses the limit of the artist's chances in society. By civic professions we mean those which promise a certain financial security through industry and patience and therefore give to those who follow them a certain prestige in capitalist society. The prestige of the civic professions

---

[1] It is significant that Schiller, for example, felt released when he was granted an unpaid professorship in Jena (1787). "So far," he said, "I have always been haunted by the curse which public opinion has put on that frivolity of the mind—poetry." Cf. H. Lilienfein, *Schiller und die Deutsche Schiller Stiftung*, Weimar, 1934, p. 16.

is based principally on security, that of the artistic professions on fame. The careers of the writer, artist and official present especially the most vivid contrast. The prestige of the official is characterized by his relation to an institution which offers him security and honour. According to Karl Mannheim, it is a "borrowed prestige."[1] The official is legitimized in society not so much by his personal achievement as by the institution to which he belongs. His career is regulated by his superiors, whose position is usually governed by seniority. The writer, on the other hand, can acquire his prestige almost entirely only by his own achievement and has to maintain it in a permanent competitive struggle.

It is important for the economic and social status of an author whether writing is his main occupation or merely a side-line. The author to whom writing is a side-line is not necessarily an outsider in society. His economic and social position is very often secured through his main profession. He often fits better into society on account of his double activities, which give him an added attraction. Such was the case with a noble poet and estate-owner of the Middle Ages, Neidhart von Reuenthal, for instance, as well as with the meistersingers in the German towns of the fifteenth century, and with the numerous authors who were officials in the eighteenth and nineteenth centuries. To give only a few examples: Immermann and Th. Storm were judges, Eichendorff and E. Th. A. Hoffmann government officials, etc. Their double activities gave them entry into the circles of two professions, but also had the disadvantage of frequent tension between duty and inclination, office and leisure. In any case these writers had a more secure economic position to rely on in the event of failure and defeat when they were ousted by the younger generation, or when their productivity began to decrease. Very different was the case of the

---

[1] K. Mannheim, *The Place of Sociology*, p. 7 (Papers of the Conference on the Social Sciences, London, 1935).

author who relied on writing only. He had no backing from a normal civic existence, he was economically dependent on the reception of his works by the public as well as by his critics. He was judged purely on his literary achievements.[1]

The reactions of the artist to the existence of the bourgeois in the nineteenth century were often very complicated. The artist mocked at his dullness, but secretly envied his economic efficiency. He felt superior to the bourgeois because of his greater gifts, but inferior because of his lack of social superiority.[2]

The contrast between a middle-class and free-lance literary existence has not only been dealt with in novels and essays, but also in the autobiographies of the writers themselves. By a law of social psychology, people exaggerate the compensations which they usually see in professions other than their own. Julius Grosse, for example, a writer of the Munich circle of about 1860, contrasts in his autobiography the security of the official with the insecurity of the artist and scholar in the following striking passage:

Happy the official in the hierarchy of the Civil Service. As soon as the examinations are passed *cum laude*, the candidate is admitted to the holy spirit of the caste, is appointed and then gradually promoted. A faithful fulfilment of duty, a practical application of acquired knowledge, a loyal regard for all official duties, as the proof of intelligence and capability; that is all, and cheerfully the stormless years pass, bringing further honours. How different is the free artist, the creative author! A success, a triumph, however brilliant, are only helpful to him for a time; then continued struggle and victory must follow, or ultimate defeat will destroy the former success and with it his prestige.

[1] There are differences of status, also, among authors whose main profession was writing. In the nineteenth century there was, on the one hand, the type who, as employee, editor or permanent contributor of a newspaper, lived in a certain dependence; on the other, we have the free-lance writer who gained his prestige solely through his books. Actually many authors were a mixture of the two.

[2] A longing for and envy of the normal life of the burgher combined with a consciousness of superiority is especially a leading theme in the works of Thomas Mann, particularly in his story *Tonio Kröger*.

A series of impressive achievements can establish a permanent confidence and reputation, but even then the dictum holds that conquests must be maintained by the same means by which they have been made.

An artist or scholar must, as it were, repeat his examination before the nation every year. The struggle is continuous, and woe even to a fortunate man when repeated defeats weaken the power of his fame, let loose the envy of his adversaries and bring about the victory of younger competitors. If, then, catastrophes happen by which all that has been won, including reputation, is lost again, the life of the artist is like that of the merchant who sees his ships surrender to the elements:—the sequence of events is similar: the loss of goods is followed by loss of reputation, by bankruptcy and ruin. If a remnant of the property then remains, and if vigour still remains, the courageous and resolute man can perhaps start again and successfully re-establish himself.

Karl Gutzkow overcame his defeat in the struggle with the *Grenzboten* by new victories, but he never overcame his bitter feelings. In former times the older generation withdrew, so to speak, into the background, and its vigour and good luck faded. To-day it has become the custom for the younger successor, if he is able, to remove the older contemporary by the law of the stronger, in order to make way for himself.[1]

These words brilliantly characterize the dependence of the writer on the reception of his works, the insecurity of fame in modern society, the hidden and open competitive struggles between members of the same generation as well as between the older and younger generations.

If the artist and poet of the nineteenth century was more conscious of the disadvantages of his position in comparison with that of the burgher, it was largely due to the fact that the profession of writer had meanwhile in many instances changed from a side-line occupation to a whole-time profession. In the eighteenth century most writers were either engaged in another profession, or possessed private means, and only incidentally earned money from literary work. According to Bruford, there probably existed at the end of the eighteenth century fewer professional writers in Germany than in

[1] J. W. Grosse, *Ursachen und Wirkungen*, Braunschweig, 1896, p. 372 f.

England.[1]   Lessing, at this time, was the only outstanding free-lance journalist; it was not until the end of his life that he accepted a permanent post as a librarian.   Of the romanticists, one section consisted of state officials (Eichendorff, E. T. A. Hoffmann, Novalis, Schleiermacher, A. W. Schlegel), others had independent means (A. v. Arnim), whilst the rest earned a living as free literati by their writing and also by secret political reports (Fr. Schlegel, Ad. Müller, H. v. Kleist, etc.).   Beginning with the days of the "Young German Movement" the author was given a new chance for his work by co-operation with the Press, which then was a growing power.   At the same time the new copyright law protected him and his publishers against literary pirates. The free-lance writer's chances of making money began to increase through his contributions to newspapers and journals, especially through the publication of novels and essays, which later appeared in book-form, in the *feuilletons*.   Also at that time the production of books in general increased about 150 per cent between 1821 and 1840.[2]

Comparatively few of the important and successful authors after 1830 had any other profession than that of writing.   Grillparzer was an official, Storm a judge, Keller, after many years of migratory life, became, through the mediation of his friends, Clerk of the Council of Zurich.   But the majority preferred the insecurity of the free-lance author's existence.   Very often journalism and free-lance literary productions were combined, as in the cases of Börne, Heine, Gutzkow, Spielhagen, Fontane, and occasionally the work of a playwright and writer, as in the cases of Gutzkow, Laube, Dingelstedt.

The general standard of life in other professions, as well as the income, should form the basis of a comparative judgment of the income of German novelists, but it is difficult to obtain reliable information for this purpose

---

[1] W. H. Bruford, *Germany in the Eighteenth Century*, p. 271.
[2] J. Goldfriedrich, *Geschichte des Deutschen Buchhandels*, Leipzig, 1913, iv. 199.

and we must content ourselves with a few facts.   At the end of the eighteenth century Goethe received 15 Taler for a printed sheet of his complete work, whilst 40 Taler were given to Schiller for a sheet of the *Horen*!   On the other hand, the author of a popular and simple travel novel of ten volumes received 5,000 Taler, that is to say more than Goethe and Klopstock together were till then given for their complete works.[1]

During the first part of the nineteenth century, there still existed a patriarchal relationship between the owner of a bookshop and his employees: similarly the mode of payment between publisher and author was far behind the rationalism of the modern cheque book.   Some publishers even paid their fees in kind.[2]

In the second half of the nineteenth century the income of authors increased.   Whilst the payment for all the editions of Heine's *Reisebilder* was 50 Louis-d'ors, historical novels of the following period were far more remunerative.   For example, G. Freytag made 120,000 Marks for the series *Die Ahnen* and G. E. Ebers more than a million for all his Egyptian novels.   But the literary importance and financial success of a book are not always identical.   In 1873 G. Keller claimed a fee of 2,000 Franken for one volume of his *Die Leute von Seldwyla*.   Fontane in 1887 received 400 Marks a folio from a journal.[3]   The income of a successful playwright, who was at the same time a novelist, was even larger.   Sudermann made 100,000 Marks in royalties for his dramas in the period before 1900, whilst the fee for the publication of his novel *Es war* in a periodical amounted to 20,000 Marks.

[1] W. H. Bruford, *op. cit.*, p. 278.   But Goethe later received 1,000 Reichstaler for *Hermann and Dorothea*.

[2] The authors' accounts of a well-known Berlin publisher (Georg Reimer) contained the following note of remuneration before 1840: "For A. W. Schlegel half a dozen and a dozen respectively fat geese and one supply of Teltower carrots.   For Schleiermacher a sweepstake ticket, cloth, wool, salmon, cognac, wine, and a pair of trousers, including the tailor's wages" (J. Goldfriedrich, *op. cit.*, iv. 495).

[3] E. Heilborn, *Zwischen zwei Revolutionen, Der Geist der Bismarckzeit*, Berlin, 1929, p. 64 f.

The prestige of the man of letters in society grew much more slowly than his income, but it was increasing rapidly in all European countries and therefore also in Germany.[1]   Owing to the rise of the middle-class and its cultural ideals, art and science attained a higher status. In feudal society art had principally an ornamental function; in liberal society it had an elevating one.

Between 1830 and 1914, German Classicism became a kind of substitute for religion.   As the pious Moslem made a pilgrimage to Mecca, so thousands of educated Germans followed Goethe's footsteps to Italy.   Goethe's position at court especially impressed the bourgeoisie. The upper middle-class regarded the Classics as its intellectual property and itself as the real educated class. But Schiller, even more than Goethe, was the spokesman of the liberal and national views of this stratum. The centenary of Schiller's birth (1859) clearly showed how this famous author was representative of the struggle of the bourgeoisie.   The Schiller Commemorations of that year were a sign of the advanced political consciousness of the strata of property and education.   A brochure of this centenary is characteristic.   In it we read:[2]

> Schiller is one of the great heroes of that renaissance of our literature with which the resurrection of Germany also begins. The achievement of literary popularity and the elimination of foreign influences was the first step in the awakening of popular tendencies in the political field also.   The bourgeoisie will achieve freedom in internal policy, and power and strength in external policy, only if it keeps faith with the spirit of Schiller.

The sociological position of the supporters and opponents of these celebrations corresponded to that ideology.   The educated middle - class — professors, manufacturers, guilds—attended in large numbers, a few progressive princes were in favour of them, but the reactionary groups of the aristocracy and the orthodox Church circles remained aloof.

[1] See L. L. Schücking, *The Sociology of Literary Taste*, London, 1944, chap. iii.
[2] *Die Schillerfeier der alten und neuen Welt*, Leipzig, 1860, p. 2 f.

But one could see that only a few men from old and distinguished families took part in the Centenary, the high aristocracy sent only a few representatives.   As has already been pointed out, one realizes that many have regretted it.   The English aristocracy would certainly not have thought to make itself conspicuous by not attending the celebrations in honour of Shakespeare.[1]

Having become an indispensable heritage of the middle-class, the Classics were fully canonized and taken for granted.   It was a mark of rank and prestige to give prominence in one's home, when visitors came, to the complete works of Schiller and Goethe.   After the abolition in 1864 of the privilege of printing the Classics, hundreds of thousands of cheap copies found their way to homes all over Germany.[2]   But what was the attitude of the bourgeoisie and the feudal court strata after 1830 to the writers of their own time?   It is with the answer to this question that we shall be concerned in the following section.

2. PATRONAGE

The German writers between 1830 and 1870 had a different public and a different patronage according to whether they were protagonists of liberalism and progress, of a parliament and domination from below, or of the existing régime and its opposition to the mob and the maintenance of the courts and the culture of small élites. At that time there existed a courtly aristocratic as well as a middle-class liberal patronage, and the prestige of writers increased through this pluralism of the reading public.   The author was no longer dependent on the benevolence of princes, or on the favour of small court-circles, as in the seventeenth and eighteenth centuries, and now he could also fight against them through the Press and public opinion.   He needed no longer to be

---

[1] *Die Schillerfeier der alten und neuen Welt*, p. 4.

[2] "We get," wrote a clerk in a Berlin book and art shop of that time, "Schiller, Goethe, Lessing, in hundreds and sell them by a mere display in the window." (J. Goldfriedrich, *op. cit.*, iv. 472.)

a servant of kings, but could feel himself to be a tribune of the democratic movement. A consequence of the writer's relative liberty of choice was that, at any rate before 1870, the princely holders of political power were more interested in him. He no longer needed to strive for the favour of the courts; the numerous German courts vied with each other for him. In this connection the contrast with England is striking. Since the beginning of the nineteenth century, the patronage of the English court and aristocracy had decreased; so much so that a leading statesman like Canning could say: "I am really of opinion with Dr. Johnson that the multitudinous personage called the Public is after all the best patron of literature and learned men."[1]

In Germany there existed between 1830 and 1870 the middle-class author, who openly sided with the world of the courts, and the liberal and democratic author who appealed to the upper and lower classes because of his opposition to feudalism and monarchy. Some facts may serve to illustrate the relationship between court and writer. Frederick-William IV granted pensions to the romantic writer Tieck, the poet Kopisch and the lyricist Geibel, and even, for some time, to Ferdinand Freiligrath. Frederick's successor in Prussia from 1868 onwards, William I, paid 1,300 Taler a year to Emanuel Geibel, whilst Ludwig I of Bavaria took the impecunious Graf Platen under his wing and supported Rückert by appointing him to a professorship. Max II collected a whole circle of Court Poets and Court Scholars around him and granted to the poets Geibel, Heyse and Bodenstedt a pension of 1,000 Gulden a year and a professorship. In Württemberg, Dingelstedt obtained in 1843 an appointment as reader to the King and Hofrat with a salary of 2,000 Gulden. In Coburg the liberal Duke, Ernst II, was on very friendly terms with the novelist and playwright Gustav Freytag and protected him against persecution by the Prussian police by appointing him court reader. In Weimar the Grand Duke

[1] A. S. Collins, *The Profession of Letters*, London, 1928, p. 249.

Karl Alexander endeavoured in vain to attract Geibel and Heyse by posts of honour and pensions.[1]

What were the motives of this patronage by the courts? Partly, to get the support of authors whose political ideas and cultural achievements were in keeping with their own governmental policy; partly to maintain the prestige of the court, by the establishment of a "Court of the Muses," against the competition of the numerous other German courts. Conservative soldiers like William I gave literary pensions only for reasons of State, but princes like Max II of Bavaria or Duke Ernst II of Saxe-Coburg took a deeper interest in art and science. The fact that Bavaria—in size the second state in Germany, but having a reputation for backwardness in cultural life—tried to establish a higher level by the importation of protestant scholars from Northern Germany was due to competition with Prussia, which was said to be politically and intellectually superior. This rivalry motive is also the key to the patronage of authors by small courts like Weimar and Coburg.

Attachment to a court, in its turn, not only often meant financial security to poets and artists, but also honour through direct contact with court circles and the ruling bureaucracy; in some cases it even led to ennoblement (e.g. Adam Müller, Geibel, Dingelstedt). On the other hand, large sections of the upper middle-class were sceptical of any court culture, so that court poets between 1840 and 1870 had many enemies and were often subjected to ridicule by organs of the liberal press, such as the *Kölnische Zeitung* and the *Gartenlaube*. Between 1840 and 1848, particularly, the poet and writer became a social force, and was as conscious of the fact as was the Government. The author's political influence grew with the wider extension of the Press and the new technical possibilities of a more rapid circulation. A poem by G. Herwegh, *An die Deutschen Dichter*, expresses this increased self-respect of the man of letters:

[1] Cf. Paul Heyse, *Jugenderinnerungen und Bekenntnisse*, 5th Ed., Stuttgart, 1912, i. 299.

Be proud! No gold in the world
sounds as does the gold of your strings.
No prince is so highly placed
that you should serve him!
In spite of ore and marble
he would die
if you allowed it.
The finest purple is still the blood
that you shed in your songs![1]

The conservative governments before and after 1848 acknowledged in two ways the political significance of the writer as a propagandist as well as a counter-propagandist: either by persecution and supervision of writers in disagreement with the existing régime, or by support and promotion of writers in agreement with it.

Metternich not only opposed the dangerous character of the Young German authors by forbidding their books (decision of the Bundestag in 1835), but also suggested spying out and keeping these writers under observation.[2] On the other hand, governments did their utmost to win and maintain the loyal support of writers who had great reputations. The careers of Freiligrath and Dingelstedt are two contrasting examples which illustrate the German writers' vacillation at that time between the courtly and liberal circles.

Freiligrath, the son of a schoolmaster of Detmold, found himself handicapped by a business-position.[3]   In 1841 he attacked Herwegh for his proneness to making poetry a matter of politics, claiming that poetry was remote from political life: "The watch-tower of the poet is higher than the will of a party." Herwegh defended himself energetically and found much support in the liberal Press, whilst the conservative Press was in favour

---

[1] G. Herwegh, *Gedichte eines Lebendigen,* 12th Ed., Leipzig, 1896, p. 57. How much more self-assertive is the attitude of the politically-minded poet than the resignation of forty years before which is expressed in Schiller's poem *Die Teilung der Erde* as regards the social powerlessness of the poet.

[2] Cf. in regard to Gutzkow, H. H. Houben, *Jungdeutscher Sturm und Drang,* Leipzig, 1911, p. 158 f.

[3] For the facts of Freiligrath's life, see introduction to his *Sämtliche Werke,* ed. by J. Schwering, and for the stages of his political development, cf. E. G. Gudde, *Freiligraths Entwicklung als politischer Dichter,* Berlin, 1922.

of the political neutrality of poetry. Freiligrath, having before enjoyed the favour of a Prussian princess who liked his patriotic poems, now obtained an honorary grant of 300 Taler through the mediation of Alexander von Humboldt. When he then, with Geibel, made a protest in a poem against the successful political expeditions of Herwegh in 1841, the liberal Press interpreted the step as "a poetical receipt for the royal pension," and many liberal writers renounced Freiligrath. The poet now had large sections of public opinion against him, whilst the reactionary government was on his side. Suffering both from the liberal boycott and the growing vigour of reaction, he changed front in 1843. When the censorship grew stronger and the political tension increased between the population of the Rhineland and the centralized administration in Berlin, he realized that an author, like his friend Geibel, unconsciously served the most primitive absolutism by his "conservative innocence." Freiligrath suddenly turned liberal and wrote a volume of democratic poems, *Ein Glaubensbekenntnis* (1844), against the Crown. Simultaneously with its publication he renounced his Prussian pension. The new liberal then emigrated. From our standpoint, the interest the government took in this political change of an influential writer is significant. For the government it was a political matter. The squire (*Landrat*) of the district, with whom Freiligrath had been on friendly terms, had to report officially on the affair and on his attempts to change the poet's decision. Finally the report was submitted to the King through the appropriate ministry.

Meanwhile, Freiligrath had become the martyr and hero of liberal public opinion. After a long period spent as a struggling business-man exiled in London he was to experience the favour of the liberal and democratic movement. In 1865 some German friend of his suggested a national gift to the poet of liberty, who was in financial straits. A stirring appeal made by the *Gartenlaube* was enthusiastically echoed throughout the German

Press.   The return of the exile to Germany in 1868
proved a real triumph.   He received nearly 60,000
Taler.   He welcomed the national unity brought about
by Bismarck in 1871, but did not give up his democratic
ideas.

This example shows that the intellectual in society had
greater freedom of action than had the non-intellectual.
The interplay of different possibilities, of the chances of
sudden change in position, has been described as particularly characteristic of the romantic writer.[1]   But it
has been completely overlooked that change of political
attitude and position was by no means uncommon
amongst the representatives of the later literary movements in the nineteenth century.   The case of Freiligrath demonstrates the change from royalist constitutionalism to a revolutionary democracy; and conversely
the truly romantic change from radical opposition to the
existing régime (which resulted in exile), to appointment
as court-reader and privy councillor, can be traced in
the career of another political lyricist of that time,
Friedrich Dingelstedt.[2]

There is an interesting point of contact in the careers of
Freiligrath and Dingelstedt.   When the former surrendered the
royal pension and became a democrat, he received the following
lines from the hitherto democratic Dingelstedt, who yearned to
join the court-circle: " To fling away a royal pension so that the
liberal rabble, with its importunate collections and subscriptions,
may bring you its public offering with peasant pride?   Good
heavens, Freiligrath, not that!"[3]   And he recommended him,
instead, to stay in Stuttgart and make friends with the amiable
and simple people of the court there.

Dingelstedt was brought up in restricted circumstances in a small German state (Kurhesse).   His father
was a narrow-minded petty-official who looked with awe

---

[1] Cf. C. Schmitt, *Politische Romantik*, 2nd Ed., Munich, 1925, especially
chaps. i and iii.

[2] See Fr. Dingelstedt, *Blätter aus seinem Nachlass*, ed. J. Rodenberg, 2 vols.,
Berlin, 1891, and *Allg. Deutsche Biographie*, vol. 47, pp. 707-25.

[3] *Freiligraths Werke*, ed. J. Schwering, Introduction, pp. lxx ff.

upon his superiors, the privy councillors. The son, an easy-going, placid person, very early displayed his poetical talent, as well as a desire to attain to a higher social level. But the pressure of the ruling régime, operating mainly through the police in his home country, and the general liberal tendencies of the young generation gave rise, for the time being, to a decisive liberal attitude in the ambitious youth. As a student he first devoted himself—like Laube, Gutzkow and Wienbarg before him—to the study of theology, but in order to satisfy his father forsook it for teaching. Despite his democratic tendencies, he liked, as a student, to mix in aristocratic circles, and became a member of a corps. In 1836 he was appointed teacher at a gymnasium at Kassel and in his leisure time edited the literary supplement of a local newspaper. He got into touch with other poets of a similar tendency in the province, and found a benefactor in a general who was later war minister of Kurhesse during the revolution. As a consequence of his liberal writings, he was transferred to another post of the province and his superiors forbade him to use the title of Doctor, because he had obtained it "abroad," that is, in a neighbouring German state. Eventually the free-lance writer got the upper hand of the official in him, the need for individual development conquered the desire for security.

In 1841 he gave up his post as a state teacher, and published the sarcastic, radical *Lieder eines kosmopolitischen Nachtwächters*. The tyranny of the pettyrulers of the German territorial state as well as the philistinism of the German middle-class are here shrewdly and caustically ridiculed. With this book Dingelstedt made his name in the literary world. In the same year he became a permanent correspondent of the *Augsburger Allgemeine Zeitung*, a post very much desired by the freethinking men of letters of that time.[1] For this influ-

---

[1] An interesting characteristic of this versatile man of letters is to be found in some information given to Baron Cotta by Hofrat Fr. Murhard at that time (1837). Cf. *Briefe an Cotta*, Stuttgart, 1934, iii. 394–6.

ential and excellent newspaper he went to Paris, London and Vienna.   The world was revealed to the provincial.[1] He met the leading French politicians, as well as other German writers of the opposition such as Heine, Herwegh, Freiligrath; but it was in these very circles that his inner convictions began to change.   The emigré coteries seemed to him shallow and empty; in the depths of his heart lay a strong desire to rise into society, as well as ambition to be in a good social position for the sake of his fiancée, a celebrated Austrian actress.   In 1848 he left the liberal camp and obtained an appointment as court librarian and reader to the King of Württemberg on the recommendation of Baron von Cotta and of some aristocratic ladies.   How the craving for courtly favour had long obsessed him is unconsciously shown in the delightful self-mockery *Wohlgeboren und Hochwohlgeboren von zwei deutschen Dichtern in Paris* (1841), which he had written a year before with Herwegh.

> There's still a God to reward merit
> and still many a noble house of princes.
> God distributes crowns among the princes,
> the princes distribute titles among us.
> Surely, surely, I shall find it,
> my ultimate aim on this earth;
> if only for the sake of an obituary by Voigt:—
> I *must* become a Privy Councillor![2]

A year later, Dingelstedt became a privy councillor

[1] The following letter of Dingelstedt, written from Paris to an intimate friend who was a lawyer in Kassel, is significant of the contrast between the stagnating life of a German petty-state province and the wide world:
"You will remain in Kassel your whole life long; if the Kurprinz should take it into his head to reduce your salary, you will still worry yourself with documents in the morning and with people in the evening, and will not know which of them is the dustier; every sneaking rascal will look into your head or into your pot, envying or despising you according to whether he comes from the nobility or from the canaille. . . .
"To-morrow I am invited to Guizot's to a political soirée, the day after to-morrow to dinner at Janin's; gracious, what man can become! if one did not still have a German conscience or a philistine one, one might sell oneself to these French dogs, and get 12,000 francs, at least." (F. Dingelstedt, *Blätter aus seinem Nachlass*, i. 193.)
[2] See Herwegh's *Gedichte eines Lebendigen*, 12th Ed., Leipzig, 1896, p. 200.

at the Court of Stuttgart. As before he had detested German provincialism, he now delighted in the courtly atmosphere of this residence which earned him his livelihood. With a curious sentimentality, this one-time rebel wrote to his father of his appointment which carried 2,000 Gulden a year:

> This extraordinary graciousness of my King and Lord.[1] God in Heaven! [he exclaimed], how deeply and easily I breathe in this atmosphere. To be released from the pressure of toil, to move about in a circle of the most amiable people whose interests are completely my own; the phantastic dream of a Tasso- and Goethe-world, are all combined in this sphere and I scarcely know whether I am awake or dreaming.[2]

In Dingelstedt the desire for an idealized world of court-circles was stronger than the urge of opposition and the feeling of solidarity with the middle-class. With considerable satisfaction the renegade wrote to his friends about his social rise. From the chrysalis of an obscure writer, "he was metamorphosed into a brilliant courtly butterfly," and he had nearly forgotten "the slow schoolmaster caterpillar." Yet two years ago he was still mocking at the function of court-poets.[3]

> Blessed of all countries the country
> that decorates councillors and judges with laurels
> and poets with the ribbons of ministerial orders.
> Only one question I can hardly suppress:
> Are the latter more than ministers or judges?

Now the courtly self-confidence of the *arriviste* provincial knew no bounds.

> You can well imagine how much I am in demand here. The King often sends for me when I am not on duty, speaks to me in the street, even invites me to dinner; consequently the princesses do the same, the court still more, the whole city most of all.[4]

The King's reader lost his post in 1848, and therefore grew resentful of the democratic movement. "The

---

[1] F. Dingelstedt, *Blätter aus seinem Nachlass*, ii. 10 ff.   [2] *Ibid.*, p. 7.
[3] *Lieder eines kosmopolitischen Nachtwächters*, 2nd Ed., p. 66.
[4] F. Dingelstedt, *Blätter aus seinem Nachlass*, ii. 14.

Press and the barristers rule the world," he complained
with indignation.[1]   In 1851 he was appointed superintendent of the royal theatre in Munich, but suffered
from being excluded from the symposia of the King.
After a short interlude as superintendent of the theatre
in Weimar in 1870, his greatest ambitions were fulfilled.
As a director of the K.K. Burgtheater in Vienna and
K.K. *Hofrat* (Privy-Councillor), he was ennobled in
Austria.   But meanwhile his literary productivity had
considerably decreased.   One of his contemporaries
called the one-time author of anti-feudalist songs "the
rhymester *Hofrat*," and "drawing-room chameleon." [2]
The critic of Dingelstedt was right who in 1837 wrote
to Cotta: "As to Dingelstedt's character, he seems to
have little firmness.   He might well serve anyone who
pays him." [3]

After 1870 the likelihood of gaining the support of
the court diminished considerably in the Empire.   The
Prussian court was no longer interested in gifted writers.
The rôle of the third-rate writer Joseph von Lauff as
poet laureate to William II is as characteristic as the
rejection of a really great dramatist—Gerhart Hauptmann—by the same ruler.   The prestige of the writer
in the eyes of the ruling class began to diminish.

A shrewd observer like Fontane, who had himself
experienced a good deal of disappointment during his
career, had, in the last quarter of the century, some
melancholy reflections to make on the situation of the
author in comparison with that of the publisher: [4]
"Those who trade in literature and journalism become
rich, those who work in these professions either starve
or just muddle through."   Why was the writer suspect

---

[1] Dingelstedt subsequently became enthusiastic for the aristocracy of blood,
glorified the Christian entrepreneur and expressed sharp anti-semitic feeling
against Jewish business and journalism in his novel, *Die Amazone* (Stuttgart,
1868, 2 vols.).

[2] F. Dingelstedt, *Blätter aus seinem Nachlass*, ii. 232.

[3] *Briefe an Cotta*, iii. 396 (Friedrich Murhard).

[4] See the anonymous article *Die gesellschaftliche Stellung des Schriftstellers*,
Das Magazin für Literatur, 1891, vol. 60, pp. 818 ff.

in society? Fontane finds three reasons for it: firstly, a certain penetration which gave the professions something of the character of a detective; secondly, the fact that these professions were not considered essential, it being claimed that *belles lettres* was the only profession which had little connection with the real needs of men; thirdly, the lack of acknowledgment of this profession by the State. In a society whose models are the officer and the official, the writer, being an individualist and outsider, counts for little. Only authors who hold public positions enjoy a higher prestige. Fontane cites as examples A. F. von Schack, the director of an art-gallery, and Paul Lindau, director of a theatre.

As in the period of "Storm and Stress" at the end of the eighteenth century, the system of the ruling-class was unfavourable to the creative intellectual.

The idea that only examination, testimonials, degrees, offices, titles, medals—in short, everything that is a manifestation of state power—has value and significance, rules the mind more than ever, and the free geniuses, the "savages," having always been suspect, are now more suspect than ever. The social precedence of kindred groups of artists such as painters and sculptors is evident.[1]

Declining to have anything to do with revolutionary changes, but striving for an improvement of the social status of his profession, Fontane asks that his colleagues be given those honours, small or great, which alone guarantee social prestige in Germany. He suggests invitations from society circles (not only—as is usual—from bankers in the Tiergartenstrasse, but also from princes and ministers of state, who hitherto were in the habit of receiving painters and musicians) and orders and honours, not for the sake of vanity, but with a view to increasing the prestige enjoyed by those who hold them, particularly in Prussia.

3. THE ARISTOCRATIC WRITER

In the earlier chapters we have several times touched upon the vacillation of the non-aristocratic writer towards

[1] *Ibid.*

the aristocracy. We have seen that the middle-class men of letters experienced an inner conflict between their origin and political ethics which inspired hostility towards the aristocracy and their æsthetic needs which led them to sympathize with it. We now intend to give a brief analysis of the situation of the writer of aristocratic descent. The term "aristocratic writer" involves an antinomy, a certain self-contradiction. For it has been pointed out previously that the German aristocracy in the nineteenth century was indifferent and even hostile to literature, because of its deep distrust of the destructive tendencies of writers.[1]

"Thrones and those who stand near them," says an aristocratic writer in 1860, "have ceased to be patrons of literature, which now draws its patrons and readers from the whole of the educated middle-class."[2]

Being a member of the intelligentsia, the aristocratic writer was, in the nature of things, more critically minded than the majority of his compeers, and his outlook on life was by no means always analogous with the ideology of the class from which he came. Sometimes he dissociated himself from it after serious inner conflict. He often had to adapt himself to changed conditions and seek his public in middle-class circles. Owing to an implicit code, writing was taboo for the aristocracy, a fact which is evidenced by the not infrequent publications of works of aristocratic authors under non-aristocratic pseudonyms, especially in the case of Austrian aristocrats, e.g. Graf Auersperg (Anastasius Grün), Niembsch Edler von Strehlenau (Nikolaus Lenau),

---

[1] To a certain extent the bias of aristocracy against intellectualism was international; cf., even in regard to England, the remarks of A. Ponsonby in *The Decline of Aristocracy*, London, 1912, p. 92.

[2] "No haughty disregard of poets, no sneers, no legitimate ban, will avail. The courts and the aristocracy must adapt themselves to the new taste or not read at all. The latter is the case now, but the future will show how long they can stand it. The tendency towards village fiction is already symptomatic of a democratic inclination." (A. v. Ungern-Sternberg, *Erinnerungsblätter*, 1860, vi. 4.)

Freiherr von Münch-Bellinghausen (Friedrich Halm), and also Prinz Georg von Preussen (G. Conrad).[1] The aristocratic writer very often found himself isolated or even boycotted by his own family, even when he fought for patriotic and national aims as in the case of H. von Kleist or when he wrote conservative tales as in the case of the Baroness A. von Droste-Hülshoff. In the latter case a conflict arose between class tradition and individual inclination. Heinrich von Kleist, for example, first embarked on the usual career of a Prussian Junker —the army—but gave it up to devote himself to philosophy and poetry.[2] This aroused the resentment of his family.[3] The Catholic Westphalian family of the Baroness Droste-Hülshoff reacted similarly to the publication of her first poems. "One found fault with her approach to the public as one would with a false step, quite apart from her people's lack of judgment on the subject of poetry."[4]

The aristocratic author wrote at a time when his own class was very much attacked in literature. Education for all, democracy, parliamentarism, were demands which the aristocracy disliked. To the aristocratic author many things which were self-evident to his compeers seemed problematic. Three main possibilities of an approach to the aristocracy and the middle-class were open to him:

A defence of the old status and privileges of aristocracy, or a function as mediator, working for a reconciliation between the two strata by recommending the values of

---

[1] Cf. L. L. Schücking, *The Sociology of Literary Taste*, p. 17. But Schücking overlooks the fact that these authors are all Austrian. In Prussia, the books were nearly always published without pseudonyms. (See the cases of Heinrich v. Kleist, Annette v. Droste-Hülshoff, Prinz v. Schönaich-Carolath, Ernst v. Wildenbruch, Freiherr Börries v. Münchhausen. An exception is Prince Georg von Preussen (1826–1902), who published dramas under the name of G. Conrad.)

[2] Similar was the development of a younger aristocratic writer, Franz Freiherr von Gaudy. (Cf. J. Reiske, *Franz Freiherr von Gaudy als Dichter*, Berlin, 1911.)

[3] See the article: H. v. Kleist, *Allgemeine Deutsche Biographie*, xvi. 128.

[4] Fr. Gundolf, *Romantiker, Neue Folge*, Berlin, 1931, p. 198 f.

the middle-class to the aristocracy, and, conversely, aristocratic values to the middle-class, or conversion to liberalism and a demand for the reform of the nobility varying in degree from sober criticism of the aristocracy to destructive hatred.

Let us take these three points separately: There is a characteristic dearth of outspoken champions of an aristocratic régime amongst the aristocratic writers after 1830. A French emigrant like Fouqué or an illegitimate offspring of the royal family like Ernst von Wildenbruch were the writers who tried to glorify nobility and a noble attitude in their works. This type of aristocratic writer often seeks the favour and patronage of the court, as did Count Platen and Wildenbruch, the latter's dramas being accepted for the stage by the Duke of Meiningen, who was a great lover of art. The successful Austrian playwright Freiherr von Münch-Bellinghausen obtained a sinecure, and also became principal of the court library and superintendent of the court theatre.

Far more aristocratic writers come into the category of "middle-men," who combine a positive attitude to the class of their origin with a moderate criticism of it, and try to build a bridge between tradition and achievement, between the aristocracy of blood and the aristocracy of culture. Amongst them are not only great figures like Wilhelm von Humboldt and Alexander von Humboldt —the latter taking the widest advantage of his position as Chamberlain to the Prussian King to patronize young poets and scholars [1]—but writers of the last third of the century such as W. von Polenz, Georg von Ompteda and Prince von Schoenaich-Carolath also come into this category. This type assumes the function of arbitrator, of conciliator. It demands the amalgamation of the healthy aristocratic and middle-class elements, and sums up the social defects of the two classes with remarkable frankness. Prince von Schoenaich-Carolath, for

---

[1] See in this connection K. Gutzkow, *Rückblicke auf mein Leben*, Berlin, 1875, p. 243. At the same period the poet and banker, Samuel Rogers, fulfilled in England a similar function as patron of young talent.

example, wrote two volumes of short stories, *Adliger Tod*
and *Bürgerlicher Tod*, in which he describes the typical
phenomena of decomposition in the aristocracy and in
the bourgeoisie.

With the third type which goes over to liberalism,
we often find that the motive is a subconscious wish to
spite the father. The aristocratic self-confidence im-
planted in childhood is impaired in adolescence and
transforms itself into a strong critical attitude towards
the aristocratic world. Alliance with the free sphere of
literature, as well as estrangement from feudalism, can
take a stronger or weaker form. If perchance such an
aristocratic writer is brought into contact with a court
which is a kind of self-hatred. The attitudes of Freiherr
von Schack on the one hand and of Ernst von Wolzogen
If, however, he has to earn his living as a writer, his
estrangement from the aristocracy becomes greater; it
may even take the form of a hatred of the aristocracy
which is a kind of self-hatred. The attitude of Freiherr
von Schack on the one hand and of Ernst von Wolzogen
on the other are typical examples of these two forms of
liberalism.

Freiherr von Schack was born a member of the
Mecklenburg country-nobility.[1] His father was later
appointed minister to the Bundestag in Frankfurt, and
although on friendly terms with some of the Romanticists, shared the typical aristocratic prejudice against
writing as a profession. He would therefore only allow
his son to take up a career befitting an aristocrat and
thought a position at a court more suitable than a professorship in philology or philosophy. His son reacted
strongly and became secretly an enthusiast for the heroes
of liberalism. As a young man he attended the debates
of the *Landtag* of Baden and was enthusiastic about
K. Welker, the liberal leader of the opposition.

It was precisely the hostile and disdainful tone [he says later,
in analysing his own attitude] in which this man and his com-

[1] Cf. the memoirs of A. F. v. Schack, *Ein halbes Jahrhundert*, 3 vols., Stuttgart, 1888.

rades were spoken of in the circles in which I moved, which inspired me to an admiration exceeding the measure that was really his due.[1]

It was not political struggle, however, but culture, which became the real interest of this refined aristocrat, who later made a name as a distinguished translator and art-collector. In the Bavarian Court in Munich he found the proper field for his cultural inclinations. A far more radical criticism of the aristocracy was expressed by E. von Wolzogen, particularly in his pamphlet *Linksum kehrt—schwenkt Trab, Ein ernstes Mahnwort an die herrschenden Klassen und insbesondere den deutschen Adel* (1895). Wolzogen demanded that the aristocracy should change over to democracy and, what amounted to the same thing, to modern literature. There is perhaps nothing more characteristic of the tension between aristocracy and bourgeoisie than this pamphlet. Lack of adaptability and pride of caste are alleged to be the main faults of the nobility:

> Anyone who likes to belong to the caste of the chosen is forbidden to differ, in his outward behaviour as well as in his thinking and feeling, from his caste-fellows. To have the courage of one's convictions is no longer regarded as a virtue, but as impertinent and lacking in taste; the enlightened must therefore become hypocrites.[2]

In the new empire the stereotyped ideal of the aristocracy is embodied in the officer. "The manners of the officer, his whole social training, are zealously imitated, and the youth of our noblest circles almost goes so far as to regard as a social outsider the man who could not be recognized as an officer when in mufti." [3]

Here again the English aristocracy is held up in contrast to the German, taking such examples as Immermann, Riehl, and Schack. In England, the younger

---

[1] A. F. v. Schack, *Ein halbes Jahrhundert*, i. 69.

[2] Ernst v. Wolzogen, *Linksum kehrt—schwenkt Trab! Ein ernstes Mahnwort an die herrschenden Klassen und den deutschen Adel insbesondere*, 6th Ed., Berlin, 1895, p. 11.

[3] E. v. Wolzogen, *loc. cit.*, pp. 18 ff.

sons of the aristocracy could become bankers, merchants, clergymen, scholars, artists—"in short, everything for which they possessed inclination or talent." [1]   But this progressive aristocrat, with his exhortations to the aristocracy to adapt themselves to the new age, remains a voice crying in the wilderness.   "The horrors of the great revolution ought to have taught us that the true aristocrat is the born champion of new ideas, from wherever they may come." [2]

Further, not only was the aristocracy biassed against modern development, but aristocratic writers had also to suffer from the prejudice of their middle-class competitors.   Their position between the unliterary aristocracy and the self-assured man of letters of middle-class origin was not an easy one.[3]   In the literary struggle which Heine and Immermann waged against the aristocratic poet Platen, their anti-aristocratic bias played no small part.   Even the progressive aristocratic poets were subject to the criticism of their middle-class colleagues during the revolutionary period of 1848. The liberal poet Anastasius Grün (Graf Auersperg) had in 1839 married an Austrian Countess.   Her rank as a lady of the *Sternkreuzorden* led him for formal reasons to ask for the title of an Austrian chamberlain.   Having become a chamberlain, he was entitled to attend court-receptions with his wife.   Democratic writers were very indignant at this subservience to court ceremonial, and

---

[1] *Op. cit.*, p. 30.

[2] *Op. cit.*, p. 22: "Rid yourself of the outmoded knightly equipment of prejudice, dare to be modern, learn to understand our times, and open your ears to the tidings it brings you!"

[3] The complaint of one aristocratic writer is significant of the bias of the non-aristocratic critic: "Criticism before 1848 was full of bitterness and anger, which was the stronger the less it dared to come out into the open.   It was not talent versus talent, but the little word 'von' versus the simple name without a 'von' " (A. v. Ungern-Sternberg, *Erinnerungsblätter*, Berlin, 1855, i. 14).

A characteristic example of the intermediate position of the aristocratic artist who cannot be counted as belonging entirely to one group, is given by Fontane in his *Tunnel an der Spree*; he explains the lack of popularity of an aristocratic painter (H. v. Blomberg) by the fact that the Barons regarded him as a painter, but the painters in their turn regarded him as a Baron. (Th. Fontane, *Von Zwanzig bis Dreissig*, Berlin, 1925, 19th Ed., p. 262.)

one of the most influential expressed his disgust in the following verses:

> May one desecrate the temple for a woman's sake?
> And dance with a woman round idols of gold?
> You want to take the liberty of being free
> And to place your sword
> like a little cross on your breast?
> I look for the poet only in *our* ranks.
> Farewell! Farewell!
> I leave you to your courtiers!
> Already I can hear you say:
> "My heart, my heart, no longer so warm!
> We are going to court, countess, please, your arm!"[1]

The difficulty of compromise between traditional sentiments and clear recognition of the changed social situation has tormented more than one aristocratic writer. The development of Alexander von Ungern-Sternberg (1806–68) is characteristic of this.[2] He was neither taken seriously by his own caste, nor did he manage to establish an alliance with the bourgeoisie at the right time. This individualistic figure came from a cosmopolitan aristocratic family, his father being Vice-Chancellor of the university of Dorpat and a freemason. Rather spoiled by his education, he at first became a chamberlain at the Court of the Grand Duchess of Baden. In 1838 he published his first novel, a parody on the Young Germans. After that he lived for some time in Stuttgart as a member of two very different circles, participating in the middle-class idyll of the *Schwäbische Dichterschule* and in the splendour of the drawing-room of the Queen of Württemberg. When in 1834 his allowance from his father was stopped, the gifted young man had to earn a living with his pen, and now had the choice of entering the service of the Russian Reaction, or of joining the drawing-room liberalism of Varnhagen von Ense, which he so much admired. This alternative determined his whole future status. In 1848 Sternberg still showed a reactionary attitude in his *Neu-*

---

[1] G. Herwegh, *Gedichte eines Lebendigen*, 12th Ed., p. 61.
[2] Cf. A. v. Ungern-Sternberg, *Erinnerungsblätter*, vol. i–vi, Berlin, 1855–60; further E. Weil, *Alexander von Sternberg*, Berlin, 1932.

preussische Zeitbilder. But only a few years later he retracted his views and revoked his royalist opinions. Through his demands for a reform of the aristocracy he fell out with both parties; the aristocrats were annoyed with the impoverished critic of noble blood, and the liberals distrusted his haughtiness. He was more and more isolated and a prey to inner conflict.[1] This is clearly shown in the reflections of the aristocratic Alcidor in Sternberg's amusing *Palmyra oder das Tagebuch eines Papageien*. The vacillation of this spirited individual between thought and feeling, between recognition of the inevitability of the new social development and a sense of superiority as a member of a formerly ruling-class, is realistically demonstrated:

He was an aristocrat of an old and good family, who had always enjoyed, with modesty, the privileges which were formerly granted them and which the changed social order now gives to other classes. Alcidor was too clever not to realize that an old injustice was thereby repaired; but his personal pride was hurt.[2]

The hero of this book suffers from the problematic position of the aristocrat in a changed society: "Aristocratic birth, formerly a special favour of providence, now became a dangerous thankless position."[3] The dangerous situation engendered a lack of balance in this arrogant man of letters: "An aristocrat from top to toe, he could sometimes become a democrat," as one of his contemporaries says,

he could even show some revolutionary tendencies. Poor as he was, and dependent on a living from his pen, he scolded the state, the church, the society, as long as he had to work for his living. But when he had earned money and was well off, he at once became aristocratic and haughty again.[4]

---

[1] See the remarkable confession of this author quoted above, chap. iii, p. 99.
[2] *Palmyra*, p. 172.   [3] *Ibid.*, p. 173.
[4] F. Wehl, *Zeiten und Menschen*, vol. ii, quoted in E. Weil, *op. cit.*, p. 137.

CHAPTER IX

LITERARY ASSOCIATIONS

THE writer in the age of liberalism is, to a large extent, characterized by an individualistic approach to life. With a few exceptions, he is a product of that typical modern spirit which finds the individual interesting as such, and which insists on free development. But the author of this age is also, in the nature of things, a social being, and is dependent on social contact in spite of all his self-glorification. The old antinomy of individualism and of collectivism, of loneliness and of co-operation, of self-reliance and of dependence on the public, has here been embodied in an unusual shape. Competition forces every author to try to develop a literary tone of his own. But, in addition to this, the writer of the nineteenth century is largely a supporter of that kind of personality which is characterized by Goethe's much-quoted and much-misquoted saying:

Höchstes Glück der Erdenkinder ist doch die Persönlichkeit.

The author and poet, whom one should not confuse with the political writer, is mainly concerned with expressing and moulding himself, his ideas and his feelings. He is mostly a differentiated type who thinks independently and seldom, therefore, identifies himself prominently with any group or class. Moreover, his work is not performed in a commercial undertaking or in a state department, he is not so much affected by the division of labour; his activities, like those of certain groups of scholars, are confined to the loneliness of the desk. On the other hand, the writer, as a social being, is like any other professional type, subject to various kinds of association in his private as well as in his professional life.

Roughly speaking, we can distinguish three main forms of social groupings:

(1) Intercourse with colleagues, either in strictly professional unions, like the modern Pen Club, or in literary circles, schools, and movements of a stronger or weaker coherence, which share common æsthetic or cultural tendencies.

(2) Intercourse with friends of literature and laymen, in communities which acknowledge a specific poet or writer as their spiritual leader and propagate his works.

(3) Intercourse outside the professional sphere proper; common, political or social or religious interests bringing about an association, and the writer then often having the function of spokesman or literary exponent.

Milton and the Puritans, Byron and Philhellenism, Brentano and the *Christlich-deutsche Tischgesellschaft* in Berlin, Börne and the German emigrant-artisans in Paris, provide examples of such literary groupings.

Here we shall deal only with a few cases of association amongst German writers in the nineteenth century. For this purpose it is not so much the historical sequence of these examples that is important, as the relation of the authors to different social forces. We shall be concerned with describing and analysing:

(i) The Young German writers as the type of a grouping of mobile and radical intellectuals.

(ii) A "neutral" union of writers and friends of literature of different political opinions.

(iii) A combination of conservative and liberal intellectuals connected with court-circles.

1. Progressive Intelligentsia: The Young Germans

An important formula of the sociology of culture distinguishes between mobile intelligentsia and autochthonous intelligentsia.[1] Whilst the autochthonous in-

[1] Cf. K. Mannheim, *Man and Society in an Age of Reconstruction*, London, 1940, pp. 92–94.

telligentsia is steeped in the cultural heritage and the regional tradition of certain districts and provinces, the mobile intelligentsia is characterized ·by relative independence of local traditions, a tendency to pursue change of place as well as of ideas.   The function of the intelligentsia dominated by tradition is the expression of national or regional heritage.   The function of the mobile intelligentsia, on the other hand, is to propagate new ideas and to criticize the existing social order. Through its greater versatility, the mobile intelligentsia obtains comparative criteria for the values of different social strata and nations and makes possible an exchange between them, thus serving as a kind of intermediate link.

Whilst the autochthonous intelligentsia lays chief stress on the power of tradition, of history, of *Volkstum*, the mobile one is led rather by abstract principles, such as salvation of the soul, science, progress, etc.   It has rightly been said [1] that it would be possible and fruitful to write a history of the intellectual movements from the point of view of the interchange between autochthonous and mobile intellectual élites, but if one begins such an approach from a one-sided positive valuation of the autochthonous intelligentsia, as is done, for example, by Joseph Nadler,[2] the peculiarity and function of the mobile groups in history is easily subject to misinterpretation.[3]   For types like the wandering students of the Middle Ages, the humanists of the sixteenth century and the literati of naturalism and expressionism in our modern big cities, cannot be primarily explained by the national factor; therefore it does not show a scientific attitude to stigmatize them as "the uprooted."

Young Germany is the first definitely mobile intellectual élite of Germany in the nineteenth century.   The

[1] K. Mannheim, *ibid.*, p. 70.

[2] J. Nadler, *Literaturgeschichte der deutschen Stämme und Landschaften*, Regensburg, 1912–28, 4 vols.

[3] For this reason Nadler has no understanding at all of Börne and Heine. See his very biased exposition of the German emigrants in France after 1848 (*Literaturgeschichte*, iv. 64).

early romanticists had, it is true, displayed an attitude by no means corresponding to national tradition, although the later romanticists had partly turned supporters of a conservative status-ideology. But Young Germany was not only a mobile group of intellectuals like the early romanticists, it was also outspoken, progressive and open-minded. These writers did not merely discover this or that country, but the "world," the social reality, with all its shades, with its abundance, and with its tensions.

Their movement was a movement of protesting people and was characterized for a long time by its antagonism against the ruling-class. The Young German liked to vary the place as well as the kind of his activities. He scattered his numerous reflections and ideas here and there, and thus overcame the paralysing narrowness of the German territorial states.

As often happens in intellectual history, it was the opponents of the movement who stigmatized as a secret society the loose alliance of its writers, and thereby forced them to greater solidarity. In the period of the persecution of the demagogues and of secret political unions the German governments suspected that the loose literary contacts of these intellectuals were, in fact, the basis of a hidden conspiracy. As a consequence they confused the homonymous German section of a revolutionary secret society, *Junges Europa*, with the literary group, *Junges Deutschland*, which, as a matter of fact, consisted only of dedications of books.[1]

Under the name of "Young Literature" [to quote from, for instance, a decree of the government of Baden], a union of several writers has been formed, the supposed intention of which was to bring about an anarchy in social relations through the overthrow of all usual ideas of Christianity, authority, property, marriage, etc., and to prepare a general revolution.[2]

[1] J. Proelss, *Das junge Deutschland*, Stuttgart, 1892, pp. 611 ff.
[2] H. Houben, *Jungdeutscher Sturm und Drang*, Leipzig, 1911, p. 76. Amongst the four writers denounced there was only one Jew; but an appeal was made to anti-semitic instinct by falsifying the facts. The Bavarian government issued an order against Heine, Karl Gutzkow, Theodor Mundt, and Ludolf Wienbarg as being of Jewish descent (H. Houben, *ibid.*, p. 96).

In other words: the progressive élite was branded as a
secret society hostile to the existing state. What were
the real facts of the situation? There were loose personal contacts; some of the Young German authors knew
each other, all corresponded with one another, discussed
literature in an aggressive manner, but a proper organization never existed.[1]

For the formation of a literary school was prevented
by the competition existing between these writers who
lived at different places. Every author wished to
succeed and had therefore to think of his own interests.
Common ideas and common opponents caused co-
operation, the search for success and fame in its turn
engendered the fear of competition amongst this useful
and bold literati.

The Young Germans can be divided into two groups:
the Jewish group (Börne-Heine) and the non-Jewish
group (Gutzkow, Laube, Mundt, Wienbarg, Kühne).
The active co-operation of Jews and non-Jews in this
movement was a new feature; it was much discussed by
their supporters as well as by their opponents. At the
same time it meant the introduction of a larger group
of Jews into German literature.

With remarkable shrewdness Wienbarg had already
recognized the correlation between Heine's wit and his
situation as a Jewish outsider.

Heine was—so to speak—destined for the keenest unsparing
satire, which always knows how to hit the nail on the head, by
a destiny which had raised him from the trading Jew to the student
of Göttingen and to a German writer. No Frenchman, no
foreigner, is able to realize and to ridicule the follies, the weaknesses, the pride in ancestors, and the pedantry of the Germans
better than a Jew, born in Germany, who being likewise strange
to the heart and to the history of the nation has a special bent

---

[1] See the significant words of Gutzkow in his preface to a book of Hogarth's
engravings: "We young people, who claim to continue and revive the tradition
of German literature, maintain a lively correspondence behind the scenes; we
exchange slogans, prepare attacks and reciprocally correct one another, in
short, we have a conspiracy, but this cannot be called a criminal one" (H.
Houben, *loc. cit.*, p. 42).

for satire, which the foreigner lacks; I mean the stimulus which sprang from the contempt which his co-religionists had hitherto to stand, the wounded feeling of a nation, ill-treated through the centuries, and until recently forced to silence.[1]

Börne and Heine differed from the gentile Young Germans in age as well as in origin. Their fame was already established in 1830, whilst the reputation of the other Young Germans was purely a result of their pamphlets and publications after the French July Revolution. Their fathers were merchants whilst nearly all of the Christian Young Germans came from the circles of artisans and of lower officials.[2] The different training through which the members of the two groups passed before they became professional writers was also significant: Börne was an employee in the town council of Frankfort-on-Main, his native town, Heine studied law and took the degree of doctor of law, but Laube, Wienbarg and Gutzkow started with theology, partly because it was the cheapest study and the quickest road to a post. Yet none of the latter completed his studies; all turned very soon to modern philosophy and journalism. Gutzkow at the age of twenty was editor of the *Forum der Journalliteratur*; Laube at the age of twenty-three became a dramatic critic in Breslau; Wienbarg caused some sensation by his vigorous lectures *Ästhetische Feldzüge*, which he delivered and published when he was thirty-one.

What characterized the critical approach of the Young Germans? Similarly to the "Storm and Stress," it was directed on the negative side against old and lifeless social powers and conventions; against feudalism and middle-class philistinism; on the positive it represented a kind of aristocratic vanguard of the slowly beginning process towards democratization.[3]

[1] L. Wienbarg, *Ästhetische Feldzüge*, 1834, pp. 287 ff.

[2] See R. Horovitz, *Vom Roman des Jungen Deutschland zum Roman der Gartenlaube*, p. 114.

[3] A convincing exposition of the aims of the Young Germans from another point of view is to be found in R. Kayser, *Dichterköpfe*, Vienna, 1930, pp. 48–87.

With impressive power these young literati attacked the old Germany in its threefold shape as incompetent aristocrats, pedantic scholars and dull philistines. They turned against bad university, court and other stiffening atmospheres.[1] In treating politics æsthetically and æsthetics politically, they thought to spiritualize the sensual and sensualize the spiritual. They protested with passion

against the benumbing of the youthful mind in our schools, against the treatment of the sciences as a trade at the universities, against the laziness of bureaucracy, against the tolerance of evil because it is legitimized by tradition, against the whole feudal-historical school which would nail us alive to the cross of history.[2]

This anti-conservative attitude was the outcome of the courage to face reality; they mocked at the trivial glorification of the ancient world, at the endless interpretation of Greek writers which had nothing to do with the life of the present. The enthusiasm for Greece meant an escape for the classical writers from the misery of the political impotence of the middle-class.[3] At first the Young Germans attempted to overcome this political impotence, and consequently declined this avenue of escape. Like the representatives of the preceding literary movements they propagated ideas, but only those which had some connection with the social situation of the time. They wanted to fill society with the spirit of liberty. Therefore, the two opposite types who were attacked by the Young Germans were on the one hand the philistine, and on the other the non-political *bel esprit*. Both were said to be too indolent, they adapted themselves to the real or to the imaginary world without altering or decisively influencing social conditions.

It was precisely the lack of *Gemütlichkeit* that Wienbarg called *the* criterion of the æsthetics of the new literature in contrast to the prose of Goethe and of Jean

[1] L. Wienbarg, *Ästhetische Feldzüge*, 1834, p. vi.

[2] L. Wienbarg, *ibid.*, p. 34.

[3] Cf. W. H. Bruford, *Germany in the Eighteenth Century*, p. 307.

Paul.[1]   And indeed the new movement did not shrink from the fate of a persecuted élite.   Although devoted to the enjoyment of life, its members had to face imprisonment and denunciation by the government.   It is a characteristic objection of the Young Germans against romanticists, when they warn the poets and novelists

they could not always hover so softly and ethereally, truth and reality now would impress them profoundly and with this reality they would have to contend so long as the actual were no longer synonymous with the vulgar, which is opposed and hostile to the ideal.[2]

This intention of reconciling reality and ideal, of making reason palpable, and society reasonable, shows the connection of the movement with the philosophy of that time, a certain affinity to the doctrines of Hegel and the Young Hegelians.[3]   Discomfort appeared a virtue to the Young Germans.   Therefore, before 1848, nothing was more hateful to them than security, prolonged residence at one place, and the lack of versatility.   Their natural form of life was mobility.[4]

How can this mobility be explained?   To a large extent it was the product of the new technical and economic situation.   A new type of journalist and writer was needed, able to combine knowledge with experience of the world in an era of industrialization and growing political interest.   At a time when the whole German system of communication was reformed by people like Fr. List and the brothers Harkort, journalism also changed its face.   The travelling writer, the reporter, now became an institution.   The pleasures of travel increased with the quicker methods of transport, and the attractions of journalism received a new stimulus.   "To see double the amount in half the time, meant four

---

[1] L. Wienberg, *op. cit.*, p. 297.   [2] L. Wienberg, *ibid.*, p. 299.

[3] As regards the similar turning of the Young Hegelians to political reality see J. Löwenstein, *Hegels Staatsidee, ihr Doppelgesicht und Einfluss im 19. Jahrhundert*, Berlin, 1927, p. 80.

[4] Quotations referring to the Young German idea of movement are given in R. Horovitz, *op. cit.*, p. 19.

volumes instead of one." [1]   From 1835 onwards, the correspondence of the great newspapers and journals grew to quite new dimensions, and whoever was not tied to one place devoted himself, at least for some weeks, to the life of a vagrant man of letters, sending impressions of a journey, sketches, views of abroad, to all editors.

These *Reisebilder* provide a better expression of the mentality of the Young Germans than any other literary product.   They contain either poetry and poetical satire or sketches from the history of culture.   Besides the different parts of Germany, France, Italy, Poland and Holland are favourite subjects.   Börne, Heine and Gutzkow wrote letters from Paris, Laube described conditions in Poland, Wienbarg gave an account of Holland from 1831 to 1832.   To the younger generation of 1830 a life of travel seemed the only kind of life worth while.

What could the homeless German literature do better than tramp about? [asks Theodor Mundt in the postscript to *Madonna. Unterhaltungen mit einer Heiligen*].   The author has written all these sketches in inns, he has invented some in a swaying mail-coach, and dreamt others on the roadway in blizzard and storm.[2]

Here, travelling means more than a mere change of place, it symbolizes an inner movement and has its cause in the homelessness of the progressive intellectual.

Still more do I pity [says Mundt] those who can feel comfortable to-day in the contemporary conditions of their country, who are autochthonous, and are not ready at a moment's notice to quit.   Faithfulness to the soil means nothing if the soil suppresses the intelligence.[3]

More realistic is the mocking interpretation of the mobile attitude of the Young Germans by one of their opponents.

The German poets have become disquieted, they no longer want to stay in obscure towns and villages, they emigrate to

---

[1] H. Houben, *Jungdeutscher Sturm und Drang*, p. 356.
[2] Th. Mundt, *Madonna*, Leipzig, 1835, p. 431 f.   [3] *Ibid.*, p. 4.

Rome, Naples, London or Paris.   It is no longer sufficient to describe how Walter and Luise gather strawberries, or how the old, honest parson is sleeping in his armchair beside the stove; the author only expects success for his book if he is able to say in it that he has exchanged a few words with Prince Talleyrand.[1]

Laube's *Neue Reisenovellen* (1837), for instance, is a record of a journey through Germany from the South via Thuringia and Berlin to Pomerania.   The book deals with people and country and criticizes the social conditions.   Besides Laube, the travel sketches by L. Wienbarg impress us as particularly interesting.   The first number of the *Deutsche Revue* [2] contains his impressions of a journey under the title of *Elbe und Nordsee*. In a small town of Holstein the social limits of the different strata are pictured and the problem of intermarriage between Jews and Christians is discussed from a liberal point of view.   Or he exposes the relics of feudalism in Denmark, drawing on his experience during his time there as a tutor.   "What had I to see at Seeland and at Fähren?   A poor woman came creeping on her knees into the room of the gracious countess in order to beg something of her.   She kissed the train of her silk dress." [3]

An active attitude, which believes in the possibility of a more reasonable and just society in the future, was behind the social criticism of this vehement writer.   The outlook of Young Germany is brought about by the transition from the conservative spirit of the Romantics to the Realism of a democratic society.[4]   This transition, which can be demonstrated in regard to æsthetics as well as the social philosophy of the Young Germans, presents great difficulties in the interpretation of this movement, which is often overcrowded with ideologies

[1] A. von Ungern-Sternberg, *Palmyra*, p. 237.

[2] See the edition of *Die Deutsche Revue* by J. Dresch, in *Deutsche Literaturdenkmale des 18. und 19. Jahrhunderts*, No. 132, Berlin, 1904. The very first number of this review, which Wienbarg published with Gutzkow, was suppressed by the reactionary police.

[3] *Die Deutsche Revue*, p. 20.

[4] Cf. L. Wienbarg, *Ästhetische Feldzüge*, p. 116.

and characterized by an undisciplined and ambiguous style.

The Young Germans still shared with the Romantics the predilection for an aphoristic playful mind. (Friedrich von Gentz, the political romanticist, for instance, therefore admired Heine.) They liked to display their brilliance in the salons of clever women like Rahel Varnhagen, or later Therese von Bacheracht.[1] On the other hand they recognized the great political and social changes in Europe during this period. The individual has only a small part in society, but his elevation to a more dignified status in a reformed state is a worthy aim. The Young German travelling-sketches often represent a curious mixture of subjective ideas and objective observations. Similarly their æsthetics waver between idealism and realism, their social philosophy between democratic and aristocratic tendencies. Although the different young German authors incline more to one direction or the other, and change their views in the course of their development, this dualism is characteristic of most of their publications.

At first, the collectivism of the new literary age, which is called republican, is contrasted with the individualism of the aristocratic classicism and romanticism. The illusion that the individual can set himself, as a cosmos in himself, against the world, is rejected as the ideology of an uneasy aristocracy. The idea of present equality is welcomed and this age is regarded as a period "when fewer single individuals tower like giants" and "an evenly distributed lively activity tends to produce a general happy and harmonious condition of civilization."[2]

One of these writers later tried to demonstrate the idea of immanence as a guiding line of the general outlook as well as of the æsthetics and social ideology of

---

[1] A radical Young Hegelian like Arnold Ruge in his manifesto *Der Protestantismus und die Romantik*, 1839, speaks scornfully of romanticism as the "dangerous twilight" of German intellectual life from Luther to the Young Germans, those "French romanticists." Cf. W. Neher, *Arnold Ruge als Politiker und politischer Schriftsteller*, Heidelberg, 1933, p. 59.

[2] Th. Mundt, *Kritische Wälder*, 1833, p. 180.

this group.[1]   This immanence is contrasted with the transcendency, which had hitherto prevailed in all spheres. The new outlook on life gives up the formerly valid but noxious separation of idea and reality, "recognizes the necessarily divine vital power of reality and has made it the principle of the whole structure of existence." [2] This idea of immanence is connected with the idea of purity.

That view of life is called immanent which has advanced to the idea that matter, world, reality, are not impure and that God could not therefore be imagined only beyond them, but that they are pure and dignified in order to involve God and to represent Him in them.[3]

Immanence also has its analogy in the sphere of the State.

Immanence [Mundt declares] we call that political view resulting from this *Weltanschauung* which does not accept the common belief that the people are an impure and undignified substance, over whom an absolute ruler is enthroned, capriciously sending sunshine or rain.[4]

The idea of immanence as the guiding thought of the republican period of literature has important consequences for the rôle of literature in society, for it means a decrease in social distance and an increase of democratization. According to the Young Germans the distance between prince and nation ought to be given up as well as the distance between author and public. "In classic and romantic literature," says Wienbarg, "the poet was transcendent to the public; in the new age he becomes a part of the public itself." [5]   Till then the famous author had been like a prince to whom the people paid homage; now he must become its partner, on the same level as itself.

Those former *grandees* of our literature lived in a sphere separated from the real world; they existed in an enchanted, ideal

---

[1] Th. Mundt, in his *Ästhetik, Die Idee der Schönheit und des Kunstwerks im Lichte unserer Zeit*, Berlin, 1845.

[2] Th. Mundt, *Ästhetik*, p. 16 f.   [3] *Ibid.*   [4] *Ibid.*, p. 17.

[5] L. Wienbarg, *Ästhetische Feldzüge*, p. 298.

world of their own, softly and warmly bedded, and like mortal
gods looked down upon the sufferings and enjoyments of the real
world, supporting themselves on the exhalations of the offerings
of the public's feelings and wishes.[1]

But soon a counter-tendency arose in the hearts of the
Young Germans themselves against the democratization
of poetry. The poet was to become part of the public,
but could he really identify himself completely with it?
He declared himself a democrat, but could he then
renounce the individualism of the modern writer? That
would be possible only for a short time. Therefore,
a strong plea for reserve soon becomes apparent,
demanding once more a certain distance between the
cultural élite and the public. It is characteristic that
this desire is felt especially by those Young Germans
who came from the lower middle-class and by no
means wanted to renounce the chance to rise via the
cultural élite.[2] Whilst Wienbarg in 1834 distinguishes
between the unproductive educated public and the
masses, deeming only the latter of any value, the valuation of the always resentful Gutzkow is quite different.
He contrasts the exclusive public of the connoisseurs
with the nation. In a leading article of the *Deutsche
Revue* he says:

> Literature ought to be the mirror of our national life—that
> is certain; but ought it not be more? ... One utters cautions
> against an aristocratic literature. I think one ought to give
> warnings against a literature which flatters the masses.[3]

Literature according to Gutzkow has definitely done
away with the auxiliary services it performed for the
petty-bourgeoisie as late as the eighteenth century. Its
prestige has increased enormously since classicism, it no
longer has the function of making marriage odes for
wealthy burghers or of phrasing invitations addressed to
the burghers to elect a county council.

[1] *Ibid.*

[2] The argument, therefore, of H. v. Kleinmayr, *Welt-und Kunstanschauung
des "Jungen Deutschland,"* Wien, 1930, p. 163, that the Young Germans
showed no tendency towards the aristocratism of the mind is definitely wrong.

[3] *Die Deutsche Revue,* p. 32.

"In using the word 'literature' we shall not shake hands with every neighbour or visit their homes near by and ask after the state of health of the worthy lady who is in the family way." [1] Gutzkow's ideal public consisted of an exclusive cultured aristocracy; he wanted "to imagine before him only so many listeners as there are educated, cultured people with good taste." [2]

From the beginning of his career Gutzkow fought for this ideal of an intellectual aristocracy and, as late as 1849, tried to express it in *Die Ritter vom Geiste*. On the other hand, one of his colleagues, Laube, went through a long development before he began to doubt the validity of middle-class ideals. Laube, who as a tutor amongst the Silesian aristocracy had learned to know and detest this class, subsequently became an opponent of the aristocracy of blood, but a champion of the aristocracy of the mind. The young democrat was pleased to attack the Silesian aristocracy and to challenge its anti-middle-class bias.[3] In the course of years, after much political persecution, strong doubts arose in Laube as to whether it would be wise to supersede the old power of the aristocracy by the new power of the bourgeoisie, which was no less ugly. Was this free writer's devotion to the destruction of aristocratic domination and to the building of a new society based on the middle-class, really justified? Was not the actual result of the process towards democracy quite different from the intention of these progressive writers?

It is true [Laube himself admits] that the development of the revolution has become different from what we had anticipated, it seems sometimes as if a spirit were playing about with us, as if the new were worse than the old, the merchant with his purse

---

[1] *Loc. cit.*, p. 33.   [2] *Ibid.*

[3] A correspondent of the *Zeitung für die elegante Welt*, 1833, addressing Laube, sketched this attitude of the Silesian aristocracy as follows: "You must die early, if not from an infantile disease, at least of some cause which privileged male and numerous female tongues pronounce against the author of the New Century. Friend, you have broken into a wasp's nest" (quoted in P. Przygodda, *H. Laubes literarische Frühzeit*, p. 46 f.).

in his hand more disgusting than the old aristocrat with his genealogical tree.[1]

Just as the Young Germans did not surrender completely to the mass society of the nineteenth century, so they could not make up their minds to the unqualified reception of realism in the art which it produced. Their approach to reality was always counterbalanced by a subjective idealism. They looked upon reality more as a philosophical construction, but they did not observe its features with scientific precision.

Theodor Mundt, for example, wrote in 1834 against empiricism in art, even repudiating the realistic picture of the weaving trade given by Goethe in *Wilhelm Meister's Wanderjahre*.[2] In 1845 Laube still distinguished sharply between "poetical" truth and crude truth, and Gutzkow was disgusted by the realism of his competitor Freytag, which he attacked. To work without any purpose meant for him to work without ideas; that was the keenest objection which a supporter of the German philosophical tradition could raise at that time.[3] The cause of this lack of naturalism consequent in the Young Germans has been justly attributed to their not very extensive knowledge of society, which, in its turn, was due to the career of this type of writer.[4]

These authors, as we have pointed out, proceeded mainly from the study of theology and philosophy to the profession of writing; they lacked therefore that training in the natural and in the social sciences which was at the disposal of the naturalists fifty years later. "Reality" for them was—in contrast to Balzac and Zola—a vague

---

[1] H. Laube, *Gesammelte Schriften*, vol. vi, *Die Krieger*. Similarly Wienbarg regards the old as well as the new power as destructive. Cf. the end of the *Ästhetische Feldzüge*, p. 308.

[2] Th. Mundt, *Kritische Wälder*, Leipzig, 1833, p. 186 f.

[3] The influence of Hegel's ideas on the Young Germans is significant, e.g. the following declaration of the hero in Laube's *Die Krieger*: "If the idea, if the theory should no longer be right, then reason on earth and with it the earth itself must perish. For thought is the spirit of God" (H. Laube, *Gesammelte Schriften*, vi. 160).

[4] H. v. Kleinmayr, *loc. cit.*, p. 72.

idea, but not yet the field of an exact microscopical research.[1]

2. NEUTRAL INTELLIGENTSIA : *DER TUNNEL ÜBER DER SPREE*

The tendency to separate society into different spheres —political, economic, religious, artistic—is characteristic of the liberal, more or less democratic, period. A social system which involves pluralism of parties implies also a relative autonomy of the different spheres of activity. In a totalitarian state, politics, art, science and private life are controlled by a central political power and are subject to its interference. In the liberal-democratic state, political power and culture are not identical. Cultural interests can here operate as a relatively autonomous socializing principle and can unite people of different religions and different political views.

Between 1840 and 1870 in Germany, it was possible for the promotion of culture to be regarded as an important function of the higher officials and the educated middle-class; it therefore neutralized, to a certain extent, the political contrasts. In England, at the time, the political contrasts were bridged by a certain necessary minimum standard of good manners and by a widely accepted code of fairness. In Germany it was an æsthetic culture which brought about a rapprochement amongst members of different social strata.

Between 1840 and 1860 the literary club, *Der Tunnel*

---

[1] Even the stimulating study by F. Strich, *Die Romantik als europäische Bewegung, Festschrift für Heinrich Wölfflin*, Munich, 1924, pp. 48–61, contrasts the Young German movement too one-sidedly with German romanticism. Certainly the Young Germans had, in contrast to the Young Romantics, the watchword of liberalism, realism and disillusion in common with the West-European romantics. But on the other hand the empirical and constructive realism of Stendhal and Balzac is very different from the subjectivism and the vague philosophical ideas of the Young Germans. It is true that the Young Germans put in the place of a dreaming lyricism a wordly, realistic prose, but this prose is not objective, not intent on describing reality, but often reflective, playful and distracted. Their attitude towards social reality is full of contradictions.

über der Spree, fulfilled this function.[1]   It represented a union of the producers and the friends of literature from different professions and political circles.   This club differed from similar predecessors (such as the Berlin salons of about 1800 or the *Christlich-Deutsche Tischgesell-schaft*) by its strict rule of political neutrality.   One can distinguish different phases of this *Herrenclub* for the cultivation of literature.   In the early stage between 1827 and 1840 it consisted primarily of young people: students, young barristers, merchants, officers and actors.

Between 1844 and 1860, according to Fontane's notes [2] four different groups were to be found there. The first group embraced the ministerial bureaucracy, legal officials and professors.   Among them were twelve assessors, three of whom subsequently became Ministers of state,[3] one district education officer, one senator, and two future professors.   The second group consisted of officers with a literary bent, among them a major, four colonels and five lieutenants.   The third group was mainly made up of poets, professional writers and artists, principally with a conservative or national tendency.   It included the writers Graf Strachwitz, Emanuel Geibel, Theodor Storm, Chr. F. Scherenberg, Paul Heyse, Georg Hesekiel, Heinrich Seidel, Felix Dahn, and also three literary historians.   Members of various profes-sions formed the fourth group; for instance, a doctor, an educationist, a scientist, and a captain of industry. There were also some Jewish members of the *Tunnel*, such as Dr. Löwenstein, the editor of the satirical *Klad-*

---

[1] Cf. the exposition by Th. Fontane, who was for some time a member of the *Tunnel*, in *Chr. Fr. Scherenberg und das literarische Berlin von 1840–1860*, chaps. 4, 5 and 9 (1885), and in his autobiography, *Von Zwanzig bis Dreissig*, 19th Ed., pp. 174–355.

Also, on the early period of the *Tunnel*; Fr. Berend, *Der Tunnel über der Spree*, i. *Kinder- und Flegeljahre, 1827–1840*, Berlin, 1919.

[2] Fontane gives a different survey of the groups in *Chr. Fr. Scherenberg, etc.*, pp. 36–8, for the years 1840 to 1845, and in *Von Zwanzig bis Dreissig*, pp. 175–9, for the period around 1844 and the subsequent fifteen years.

[3] They included the future minister of justice Friedberg, who was also Scherenberg's patron, and the future minister of education, von Mühler.

deradatsch, and S. Stern, eventually director of a school and leader of the Jewish reform movement.

These groups shared the idea that they were supporters of a literary culture; and on this common ground, differences of political view and discrepancies of age were to take second place. Such differences seemed to be eliminated in two ways: Firstly a pseudonym was assumed —the name of some great historical figure with whom the new member felt a certain affinity and secondly politics were absolutely forbidden as subject-matter for discussion. Politicians respected the literati, and writers, in their turn, were gratified by contact with the administrators of political power. Only the exclusion of politics made possible the rare—in comparison with England— phenomenon in Germany of officials of a conservative Prussian ministry sitting side by side with such thorough liberals, as, for instance, the editor of a satirical journal of the opposition.

The main feature of the meetings was usually severe criticism of the poetical work of the members. As striking as their differing political attitudes was the agreement in literary taste among the majority. This taste, which was to a large extent restricted by the political ideology of the upper stratum, was characterized by two antipathies. The majority of the *Tunnel* rejected all songs of liberty in the Herwegh style, and it had as little sympathy with the refined formal art represented in the Club by a small group of æsthetes. Fontane's debut, therefore, with a liberal poem entitled *Herwegh* was not a success, and he met with approval only by the later recitation of his ballad: *Der alte Derfflinger*. The popular ballad with a national bias, particularly those of Count Strachwitz or of Chr. Fr. Scherenberg, exemplified the literary pattern of this club.

For this reason the formal æsthetics of the *Geheimer Regierungsrat Kugler* group, of which young Paul Heyse was an outstanding figure, won the respect but not the sympathy of this circle. This subgroup seemed to the majority "too refined, too academic, too

independent."[1]   According to Fontane, the *Tunnel* on
the whole—in spite of an occasional liberal disposition—
was led by that Old Prussian attitude which is mainly
characteristic of conservatism.

Very soon, therefore, Hohenfriedberg and the *Zittenritt*, Ligny
and Waterloo became once more favourite subjects.   Certainly
Heyse mastered the form—he was brilliant—but the real talent
of the *Tunnel*, best corresponding with its constitution, was and
remained Scherenberg.[2]

Of the literary taste of this circle as well as that of
the whole upper stratum of Berlin in the Biedermeier
period, nothing is more significant than Scherenberg's
reception.   Scherenberg was the author of stirring battle
poems like *Ligny* (1846) and *Waterloo* (1849), depicting
the heroic deeds of the Prussian army in glowing colours.
The theme as well as the grandiose language roused
the emotion and enthusiasm of the courtly and feudal
circles.   The tendency of these poems was ambiguous,
and the glorification of the Prussian army of 1813 suited
the liberal supporters of the *Landwehr* and the democratic
army[3] as well as the patriotism of the court.   Not only
generals and courtiers, but also liberal intellectuals, like
Robert Prutz and Kinkel, praised it, and even Lassalle
was deeply moved by Scherenberg's fervour.[4]

Scherenberg, as the poet of the *Tunnel*, rose by way
of this circle.   Here he was discovered by Assessor
Friedberg, subsequently minister of justice, who introduced the poet to his home, where congregated the
Tunnel aristocracy of blood as well as of brain.[5]   The
new patron also had Scherenberg's first poems printed
in 1845, and procured him a minor post as assistant
librarian in the Ministry of War.   The sale of the poems

---

[1] *Von Zwanzig bis Dreissig*, 19th Ed., p. 197.

[2] *Ibid.*, p. 206 f.   Scherenberg has been hitherto neglected by historians of
German literature.

[3] See particularly the glorification of the national army of 1813 in *Waterloo*,
p. 3, and further the realistic comments of Fontane on the struggle between
patriots and democrats in the *Tunnel*, both claiming Scherenberg as a spokesman (*Von Zwanzig bis Dreissig*, p. 275).

[4] Th. Fontane, *Chr. Fr. Scherenberg, etc.*, p. 205.   [5] *Ibid.*, p. 46.

was at first small, but the patriotic songs roused the interest of high officers like the governor of Berlin, General Field-Marshal von Müffling, and General von Nostiz, who had been aide-de-camp to Blücher at the battle of Ligny. "Acquaintance with him [Friedberg] stimulated Scherenberg," as Fontane puts it, "to deal with the military literature of the Wars of Liberation, especially the Campaign of 1815, and his first epic battle poem *Ligny* was the result."

This poem, dedicated to General von Nostiz as an "expression of deepest reverence," strengthened the poet's reputation in ruling circles. The military Press praised his knowledge of the subject and his convictions. When Louis Schneider, the King's reader, and also a prominent member of the *Tunnel*, read to the King parts of the manuscript of Scherenberg's next epic battle poem *Waterloo*, Frederick-William IV was delighted and had this and other unprinted poems published at his own expense. The poem, which glorified the victory of the Prussians and the English at Waterloo, was dedicated to "Prussia's flags," i.e. the old and the young Prussian army. Whilst army- and court-circles, of course, praised a work which reflected their ideology, the liberals—for reasons difficult to understand to-day—thought highly of its æsthetic qualities.[1] The counter-revolutionary wave after 1848 saw in Scherenberg its literary exponent. The poet became a legend. Dozens of travelling orators recited his battle poems in the provinces, young poets sought his protection or criticism, directors of schools praised and circulated his works. Hundreds of sonnets were poured out in homage to the master, and in a Stettin newspaper a long essay even was published entitled *Chr. Fr. Scherenberg, the Pomeranian Shakespeare*.[2]

The successful poet of court and army received all the honours which a monarchy could bestow on a poet faithful to its ideology. Through the good offices of Count Bismarck-Bohlen, he obtained from 1854 onwards a royal pension of 300 Taler a year. He was admitted

---

[1] Th. Fontane, *Chr. Fr. Scherenberg, etc.*, p. 77.   [2] *Ibid.*, p. 173.

to the court, and also received a gracious letter of acknowledgment from the King of Bavaria.   As a court-poet
he was asked to write the text of an album dedicated to
the Empress of Russia and illustrated by Adolf Menzel,
for which he was granted a Prussian as well as a Russian
"honorary remuneration."   His regular income also
rose considerably, for he was getting a thousand Talers
or more from the sale of his old and new poems.

   After 1856 this poet's prestige suddenly declined.
The new self-estimation of the liberal bourgeoisie,
which had become so outspoken in the period of the
Prussian military conflict, flatly refused to glorify the
army through Scherenberg's lyrics.   "Political circumstances had raised Scherenberg and political circumstances
cast him down again." [1]

   But the political situation alone does not account for
this change in the reception of Scherenberg's poetry.
For had not liberals and democrats also unceasingly
praised Scherenberg's work?   The emigrant Kinkel
had looked upon him as the "most significant and
characteristic poet" of his age.   The taste of the whole
educated-class between 1830 and 1865 had been un-
realistic, preferring the high-flown tone, as is shown by
lyric writers of the right-wing like Strachwitz and
Scherenberg, as well as of the left-wing like Herwegh.
But after 1865 the taste of the cultural élite in Berlin
turned towards the realistic.   The cause lay not so much
in the changed distribution of political power, which did
not take place very widely, as in technical development
and industrialization.

   Fontane considers Scherenberg's rhetoric to be the
expression of a bygone age—what we would to-day call
the *Biedermeier* period—and Gustav Freytag's realism
that of the new industrial age.   These two popular
authors were both national, but with a different bias.
The *Tunnel* belonged to the first category because of its
predilection for Scherenberg.   Its political "neutrality"
was based on a common love of rhetoric and lyricism,

[1] Th. Fontane, *Chr. Fr. Scherenberg, etc.*, p. 211.

and its inner decay was not a little due to this change
in literary taste.

One wanted [as Fontane expresses it] present not past, reality
not appearances, prose not verse. But what one wanted least
of all was rhetoric. A new age dawned in which, after centuries
of overproduction of lyrics and epics with a lyric touch, comparatively few poems were written and read. In other words,
thus was consummated the great transformation which brought
about the victory of realism.[1]

3. LIBERALISM OF THE COURT

Up till now literary history has not sufficiently recognized the sociological significance of the lesser German
poets in the second half of the nineteenth century.
Whereas formerly the courts of Weimar, Darmstadt and
Düsseldorf played a cultural rôle, now Munich, Weimar,
Coburg became the places where, owing to courtly
patronage, single individuals or whole groups of artists
and scholars gathered. We suggest calling this co-
operation of enlightened princes and middle-class men
of letters "liberalism of the court."

"Liberalism of the court" means a combination of
aristocratic tradition and middle-class culture. The
princes and kings here displayed an interest in art and
science regardless of the origin of their representatives.
For non-aristocratic scholars and artists there was a
chance of social rise, of mixing with aristocrats and in
some cases of winning the princes to liberal ideas.

In the nineteenth century some well-known liberal
and democratic writers had direct contact with princes.
Paul Heyse, the liberal æsthete and non-political liber-
tine, and his connections with the court of Max II, have
already been mentioned. Similar were the relations of
the democratic Jewess, Fanny Stahr-Lewald, to the Grand
Duke Carl Alexander of Saxe-Weimar, of Spielhagen to
the Crown Prince and later Emperor Frederick William;
and last, but not least, the connection of Gustav Freytag
with Duke Ernst of Coburg-Gotha. *Bildung* in the

---

[1] Th. Fontane, *Chr. Fr. Scherenberg, etc.*, p. 210.

sense of Weimar classicism led in these places to a formation of élites not characterized by common origin and
political conviction, but by a common interest in culture.
The function which the work of Goethe and of Weimar
classicism thereby had is striking. Goethe's style and
principles called forth many imitations. The Goethe
cult caused an integration of people of different origin
and position. An example of this is the friendship between the Grand Duke Carl Alexander of Saxe-Weimar
and the writer, Fanny Stahr-Lewald.[1] The Prince,
whose education had been supervised until he was fourteen years old by Goethe himself, lived completely in the
classical tradition of Weimar. As a result of his training at German universities and of his extensive travel in
Western and Eastern Europe, he took much interest
in musicians and artists and invited them to his Court.
He became an intimate friend of Franz Liszt. Just as
Fanny Lewald played the active part in their correspondence, so it was she who endeavoured to stimulate
the interest of the Prince in liberalism and the rights of
the people. From the common basis of a veneration for
Goethe, the shrewd and resolute Jewess tried to bring
about a rapprochement between the Prince and democracy. Thus she said, for instance, at her first meeting
with the Grand Duke:

> The greatness of our time is not only that the people are win-
> ning emancipation, but that they also wish to emancipate the
> princes from their lonely position where they stand between flat-
> tery and deceit removed from their fellow-beings. But you,
> Your Highness, stand beside us and therefore we can talk so
> easily with you.[2]

The relationship of superordination and subordination
between Prince and people will now be replaced by
equality. The enlightened author attacked the remnants
of the theory of the divine rights of kings, but Carl Alexander, owing to a somewhat democratized patriarchal

[1] *Grossherzog Carl Alexander und Fanny Lewald in ihren Briefen 1848–1889*,
ed. R. Göhler, Berlin, 1932, 2 vols.
[2] *Briefwechsel*, i. p. xviii.

tradition, regards his country as a fief entrusted to his care by God, for which he has to give an account both to God and to the people.[1]

(i) *Coburg*

Especially significant for liberalism is the relation between Gustav Freytag and the Duke Ernst of Coburg-Gotha; the former a prominent writer, the latter an outstanding politician between 1850 and 1870. For a better understanding of this characteristic relationship a précis of Freytag's career up to his first meeting with the Duke will be given.[2] Freytag was born in 1816 in a small town of Upper Silesia, his father being a doctor and an honorary burgomaster, his mother the daughter of a clergyman. Two factors therefore moulded his youth: his ancestors, who included Prussian notables, and experience gained from living near a frontier. His father embodied the virtues of a Prussian official and displayed a complete loyalty to the State, an attitude which was adopted later by Gustav Freytag.

The son of a professional man, he passed through a secondary school in Silesia and from 1835 studied German literature and history in Berlin. From 1838 until 1844 he was a lecturer in German at the University of Breslau. In 1844 he became an independent writer, then a playwright, later a successful novelist and historian of civilization. In the year 1848 together with Julian Schmidt, he edited the Journal, *Die Grenzboten*, and made it the leading periodical of the *Kleindeutschen*.[3] It maintained a middle position between the radicalism of the democrats

[1] Cf. *Briefwechsel*, i. 7.

[2] On the life of Freytag see the article in *Allg. Deutsche Biographie*, vol. 48, pp. 749–67, and the book by H. Lindau, *Gustav Freytag*, Leipzig, 1907; further, the autobiography *Erinnerungen aus meinem Leben*, 1887, and *Gustav Freytag und Herzog Ernst von Coburg-Gotha im Briefwechsel 1853–1893*, ed. E. Tempeltey, Leipzig, 1904. A careful analysis of Freytag's early development from the sociological point of view has been recently set forth by O. Herrmann, *Die Anfänge Gustav Freytags*, Ph.D. Thesis, Hamburg, 1934.

[3] The new editors intended, according to their programme, "to represent a decisive democracy towards the Government, an aristocracy of education and of rights towards the stupidity of the masses." Cf. H. Lindau, *Gustav Freytag*, p. 368.

and the conservatism of the Government. In this way Freytag became the favourite spokesman of the North-German well-to-do bourgeoisie, of the higher officials and professional men. The versatile author combined the objectivity of a scientific mind with the elasticity of a journalist.[1] He came into contact with all sections of the population which on account of their social position inclined towards liberalism: in Breslau he had intercourse with educated merchants, in Leipzig with actors, scholars and publishers, and in the country he made the acquaintance of an enlightened prince—Ernst, Duke of Saxe-Coburg. Mutual political conviction formed a common basis between the middle-class journalist and the liberal ruler of a small German state. They formed together the *Literarischen-Politischen Verein.*

Duke Ernst of Coburg-Gotha (1828–93) is an example of the enlightened duodecimo prince, who tried to play a greater rôle in German politics with the help of his kindred relations in the great European courts. The family of this Duke had at that time considerable European significance, for Leopold of Saxe-Coburg, the uncle of Duke Ernst, was King of Belgium, whilst Ernst's brother Albert became the consort of Queen Victoria. Through an all-round education which Ernst von Coburg received, together with his brother, as well as through his sojourn at the courts of England, France and Belgium, the outlook of the young prince was wider than that of most of his compeers. In 1842 he ascended the throne of Saxe-Coburg. He wanted to achieve a liberal reform of the constitution, but he met with the firm opposition of the aristocracy and bureaucracy, by whom he was regarded as "the sole democrat of the country." The Duke in his turn sharply criticized the

[1] How much the German professors regarded Freytag as their literary spokesman can be traced from the address when an Honorary Doctor's Degree of the Berlin Philosophical Faculty was conferred on him: "And when the Germans of future generations learn from our poetry the feelings of the sons of the nineteenth century, they will also understand why it was in our days a pride and a pleasure to be a German professor." (G. Freytag und H. von Treitschke, *Briefwechsel,* Leipzig, 1900, p. 183.)

backwardness of his fellow-princes: "We princes," he said, "are losing ground because we have too little intelligence, courage and understanding of the spirit of the time." In 1848 the Duke sympathized with the democratic parliament in Frankfort, but he quickly realized the futility of its methods. Later he decided more and more in favour of the idea of a united Germany under Prussian leadership. He was in direct contact with the Great Powers on the one hand (his friendship with William of Prussia dated from 1852), and on the other hand with the liberal professionals and the masses of the bourgeoisie whom he patronized at the shooting, gymnastic and singing festivals. Therefore, he preferred moderate reform from above to radical revolution from below. The liberal Duke was extraordinarily popular amongst the masses, but this popularity awakened the distrust of his peers as well as of the radical democrats. A dilettante himself, he was predestined through his love for music and poetry to become a patron of the arts.

Both Gustav Freytag and the Duke have emphasized the independence in their friendly relations.[1] The successful writer and journalist, in 1853, when he met the princely politician for the first time, was already acknowledged. The Duke certainly was pleased to come into closer contact with the famous man of letters who, moreover, could provide him with important information.[2] The middle-class writer, on the other hand, felt flattered by the friendship and the patronage which the popular Duke accorded him. Freytag's attitude towards the Duke wavered between the self-confidence of the poet who no longer needs titles and decorations[3] and

---

[1] See Freytag's *Erinnerungen aus meinem Leben*, pp. 67 ff., and Herzog Ernst's book, *Aus meinem Leben und aus meiner Zeit*, Leipzig, 1889, 6th Ed., ii. 317.

[2] The Grand Duke of Saxe-Weimar, a neighbour and to a certain extent a rival of the Duke of Saxe-Coburg, tried, when Freytag was visiting him, to win him permanently for his court. See the humorous report which Freytag gave about his visit to the Duke of Coburg (*Briefwechsel*, pp. 40-3).

[3] After having received decorations from different German States he refused rather brusquely one from Duke Ernst, which appeared to him to be too insignificant (*ibid.*, p. 261).

the servility of a subject who observes exactly every
formality of courtly etiquette.[1]　At one time he regards
the Duke as his Sovereign, at another as a friend of
high rank who is open to praise as well as to frank
criticism.　Both felt the benefit of this relationship:

born under different stars, brought up in a different manner, in
different circumstances, we have found each other without any
special purpose. . . .　Neither of us could fit in completely with
the other's position to his own advantage and to the advantage
of the world.[2]

"Liberalism of the court" characterizes therefore not a
surrender of the courtly or of the middle-class position,
but a rapprochement, a diminution of the limits and an
increased understanding between two hitherto little-
connected worlds.

(ii) *Munich*

We have dealt so far with relations between Prince
and one particular author.　We now go on to describe
the courtly liberalism at Munich, where not an individual
author, but a whole circle was involved.　The circle
represented a striking double combination—firstly, of
courtiers with scholars and poets; secondly, of North
German Protestants with South German Catholics.
Whilst at a North German university the King of
Bavaria, Max II, had come to realize the superiority of
the Protestant culture of the North, and was ambitious
to raise the level and prestige of his court through an
invitation to leading scholars and poets from North
Germany.

In Berlin at that time the culture of the court was
restricted, owing to the mentality of a conservative soldier
king like Wilhelm I, to an alliance of throne and pulpit,
of hymns and military marches; in Munich Max II
tried to create a centre of refined culture corresponding
to the gentler atmosphere of the South.　This step of

[1] See the servile begging letter to the Duke (*ibid.*, p. 72).
[2] *Ibid.*, p. 95 f.

the Bavarian King is explained by a double motive: by his true love of art and scholarship, as well as by his fear of the political hegemony of Prussia. Already one contemporary has explained the contradictions of his attitude towards North Germany as an "incompatible double emotion of love and hatred, of sympathy and deepest distrust." The king loved the North as

the home of the sciences and of the friends of his youth, Wendland and Dönniges who brought about the later appointments (of the North German intellectuals). He hated it as a political power which he believed he ought to fear as a Wittelsbach.[1]

What was the composition and function of this Munich circle, which was at its best during the years 1854–64? Max II was even more interested in scholarship than in art. He appointed particular scholars, who were semi-poets, like W. H. Riehl, Franz Kobell, or he gave poets a professorship as in the cases of Geibel, Heyse, Bodenstedt, who could therefore enjoy comfortable sinecures.[2] In his circle the King gathered together these loyal poets and scholars, often several times in one week, to discuss subjects of learning and *belles lettres*.[3] Here the courtly poets and scholars met the aides-de-camp and high officers of the King.

Using an expression from the history of the German parties in the nineteenth century, the attitude of this circle can be characterized as free-conservative, or, in our term, "courtly liberal." For conservatives like Riehl and Geibel, reactionaries like Bodenstedt (who had

[1] J. Grosse, *Ursachen und Wirkungen, Lebenserinnerungen*, p. 321.

[2] P. Heyse, for example, was appointed at the age of twenty-four with an annual salary of 1,000 Gulden without any special duties except attendance at the symposium of the King (*Jugenderinnerungen und Bekenntnisse*, i. 185).

[3] We give here the following sources for the Munich circle besides the book of Grosse, mentioned above. P. Heyse, *Jugenderinnerungen und Bekenntnisse*, 5th Ed., Stuttgart, 1912, vol. ii, pp. 184–301, and A. F. v. Schack, *Ein halbes Jahrhundert*. See further the biography of Geibel in the introduction to the *Historisch-Kritische Ausgabe* of his works, edited W. Stammler, the article, *Münchner Dichtergruppe*, by E. Petzet, *Reallexikon der deutschen Literaturgeschichte*, vol. 11, pp. 415–23, and the introduction to *Der Münchner Kreis*, by E. Stemplinger, *Deutsche Literatur, Reihe Formkunst*, Leipzig, 1933, vol. 1.

praised the Emperor of Russia in a poem) or like the *arriviste*, Dingelstedt, mingled here with the supporters of a freer *Weltanschauung*, like the essayistic Epicurean, Paul Heyse, or the liberal aristocrat, Graf von Schack. During the symposia there was complete liberty of speech, the King listening with the respect of a layman to the representatives of art and scholarship.

The function of this circle can best be understood from the reactions of its opponents. These were divided into two groups: one of native poets and scholars, who realized with resentment and indignation the successful invasion of these North German competitors; the other of aristocratic Bavarian families, who could scarcely make a serious objection against the loyalty of these imported intellectuals but were jealously antagonistic because "these scholars and writers, below themselves in rank, were granted an intimate intercourse with His Majesty, which was denied to them." [1]

The literary section of this Munich circle was opposed to the overheated and formless diction of the Young Germans; they wanted to be masters of form, but not semi-journalists; they wished to idealize the world and reflect its beauty, but not to reveal its defects and contradictions. There was no reason for these ecstatic holders of royal sinecures to stress the ugliness of reality; like every other classicism in history, this one also preferred form to content, rhyme to reality.

But the ideological differences within this circle were remarkable. On the one hand, W. H. Riehl, the conservative sociologist and opponent of the revolution, was in favour of a restoration of the conservative forces, such as family and *Volkstum*, and denounced the libertinism of the intellectual proletariat of the left. [2] On the other hand, Paul Heyse belittled one of the main pillars of the existing order, Christianity, but as he only portrayed

---

[1] P. Heyse, *op. cit.*, i. 218.

[2] Riehl was regarded by the victorious Bavarian reaction as a prophet, not without justification, although he himself protested against it. (See J. Grosse, *op. cit.*, p. 199.)

the defects of the Protestant Church and of its ministers and did not touch upon the Catholic Church (as revealed, for instance, in the novel *Kinder der Welt*, 1873), his liberalism was not dangerous in Bavaria. By his exposure of the outlook and of the love affairs of members of the free intelligentsia, such as lecturers and artists, actors and even canonesses, this æsthete did not go beyond the problems of academic circles, the members of which enjoyed a secure and comfortable life.[1] Antipathetic to all extremes, he kept far from the radicalism which characterized the Young Germans.

Moreover, from the dispassionate standpoint of historicism, the Munich circle dealt with the poetry of exotic nature and escaped into a historical and romantic *Weltanschauung* which did not exclude a German national tendency. Learning and imagination worked closely together. Heyse and Geibel translated a Spanish Romanzero; Bodenstedt, Russian and English poetry, whilst Geibel was deeply interested in subjects of the antique world. Besides this, works of Geibel like *Gudrun* and *Volker's Nachtgesang*, the epic *König Sigurt's Brautfahrt* and the tragedy *Brunhild*, clearly displayed the national romantic trend, which later brought about the alliance between Ludwig II and Wagner. In spite of all its own claims this literary school was as little unbiassed as the Young Germans whom it attacked so violently.

The purely human element of all ages [one of the supporters of the school says rather naïvely [2]] was stressed again in contrast to the earlier poetry of the Young Germans; and when finally these efforts culminated in the German national romanticism, the most triumphant expression of which, namely, the music of Wagner, must not be overlooked, this development was to a large extent the result of the work of the Munich school.

---

[1] On Heyse's position as an outsider of the bourgeoisie see also the remarks in E. K. Bennett's *A History of the German Novelle from Goethe to Thomas Mann*, Cambridge, 1934, pp. 206 ff.

[2] J. Grosse, *op. cit.*, p. 265.

The ideological exponent of this school was Emanuel Geibel. His position as a kind of herald of the nation became so typical and successful that we should take a quick glance at his career.

Geibel, the son of a clergyman, was born in Lübeck in 1815. His poetry never could conceal certain clerical characteristics, and even his career seemed to be determined by that of his father. At first he studied theology and philology and became a tutor to the children of the Russian ambassador in Athens. From this time his association with the conservative and aristocratic circles became permanent. His decision not to accept a post as secondary school-teacher, in the interest of his literary production, led to considerable financial trouble. But at last he found a patron of noble rank in the Hesse Chamberlain, Karl von der Malsburg, who was a friend of his father. The impecunious poet dedicated the first edition of his poems *Zeitstimmen* (1841) to this patron. As a nationalist he appealed to the newly restored European reaction for a crusade to free Jerusalem, and he denounced France as "the snake in the West." In the same year he was the guest of another aristocrat, Prince Carolath, in Silesia and found a friend in the conservative poet Graf Moritz Strachwitz. Geibel's attack on the revolutionary lyric of Georg Herwegh was viewed with considerable satisfaction by the court circles. With some pride he declared in his poem *An Georg Herwegh* [1] (1842):

> I sing not for the favour of any king,
> Where I was born, there ruled no prince.
> As a free priest of free art,
> have I taken an oath
> to serve only Truth.[1]

But when his conservative attitude was rewarded by a pension of 300 Taler from Frederick-William IV he proclaimed his mission as a poet of the court, as a champion of the existing order.

---

[1] E. Geibel's *Gesammelte Werke,* Stuttgart, 1883, i. 220.

God help me, that I use with joy
the gift granted to me;
that I loyally uphold
the banner of German honour, discipline and nature.
Far away from the crowd
which blindly shatter altar and heart,
may the sacred well of poetry flow for me
from the rock, which holds the Church.[1]

Honoured by kings and nobles, Geibel now attempted to make himself completely equal to the aristocratic stratum by marriage, but his attempt to win the daughter of his first patron failed because of his middle-class blood. In 1855 he was granted an audience by Frederick-William IV, and after that the Berlin æsthetic circles opened themselves to him, amongst them the house of *Geheimrat Kugler*, where he met Heyse, Jakob Burckhardt, Fontane and others. The year following his marriage in 1851 to the daughter of a Lübeck lawyer, brought the great turning-point in his life—the call to the court of the Muses in Munich. He received an annual pension and an honorary professorship in German language and literature. As influential adviser of the King, the poet soon became the central figure of the Munich circle and as the court-poet was decorated with the royal order and granted personal nobility.

When, however, after 1866 the political tension between Bavaria and Prussia broke into open war, the North German Protestant found himself in a difficult situation. Two years afterwards Geibel celebrated the sojourn of William I in his native town of Lübeck with a rapturous poem. This aroused the jealousy of the Bavarian Press against the "pensionary of the Bavarian exchequer" and Ludwig II informed him of the termination of his pension because of the tendency expressed in his poems.

Significant of the twofold possibility of patronage at the disposal of the man of letters is the fact that Geibel now received offers from other courts like Weimar and

[1] *Au den König von Preussen*, December, 1842, *loc. cit.*, i. 227.

Berlin, and also an offer from the national-liberal Press, for the *Kölnische Zeitung* wanted at that time to arrange a national collection for him. But he proudly rejected this. Turning again to the other side he received from King William I, whom he had exalted in his poem, a further pension of 1,000 Taler in addition to his present one of 300. For the rest of his life Geibel lived in Lübeck. There the freedom of the City was conferred on him in 1868 and, as Heyse realized on a visit, his friend assumed the rôle of a "city saint" (*Stadtheiliger*).

According to the fashion of the time, Geibel clothed his contemporary problems in an historical dress and precisely through his exaggerated style achieved a completely unhistorical effect. If, at that time, in the mocking words of Gottfried Keller, "the Brunhild cult began to appear on the horizon as the aspiration of German youth and to displace the shadows of the housewifely Thusnelde," [1] then Geibel was a most influential propagandist of such Teutonic echoes. It was he who wrote the lines so often quoted—especially during the World War:

> And the German character may
> still restore the world one day! [2]

The intellectual domination of the Munich circle of poets did not long persist, even in the home of its activity. As if in accordance with a law of dialectics in intellectual history, the succeeding generation of South German poets and writers turned in sharp opposition against the restriction of art to purely æsthetic and private matters which, in their opinion, closed its eyes to the continually increasing power of social problems in the reality of life. The naturalism of the circle gathered around the periodical *Die Gesellschaft*, and keenly opposed the false elegance of this courtly liberalism which, it alleged, "had been bred in the drowsy and benumbing emotional

---

[1] Gottfried Keller, *Der Grüne Heinrich*, 2nd version, part iv, chap. ii.
[2] E. Geibel, *Deutschlands Beruf*, 1861, *Gesammelte Werke*, iv. 214.

intellectual atmosphere of the higher nurseries, of pedantic cultural gossipers and of police-fearing hypocrites."[1] The contrast that found expression here was partly one between respected and secure notabilities and paterfamilias, and a still bohemian mobile and insecure artistic youth. Naturalism gained a rapid victory with the impetuosity of the new and the radical, but an analysis of its structure and function lies outside the scope of this work.

---

[1] See the programme of the circle in *Die Gesellschaft*, Leipzig, 1888, vol. i, no. 1. The vigour of the attacks in this periodical explain why a spokesman of the Munich circle, like Paul Heyse, sharply opposed the naturalist tendency at this time. See, for example, his novel *Merlin*, Berlin, 1892, 3rd Ed., vol. ii, pp. 204–11.

CONCLUSION

I

In the introduction the question was raised whether the writers were spectators or participants in the struggle between aristocracy and bourgeoisie, and whether they were class-conscious or more or less indifferent to the class-issues. After a detailed analysis, this question can now be answered. As intellectuals the writers could choose between different classes and groups: they could make a livelihood and win prestige with the old feudal powers as well as with the new middle-class. This relative liberty in the choice of position was, before 1870, still further increased by the political and cultural variety in the German territorial states. In contrast with England and France, the still continuing decentralization in Germany played no less important a part than did the contradictions between a politically influential feudal caste and an economically powerful bourgeoisie. Further, the quick sequence of antagonistic literary and intellectual movements, which often joined different political camps, is characteristic of the situation of the writers. The romantic movement became, in its later phases, more and more attached to nobility and Church (Catholic), whilst the Young German writers attacked them without, however, always being in agreement with the middle-class. But the large majority of authors coming from the former *tiers état* definitely took its side. Their pleading for recognition of the demands of the bourgeoisie did not mean that they identified themselves completely with them: they thought and wrote as champions of this class so long as its claims were not fulfilled. But as these demands became a commonplace, the writers dealt with them in a more critical and sometimes sarcastic manner. Even when, from the political point of view, some authors were only passive spectators of the class struggle, from the cultural aspect (i.e., as regards their modes of life), in spite of their hidden longing for the aristocratic sphere, they were practically followers of the middle classes.

The German novel of the nineteenth century, after the period of Goethe, had undoubtedly a greater sociological than æsthetic importance. One reason for this was the power of middle-class provincialism from which many writers originated, the influence of which they could never completely overcome. With a few exceptions like Heine, Heyse, Fontane, and aristocrats like Fürst Pückler, E. von Wolzogen, etc., they could never conceal that solid but clumsy artisan attitude, which was so deeply rooted in the inhabitants of provincial towns. The middle-class gospel of labour was not only proclaimed by individual authors like Auerbach, Freytag and E. von Wolzogen, it was also represented by most of the writers. For the German man of letters after the period of the romantics is, with a few exceptions, not an æsthete and a bohemian, but a propagandist of ethical ideas, an educationalist, a preacher of continuous work, and therefore more or less a specific type of burgher.

"The efficiency of the artisan"—as has been cleverly said with reference to the German provincial poet of the nineteenth century *à la Storm*—"characterizes this æstheticism, and it is inseparably and deeply connected with that attitude towards life which they show for the last time together with the primitive middle-class decency of the artisan." [1]

The main experience, the central subject of most of the writers dealt with in this book, was formed by *Heimat* and class. Although occasionally they criticized these social factors, they never could really rise superior

[1] G. v. Lukács, *Bürgerlichkeit und l'art pour l'art* in *Die Seele und die Formen*, Berlin, 1911, p. 133.

to them.   Therefore German literature of the nineteenth century, after Heine, lacked on the whole any European significance.   When, only after the end of the century, authors like Nietzsche and Thomas Mann, George and Sternheim again achieved a truly European level, it was not by accident that they were penetrating critics of the bourgeoisie.   With all its philosophical terminology, apparently indispensable in Germany, literature after 1830 was primarily didactic and moralizing.   Honest and solid work constituted the model the writers tried to achieve; artistic versatility was not regarded with such adoration as it once was by romantics like Fr. Schlegel. The bulk of the German writers were not active members in the struggle of the bourgeoisie for prestige and power, but sympathizing spectators, who cheered the middle-class team, even when the face or the behaviour of some single member did not appeal to them.

They thought in a middle-class manner, even when they lived somewhat bohemian lives, and they lived quite often in middle-class style, even when they did not think like commoners.   This literary middle-class approach to the world could be polemizing as with Spielhagen, proud as with Freytag, mellow as with Storm or self-conscious as with Keller: it could be more aggressive, as before 1870, or more condoning, as after 1870; in any case it formed a striking feature of the fiction and of much of the poetry produced between 1830 and 1900.

II

But literature is not only formed by society, it is also itself a social force.   Its influence on society in this period, its effect on the reading public, is less clearly defined than the connection of writers with the middle-class.   The reading public of these middle-class writers is heterogeneous and subject to constant change; the causes of literary success or failure are not always apparent and cannot easily be reduced to a formula.   The blunt political lyricists, the politically biassed but more courte-ous novelists enjoying popular success and the so-called

ability and adaptability which permitted the
...dmirer of Herwegh, the disciple of Scheren-
the friend of Paul Heyse, to become later an
...for the greatest poet of the younger genera-
...: 1870,—for Gerhart Hauptmann and his
... There existed a strange affinity between
...aturalism and Fontane's work, although Fon-
...more subtle and wiser than the youthful and
...Naturalists. Perhaps it was caused by the fact
...Naturalists and Fontane did not cast in their lot
...th the aristocracy or with the bourgeoisie, that
...: at a distance from both, although the younger
...n did actually face them with analytic pitiless-
...the old Fontane with mature understanding.
..., whose early works met with some success, was
...to the shade after 1870 by contemporary cele-
...ke Paul Lindau and Felix Dahn; in the frenzy
...oom period, in the exultation of the era of suc-
...ourgeois finance, his pietistic mixture of *Inner-*
...individualism and diffident pessimism found no
...amongst the bourgeoisie. Through this fact,
...stle of the German soul became involuntarily
...der of a local sect, just as later in the twentieth
...the lyricist, Stefan George, became voluntarily
...tle of intellectual predestination and the founder
...rary sect.

Fontane and Raabe found support in a period of
...y in a company of like-minded men, Fontane in
...nel über der Spree, Raabe in the circle of the
...eller in Brunswick. But whilst Fontane joined
...nnel before writing his novels, Raabe entered
...iderseller when he was a fully-fledged novelist.[1]
Tunnel über der Spree was a circle of men of the
...of the most varying political and æsthetic convic-
...the capital of Prussia, where merchant sat side
...e with officer, the *Kleiderseller* were a modest
...tisch of provincial intellectuals in a residential town
...etty state. Founded as "a loose group for the

[1] ...he *Kleiderseller* see H. Spiero: *Raabe*, Darmstadt, 1924, p. 172 ff.

unpolitical novelists who achieved success with difficulty, had different types of reading public, and the
duration as well as the intensity of their success was
dependent upon different sets of rules.

The political lyricists between 1840 and 1850 were
political writers in the real sense of the word.[1] Their
fiery conservative or democratic songs became watch-
words and battle-cries for large groups of the bourgeoisie.
Some cast in their lot with the courtly-conservative front
like the worthy Geibel or the amiable ballad-makers
Scherenberg and Graf Moritz Strachwitz, and thereby
obtained patrons and public in the circles around
Frederick-William IV or Max II. In contrast with
these were the more numerous and more vigorous lyricists
of the liberal-democratic mass-movement, like Herwegh,
Hoffmann von Fallersleben, Freiligrath, R. Prutz, etc.;
they found a more powerful response because they
fought on the side of a rising movement and gave
dramatic expression to the grievances of a politically
repressed class. When Herwegh began his journey
of triumph through Germany in 1842, and was acknowledged in audience by Frederick-William IV as an
"honourable enemy," he was cheered by the bourgeoisie
like a modern film-star. Freiligrath, too, became the
apostle of the uncompromising liberal opposition with the
publication of his pugnacious poems in 1844, as well as
the pride of the bourgeoisie, when he was able to return
in triumph to Germany in 1868 from his English exile.

The consciousness that political lyricists and writers
were coveted by both political fronts in the period of
industrialization, that they, as has been shown in the
contrasting examples of Freiligrath and Dingelstedt,
had the possibility of changing from the conservative to
the liberal-democratic side and vice versa, gave them new
prestige and increased confidence. Conversely, this
situation caused a rapprochement between the German
courts and the middle-class intelligentsia and produced

[1] Cf. Chr. Petzet, *Die Blütezeit der deutschen politischen Lyrik von 1840–1850*, Munich, 1903,—a book rich in material, although not very profound.

the courtly liberal type.   The conciliatory liberal writer, like Freytag and Heyse, appeared side by side with the "enlightened" petty princes like Max II of Bavaria and Duke Ernst of Saxe-Coburg.

For obvious reasons the political novel is, in general, less crude than the political lyric, chiefly because of the different character of the two literary forms.   The political lyric is essentially an inspiring appeal, it can be set to music, and thereby serves as an instrument for mass-propaganda.   The novel, on the other hand, even if tendencious and filled with ideologies, is always more sided, more colourful, more descriptive, and therefore appeals no less to the intellect than to the emotions. In the period before 1850, triumphal processions were organized for the political lyricists and their poems were recited at public gatherings; but the novels of widely-read authors like Freytag or Spielhagen exercised a more enduring influence in the reactionary period after 1850 and propagated the gospel of labour of the self-confident bourgeoisie.   The link between politics and literature was indeed more indirect than direct with both the national-liberal Freytag and the more radical Spielhagen, but it endowed all their works with an unmistakable note. If these male writers preached explicitly "manly pride before the thrones of kings," that is, the self-confidence of the industrious bourgeoisie in face of the indolent and unproductive aristocracy, then the female writers of the middle-class of that time turned this note into senti-mentality and caricature.   The strong response which they evoked is not only indicated by the rising circulation of the family journals; when E. Marlitt, the originator of the family journal novel, died in 1887, both her brother and the editor of the *Gartenlaube* received masses of letters of condolence and elegaic poems from her circle of readers, from society-ladies as well as from simple house-wives, but most of them came from the petty-bourgeois and working-class and expressed personal grief at the death of "their" authoress.[1]   How strongly this woman

[1] See L. Marlitt's obituary in *Die Gartenlaube*, 1887, p. 476.

appealed to the taste of m
by the fact, astonishing to
than Gottfried Keller sp
praised her powers of d
being unrivalled.[1]   It mi
really not so much the a
sense of middle-class ind
link between the taste of
incomparably more origi
writer.

The   politically-biassed
nouncedly liberal novelists
masses; they achieved a r
much because of their litera
timely political and social
open, more or less anonym
ferent was it with a third gr
authors, who were too inc
represent the group-taste or
if they do reflect liberal and
these tendencies are either
background and overshadov
tives.   Fontane and Raabe e
acteristic manner.   Both wri
in life and were for a long t
brities of the moment; both t
and the rugged Raabe suffere
tion and from the material w
their families which it involve
with Fontane's development,
aristocratic ideal public and
Jewish public.   If Fontane a
old age, then this was not
quality of his work which ha
of observation with a melanch
was also due, as has already t

[1] Cf. R. Horovitz, *Vom Roman der Junga
laube*, p. 4.
[2] Cf. H. Spiero, *Fontane*, Wittenberg, 192

his chang
youthful
berg and
advocate
tion afte
naturalis
young N
tane was
vigorous
that the
either w
they kep
generati
ness an

Raab
thrust i
brities l
of the b
cessful
lichkeit,
demand
this ap
the fou
century
the apo
of a lit

Both
difficul
the *Tu*
Kleider
the *T*
the *K*
If the
world
tions
by si
Stamm
of a

[1] For

collection of local antiquities and memories of every kind," it finally became a small club for men seeking intellectual intercourse, a kind of guild of congenial spirits, where Raabe lorded it as a *primus inter pares*. Amongst its chief members were a philologist, a lawyer, an editor, an engineer, an architect and other professional men. Not a few of them regarded themselves secretly or openly as poets, and they all honoured Raabe as their intellectual head.

The speech which Raabe made to this circle on the occasion of his fiftieth birthday (1881) clearly reveals the character of this exclusive group, which possessed a strong consciousness of superiority. Neither age, profession nor wealth were of importance, only the general values of originality, independence and art in the sense of the provincialism of Raabe. The hostility and opposition of these small-town intellectuals shown to philistines, whilst taking over completely their outward forms of life, characterizes this club and its conventions as a social phenomenon of a kind that was probably only possible in a German provincial-town of the nineteenth century.

We are the people—[said Raabe, with emphatic collective consciousness] who go freely through the world of philistines, and if we on occasion specially select one of ourselves (as on this evening), in order to vent our high spirits on him and to celebrate in his person what is called a jubilee amongst the philistines, then this also always happens *sub specie aeternitatis*, in the face of eternity of the time indestructible brotherhood of the Kleiderseller of Brunswick. We only celebrate communal festivals, and the individual Kleiderseller has to suffer calmly what one does with him! [1]

After his death this droll circle of Raabe-ites grew into the *Gesellschaft der Freunde W. Rabbes*, still existing to-day, which propagates Raabe as a model for the life and thought of the German people.[2]

---

[1] *Ibid.*, p. 175 f.

[2] Cf. *W. Raabe und sein Lebenskreis. Festschrift zum 100. Geburtstag des Dichters*, ed. H. Spiero, Berlin, 1931, p. 9. This *Festschrift* also contains various articles on some members of the Kleiderseller-circle.

It is a peculiar irony of German development that the two figures and interpreters who were for so long "unsuccessful," the Prussian humanist Fontane and the pietist Raabe, only found in their old age, and still more after their death, that acknowledgment which their rivals, because they represented the bourgeois group-spirit more definitely and more palpably, enjoyed earlier, but which was also earlier withdrawn from them as history pursued its course. These independent and lonely realists were not spoilt by the applause of contemporaries and the pleasure of receiving approbation, as perhaps were Spielhagen and Heyse. The importance of their works is not lessened by the fact that they regarded the society, in which they lived, without illusions and that they inevitably pursued their way in it with the tenacity of real talent.

Throughout my life [the old Fontane once wrote significantly to his family],[1] I have been unassuming, because I *had* to be. I always had an eye for the facts of reality, and the facts of reality prescribed modesty for me. It has been likewise with my social position. But in my *heart* I have never lacked self-confidence. After all, what otherwise would have become of me?

[1] Th. Fontane, *Briefe an seine Familie,* ii. 99 (17/6/1884).

BIBLIOGRAPHY

The following list refers mainly to books mentioned in the footnotes. The section dealing with "Sociology of Literature," however, includes books not directly used in this work as it is felt that a more detailed list for this recently developed aspect of literature may be useful. It does not claim to be complete.

I. GENERAL SOCIOLOGY AND SOCIAL PSYCHOLOGY

L. FEUCHTWANGER, *Die freien Berufe*, Munich, 1922.

S. FREUD, *Massenpsychologie und Ich-Analyse*, Leipzig, 1921.

M. GINSBERG, *Sociology*, Home University Library, London, 1934.

H. HELLER, *Allgemeine Staatslehre*, Leiden, 1934.

B. LAZAR, *L'Antisémitisme*, Paris, 1934.

E. MANHEIM, *Die Träger der öffentlichen Meinung*, Brünn, 1933.

K. MANNHEIM, *Ideologische und soziologische Interpretation geistiger Gebilde, Jahrbuch für Soziologie II*, Karlsruhe, 1926.

—— Article, *Wissenssoziologie, Handwörterbuch der Soziologie*, ed. A. Vierkandt, Stuttgart, 1931.

—— *Mensch und Gesellschaft im Zeitalter des Umbaues*, Leiden, 1935.

—— *Ideology and Utopia*, London, 1936.

A. MEUSEL, *Die Abtrünnigen, Kölner Vierteljahresschrift für Soziologie*, vol. iii, 1924.

R. MICHELS, *Probleme der Sozialphilosophie*, Leipzig, 1914.

V. PARETO, *Les Systèmes Socialistes*, 2 vols., Paris, 1902.

—— *Traité de Sociologie Générale*, 2 vols., Paris, 1919.

A. RUPPIN, *Soziologie der Juden*, 2 vols., Berlin, 1931.

—— *The Jews in the Modern World*, London, 1934.

MAX SCHELER, *Abhandlungen und Aufsätze*, vol. i, Leipzig, 1915.

GEORG SIMMEL, *Soziologie*, Munich, 1908.

G. TARDE, *Les Lois de l'Imitation*, Paris, 1907.

R. H. TAWNEY, *Equality*, London, 1931.

TH. VEBLEN, *The Theory of the Leisure Class*, 2nd Ed., London, 1924.

MAX WEBER, *Gesammelte Aufsätze zur Soziologie und Sozialpolitik*, Tübingen, 1924.

—— *Religionssoziologie*, Munich, 1920.

—— *Wirtschaft und Gesellschaft. Grundriss der Sozialökonomik*, III, 1, Tübingen, 1922.

Encyclopædia of the Social Sciences, ed. E. R. A. Seligmann, New York, 1930.

Handwörterbuch der Staatswissenschaften, ed. by L. Elster and others, 4th Ed., Jena, 1923–9.

Papers of the Conference on the Social Sciences: Their Relations in Theory and in Teaching, London, 1935.

II. Political, Economic and Social History

1. *Primary Sources*

Fr. Baron de la Motte-Fouqué und Fr. Perthes, *Etwas über Deutschen Adel, über Ritter-Sinn und Militär-Ehre in Briefen*, Hamburg, 1819.

Chr. Garve, *Versuch über verschiedene Gegenstände aus der Moral, der Literatur und dem gesellschaftlichen Leben*, 5 parts, Breslau, 1802/1804.

Ch. G. Goehrum, *Geschichtliche Darstellung der Lehre von der Ebenbürtigkeit nach gemeinem deutschen Reche*, Tübingen, 1846.

B. Goltz, *Typen der Gesellschaft*, 3rd Ed., Berlin, 1864.

Hannoversches Magazin, vol. 1830, Hanover.

Joh. Mich. von Loen, *Der Adel*, Ulm, 1752.

L. von der Marwitz, *Preussischer Adel*, ed. Fr. Schinkel, Breslau, 1932.

A. Müller, *Die Elemente der Staatskunst*, Berlin, 1809.

A. W. Rehberg, *Über deutschen Adel*, Göttingen, 1803.

W. H. Riehl, *Die bürgerliche Gesellschaft*, 5th Ed., Stuttgart, 1858.

—— *Die Familie*, 9th Ed., Stuttgart, 1882.

Caroline von Rochow, *Vom Leben am Preussischen Hofe, 1815–1852*, ed. L. von der Marwitz, Berlin, 1908.

Soziale Praxis, vol. iv, Berlin, 1895.

R. Springer, *Berlin's Strassen, Kneipen und Clubs im Jahre 1848*, Berlin, 1850.

A. F. C. Streckfuss, *Über das Verhältnis der Juden zu den christlichen Staaten*, II, Schrift, Berlin, 1843.

H. v. Treitschke, *History of Germany in the 19th Century*, vol. iv, London, 1918.

A. Wolff, *Berliner Revolutions-Chronik. Darstellung der Berliner Bewegungen im Jahre 1848 nach politischen sozialen und litararischen Bezichungen*, Berlin, 1852, 3 vols.

E. von Wolzogen, *Linksum kehrt—schwenkt Trabe! Ein ernstes Mahnwort an die herrschenden Klassen und den deutschen Adel insbesondere*, 6th Ed., Berlin, 1895.

2. *Secondary Sources*

R. Aris, *History of Political Thought in Germany from 1789 to 1815*, London, 1936.

F. C. Biedermann, *1840–1870. 30 Jahre Deutscher Geschichte*, 2 vols., Breslau, 1896.

M. von Boehn, *Biedermeier. Deutschland von 1815–1847*, Berlin, n.d.

K. Brandt, *Junkers to the Fore Again. Foreign Affairs.* vol. xiv, New York, 1935.

C. Brinkmann, *Die Aristokratie im kapitalistischen Zeitalter. Grundriss der Sozialökonomik,* ix, 1, Tübingen, 1926.

—— *Die Umformung der kapitalistischen Gesellschaft, op. cit.,* ix, 1, Tübingen, 1926.

—— *Wirtschafts- und Sozialgeschichte,* Munich, 1925.

W. H. Bruford, *Germany in the Eighteenth Century. The Social Background of its Literary Revival,* Cambridge, 1935.

A. Buchholtz, *Die Literatur der Berliner Märztage. Deutsche Rundschau,* vol. 94, Berlin, 1898.

K. Demeter, *Das Deutsche Offizierscorps in seinen historisch-soziologischen Grundlagen,* Berlin, 1930.

W. Dibelius, *England,* 2 vols., Stuttgart, 1923.

S. Dubnow, *Weltgeschichte des jüdischen Volkes,* vol. ix, Berlin, 1929.

F. C. Endres, *Soziologische Struktur und dazu gehörige Ideologien des deutschen Offiziercorps vor dem Weltkriege, Archiv für Sozialwissenschaft und Sozialpolitik,* vol. 53, Tübingen, 1924.

H. Gerth, *Die sozialgeschichtliche Lage der bürgerlichen Intelligenz um die Wende des 18. Jahrhunderts,* Berlin, 1935.

J. Goldfriedrich, *Geschichte des deutschen Buchhandels,* iv, Leipzig, 1913.

K. Griewank, *Vulgärer Radikalismus und demokratische Bewegung in Berlin, 1842–1848, Forschungen zur Brandenburgischen und Preussischen Geschichte,* vol. 36, Munich, 1924.

W. Hallgarten, *Vorkriegsimperialismus,* Paris, 1935.

F. Hartung, *Verantwortliche Regierung, Kabinette u. Nebenregierungen im konstitutionellen Preussen. 1848–1918. Forschungen zur Brandenburg. und Preussischen Geschichte,* vol. 44, Munich, 1931–2.

H. Haupt, *Quellen und Darstellungen zur Geschichte der deutschen Burschenschaft und der deutschen Einheitsbewegung,* vol. i, Heidelberg, 1910.

G. Hermes, *Statistische Studien zur wirtschaftlichen und gesellschaftlichen Struktur des zollvereinten Deutschland, Archiv für Sozialwissenschaft und Sozialpolitik,* vol. 63, Tübingen, 1929.

A. Hoyler, *Gentleman-Ideal und Gentleman-Erziehung, mit besonderer Berücksichtigung der Renaissance,* Leipzig, 1933.

E. Jordan, *Die Entstehung der konservativen Partei und die preussischen Agrarverhältnisse von 1848,* Munich, 1914.

H. Kantorowicz, *Der Geist der Englischen Politik und das Gespenst der Einkreisung,* Berlin, 1929.

R. Koser, *Geschichte Friedrichs des Grossen,* 3 vols., Stuttgart, 1912–14, 4th Ed.

P. Kosok, *Modern Germany,* New York, 1933.

Max Lenz, *Geschichte der kgl. Friedrich-Wilhelms-Universität zu Berlin,* 5 vols., Halle, 1910–19.

R. Lewinsohn (Morus), *Das Geld in der Politik,* Berlin, 1930.

A. Lotz, *Geschichte des Deutschen Beamtentums*, Berlin, 1909.

K. Mannheim, *The Crisis of Culture in the Era of Mass-Democracies and Autarchies, Sociological Review*, vol. 26, London, 1934.

F. Meinecke, *Radowitz und die deutsche Revolution*, Berlin, 1910.

Th. Mundt, *Geschichte der deutschen Stände nach ihrer gesellschaftlichen Entwicklung und politischen Vertretung*, Berlin, 1854.

E. von Nathusius, *J. G. Nathusius. Ein Pionier deutscher Industrie*, Stuttgart, 1915.

W. Neher, *Arnold Ruge als Politiker und politischer Schriftsteller*, Heidelberg, 1933.

F. Neumann, *Der Hofmeister, Hallische Pädagogische Studien*, no. 9, Halle, 1930.

S. Neumann, *Die Stufen des Preussischen Konservatismus*, Berlin, 1930.

H. Oncken, *Rudolf von Bennigsen*, 2 vols., Berlin, 1910.

F. Paulsen, *Geschichte des gelehrten Unterrichts*, 3rd Ed., ed. R. Lehmann, Berlin, 1919.

H. von Petersdorff, *König Friedrich Wilhelm IV.* Stuttgart, 1900.

K. L. Pinson, *Pietism as a Factor in the Rise of German Nationalism*, Columbia Studies in History, Economics and Public Law, no. 398, New York, 1934.

A. Ponsonby, *The Decline of Aristocracy*, London, 1912.

H. Preuss, *Die Entwicklung des Deutschen Städtewesens*, i, Leipzig, 1906.

W. Rathenau, *Von kommenden Dingen*, Berlin, 1917.

A. Rosenberg, *Die Entstehung der Deutschen Republik, 1871–1918*, Berlin, 1928.

H. Rosenberg, *Rudolf Haym und die Anfänge des klassischen Liberalismus*, Munich, 1933.

—— *Die Weltwirtschaftskrise von 1857–59*, Stuttgart, 1934.

—— *Theologicher Rationalismus und vormärzlicher Vulgärliberalismus, Historische Zeitschrift*, vol. 141, Munich, 1929.

A. Sartorius von Waltershausen, *Deutsche Wirtschaftsgeschichte, 1815–1914*, Jena, 1920.

F. Schnabel, *Deutsche Geschichte im 19. Jahrhundert*, vols. 1–3, Freiburg i. Br., 1929–1934.

W. Sombart, *Der Bourgeois. Zur Geistesgeschichte des modernen Wirtschaftsmenschen*, Munich, 1913.

—— *Deutsche Volkswirtschaft im 19. Jahrhundert*, 7th Ed., Berlin, 1927.

—— *Der moderne Kapitalismus*, vol. 1 and 2, 2nd Ed., Munich, 1916.

H. Schroth, *Welt- und Staatsideen des deutschen Liberalismus in der Zeit der Einheits- und Freiheitskämpfe. 1859–1866. Ein Beitrag zur Soziologie des deutschen politischen Denkens*, Berlin, 1931.

J. Schultze, *Die Auseinandersetzung zwischen Adel und Bürgertum in den deutschen Zeitschriften der letzten drei Jahrzehnte des 18. Jahrhunderts (1773–1806)*, Berlin, 1925.

G. Schuster, *Die Geheimen Gesellschaften, Verbindungen und Orden*, ii, Leipzig, 1906.

H. von Srbik, *Deutsche Einheit*, 2 vols., Munich, 1935.

L. D. Stirk, *Die Aristokratie und die industrielle Entwicklung in England vom 16. bis zum 18. Jahrhundert*, Breslau, 1933.

F. Tönnies, *Deutscher Adel im 19. Jahrhundert, Neue Rundschau*, vol. ii, Berlin, 1912.

E. Tröltsch, *Protestantisches Christentum in der Neuzeit, Die Geschichte der christlichen Religionen* (*Die Kultur der Gegenwart*), i, 2, 2nd Ed., Berlin, 1909.

V. Valentin, *Geschichte der deutschen Revolution, 1848–1849* 2 vols., Berlin, 1931.

M. Weber, *Wahlrecht und Demokratie in Deutschland*, Berlin, 1918.

W. Wenck, *Deutschland vor 100 Jahren*, 2 vols., Leipzig, 1890.

J. Ziekursch, *Politische Geschichte des neuen deutschen Kaiserreichs*, 3 vols., Frankfort-on-Main, 1925–30.

III. Literary History and History of Thought

1. *Primary Sources*

A. Fiction

B. Auerbach, *Das Landhaus am Rhein*, Stuttgart, 1869.

F. Dingelstedt, *Die Amazone*, 2 vols., Stuttgart, 1868.

—— *Lieder eines kosmopolitischen Nachtwächters*, Cassel, 1842.

B. Disraeli, *Endymion*, London, 1880.

—— *Sybil, or the two nations*, World Classics, vol. 291, London, 1925.

M. v. Ebner-Eschenbach, *Zwei Komtessen*, 4th Ed., Berlin, 1874.

J. v. Eichendorff, *Krieg den Philistern*, Berlin, 1824.

Th. Fontane, *Die Poggenpuhls*, Berlin, 1896.

—— *Ausgewählte Werke. Mit Einleitung von Th. Mann*, n.d. (Reclam).

F. Freiligrath, *Sämtliche Werke*, vol. i, ed. I. Schwering (Bong), n.d.

G. Freytag, *Gesammelte Werke*, Leipzig, 1887/88.

—— *The Lost Manuscript* (Translation), London, 1887.

I. Geibel, *Gesammelte Werke*, vol. i, Stuttgart, 1883.

J. W. v. Goethe, *Sämtliche Werke. Jubiläumsausgabe*, ed. E. v. d. Hellen, Stuttgart-Berlin, 1902–07.

—— *Wilhelm Meister's Apprenticeship and Travels*, translated by Th. Carlyle, London, 1872.

K. Gutzkow, *Die Ritter vom Geiste*, 9 vols., 1st Ed., Leipzig, 1850/51.

I. Hahn-Hahn, *Aus der Gesellschaft*, Berlin, 1838.

E. Heimburg, *Lumpenmüllers Lieschen*, 45th Ed., Stuttgart, 1928.

H. Heine, *Gesammelte Werke*, ed. O. Walzel, vol. x, Leipzig, 1918.

—— *Works*, translated by Ch. G. Leland, London, 1891–1903.

G. Herwegh, *Gedichte eines Lebendigen*, 12th Ed., Leipzig, 1896.

P. Heyse, *Die Kinder der Welt*, Berlin, 1873.

—— *Merlin. Roman*, 3 vols., 3rd Ed., Berlin, 1892.

K. Immermann, *Werke*, ed. W. Deetjen, 6 vols. (Bong), n.d.

G. Keller, *Der Grüne Heinrich*, 2nd version.

H. Laube, *Gesammelte Schriften*, vol. vi, Vienna, 1876.

—— *Neue Reisenovellen*, 2 vols., Mannheim, 1837.

F. Lewald, *Gesammelte Werke,* 10 vols., Berlin, 1870/71.
Th. Mann, *Buddenbrooks. Verfall einer Familie,* 3rd Ed., Berlin, 1903.
E. Marlitt, *Reichsgräfin Gisela,* Leipzig, 1870.
—— *The Countess Gisela* (translation), London, 1870.
—— *Gold Else* (translation), London, 1873.
—— *Die Zweite Frau,* 2 vols., Leipzig, 1874.
Der Münchner Kreis, ed. E. Stemplinger, *Deutsche Literatur. Reihe Formkunst,* i, Leipzig, 1933.
G v. Ompteda, *Deutscher Adel um 1900,* 3 vols., Berlin, 1900.
W. v. Polenz, *Die Grabenhäger,* 2 vols., Berlin, 1898.
Politische Lyrik. 1756–1871, ed. B. v. Wiese, Berlin, 1933.
W. Raabe, *Sämtliche Werke,* Series i, vol. 5, n.d.
—— *Der Hungerpastor,* 55th Ed., Berlin, n.d.
—— *Abu Telfan, oder die Heimkehr vom Mondgebirge,* 2nd Ed., Stuttgart, 1870.
Chr. F. Scherenberg, *Ligny. Ein vaterländisches Gedicht,* Berlin, 1846.
—— *Waterloo. Ein vaterländisches Gedicht,* Berlin, 1849.
L. Schücking, *Ausgewählte Romane,* 2nd Ed., Leipzig, 1864.
—— *Eine Aktiengesellschaft,* 3 vols., Hanover, 1863.
F. Spielhagen, *Sämtliche Werke,* Leipzig, 1872/73.
—— *Sturmflut,* 3 vols., Leipzig, 1877.
W. Thackeray, *Miscellanies. Prose and Verse,* vol. i, London, 1854.
A. Trollope, *Dr. Thorne,* 3 vols., London, 1858.
A. v. Ungern-Sternberg, *Palmyra oder das Tagebuch eines Papageis,* Stuttgart, 1838.
—— *Die Royalisten,* Bremen, 1848.
E. v. Wolzogen, *Ecce Ego. Erst komm' ich,* Berlin, 1895.

B. Non-Fiction
Album des Literarischen Vereins in Nürnberg, 1854.
Anonymous, *Die Schillerfeier der alten und neuen Welt,* Leipzig, 1860.
M. Arnold, *Essays in Criticism.* With an introduction by A. Miles. Notes by Leonard Smith, Oxford, 1918.
—— *Culture and Anarchy,* London, 1869.
—— *Friendship's Garland,* London, 1871.
B. Auerbach, *Der gebildete Bürger,* Karlsruhe, 1843.
L. Börne, *Gesammelte Schriften. Vollständige Ausgabe,* 3 vols., Leipzig, 1878.
C. Brentano, *Gesammelte Schriften,* vol. v, Frankfort-on-Main, 1852.
Th. Carlyle, *Past and Present,* London, 1843.
Cotta, *Briefe an Cotta,* ed. H. Scheller, vol. ii, Stuttgart, 1934.
Daheim, *Ein deutsches Familienblatt mit Illustrationen,* vols. 1–36, Leipzig, 1865–1900.
L. Deibel, *Die Gartenlaube. Eine Kritik,* Munich, 1879.
Die Deutsche Revue. Edition by J. Dresch, in *Deutsche Literaturdenkmale des 18. und 19. Jahrhunderts,* no. 132, Berlin, 1904.
Fr. Dingelstedt, *Blätter aus seinem Nachlass,* ed. J. Rodenberg, 2 vols., Berlin, 1891.

J. v. Eichendorff, *Der Adel und die Revolution* in *Sämtliche Werke*, Historisch-kritische Ausgabe von Th. A. Becker, W. Kosch, A Sauer, vol. x, Regensburg, 1911.

Th. Fontane, *Ein Sommer in England*, Berlin, 1854.

—— *Wanderungen durch die Mark Brandenburg*, 4 vols., Berlin, 1892.

—— *Meine Kinderjahre*, 2nd Ed., Berlin, 1894.

—— *Von Zwanzig bis Dreissig*, 19th Ed., Berlin, 1925.

—— *Chr. Fr. Scherenberg und das literarische Berlin von 1840–1860*, Berlin, 1885.

—— *Aus dem Nachlass*, ed. I. Ettlinger, Berlin, 1908.

—— *Das Fontanebuch*, ed. E. Heilborn, Berlin, 1919.

—— *Briefe an seine Familie*, ed. by K. E. D. Fritsch, 2nd Ed., 2 vols., Berlin, 1905.

—— *Briefe Theodor Fontanes*, 2. Sammlung, ed. O. Pniower und F. Schlenther, 2nd Ed., 2 vols., Berlin, 1910.

G. Freytag, *Erinnerungen aus meinem Leben*, Leipzig, 1887.

—— *Gesammelte Aufsätze*, 2 vols., Leipzig, 1888.

—— *Vermischte Aufsätze aus den Jahren 1848–1894*, ed. E. Elster, 2 vols., Leipzig, 1901–3.

—— *G. Freytag und Herzog Ernst von Coburg-Gotha im Briefwechsel, 1853/93*, ed. E. Tempeltey, Leipzig, 1904.

—— *G. Freytag und H. Treitschke im Briefwechsel*, ed. A. Dove, Leipzig, 1900.

Die Gartenlaube, Illustriertes Familienblatt, vols. 1–50, Leipzig, 1853–1902.

G. G. Gervinus, *G. G. Gervinus' Leben. Von ihm selbst*, Leipzig, 1893.

—— *Geschichte der deutschen Dichtung*, 5 vols., 4th Ed., Leipzig, 1853.

Die Gesellschaft, Monatsschrift für Literatur und Kunst, ed. M. G. Conrad, vol. i, Leipzig, 1888.

Goethe-Schiller, *Xenien, 1796*, ed. E. Schmidt und B. Supan, *Schriften der Goethe-Gesellschaft*, Weimar, 1893, vol. 8.

I. W. Grosse, *Ursachen und Wirkungen. Lebenserinnerungen*, Braunschweig, 1896.

Grossherzog Carl Alexander und Fanny Lewald-Stahr *in ihren Briefen 1848/89*, ed. R. Goehler, 2 vols., Berlin, 1932.

K. Gutzkow, *Gesammelte Werke*, vol. iii, Frankfort-on-Main, 1845.

—— *Rückblicke auf mein Leben*, Berlin, 1875.

H. Heine, *Gespräche mit Heine*, ed. H. H. Houben, Frankfort-on-Main, 1925.

—— *Kahldorf über den Adel in Briefen an den Grafen M. v. Moltke*, Nürnberg, 1831.

Herzog Ernst von Sachsen-Coburg, *Aus meinem Leben und aus meiner Zeit*, 6th Ed., 3 vols., Berlin, 1889.

P. Heyse, *Jugenderinnerungen und Bekenntnisse*, 5th Ed., Stuttgart, 1912.

A. Jung, *Briefe über Gutzkows Ritter vom Geiste*, Leipzig, 1856.

F. Lassalle, *Herr Julian Schmidt, der "Literarhistoriker,"* Berlin, 1852.

H. Laube, *Politische Briefe*, Leipzig, 1833.

—- *Moderne Charakteristiken*, vol. ii, Mannheim, 1835.

—— *Gans und Immermann*. *Deutsche Pandora*, Berlin, 1841, vol. iv.

Fanny Lewald, *Gefühltes und Gedachtes (1838–1888)*, ed. L. Geiger, Dresden, 1900.

Das Magazin für Literatur, vol. 60, Berlin, 1891.

A. Menzel, *Deutsche Dichtung von der ältesten bis auf die neueste Zeit*, 3 vols., Stuttgart, 1858/59.

L. Mühlbach, *Erinnerungsblätter aus dem Leben Luise Mühlbachs*, ed. Th. Ebersberger, 1902.

Th. Mundt, *Ästhetik*. *Die Idee der Schönheit und des Kunstwerks im Lichte unserer Zeit*, Berlin, 1845.

—— *Madonna, Unterhaltungen mit einer Heiligen*, Leipzig, 1835.

—— *Kritische Wälder*. *Blätter zur Beurteilung der Literatur, Kunst und Wissenschaft unserer Zeit*, Leipzig, 1833.

Fürst H. Pückler-Muskau, *Briefe eines Verstorbenen*, 3 vols., Stuttgart, 1831.

A. F. v. Schack, *Ein halbes Jahrhundert*. *Erinnerungen und Aufzeichnungen*, 3 vols., Stuttgart, 1888.

Fr. Spielhagen, *Finder und Erfinder*. *Erinnerungen aus meinem Leben*, 2 vols., Leipzig, 1890.

A. v. Ungern-Sternberg, *Erinnerungsblätter*, vols. i–vi, Berlin, 1855–60.

K. A. Varnhagen von Ense, *Tagebücher*, vol. i, Leipzig, 1861.

F. Wehl, *Das Junge Deutschland*, Hamburg, 1886.

L. Wienbarg, *Ästhetische Feldzüge*, Kiel, 1834.

2. Secondary Sources

B. Alberts-Arndt, *Die englische Gesellschaft im Spiegel der Romane von Meredith*, Karlsruhe, 1931.

Anonymous, *Fritz Reuter und die Juden*, Dresden, 1895.

S. v. Arnim, *Goethe und Fürst Pückler*, Dresden, 1932.

G. M. Bacon, *The Personal and Literary Relations of H. Heine to K. Immermann*, Ph.D. Thesis, University of Michigan, 1910.

Fr. Behrend, *Der Tunnel über der Spree. 1. Kinder- und Flegeljahre 1827–40. Schriften des Vereins für die Geschichte Berlins*, no. 1, Berlin, 1919.

R. Bender, *Manuskript eines Romans—die hochdeutsche Urgestalt der "Stromtid,"* Halle, 1930.

E. K. Bennett, *A History of the German Novel from Goethe to Thomas Mann*, Cambridge, 1934.

H. Bieber, *Der Kampf um die Tradition. Die deutsche Dichtung von 1830–80*, Stuttgart, 1931.

Georg Brandes, *Die Literatur des 19. Jahrhunderts in ihren Hauptströmungen dargestellt*, vol. vi, Leipzig, 1891.

W. Brandes, *Wilhelm Raabe*, Wolfenbüttel, 1901.

E. M. Butler, *The Saint-Simonian Religion in Germany. A Study of the Young German Movement,* Cambridge, 1926.

—— *The Tempestuous Prince,* Cambridge, 1929.

W. Dilthey, *Das Leben Schleiermachers,* vol. i, Berlin, 1870.

J. Dresch, *Le Roman social en Allemagne, 1850–1900. Gutzkow-Freytag-Spielhagen-Fontane,* Paris, 1913.

A. Ehrhard, *Le Prince Pückler,* vol. i, Paris, 1925.

K. Feisskohl, *Ernst Keils publizistische Wirksamkeit und Bedeutung,* Berlin, Leipzig, 1914.

H. Freyer, *Die Bewertung der Wirtschaft im philosophischen Denken des 19. Jahrhunderts,* Leipzig, 1921.

J. und O. H. Geffken, *Karl Immermann. Eine Gedächtnisschrift zum 100. Geburtstag des Dichters,* Hamburg, 1896.

R. v. Gottschall, *Die deutsche Nationalliteratur des 19. Jahrhunderts,* 6th Ed., Breslau, 1892.

G. P. Gooch, *History and Historians in the Nineteenth Century,* London, 1913.

E. G. Gudde, *Freiligraths Entwicklung als politischer Dichter. Germanische Studien,* no. 20, Berlin, 1922.

Fr. Gundolf, *Romantiker, Neue Folge,* Berlin, 1931.

O. Herrmann, *Die Anfänge Gustav Freytags,* Ph.D. Thesis, Hamburg, 1934.

I. A. Hess, *Heine's Views on German Traits of Character,* New York, 1929.

R. Horovitz, *Vom Roman der Jungdeutschen zum Roman der Gartenlaube. Ein Beitrag zur Geschichte des deutschen Liberalismus,* Breslau, 1937.

H. H. Houben, *Jungdeutscher Sturm und Drang,* Leipzig, 1911.

R. Kayser, *Dichterköpfe,* Vienna, 1930.

W. H. Klein, *Immermanns Deutschheit. Zeitschrift für Deutschkunde,* vol. 49, Leipzig, 1935.

H. von Kleinmayr, *Welt- und Kunstanschauung des "Jungen Deutschland." Studien zur Geistesgeschichte des XIX. Jahrhunderts,* Vienna, 1930.

V. Klemperer, *Die Zeitromane Fr. Spielhagens und ihre Wurzeln. Forschungen zur neueren Literaturgeschichte,* ed. F. Munker, Nr. 43, Weimar, 1913.

P. Kluckhohn, *Persönlichkeit und Gemeinschaft. Studien zur Staatsauffassung der deutschen Romantik,* Halle, 1925.

W. Kockjoy, *Der deutsche Kaufmannsroman. Der deutsche Roman in Gruppen- und Einzeldarstellungen,* vol. i, Strasbourg, 1933.

A. Krüger, *Der junge Raabe,* Leipzig, 1911.

H. Lilienfein, *Schiller und die Deutsche Schiller-Stiftung,* Weimar, 1934.

H. Lindau, *Gustav Freytag,* Leipzig, 1907.

E. Löwenthal, *Studien zu Heines Reisebildern,* Palästra Nr. 138, Berlin, 1924.

W. Manggold, *Der deutsche Adelsroman im 19. Jahrhundert*, Ph.D. Thesis, Freiburg-i.-Br., 1931. (Typewritten.)

L. Männer, *Gutzkow und der demokratische Gedanke*, Munich, 1921.

O. Mann, *Der Dandy, Philosophische Forschungen*, ed. K. Jaspers, Nr. 1, Berlin, 1925.

K. Mannheim, *Das konservative Denken, Archiv für Sozialwissenschaft und Sozialpolitik*, vol. 57, Tübingen, 1927.

H. Maync, *Immermann*, Munich, 1921.

Mielke-Homann, *Der Deutsche Roman des 19. und 20. Jahrhunderts*, 7th Ed., Dresden, 1920.

J. Nadler, *Literaturgeschichte der Deutschen Stämme und Landschaften*, 4 vols., Regensburg, 1912–28.

J. Petersen, *Fontanes Altersromane. Euphorion*, vol. 29, Stuttgart, 1928.

Chr. Petzet, *Die Blütezeit der deutschen politischen Lyrik von 1840–1850, Ein Beitrag zur deutschen Literatur- und Nationalgeschichte*, Munich, 1903.

K. Pinthus, *Die Romane Levin Schückings*, Leipzig, 1911.

L. M. Price, *The Reception of English Literature in Germany*, Berkeley, 1932.

J. Prœlss, *Das junge Deutschland*, Stuttgart, 1892.

P. Przygodda, *H. Laubes literarische Frühzeit. Berliner Beiträge zur Germanisch-Romanischen Philologie*, Nr. 42, Berlin, 1910.

B. Radau, *Der deutsche Adelsroman in der 2. Hälfte des 18. Jahrhunderts*, Ph.D. Thesis, Freiburg-i.-Br., 1931. (Typewritten.)

I. Reiske, *Franz Freiherr von Gaudy als Dichter, Palästra Nr. 60*, Berlin, 1911.

J. F. W. R. Renwanz, *Matthew Arnold und Deutschland*, Ph.D. Thesis, Greifswald, 1927.

M. Rychner, *G. G. Gervinus, Ein Kapitel über Literaturgeschichte*, Berne, 1922.

E. I. Schmid-Jürgens, *Ida Gräfin Hahn-Hahn Germanische Studien, Nr. 144*, Berlin, 1933.

Carl Schmitt, *Politische Romantik*, 2nd Ed., Munich, 1925.

M. Schönfeld, *Gutzkows Frauengestalten, Germanische Studien, Nr. 133*, Berlin, 1933.

M. Sommerfeld, *Goethe in Umwelt und Folgezeit. Gesammelte Studien*, Leiden, 1935.

H. Spiero, *Raabe. Leben-Werk-Wirkung*, Darmstadt.

—— *W. Raabe u. sein Lebenskreis. Festschrift zum 100. Geburtstag. des Dichters*, Berlin, 1931.

—— *Fontane*, Wittenberg, 1928.

G. Steinhausen, *Geschichte der deutschen Kultur*, 5th Ed., Leipzig, 1929.

Cl. Stockmeyer, *Soziale Probleme im Drama des Sturms und Drangs, Deutsche Forschungen, Nr. 5*, Frankfort-on-Main, 1922.

F. Strich, *Die Romantik als europäische Bewegung. in Festschrift für Heinrich Wölfflin*, Munich, 1924.

H. Taine, *History of English Literature*, vol. ii, Edinburgh, 1870.

W. Wätzold, *Deutsche Kunsthistoriker*, 2 vols., Leipzig, 1921–4.

K. Wandrey, *Theodor Fontane*, Munich, 1919.

H. Weil, *Die Entstehung des deutschen Bildungsprinzips*, Bonn, 1930.

R. Weil, *Alexander von Ungern-Sternberg. Ein Beitrag zur Literatur- und Kulturgeschichte des 19. Jahrhunderts*, Berlin, 1932.

H. Wuttke, *Die deutschen Zeitschriften und die Entstehung der öffentlichen Meinung*, 13th Ed., Leipzig, 1875.

H. Zang, *Die Gartenlaube als politisches Organ*. Ph.D. Thesis, Würzburg Coburg, 1935.

M. I. Zwick, *Berthold Auerbachs sozialpolitischer und ethischer Liberalismus*, Stuttgart, 1933.

Allgemeine Deutsche Biographie, vols. 1–36, Leipzig, 1875–1912.

Reallexikon der Deutschen Literaturgeschichte, ed. P. Merker and W. Stammler, 3 vols., Berlin, 1925.

IV. Sociology of Literature—Theory of Literature

L. Balet, *Die Verbürgerlichung der deutschen Kunst, Literatur und Musik im 18. Jahrhundert*, Strasbourg-Leiden, 1936.

W. H. Bruford, *Goethe's Wilhelm Meister as a Picture and a Criticism of Society*. In *Publications of the English Goethe Society*. vol. ix, New Series, London, 1933.

G. D. H. Cole, *Politics and Literature*, Hogarth Lectures No. 11, London, 1929.

A. S. Collins, *Authorship in the Days of Johnson*, London, 1928.

—— *The Profession of Letters*, London, 1928.

H. Epstein, *Der Detektivroman der Unterschicht. I. Die Frank-Allan-Serie*, Frankfort-on-Main, 1930.

H. Fehr, *Das Recht in der Dichtung*, Berne, 1931.

A. Guérard, *Literature and Society*, Boston, 1935.

G. Keferstein, *Bürgertum und Bürgerlichkeit bei Goethe* [*Literatur und Leben*, vol. 1], Weimar, 1933.

L. C. Knights, *Drama and Society in the Age of Jonson*, London, 1937.

E. Kohn-Bramstedt, *Probleme der Literatursoziologie. Neue Jahrbücher für Wissenschaft und Jugendbildung*, vol. vii, Leipzig, 1931.

Q. D. Leavis, *Fiction and the Reading Public*, London, 1932.

Article *Literature*, *Encyclopædia of the Social Sciences*, vol. ix, New York, 1933.

L. Löwenthal, *Zur gesellschaftlichen Lage der Literatur. Zeitschrift für Sozialforschung*, vol. i, Frankfort-on-Main, 1932.

—— *Conrad Ferd. Meyers heroische Geschichtsauffassung. Zeitschrift für Sozialforschung*, vol. ii, Frankfort-on-Main, 1933.

G. v. Lukacs, *Die Seele und ihre Formen*, Berlin, 1911.

R. Mayreder, *Family Literature* in *A Survey of the Woman-Problem*, translation, London, 1913.

F. Mehring, *Gesammelte Aufsätze zur Literaturgeschichte*, 2 vols., Berlin, 1930.

H. Meuter, *Die Romane Zolas Rougon-Macquart. Schriften der Deutschen Gesellschaft für Soziologie*, vol. v, 1927.

E. Muir, *The Structure of the Novel. Hogarth Lectures, no. vi*, London, 1928.

A. Nollau, *Das literarische Publikum des jungen Goethe von 1770 bis zur Übersiedlung nach Weimar.* [*Literatur und Leben*, vol. 5,] Weimar, 1935.

G. Roethe, *Vom literarischen Publikum in Deutschland*, Göttingen, 1902.

H. V. Routh, *Money, Morals and Manners as Revealed in Modern Literature*, London, 1935.

H. Schoeffler, *Protestantismus und Literatur. Neue Wege zur englischen Literatur des 18. Jahrhunderts*, Leipzig, 1922.

L. L. Schücking, *Die Soziologie der literarischen Geschmacksbildung*, 2nd Ed., Leipzig, 1931.

L. Stephen, *English Literature and Society in the Eighteenth Century*, London, 1904.

D. Waples and R. W. Tyler, *What People Want to Read About*, Chicago, 1931.

R. Wellek, *The Theory of Literary History. Travaux du Cercle Linguistique de Prague, No. 6*, Prague, 1936.

W. Wittich, *Der soziale Gehalt von Goethes Roman "Wilhelm Meisters Lehrjahre," Erinnerungsgabe für Max Weber*, vol. ii, Munich, 1923.

REFERENCES FOR SECOND EDITION

D. Barlow, *Fontane and the Aristocracy. German Life and Letters*, New Series, vol. viii, 1955.

E. K. Bramsted, *Marriage and Misalliance in Thackeray and Fontane. German Life and Letters*, vol. iii, 1939.

Peter Demetz, *Marx, Engels und die Dichter*, Stuttgart, 1959.

S. Freud, *Group Psychology and the Analysis of the Ego*, London, 1922.

Heinz Gollwitzer, *Die Standesherren: Die politische und gesellschaftliche Stellung der Mediatisierten; Ein Beitrage zur deutschen Sozialgeschichte*, Stuttgart, 1957.

G. P. Gooch, *History and Historians in the Nineteenth Century*, Rev. Ed., London, 1952.

G. Lukas, *Deutsche Realisten des 19. Jahrhunderts*, Berlin, 1951.
Studies iu European Realism, London, 1950.

P. Magill, *The German Author and His Public in the Mid-Nineteenth Century. Modern Language Review*, vol. cxliii, 1948.

Karl Mannheim, *Essays on Sociology and Social Psychology*, ed. by Paul Kecskemeti, London, 1953.
Man and Society in an Age of Reconstruction, London, 1940.

Harold March, *The Two Worlds of Marcel Proust*, London, 1948.

FRITZ MARTINI, *Die Deutsche Literatur des Bürgerlichen Realismus 1848–1898*, Stuttgart, 1962.
  Deutsche Literatur in der Zeit des Bürgerlichen Realismus: Ein Literaturbericht. Deutsche Vierteljahrschrift für Literaturwissenschaft und Geitesgeschichte, vol. xxiv, 1960.
HANS MAYER, *Der Deutsche Roman des 19. Jahrhunderts. Deutsche Literatur und Weltliteratur: Aufsätze*, Berlin, 1955.
WERNER OBERLE, *Der Adelige Mensch in der Dichtung: Eichendorff, Gotthelf, Stifter, Fontane*, Basel, 1950.
ROY PASCAL, *The German Novel*, Manchester, 1953.
A. ROSENBERG, *The Birth of the German Republic, 1871–1918*, London, 1931.
L. L. SHÜCKING, *The Sociology of Literary Taste*, London, 1944.
RENÉ WELLEK, *The Concept of Realism in Literary Scholarship*, Groningen, 1961.
and AUSTIN WARREN, *Theory of Literature*, London, 1949.
RAYMOND WILLIAMS, *Culture and Society, 1780–1950*, London, 1958.

INDEX*

Actual public, see Public

Æsthetic writer and society, 4 f., 26

Agrarian romanticism, 66 f.

Albert, Prince of Saxe-Coburg-Gotha, 322

Alberti, 110

Althaldensleben, 58

Ambiguity of emotions (*Ambivalenz*), 182 ff.

Amyntor, Georg von, 208

Andersen-Nexö, 262

Anti-aristocratic tendencies of middle-class writers, 34 f., 47 f., 54 f., 121 f., 127, 177, 185 ff., 195, 204 f., 209 ff., 232 f., 280 f., 295 f., 304, 311

Anti-semitism, 132 ff., 288, 301

Aristocracy, see also Nobility

  in Austria, 42, 229, 288, 290 ff.

  in Bavaria, 326

  in Denmark, 307

  in England, 10, 63, 156, 165, 169 f., 183, 224 ff., 229, 245, 260, 262, 265, 279 f., 290, 294 f.

  in France, 10, 23, 32, 229

  in Prussia, 11, 36 f., 41 ff., 45 f., 69, 72, 81 ff., 100 f., 153, 183, 198, 228 ff., 257, 264 ff.

  and capitalism, 45 ff., 55 f., 122 f., 228 f.

  economic decline, 47 f., 54, 57, 67, 121 ff.

  as literary public, see Public

Aristocratic attitudes, conciliatory attitude, 151, 166 f.

— exclusive attitude, 151 ff.

liberal officer, 178 ff.

liberal politician, 167, 174 ff.

writer, 37 f., 63, 98, 168 ff., 208, 231, 233, 240 ff., 263, 289 ff.

Arnim, Achim von, 276

Arnim-Boytzenburg, Count Adolf Heinrich von, 79

Arnold, Matthew, 223 ff.

Ars amandi, 60

Assessorismus, 239

Auer, A. von, 216

Auerbach, B., 109 ff., 118, 333

Auerswald, Alfred von, 175

Baader, Franz von, 38, 168

Bacharacht, Therese von, 79, 308

Baden, 293, 296, 301

Ballestrem, Count, 46

Balzac, 2, 5, 8, 75, 91, 196, 312 f.

Balzer, Protestant priest, 205

Bavaria, 179 f., 208, 318

Beer, M., 51

Bennigsen, Rudolf von, 174 ff., 206

Berlin, 25, 34, 37, 39 f., 77 ff., 88, 94, 100, 104, 134, 154, 178, 208, 236, 247, 258, 263, 277, 283, 299, 316, 321, 329 f.

Biedermann, 236 f.

Biedermeier period, 318

Bismarck, Otto von, 11, 43, 83, 97, 176, 193, 207 f., 235, 284

Bismarck-Bohlen, Count, 317

* This index has been arranged with the kind assistance of Miss A. Hirschfeld.